Introduction To

Bibliology

Introduction To

Bibliology

What Every Christian Should Know

About the Origins, Composition,
Inspiration, Interpretation, Canonicity,
and Transmission of the Bible

Jefrey D. Breshears

WIPF & STOCK · Eugene, Oregon

INTRODUCTION TO BIBLIOLOGY
What Every Christian Should Know About the Origins, Composition, Inspiration, Interpretation, Canonization, and Transmission of the Bible

Wipf & Stock
An Imprint of Wipf and Stock Publishers
199 W. 8th Ave., Suite 3
Eugene, OR 97401

www.wipfandstock.com

PAPERBACK ISBN: 978-1-5326-1719-5
HARDCOVER ISBN: 978-1-4982-4171-7
EBOOK ISBN: 978-1-4982-4170-0

Manufactured in the U.S.A.

In memory of my parents,
Edd and Lucille Breshears,
who loved God with all their
heart, soul, mind, and strength,
and who taught me from an early age
to revere the Bible as
God's holy and inspired Word.

"Your Word is a lamp to my feet,
and a light for my path"
– Psalm 119:105

"From this time many of Jesus' followers
turned back and no longer followed him.
'You do not want to leave also, do you?'
Jesus asked his disciples.
Simon Peter answered, 'Lord, to whom
would we go? You alone have the words
of eternal life.'"
– John 6:66-68

Contents

Preface

Like many Christians, my wife and I have been involved in Bible study groups in the past that started amid high expectations, only to flounder and eventually disintegrate as people lost their zeal and commitment. I recall one group in particular many years ago that even ended in an angry explosion over differences of interpretation. The failure of such groups is usually due to one or more factors such as poor leadership, simmering personality conflicts, lack of substantive insight and depth into the subject matter, unwarranted dogmatism on the part of one or more group members, competing priorities and agendas, and/or irreconcilable theological differences. And although most such groups fizzle out rather than explode, the effect can nonetheless cast a pall over people's spiritual lives and dampen their enthusiasm for studying the Bible together. It can even deter some Christians from ever again wanting to be involved in serious Bible study.

In ruminating on this problem over the years, I've begun to realize that a major contributing factor to unsatisfying Bible study experiences is that few Christians have anything approaching an informed and thoughtful philosophy of the Bible. People come together to study the Bible with wildly varying (and sometimes irreconcilable) views of the nature, the purpose and the message of Scripture. Therefore, it should come as no surprise that differences eventually surface and discussions often degenerate into competitive power struggles.

Many years ago I read Gordon Fee and Douglas Stuart's book, *How To Read the Bible for All Its Worth* (Zondervan, 1983). Afterward, I told my wife (somewhat facetiously) that I would never want to be part of any Bible study group that didn't first take a few weeks to read and discuss this book. I was convinced that if people were not sufficiently committed to take the necessary time to process and understand the basic principles of biblical hermeneutics (i.e., the basic principles of biblical interpretation), then any attempt at a serious and substantive Bible study would probably be an exercise in futility. Furthermore, I was convinced that if people *would* take the time to read and process the book, most of the theological and hermeneutical problems that cause discord among Christians would be minimized. Of course, nothing can eliminate all sources of conflict, since many of these relate to personality

I

differences and complex social and psychological factors. But a sober understanding of basic biblical hermeneutics should certainly reduce the potential for conflict that stems from bizarre theories and eccentric misinterpretations of Scripture.

Since then, I've come to believe that as valuable and necessary as a book such as *How To Read the Bible for All Its Worth* may be, Christians need something broader and more inclusive. We live in an age of religious pluralism in which the exclusive truth-claims of the Christian faith are met with skepticism if not outright ridicule. Therefore, it is essential that Christians develop an informed, thoughtful, and realistic understanding of the Bible so as to be convinced in their own mind that the Bible is a credible source of divinely inspired Truth. Only then can we live with confidence and present an effective defense of the Gospel of Jesus Christ in the midst of a hyper-skeptical society that is increasingly intolerant of traditional Christian beliefs and values.

In I Peter 3:15 we read, "But let Christ be the Lord of your heart. Always be prepared to give an answer for the hope that you have. But do this with gentleness and respect." In order to carry out this mandate effectively, we must have confidence that the Bible is indeed the divinely inspired written Word of God. We must also be able to explain *why* we believe this is true. In other words, Christians need to develop an informed and thoughtful Bibliology that provides satisfactory answers to fundamental questions such as:

- What *is* the Bible? If asked to define the Bible without using the familiar cliche, "The Bible is the written Word of God," what would you say?
- Does the Bible present a coherent, consistent and comprehensive worldview and philosophy of life – and if so, what are the basic tenets of a biblical worldview?
- Is there a qualitative difference between the kind of inspiration that we encounter in the Bible and that which motivates gifted writers, speakers, preachers, composers, and artists to produce their works?
- Why is it reasonable to believe that the Bible was divinely inspired?
- What are the basic fundamental principles that should guide our interpretation of Scripture?
- What are the origins of the Bible, and how were the early manuscripts composed?
- What are the earliest and best extant (i.e., surviving) biblical manuscripts?
- Why were certain books included and excluded from the Bible?
- What is the Apocrypha, and why are these books included in the Roman Catholic Bible and various Orthodox Bibles but not in Protestant Bibles?

- What are the arguments that skeptics put forth in their efforts to undermine the credibility of the Bible, and how can we defend the integrity of the Bible against these attacks?
- When we read the Bible, how can we be confident that we are reading what the authors originally wrote?
- How can we know the Bible has been accurately preserved and transmitted through the centuries?
- What are the differences between the various modern translations of the Bible?

The answers to these questions are essential to our understanding of the very foundation of the Christian faith. In this _Introduction to Bibliology_ I address these and other issues so that we might better understand the Bible and defend its veracity more effectively in our dialogue with unbelievers. In Christian apologetics we understand that we can never argue someone into receiving Christ as their savior, just as we can never love someone into accepting him. The active presence and power of the Holy Spirit is absolutely crucial to anyone responding positively to the call of Christ. However, what we _can_ do is to remove any unnecessary intellectual impediments – any factual misinformation or rational misunderstandings – that might confuse, distract or otherwise deter one from accepting the veracity and credibility of the Christian faith. In the process our own confidence in the truthfulness and reliability of the Bible is further strengthened.

My hope is that every sincere and dedicated Christian who is involved in serious Bible study will read and digest this book. This is why I subtitled it, _What Every Christian Should Know About the Origins, Composition, Inspiration, Interpretation, Canonicity, and Transmission of the Bible_. I believe that if Christians had a thorough understanding of Bibliology, many of the issues that divide the Body of Christ would be eliminated. Then, we could go on to concentrate on those perplexing social and psychological factors – issues that are often manifestations of our own human limitations and our inherently egocentric sinful nature – that continue to disrupt our unity in Christ and impede our unified witness to the world.

Likewise, I pray that non-Christians who are earnest spiritual seekers will read this book. In the process, it should answer many questions and clarify many of the popular misconceptions concerning the Bible, how it was written, why it is reasonable to believe that it is historically reliable and doctrinally and morally authoritative, and why Christians believe it contains the Words of Life.

Finally, a word of sincere gratitude and appreciation to those who reviewed, edited and critiqued this work-in-progress – especially to Eric Smith, Randall

Hough, David Ott, and Sophia Freaney. Your editorial comments saved me much embarrassment, and I absolve you of any responsibility regarding any further criticism that this work warrants. Likewise, thanks to all those who participated in our Areopagus seminars in Bibliology at Perimeter Church (PCA), Johnson Ferry Baptist Church, and Mt. Bethel United Methodist Church in the Atlanta area. Your involvement and input helped immeasurably as I continued to think through many of these issues. And finally, special thanks to Wayne Whitaker for his assistance in preparing this manuscript for publication and the development of the cover artwork.

— *Jefrey D. Breshears*

Introduction

The Bible and Christian Apologetics

When I was growing up, my father spent a lot of time in jail. Actually, and more accurately, for a number of years he had a ministry in which he taught a Bible study every Sunday morning to inmates in our city's detention center. Although he had (literally) a captive audience, most of his "students" showed him due respect, and some even seemed to genuinely appreciate his teaching. Over the years he led quite a number of men to faith in Christ, and although he encountered a lot of apathy he rarely met with any serious opposition. But if a difference of opinion happened to surface, he could always play his trump card. The dialogue would go something like this:

Inmate: "I don't believe that" (or "I don't agree with you").

Dad: "Well, don't argue with me. That's simply what the Bible says" – whereupon he would quote the appropriate verse or passage to make his point. This was usually sufficient to satisfy the dissident, quell the protest, and settle the matter, and he could then proceed with the lesson.

But by the late 1960s my father noticed (to paraphrase Bob Dylan) that "the times, they were a-changin'," and that simply referencing the Bible didn't always have the same impact as in the past. One Sunday afternoon he related what he considered to be a rather amusing exchange with an inmate earlier that morning. Dad was teaching a lesson based on Matthew 4 about Jesus healing the sick and casting out demons when a man in the audience expressed demonstrative incredulity. When my father asked what was troubling him, the man replied, "That's just a myth – I don't believe that." Dad responded, "Well, look there in your Bible at verse 23 – that's what it says" – to which the man retorted, "Well, I don't believe just everything I read! Do you?"

Now the reason my father found this incident to be so amusing was because the very idea that someone would regard the Bible as just another ordinary book full of subjective opinions struck him as unimaginably absurd. For all I know, my father had rarely encountered an outspoken skeptic in his life. So the realization that someone was so abysmally ignorant as to question the authority of Scripture was virtually incomprehensible to him.

5

Not so anymore. Today, the Bible is under constant attack, and the respect that was generally accorded it in the past has seriously eroded. Now, we are often reminded that we are living in a "post-Christian" society and culture. In fact, America never was a "Christian nation" in anything but a nominal and superficial sense, although it was perhaps *influenced* more by biblical Christianity than any other nation in history. But regardless, those days are long gone, and there is no longer any kind of consensus in America when it comes to religious beliefs and moral values. Contemporary America is more religiously diverse and more biblically illiterate than at any time in its history. This makes Bibliology – the study of the origins, composition, philosophy, theology, divine inspiration, principles of interpretation, canonicity, and the preservation and transmission of the Bible through the centuries – more relevant and essential than ever.

Historically, Christians have reverenced the Bible as God's unique revelation to mankind. Although written by men in their own vocabulary and within their own cultural context, it was supernaturally inspired and superintended by the Holy Spirit. Therefore, the Bible is doctrinally and morally authoritative, historically reliable and scientifically accurate when properly interpreted. It also provides a coherent, consistent and comprehensive philosophical worldview that encompasses the whole of reality. As the early Church Fathers attested, the Bible was the written expression of the Christian "rule of faith," the standard by which all things should be measured and evaluated. This was a sacred conviction that went unquestioned throughout Christian history until modern times.

Virtually everything Christians believe about truth and the nature of reality is derived either directly or inferentially via Scripture. But today many people no longer consider the Bible to be an authoritative source for what they believe and how they live their lives. For more than 200 years the Bible has been subjected to intense criticism – and not only by nonbelievers but often by ministers and scholars who profess to be Christians. This is why it is so vitally important that we develop an informed, thoughtful and defensible philosophy of the Bible, and why it is imperative that we understand not only *what* the Bible teaches but *why* we should trust it as an infallible guide for what we believe and how we live our lives.

As with all religions, people identify with Christianity for a variety of reasons. For more than a thousand years, from the early 400s into the 18th century, it was often illegal in Western societies *not* to be a Christian – or at least a nominal Catholic or Protestant. (There were some exceptions granted to Jews and Muslims in certain societies at various times.) During the

Reformation era (circa 1520-1650) local rulers or city councils often decreed whether their citizens would be Catholic or Protestant, and it was hazardous to be a religious nonconformist.

Fortunately, the age of Christian sacralism[1] and coercive Christianity is long past, and in general people no longer pretend to be Christians (or a certain kind of Christian) for fear of social discrimination or even outright persecution. But nonetheless, many still identify with Christianity for a variety of erroneous reasons. For some it is primarily a matter of ethnicity or family heritage – what is sometimes referred to as "cultural Christianity." On a more personal level, many find a measure of mental and/or emotional comfort in their faith as a source of peace, joy and hope. There is, of course, some validity in this, as religious faith can certainly be a vital component when it comes to cultivating a sense of purpose and meaning in life. Others find it beneficial to belong to a church for primarily social reasons. Churches can be ideal environments for all kinds of social networking – from developing close personal friendships to business contacts and even political connections. In this respect, church affiliation can make life considerably more interesting and enjoyable. And of course for many people, there is ultimately a very pragmatic reason for identifying with the Christian faith: They reason that if there really is a God and an afterlife, then perhaps their religious faith will save them from divine judgment and the prospect of eternal hellfire and damnation.

There is some value in some of these reasons, but unfortunately they all miss the main point: **Ultimately, the only reason for being a Christian is if in fact the Christian faith is *true*. The fundamental issue is not how it makes us feel or the benefits it accords, but does it actually correspond to reality?** This takes us into the realm of Christian **apologetics**.[2] As a corollary to Christian theology, which deals with *what* Christians believe, apologetics focuses on *why* the unique truth-claims of the Christian faith are intellectually credible. In other words, apologetics sets forth the reasons why it is sensible to believe in the Bible and the Gospel message of Christ based on four factors:

---

[1] Christian sacralism denotes the unholy alliance of church and state that dominated Western civilization from the mid-4th century until modern times. In reaction to the abuses of sacralism, America's Founding Fathers set up a system that separated the institutions of church and state. However, in recent decades the principle of separatism (or separationism) has been disingenuously misinterpreted and misapplied by some to promote an exclusively secularistic socio/political agenda even to the point of excluding Christian beliefs and values from the public square.

[2] Apologetics [Greek: *apologia*] is a legal term meaning to provide a reasoned argument or defense for one's beliefs.

(1) **Facts and evidence** derived from history and the natural sciences.

(2) **Reason** derived from philosophy and logic, including the basic principles of natural (moral) law.[3]

(3) **Intuitive, aesthetic, and existential factors** derived from personal experience, including the insights gained through one's own spiritual transformation. As the 17th century French philosopher Blaise Pascal observed, "The heart has its reasons which reason does not know."[4]

(4) **Divine revelation** derived from Scripture and confirmed by the internal witness of the Holy Spirit. This kind of special revelation is essential because some truths in life are supra-rational – i.e., they transcend the limits of normal human reasoning and therefore cannot be apprehended through purely rational means. (Examples would include doctrines such as the Trinity and the Incarnation of Jesus Christ, and the biblical view of human sexuality, among others.[5]) Faith derived from Scripture does not contravene facts and reason, but it does open up avenues of perception that otherwise would remain closed.

Contrary to what many have been led to believe, Christian faith is not an irrational "leap of faith" but a sober and sensible step of faith. Our Christian convictions can (and should) engage our emotions, but personal subjective feelings should never drive our beliefs. Our faith should be grounded in sufficient evidence, not wishful thinking. Although this point is rarely addressed in most churches and Christian ministries, anyone who has thought deeply about the Christian faith understands that this is what true faith is based upon, as C. S. Lewis emphasized in his essay on Christian apologetics:

> One of the great difficulties [in sharing the Gospel] is to keep before the audience's mind the question of Truth. They always think you are recommending Christianity not because it is *true* but because it is *good*. And in the discussion they will at every moment try to escape from the issue 'True or False' into stuff about the Spanish Inquisition [or the Crusades]... or anything whatever. You have to keep forcing them back...to the real point. Only thus will you be able to undermine... their

---

[3] Natural law relates to those fundamental moral and ethical truths that are universal and transcultural, and which all people sense intuitively as a result of being made in the *Imago Dei* – the Image of God. See Jefrey D. Breshears, *Natural Law: The Moral Foundation for Social and Political Civility* (Areopagus Publishing, 2011).

[4] Blaise Pascal, *Pascal's Pensees* (E. P. Dutton & Company, 1958), p. 67.

[5] A necessary distinction should be drawn between the *supra-rational* and the *irrational*. In contrast to supra-rational truths that transcend our human capacity to fully comprehend, irrational beliefs are illogical and nonsensical and cannot possibly be true.

belief that a certain amount of 'religion' is desirable but one mustn't carry it too far. One must keep on pointing out that Christianity is a statement which, if false, is of no importance, and if true, of infinite importance. The only thing it cannot be is moderately important....

The great difficulty is to get modern audiences to realize that you are preaching Christianity solely because you think it is true; they always suppose you are preaching it because you like it or think it is good for society or something of that sort.... This immediately helps them to realize that what is being discussed is a question about objective fact – not [opinions] about ideals and points of view.... Do not attempt to water down Christianity. [C. S. Lewis, "Christian Apologetics," in Walter Hooper, ed., *God in the Dock: Essays on Theology and Ethics* (William B. Eerdmans Publishing Company, 1970) p. 101.]

As Lewis noted, the primacy of truth is always a difficult concept to convey because most people value a religion mostly for the social, psychological and pragmatic benefits it affords them. However, even some nonbelievers who understand the philosophical basis of Christianity realize that the paramount issue is the unique truth-claims that the Christian faith proclaims. Note the comment below by Bart Ehrman, a religion professor at the University of North Carolina and a prominent critic of the Bible who nonetheless grasps the essence of the Christian faith probably better than many professing Christians.

Most people today don't realize that ancient religions were almost never interested in 'true beliefs.' Pagan religions... did not have creeds that had to be recited, beliefs that had to be affirmed, or scriptures that had to be accepted as conveying divine truth. Truth was of interest to philosophers, but not to practitioners of religion.... As strange as this may seem to us today, ancient religions didn't require you to believe one thing or another. Religion was all about the proper practices: sacrifices to the gods, for example, and set prayers.... There were many gods and many ways to worship the gods, not a single path to the divine.....

Among the many things that made Christianity different from the other religions of the Roman Empire, with the partial exception of Judaism, is that Christians insisted that it did matter what you believed.... Christianity, unlike the other religions, was exclusivistic....

The Christian religion came to be firmly rooted in truth claims. [Bart D. Ehrman, *Forged: Writing in the Name of God – Why the Bible's Authors Are Not Who We Think They Are* (HarperCollins, 2011), pp. 6-7.]

The Bible does not advocate blind faith, but it does summon us to open our hearts and minds to rationally consider the evidence of God's active involvement in human history in general and our own life in particular, and to respond accordingly. Throughout the Bible we are enjoined to love and serve God not only passionately but mindfully, as in the following passages:

- In Matthew 22:36-40, a Pharisee asks Jesus, "'Rabbi, which is the greatest commandment in the Law?'"

  Jesus replies: "Love the Lord your God with all your heart and with all your soul and *with all your mind*. This is the greatest commandment. And the second is like it: 'Love your neighbor as yourself.'"
- Proverbs 19:2 warns, "It is not good to have zeal without knowledge."
- Proverbs 4:5-7 emphasizes the priority of acquiring wisdom and understanding: "Get wisdom, get understanding;... Do not forsake wisdom, and she will protect you; love her, and she will watch over you. Wisdom is supreme; therefore get wisdom. Though it cost all you have, get understanding."
- Colossians 2:8 – "See to it that no one takes you captive through hollow and deceptive philosophy, which depends on human tradition and the basic principles of this world rather than on Christ." This makes it incumbent that we learn to think rationally and critically when confronted by the false "wisdom" of this world.
- I Peter 3:15 – "Let Christ be the Lord of your heart [i.e., your mind, emotions and will]. Always be prepared to give an answer to everyone who asks you to give the reason for the hope that you have. But do this with gentleness and respect." This verse, a favorite among Christian apologists, is a clarion call to understand what and why we believe in order to effectively defend the truth of the Gospel when confronted by either honest spiritual seekers or cynical skeptics.

In a sense, much of the New Testament is an apologetic. For example:

- Each of the Four Gospels was written to make the case that Jesus Christ was the Messiah of Israel and the divine Savior of humanity.
  - Matthew, written primarily to a Jewish audience, presents Jesus as the Messiah and regularly references Old Testament prophecies fulfilled by him.
  - Mark, written initially for a Roman audience, references Jesus' defense of his ministry.
  - Luke (and the Acts of the Apostles), addressed to a literate cosmopolitan audience, bolsters the case for Christ by providing meticulous historical research.
  - John is clear about the purpose of his gospel: "These are written so that you may believe that Jesus is the Christ" – John 20:31.

- Peter, in his sermon on the Day of Pentecost (Acts 2:14*ff*), explained the crucifixion and resurrection of Jesus as the fulfillment of ancient Hebrew prophecies, whereupon he exhorted the crowd to "Repent and be baptized... in the name of Jesus Christ for the forgiveness of your sins; and you will receive the gift of the Holy Spirit."

- Stephen, in his defense before the Sanhedrin in Acts 7, cited the prophetic elements in Hebrew history from the time of Abraham, and how God's plan was consummated in the coming of Jesus of Nazareth.

- Paul, in his sermon in the synagogue in Pisidian Antioch (Acts 13:13*ff*), reviewed Hebrew history and declared that Jesus of Nazareth, a descendent of King David, was in fact the long-awaited Messiah. As proof, Paul cited Jesus' death on a cross, his resurrection, and the fact that he was seen by many witnesses over many days. (Also ref. I Cor. 15:1-8.)

- Paul, in his speech at the Areopagus in Athens in Acts 17:16*ff*, made the case that there is only one true God, and that he had recently revealed himself in the person of Jesus Christ, who had risen from the dead. Note that because he was addressing a non-Jewish audience, Paul based his arguments on universal philosophical principles rather than the Hebrew Scriptures exclusively.

- Paul, in his comments to the Jews in Jerusalem who attempted to stone him (Acts 22), declared that he had once persecuted the followers of Jesus before experiencing a supernatural personal encounter with the risen Jesus that transformed his life.

- Paul, in his trial before Antonius Felix, the governor of Judea (Acts 24), offered an *apologia* (a reasoned argument) in his own defense, arguing that his arrest and internment were illegal and that he was being persecuted solely because he preached the resurrection of Christ.

- In Acts 26, in his trial before the governor Festus and King Agrippa II, Paul testified that he had been a model Pharisee and a persecutor of the followers of Jesus before he encountered the risen Jesus, who was the fulfillment of ancient Hebrew prophecies regarding the coming Messiah. When challenged by Festus, he replied, "What I am saying is true and reasonable," and he reminded the king that all to which he testified was common knowledge among the Jews.

As Blaise Pascal once noted, the purpose of the Gospel is simply to "make [the Christian faith] attractive, make good people wish it were true, and then show them that it is."[6] Obviously, apologetics cannot force anyone to believe in Christ and the truth of the Bible against their will. What it can do, however, is to present the rational and factual bases of the Christian faith and dispel erroneous misconceptions that people hold regarding the historicity, the factuality, and the rationality of Christian beliefs. In this sense, apologetics serves three key functions:

(1) **Apologetics presents the factual evidence for the Christian worldview and demonstrates that the Christian faith is a rational, coherent, consistent, and comprehensive belief system;**

(2) **Apologetics exposes the factual errors and the incoherence, the inconsistencies, the contradictions, and the ultimate irrationality of alternative belief systems; and**

(3) **Apologetics builds a cumulative case for the Christian faith on the basis of factual evidence, reason, moral-based intuition, real-life experiences, and the inherent credibility of the Bible.**

Ultimately, apologetics is valuable and beneficial both to Christians and non-Christians alike:

(1) **Apologetics edifies and equips believers.** Apologetics deepens and strengthens the faith and confidence of Christians by providing substantive arguments and substantiating evidence that Christian beliefs are based on sound reason and factual realities, which in turn provide a coherent explanatory system for interpreting one's own life experiences.

(2) **Apologetics engages non-believers** by providing reasonable and fact-based answers to honest intellectual questions by sincere spiritual seekers.

Bibliology

In contrast to the common practice of Bible study, Bibliology is the systematic study *of* the Bible. Although Bibliology is based on a knowledge and understanding of the contents of Scripture, the goal is not so much exegesis, hermeneutics, and the practical application of particular biblical passages and principles as the development of a thoughtful philosophy of the Bible. In other words: **Bibliology is the study of the origins, the composition, and the philosophy and theology of the Bible – including issues related to divine inspiration, hermeneutics, canonicity, and biblical textual criticism** (i.e., the

---

[6] Cited in Graham Tomlin, "Profiles in Faith: Blaise Pascal." *Knowing and Doing* (Winter 2006), p. 2.

reconstruction, preservation and transmission of the biblical text through the centuries). In this regard, Bibliology addresses questions such as...

- What is the Bible?
- What is the basic philosophy of the Bible?
- What is the central message of the Bible?
- What is the nature of divine inspiration?
- Why should we believe the Bible has been divinely-inspired?
- How should the Bible be interpreted?
- How and when were the various biblical manuscripts composed?
- Why were certain books included and excluded from the biblical canon? and
- What are the oldest and best surviving biblical manuscripts, and has the Bible been accurately preserved and transmitted through the centuries?

To call attention to the title of this book, this is an *Introduction to Bibliology*. **The goal of Bibliology is the development of an informed, thoughtful, and defensible philosophy of the Bible.** In keeping with this purpose, this study addresses many of the major issues and controversies related to the field of Bibliology. This is not, however, a comprehensive treatment of any of these topics. For all of the issues and questions covered herein, there is a wealth of resource materials available for those who are motivated to delve deeper. (See the Recommended Readings section in the back of the book.) Indeed, the scholarly and popular literature related to Bibliology is voluminous. If this study sparks an interest and motivates the reader to pursue these issues further, I will have accomplished my purpose.

This study is divided into 7 chapters that address most of the seminal issues in Bibliology:

Chapter 1: What Is the Bible?
- The Bible as a communique from God.
- Three alternative views of the Bible.
- What the Bible is.
- What the Bible is not.
- The central message of the Bible.
- The uniqueness of the Bible.
- Historical and contemporary Confessions of Faith.

Chapter 2: The Philosophy of the Bible.
- The Bible as philosophy.
- The basic components of a worldview.
- The basic tenets of Christian theism.

- Christianity as religion and spirituality.

Chapter 3: Biblical Inspiration.

- Inspiration, revelation, and illumination: What is the difference?
- The uniqueness of Biblical revelation.
- Concentric circles of inspiration.
- Why should we believe the Bible was divinely-inspired?

Chapter 4: Biblical Hermeneutics.

- Basic principles of reading and interpreting Scripture.
- Biblical exegesis and hermeneutics.
- Four schools of hermeneutics.
- A note on Bible translations.

Chapter 5: Biblical Canonicity.

- Origins of the Hebrew canon.
- The Septuagint.
- The Old Testament Apocrypha.
- The Christian acceptance of the Old Testament.
- The process of Old Testament canonization.
- Origins of the New Testament canon.
- Early compilations of the New Testament canon.

Chapter 6: Composition of the Bible and the Earliest Extant Manuscripts.

- How the Bible was written.
- Extant Old Testament manuscripts.
- Extant New Testament manuscripts.

Chapter 7: Biblical Textual Criticism.

- Has the Bible been accurately preserved and transmitted through the centuries?
- The case for biblical deconstructionism.
- A critique of biblical deconstructionism.
- Manuscript production and the transmission process.
- A brief history of biblical textual criticism.
- The methodology of biblical textual criticism.

To facilitate study and retention, I have arranged the content in this book in such a way that each chapter can be read independently. One can read these chapters either sequentially (which is preferable) or in random order. Therefore, certain facts and terms are occasionally repeated from one chapter to another for the sake of clarity, but otherwise the reader is encouraged to consult the Index for any terms that might require more explanation.

The Living Word. There is great value in studying the Bible in a systematic and scholarly way, exploring not only the depths of biblical history, doctrines and principles but also the fundamental underlying worldview and philosophy set forth in Scripture. As stated earlier, the purpose of this study is the development of an informed, thoughtful, and defensible philosophy of the Bible. However, we should always keep in mind that the Bible is more than just a holy book to be studied. The Bible is to be *encountered* and *experienced.*

The Bible is unique. Unlike any other book ever written there is life in its words because it testifies to the Living Word of God, the Lord Jesus Christ. Many books contain great truths and are informative, but only the Bible is transformative. This is why we continually return to it, rereading it and absorbing it as we are illuminated and inspired (and also convicted!) by the truth of its message. As the disciple Peter proclaimed on one occasion when many of Jesus' followers were deserting him, "Lord, to whom shall we go? You alone have the words of life" (John 6:68).

But we can only comprehend the ultimate reality of the Bible to the extent that our heart and mind have been quickened by the Holy Spirit, and in accord with the spiritual perception that we are granted that enables us to recognize the truth that we encounter in Scripture. In addition, we understand that the Bible was written primarily to serve as the guidebook not so much for solitary individuals as for a corporate body of believers in Christ who have been set apart for God's work and purpose. In this sense, the Bible is best studied and lived out in the context of a confessional community of believers who are committed to one another's spiritual growth and development. And for those who read the Bible through illuminated eyes and allow its message to transform their heart and mind, the written Word of God is truly a lamp to their feet and a light for their path.

Post-Scripts

The Society of Biblical Literature and the Evangelical Theological Society. There are two professional societies of biblical scholars in the United States that are particularly significant and influential: the Society of Biblical Literature (SBL) and the Evangelical Theological Society (ETS). Both organizations are interdenominational and international.

The SBL was founded in 1880 and is the oldest and largest organization of scholars in the field of biblical studies with a membership of approximately 8,500 from more than 80 countries. Many of its members are Old or New Testament professors in seminaries and university schools of religion. From the outset the SBL was broad-based, including professing Christians as well as Jewish and even Unitarian scholars. Membership is open to anyone with the requisite academic and scholarly credentials "who shares a mutual interest in the critical investigation of the Bible and its influences." Today, a sizable number of its members identify themselves as nonreligious, agnostic or even atheist. The society's website is www.sbl-site.org.

In keeping with the times, in 2012 the SBL received a $140,000 grant from the Henry Luce Foundation to explore the formation of a Society for Quranic Studies. As with many organizations that were founded primarily by liberal Christians, over time the SBL has increasingly become not only an interdenominational but an inter-faith organization.

The ETS is an organization of professional Bible scholars, educators, pastors and students who are theologically conservative and committed to the inerrancy of Scripture. The society was established in 1949 in response to what the founders perceived to be "a need for interaction and wider dissemination of conservative research on biblical and theological issues," and it currently has a membership of around 4,200. The ETS doctrinal statement, which all members are required to sign, is succinct and unequivocal:

> The Bible alone and the Bible in its entirety is the word of God written, and therefore inerrant in the autographs [i.e., the original manuscripts]. God is a Trinity, Father, Son, and Holy Spirit, each an uncreated person, one in essence, equal in power and glory.

The ETS publishes a quarterly periodical, *Journal of the Evangelical Theological Society* (*JETS*), and its website address is www.etsjets.org. Like the SBL, the ETS sponsors annual conferences, and although the ETS is considerably more conservative than the SBL, some ETS Bible scholars are actively involved in the SBL.

American Biblical Illiteracy. Biblical illiteracy in American society is well-documented. According to a 2010 survey by the Gallup Organization, which has tracked religious trends in the United States for over 50 years, Bible reading has declined since the 1980s and "basic Bible knowledge is at a record low." Interestingly, self-identified "born-again Christians" and "evangelical Christians" are only slightly better informed regarding the Bible than other Americans – an alarming indictment of the general state of biblical education in most churches. Of course, public opinion polls are somewhat unreliable due to the fact that many respondents, although often ignorant on a particular issue, respond as if they were knowledgeable and well-informed. But although individual surveys may be suspect, over time fairly consistent patterns emerge that are reasonably accurate indications of what people actually know and believe. Unfortunately, the cumulative data is anything but encouraging.

More than 25 years ago E. D. Hirsch, a distinguished professor of English and humanities at the University of Virginia, published a book that temporarily sent the American education establishment into convulsions. *Cultural Literacy: What Every American Needs to Know* (1986) exposed the utter bankruptcy of decades of educational experimentation that had rendered most Americans abysmally ignorant of the basic core knowledge on which our culture is founded. Hirsch cited surveys that indicated that most college students and adults lack the basic knowledge to understand current events or otherwise function as informed and responsible citizens. He attributed the problem to John Dewey and other Progressive Education reformers who de-emphasized content-based learning in favor of a skills-based approach that minimized the accumulation of facts and knowledge, culminating in educational fads such as "values clarification" and (so-called) "critical thinking." Predictably, the education establishment dismissed Hirsch's book as reactionary "academic fundamentalism" although Hirsch was in fact a mainstream liberal academician.

At the time Hirsch's book was published I was a young history professor at Georgia State University in Atlanta, and troubled by my own students' apparent lack of cultural awareness, I administered a 50-question Cultural Literacy Quiz to several hundred students covering a wide range of common names, terms, events, etc., including mind-benders such as:

- List the last four American presidents.
- What river forms the boundary between Texas and Mexico?
- What is the connotation of the term, "Wall Street" (i.e., what does it symbolize)?

- What issue was decided in the *Roe v. Wade* Supreme Court decision of 1973? and
- Who wrote the songs "Blowin' In the Wind," "The Times They Are A-changin'," and "Like a Rolling Stone?"

In addition, I mixed in a number of religious-based questions that should be common knowledge, including...

- What is the name of the current pope, and what nationality is he? [Note: Much had been made of the fact that Pope John Paul II was Polish and the first non-Italian pope in several centuries.]
- What is the largest Christian denomination in the U.S.?
- Name the most influential and successful American Christian evangelist of the 20th century.
- Who wrote most of the books of the New Testament?

On a negative scale, the results far exceeded my expectations. On a standard grading scale of 0 to 100, with 60 being the cut-off mark for a passing grade, over 90% of my students failed the test. While nearly half could name the four former members of the Beatles, only about three in a hundred could list four current members of the Supreme Court. Less than a third knew the names of Georgia's two senators, and only 8% came reasonably close to approximating the population of the United States. Even more troubling, 87% could not identify *Roe v. Wade* as the landmark court decision legalizing abortion. Regarding the question concerning "the most influential and successful American Christian evangelist of the 20th century," fewer than 20% listed Billy Graham. Some answered "The pope," Jimmy Swaggert, "that PTL guy" (Jim Bakker), Jesse Jackson, and even Martin Luther King Jr. And on the question, "Who wrote most of the books of the New Testament?" less than 20% answered "Paul" or "St. Paul." Other responses ranged from Moses, John the Baptist and Jesus to "King James" and "Nobody knows."

Considering my students' lack of religious literacy in general and Bible knowledge in particular, I occasionally ruminated on the implications. Assuming that children can begin learning Bible stories and retaining basic Bible knowledge by about the age of four, and supposing that about half of my students grew up attending church at least half of the time, they would have logged nearly 400 hours in church (or 800 hours if they attended both Sunday School and worship services) by the time they entered college. Now if students were exposed to arithmetic or English grammar or U.S. history for several hundred hours, we might reasonably expect them to know something about the subject by the time they enrolled in a university. Yet very few of my students seemed to know much of anything when it came to the Bible and Christianity. Evidently, they had learned little in all their years in Sunday School and church.

The problem of religious illiteracy in general and biblical illiteracy in particular is the central theme in Stephen Prothero's book, *Religious Literacy: What Every American Needs To Know – and Doesn't* (2007). As Prothero writes:

A few years ago I was standing around the photocopier in Boston University's Department of Religion when a visiting professor from Austria offered a passing observation about American undergraduates. They are very religious, he told me, but they know next to nothing about religion....

Americans are both deeply religious and profoundly ignorant about religion. There are Protestants who can't name the four Gospels, Catholics who can't name the seven sacraments, and Jews who can't name the five books of Moses. Atheists may be as rare in America as Jesus-loving politicians are in Europe, but here faith is almost entirely devoid of content. One of the most religious countries on earth is also a nation of religious illiterates....

According to recent polls, most American adults cannot name one of the four Gospels, and many high school seniors think that Sodom and Gomorrah were husband and wife. A few years ago no one in Jay Leno's *Tonight Show* audience could name any of Jesus' twelve apostles, but everyone, it seemed, was able to list the four Beatles. No wonder pollster George Gallup has called the United States "a nation of biblical illiterates." [Stephen Prothero, *Religious Literacy: What Every American Needs To Know – and Doesn't* (HarperOne, 2007), p. 1, 6.]

As Prothero describes in his book, based on a religious literacy quiz he administered to his Boston University students in 2006:

- Most could not name the Four Gospels;
- Fewer than 10% could list the first five books of the Old Testament;
- The average student could recall only four of the Ten Commandments;
- Only about 15% knew that "Blessed are the poor in spirit" is a quote from the Sermon on the Mount; and
- Less than 20% knew that the First Amendment includes both the "free exercise" clause and the "establishment" clause.

In 2010 a highly publicized survey by the Pew Forum on Religion and Public Life supported many of Prothero's findings, including...

- Only half of American adults can name even one of the Four Gospels;
- Most Americans cannot name the first book of the Bible;
- Most Americans believe Jesus was born in Jerusalem;

- Many self-described Christians do not know that Easter commemorates the resurrection of Jesus Christ;
- Many self-described Christians do not know that the Trinity is comprised of God the Father, the Son, and the Holy Spirit; and
- Many self-described Christians have no idea who Martin Luther was.

Other less scientific surveys disclose additional interesting revelations such as...

- God created Eve from an apple;
- Noah led the Children of Israel on the Exodus out of Babylon;
- Noah's wife was Joan of Ark;
- Abraham was blinded on the road to Damascus;
- Jacob gave his son Joseph a new car of many colors;
- Moses received the Ten Commandments atop Mount Cyanide;
- In the New Testament, the epistles were the wives of the apostles;
- Matthew was swallowed by a whale; and...
- Perhaps most astonishingly: Jonah swallowed a whale!

What Do Americans Think About the Bible? A survey by the Barna Group in 2013 provides interesting insight into what Americans think about the Bible. As in the past, the Bible remains a significant cultural force, but there are definite changes in terms of how many Americans view it. It is important to keep in mind that the survey results are another reminder that only a small percentage of the American people can be considered biblically-literate, which is why in many instances the responses from question-to-question can be not only inconsistent but even contradictory.

According to the survey, nearly nine out of ten (88%) Americans own a Bible, which is a slight decline from 20 years ago when about 92% owned one. On average, Americans have 3.5 Bibles in their home, and one-quarter own six or more. While 95% of seniors (65-plus) own a Bible, 79% of young adults (18-28) own one. About 60% of atheists or "unreligious" also own a Bible.

Nearly 80% of Americans regard the Bible as "sacred literature," compared to only 8% who consider the Qur'an to be sacred literature – yet nearly half agree that the Bible, the Qur'an and the Book of Mormon are all different expressions of the same spiritual truths. One out of eight adults (12%) do not regard *any* book to be sacred – up markedly from 7% in 2011. As a further indication of just how ignorant most Americans are when it comes to biblical and religious knowledge, although 80% consider the Bible to be "sacred," a mere 4% identified the Torah as holy literature even though it constitutes the Old Testament portion of the Bible.

About three-quarters believe "the values and morals of America are declining," but whereas 56% believe the Bible has too little influence in our society, only one-third attribute our moral problems to a lack of Bible reading. Two-thirds of adults think public schools should teach values found in the Bible, but even among those who support the idea, nearly half (45%) say they would be concerned about "favoring one religion over another."

The Barna Group research indicates that neutral and negative attitudes toward the Bible are becoming more common. In 2011, 75% of adults agreed with the statement, "The Bible contains everything a person needs to live a meaningful life," but in 2013 that percentage fell dramatically to 66%. According to the Barna Group follow-up study in 2014, the number of adults who rarely if ever read the Bible and regard it as a merely human book of myths and legends has doubled in the past three years alone – from about 10% in 2011 to nearly 20% in 2014. This is about the same percentage as those who read the Bible regularly and take it seriously as the inspired written Word of God. As the survey notes, the number of biblical skeptics or agnostics "is now equal to the number of people who are Bible engaged – who read the Bible at least four times a week and believe it is the actual or inspired Word of God." Furthermore, the study concludes that "Bible skepticism will likely continue to rise."[7]

Indisputably, America is becoming a much more secular society, and although these figures are alarming, they should come as no surprise considering the moral disintegration we are witnessing in recent years. As in the days of Noah, the vast majority of Americans simply do "what is right in their own eyes" – or perhaps more accurately, in keeping with the popular sixties' slogan, they simply "do their own thing." When egocentric human beings mindlessly follow their own passions and inclinations, dire consequences are inevitable.

---

[7] To read the results of the 2013 survey, see "What Do Americans Really Think About the Bible" at https://www.barna.org/barna-update/culture/605-what- do-americans-really-think-about-the-bible#.U0WjIvldX.

To read the results of the 2014 survey, see "The State of the Bible: 6 Trends for 2014" at https://www.barna.org/barna-update/culture/664-the-state-of-the-bible-6-trends-for-2014#.U0WigPldXTo.

1
What Is the Bible?

A Communique from God?

Many devout Christians are serious students of the Bible, and some qualify as legitimate Bible scholars. They understand that the Bible is a unique book in literary history, being the product of supernatural revelation. As such, it is a font of knowledge and wisdom and the primary source of authority for our beliefs and our value system upon which we base our entire life. Yet few Christians have a well thought-out philosophy of the Bible. I'm not referring to *the* philosophy of the Bible – i.e., the explanation for reality that we encounter in Scripture as discussed in Chapter 2. Rather, I'm referring to how one perceives the Bible: What exactly is it? **If asked to explain, "What is the Bible?" without resorting to the familiar cliche', "The Bible is the Word of God," what exactly would you say?**[1]

Why is there something rather than nothing? Are we as human beings flukes of nature and the accidental by-products of random and purposeless naturalistic evolutionary processes, or were we created in the image of an omnipotent and omniscient God? If in fact there is a God and we are not alone in a strictly materialistic and impersonal universe, does this God care anything about us, and is there any intrinsic meaning to life? Do we have a destiny beyond this realm of existence? These and similar questions are what philosophers refer to as the perennial issues of life – those fundamental conundrums that have intrigued and mystified humanity for thousands of years and defined our sense of self-identity and self-worth.

Associated with the question of whether there is a God who cares is the issue of whether this God has condescended to communicate anything specifically to us regarding his will and purpose for our lives. Due to the incredibly intricate design of the universe and the very existence of natural

---

[1] Referring to the Bible as "the Word of God" might be a cliche', but this doesn't imply that it isn't true. In fact, many cliche's are true. But given the fact that cliche's can sound trite and banal, it is often helpful to express one's thoughts more descriptively.

physical laws, we reason that there must be a great Cosmic Designer who is responsible for all of this (ref. Romans 1:18-2:16). Furthermore, we would like to believe that this supernatural Being cares about us enough to communicate with us. But we can only ponder the phenomenon of the universe in a spirit of awe and wonder, as Karl Giberson comments in an article on Albert Einstein:

> We are in the position of a little child entering a huge library filled with books in many different languages. The child knows someone must have written those books. It does not know how. It does not understand the languages in which they are written. The child dimly suspects a mysterious order in the arrangement of the books but doesn't know what it is. That, it seems to me, is the attitude of even the most intelligent human being toward God. We see a universe marvelously arranged and obeying certain laws, but only dimly understand these laws. Our limited minds cannot grasp the mysterious force that moves the constellations. [Quoted in Karl W. Giberson, "The Patent Clerk from Mount Olympus." *Books & Culture*, Nov/Dec. 2005, p. 37.]

True enough: we simply cannot begin to grasp the mysterious Being that created, sustains and superintends the constellations and all life forms unless there is a personal God who has communicated with some degree of specificity his nature and his purpose to us. But of course this is precisely what those of us claim who believe in the divine inspiration of the Bible: that God, in his love for humanity, has taken great care to communicate his nature and purpose to mankind.

Christians and Jews commonly think of the terms "Bible" and "Scripture" as being synonymous, and they use these words interchangeably (although Christians and Jews define the parameters of the Bible differently – see Chapter 6). In fact, this understanding is perfectly legitimate. Scripture relates to the status of a written document that is accepted as authoritative in the formation of the orthodoxy (i.e., the doctrinal formation) and the orthopraxy (the life, mission, and worship) of a community of faith. The belief is that such a document (or collection of manuscripts) derives its authority from the fact that it was divinely-inspired. This is how devout Jews view the Old Testament, and this has been the traditional understanding of Christians toward the whole Bible. Therefore, as used in the context of the Christian faith, the terms "Bible" and "Scripture" are synonymous, and I use them interchangeably throughout this study.

As Blaise Pascal noted in his notes on Christian apologetics, *Pensees*, God has revealed himself with sufficient clarity to those with open hearts and minds who seek the truth; conversely, the reality of God's existence is vague enough so as not to coerce those whose hearts and minds are set against him:

God has willed to redeem men and to open salvation to those who seek it. But men render themselves so unworthy of it that it is right that God should refuse to some, because of their obduracy, what He grants others from a compassion which is not due them. If He had willed to overcome the obstinacy of the most hardened, He could have done so by revealing Himself so manifestly to them that they could not have doubted of the truth of His essence; as it will appear at the last day, with such thunders and such a convulsion of nature that the dead will rise again, and the blindest will see Him.

It is not in this manner that He has willed to appear in His advent of mercy, because, as so many make themselves unworthy of His mercy, He has willed to leave them in the loss of the good which they do not want. It was not, then, right that He should appear in a manner manifestly divine, and completely capable of convincing all men; but it was also not right that He should come in so hidden a manner that He could not be known by those who should sincerely seek Him.

He has willed to make himself quite recognizable by those; and thus, willing to appear openly to those who seek Him with all their heart, and to be hidden from those who flee from Him with all their heart. He so regulates the knowledge of Himself that He has given signs of Himself, visible to those who seek Him, and not to those who seek Him not. There is enough light for those who only desire to see, and enough obscurity for those who have a contrary disposition. [Blaise Pascal, *Pascal's Pensees* (E. P. Dutton & Company, 1958), p. 101.]

This being the case, we should not be surprised that opinions range from one end of the spectrum to the other when it comes to how different individuals view the Bible. For example, some affirmations from some notable individuals:

- Sir Isaac Newton: "We account the Scriptures of God to be the most sublime philosophy.... I have a fundamental belief in the Bible as the Word of God, written by men who were inspired. I study the Bible daily."

Isaac Newton

- John Locke: "The Bible is one of the greatest blessings bestowed by God on the children of men. It has God for its Author, Salvation for its end, and Truth without any mixture for its matter. It is all pure, all sincere; nothing too much; nothing wanting."

- John Wesley: "This Book had to be written by one of three people: good men, bad men or God. It couldn't have been written by good men because they said it was inspired by the revelation of God. Good men don't lie and deceive. It couldn't have been written by bad men because bad men would not write something that would condemn themselves. It leaves only one conclusion: It was given by divine inspiration of God."

- George Washington: "It is impossible to rightly govern the world without God and the Bible."
- John Adams: "Suppose a nation in some distant Region should take the Bible for their only law Book, and every member should regulate his conduct by the precepts there exhibited! Every member would be obliged in conscience, to temperance, frugality, and industry; to justice, kindness, and charity towards his fellow men; and to piety, love, and reverence toward Almighty God.... What a Utopia, what a Paradise would this region be."
- Sir Walter Scott: "The most learned, acute, and diligent student cannot, in the longest life, obtain an entire knowledge of the Bible. The more deeply he works the mine, the richer and more abundant he finds the ore."
- Immanuel Kant: "The existence of the Bible, as a book for the people, is the greatest benefit which the human race has ever experienced. Every attempt to belittle it is a crime against humanity."
- William Ellery Channing: "The incongruity of the Bible with the age of its birth; its freedom from earthly mixtures; its original, unborrowed, solitary greatness; the suddenness with which it broke forth amidst the general gloom; these, to me, are strong indications of its Divine descent. I cannot reconcile them with a human origin."
- Daniel Webster: "If there is anything in my thoughts or style to commend, the credit is due my parents for instilling in me an early love of the Scriptures. If we abide by the principles taught in the Bible, our country will go on prospering and to prosper; but if we and our posterity neglect its instructions and authority, no man can tell how sudden a catastrophe may overwhelm us and bury all our glory in profound obscurity."
- Noah Webster: "The Bible is the Book of faith, and a Book of doctrine, and a Book of morals, and a Book of religion, of special revelation from God; but it is also a Book which teaches man its responsibility, his own dignity, and his equality with his fellow man."

"The Bible is the chief moral cause of all that is good, and the best corrector of all that is evil, in human society; the best Book for regulating temporal concerns of men, and the only Book that can serve as an infallible guide to future felicity.... All the miseries and evils which men suffer from vice, crime, ambition, injustice, oppression, slavery, and war, proceed from their despising or neglecting the precepts contained in the Bible."

- Horace Greeley: "It is impossible to mentally or socially enslave a Bible reading people. The principles of the Bible are the groundwork of human freedom."
- Robert E. Lee: "There are things in the old Book which I may not be able to explain, but I fully accept it as the infallible Word of God, and receive its teachings as inspired by the Holy Spirit."
- Abraham Lincoln: "I believe the Bible is the best gift God has ever given to man. All the good of the Savior of the world is communicated to us through the Book. But for it, we could not know right from wrong."

  "I am busily engaged in the study of the Bible. I believe it is God's Word because it finds me where I am."
- Johann Wolfgang von Goethe: "The Bible grows more beautiful as we grow in our understanding of it."
- Even the agnostic biblical critic Bart Ehrman admits, "The Bible is, by all counts, the most significant book in the history of Western civilization."

Conversely, attacks on the Bible are not only unduly skeptical but often vitriolic, sometimes verging on the hysterical. A few notable examples:

- Thomas Jefferson: "The whole history of these books [i.e. the Gospels] is so defective and doubtful that it seems vain to attempt minute enquiry into it: and such tricks have been played with their text, and with the texts of other books relating to them, that we have a right, from that cause, to entertain much doubt what parts of them are genuine. In the New Testament there is internal evidence that parts of it have proceeded from an extraordinary man; and that other parts are of the fabric of very inferior minds. It is as easy to separate those parts, as to pick out diamonds from dunghills."

"Among the sayings and discourses imputed to him [i.e. Jesus] by his biographers, I find many passages of fine imagination, correct morality, and of the most lovely benevolence; and others again of so much ignorance, so much absurdity, so much untruth, charlatanism, and imposture, as to pronounce it impossible that such contradictions should have proceeded from the same being."

"It is between fifty and sixty years since I read it [i.e. the Book of Revelation], and I then considered it merely the ravings of a maniac, no more worthy nor capable of explanation than the incoherence of our own nightly dreams."

[Note: Jefferson not only rejected the belief in the divine inspiration of the Bible, but he even edited and rewrote his own gospel version of the life of Jesus (commonly known as *The Jefferson Bible*) in which he eliminated all miracles, including the Resurrection, and ended with Jesus' crucifixion and burial.]

- Thomas Paine: "It would be more consistent that we call it [i.e., the Bible] the work of a demon than the word of God. It is a history of wickedness that has served to corrupt and brutalize mankind."
- Ethan Allen: "There is not any thing which has contributed so much to delude mankind in religious matters, as mistaken apprehensions concerning supernatural inspiration or revelation."
- Robert Ingersoll: "The inspiration of the Bible depends upon the ignorance of the one who reads it."
- Friedrich Nietzsche: "One does well to put on gloves when reading the New Testament .... Everything in it is cowardice and self-deception."
- Sam Harris: "I no more believe in the Biblical God than I believe in Zeus, Isis, Thor and the thousands of other dead gods that lie buried in the mass grave we call 'mythology.' I doubt them all equally and for the same reason: lack of evidence." [Jon Meacham, "All Men Need the Gods." *Newsweek* (April 9, 2007), p. 55.]
- Richard Dawkins: "The great unmentionable evil at the center of our culture is monotheism. From a barbaric Bronze Age text known as the Old Testament, three anti-human religions have evolved: Judaism, Christianity, and Islam." [Quoted in Dinesh D'Souza, *What's So Great About Christianity* (Regnery Publishing Inc., 2007), p. 23]

"The God of the Old Testament is arguably the most unpleasant character in all fiction: jealous and proud of it; a petty, unjust, unforgiving control-freak; a vindictive, bloodthirsty ethnic cleanser; a misogynistic, homophobic, racist, infanticidal, genocidal, filicidal, pestilential, megalomaniacal, sadomasochistic, capriciously malevolent bully....

"To be fair, much of the Bible is not systematically evil but just plain weird, as you would expect of a chaotically cobbled-together anthology of disjointed documents, composed, revised, translated, distorted and 'improved' by hundreds of anonymous authors, editors and copyists, unknown to us and mostly unknown to each other, spanning nine centuries." [Richard Dawkins, *The God Delusion* (Hardcover, 2006), p. 31.]

Three Views of the Bible

1. Traditional/Conservative View.

According to the traditional view of the Bible that most professing Christians have held throughout history, the Bible is the divinely-inspired and authoritative written Word of God. This sacred view of Scripture includes a profound reverence and respect for the biblical text in keeping with the spirit of Psalm 119:105 ("Your word is a lamp to my feet and a light for my path") and Psalm 119:11 ("I have hidden your word in my heart that I might not sin against you"). However, in the interest of historical and theological accuracy, it should be noted that these references to "the word" of God, written long before there was a corpus of books that Jews or Christians would call the Bible, probably refer to the Pentateuch alone. Similarly, Hebrews 4:12 – "For the word of God is living and active. Sharper than any double-edged sword,... it judges the thoughts and attitudes of the heart." As part of the New Testament, this refers to the ancient Hebrew Scriptures as well as the spiritual illumination we receive via the internal presence of the Holy Spirit.

Traditional Christians accept the historical narratives in the Bible as reliable, including the references to direct divine intervention. Unlike modern skeptics, traditionalists believe that God *can* and *has* intervened in human affairs throughout history, and that the God of Genesis 1:1 who created all matter, energy, space and time *ex nihilo* can supervene at will the laws of nature. Therefore, the numerous examples of miracles that we encounter in Scripture are not regarded as irrational absurdities or impediments to faith. On the contrary, these accounts simply confirm the basic worldview that the Bible consistently affirms: that the omnipotent and all-loving God of the universe *can* and *has* communicated his will and purpose for humanity through human agents – prophets, chroniclers, apostles, *et al.* – who recorded these messages accurately in the inspired writings of Scripture.

Likewise, the Bible, *when properly interpreted,* is accurate when addressing science-related issues. Obviously, the Bible was never intended to be a science textbook. As John R. W. Stott once put it, "The Bible is designed to make us Christians, not scientists, and its purpose is to lead us to eternal life through faith in Jesus Christ." This is particularly significant because we should understand that when Scripture refers to the natural world it uses the common observational language that was intelligible and meaningful to ordinary people living thousands of years ago in a pre-scientific world. We should also be mindful that while the Bible is divinely-inspired and authoritative, our *interpretations* of it can be seriously flawed. Although this principle is self-evident and generally acknowledged, it is often ignored – particularly when it comes to science-related issues. This is why the study of hermeneutics, the basic principles of biblical interpretation, is so essential (see Chapter 4). When Christians fail to apply these principles to science-related issues, the credibility of the Bible is often impugned. This has been a problem throughout church history, as Augustine noted in his commentary on Genesis:

> It is a disgraceful and dangerous thing for an infidel to hear a Christian, presumably explaining the meaning of Holy Scripture, talking nonsense on [scientific-related] topics; and we should take all means to prevent such an embarrassing situation, in which people show up vast ignorance in a Christian and laugh it to scorn.... If they find a Christian mistaken in a field which they themselves know well, and [then] hear him maintaining his opinions about our [sacred] books, how are they going to believe those books on matters concerning the resurrection of the dead, the hope of eternal life, and the kingdom of heaven, when they think their pages are full of falsehoods on facts which they themselves have learnt from experience and the light of reason? [Augustine, *The Literal Meaning of Genesis* 1.42-43]

This is a point that Galileo also addressed in the context of his heresy trial – the failure to distinguish between what the Bible really says and how it is often misinterpreted. As he explained it:

> Holy Scripture can never lie, as long as its true meaning has been grasped; but I do not think one can deny that this is frequently [difficult to grasp] and very different from what appears to be the literal meaning of the words.... I do not think one has to believe that the same God who has given us senses, language, and intellect would want to set aside the use of these and give us by other means the information we can acquire with them, so that we would deny our senses and reason even in the case of physical [i.e., scientific] conclusions. [Galileo, "Letter to the Grand Duchess Christiana of Tuscany," quoted in Mark Noll, *The Scandal of the Evangelical Mind* (1994), pp. 205-6.]

In fact, early Genesis is remarkably compatible with our current understanding of the origins and constitution of the universe. One of the most astonishing insights of the Bible is its first verse: "In the beginning God created the heavens and the earth." This verse, written at a time when all other religions and mythologies presupposed an eternal cosmos, has profound implications. If this verse is true, then all other truth-claims in Scripture, including any references to miracles, are rationally unproblematical. Furthermore, regarding the origins of the universe there are only two options: Either the universe is eternal, or it had a beginning. If the universe had a beginning, it is either...

(1) Uncaused – i.e., nothing (or no one) brought it into being, which is a logical absurdity; or

(2) Self-caused, which is also illogical because if the universe created itself, it would have had to both exist and not exist at the same time.

The only logical option is that the universe had a beginning and was therefore created – a theory that corresponds both to the Bible and the modern scientific theory of Big Bang cosmology.

Regarding the doctrinal and moral authority of the Bible, the traditional Christian view was expressed by the 2nd century biblical scholar Irenaeus who referred both to the ancient Jewish writings of the Old Testament and the apostolic Christian writings of the New Testament as the "rule of faith, the standard by which we measure and evaluate all things." This principle was emphasized by many of the church's most respected theologians in subsequent centuries. As Augustine (354-430) declared, "It is to the canonical Scriptures alone that I am bound to yield such implicit subjection as to follow their teaching, without admitting the slightest suspicion that in them any mistake or any statement intended to mislead could find a place." Similarly, Anselm of Canterbury (1034-1109) accentuated the primacy of Scripture as the foundation of all truth when he wrote, "The Gospel... is the source and sum total of all our faith." Thomas Aquinas (1225-74), the premier philosopher/theologian in the millennium between Augustine and the Protestant Reformation, was equally emphatic that "canonical Scripture alone is the rule of faith," adding that "Only to those books or writings which are called canonical have I learnt to pay such honor that I firmly believe that none of their authors have erred in composing them." Correspondingly, theological conservatives accept the traditional authorship and dating of the biblical texts and believe the Bible has been accurately preserved and transmitted through the centuries.

There are, of course, variations among conservatives when it comes to the interpretation of orthodox bibliology. All accept that the Bible is **historically reliable** and **doctrinally and morally authoritative**. Some also insist that it is

inerrant (see the Chicago Statement on Biblical Inerrancy, pages 63-65). But even inerrantists concede that only the *autographa* (the original texts) were inerrant, not the generations of hand-written copies that followed. The problem, of course, is that we have none of the original manuscripts.[2] A second matter of debate relates to the issue of **verbal inspiration**. Those who hold this view argue that the Holy Spirit implanted within the minds of the writers not only the thoughts of God but the very words as well. But virtually all conservative Bible scholars reject the theory of mechanical dictation and agree that the inspiration process was concursive – i.e., each author expressed himself through his own unique personality and vocabulary and within the context of his own time and culture.

Third, many conservatives adhere to the doctrine of **plenary inspiration** – i.e., that all of the Bible was equally inspired. Others such as C. S. Lewis contend that parts of it are more authoritative than others. In *Reflections on the Psalms* Lewis wrote that "All Holy Scripture is in some sense – though not all parts of it in the same sense – the word of God." He noted, for instance, Paul's distinction in I Corinthians 7 between his own thoughts ("I speak, not the Lord") and those that were divinely-inspired ("not I, but the Lord"). He cited Luke's testimony of how he obtained his information on the life of Christ in Luke 1:1-4, and pointed to the differences in the genealogies in Matthew 1 and Luke 3. Lewis also drew a distinction between biblical stories and narratives that were historical and those that were, in his view, parabolic or mythological such as Job and Jonah. He described certain of the "deprecatory Psalms" as "ferocious," "self-pitying, "barbaric," "contemptible," "petty and vulgar," and even "devilish." Perhaps most perplexing to Lewis was Jesus' statement in the Olivet Discourse: "I tell you the truth, this generation will certainly not pass away until all these things have happened" (Matt. 24:34). Lewis regarded this passage as "certainly the most embarrassing verse in the Bible" and considered it an example of Jesus' self-limitations as a human being.[3]

Similarly, some hermeneutical schools of interpretation have understood biblical authority in the context of concentric circles of inspiration in which the

---

[2] Biblical inerrancy is a controversial issue. Some Christians regard it as a litmus test for doctrinal orthodoxy, while others consider it to be an extreme and unnecessary position. For an extended treatment of the inerrancy debate see J. Merrick, Stephen M. Garrett, and Stanley N. Gundry, eds., *Five Views on Biblical Inerrancy* (Zondervan, 2013).

[3] There are reasonable interpretations of the Olivet Discourse and Matt. 24:34 that counter the notion that Jesus was mistaken about his Second Coming. See Paul Copan, "Was Jesus Mistaken About an Early Second Coming?" in *When God Goes to Starbucks: A Guide to Everyday Apologetics* (BakerBooks, 2008).

innermost circle – the core of Scripture – is the Four Gospels that focus on the life and ministry of Jesus Christ. A second ring encompasses the rest of the New Testament, which are essentially divinely-inspired reflections and commentaries on the core Gospel of Jesus Christ. The third circle is the Old Testament, which functioned as a precursor to the New Covenant as explicated in the New Testament Epistle to the Hebrews. There is internal evidence that some of the ancient Hebrew prophets, poets and chroniclers anticipated the Gospel message, but they understood it imperfectly and only in part. Nonetheless, their writings were the product of divine revelation in the same sense as those of the apostles and other writers of the New Testament. As F. F. Bruce comments in *The Canon of Scripture*, "It would be hazardous to try to name any part of Scripture – even the genealogical tables! – in which some receptive reader or hearer has not recognized an effective and redeeming word from God."[4]

One might also conceptualize an outer ring of inspiration comprised of post-biblical Christian writings, sermons, songs, prayers, and art that illuminate the truths of Scripture. As Lewis noted, "If every good and perfect gift comes from the Father of Lights, then all true and edifying writings, whether in Scripture or not, must in *some sense* be inspired." But although such endeavors can certainly be inspired by the Holy Spirit at work in the hearts and minds of believers, there is a qualitative difference between this and the inspired revelation we encounter in Scripture. As discussed in Chapter 3, such works might best be described as the result of divine *illumination*. Although often insightful and edifying and at times even profound, they clearly lack the infallible authority of the biblical texts. We are also cognizant of the fact that throughout history Christian writers and church leaders and councils have often been wrong. Many have misunderstood and misrepresented the truths of Scripture, either unintentionally due to honest ignorance or deliberately out of ulterior motives. So although we can learn much through the writings and insights of great Christian luminaries such as Augustine, Thomas Aquinas, Francis of Assisi, Martin Luther, William Tyndale, John Calvin, Menno Simons, John Wesley, Charles Spurgeon and Feodor Dostoyevsky down to G. K. Chesterton, C. S. Lewis and Billy Graham – and although we can certainly be edified by the music of Handel, Bach and Charles Wesley as well as some of the works of contemporary Christian song writers – we understand that any truths we may glean from theses sources must correspond to our ultimate source of authority, the Bible.

---

[4] F. F. Bruce, *The Canon of Scripture* (InterVarsity Press, 1988), p. 273.

2. Liberal/Modernist View.

As a product of Enlightenment rationalism, theological liberalism holds a generally skeptical view of Scripture that questions (or outright rejects) God's active involvement in human affairs and his direct communication to mankind via the Bible. According to this view, the Bible is not particularly unique among ancient religious texts. Having been written by devout but fallible men, the Bible is a mixture of human knowledge and ignorance, wisdom and foolishness. Undoubtedly, the Bible contains some profound truths, but it also incorporates many outdated concepts regarding the character of God, human nature, the purpose and meaning of life, and morality (especially sexual morality). In essence, liberals believe that because the Bible comes to us in human form it must also be of human origin – either in part or in whole.

As typified by the Jefferson quote cited earlier, theological liberals are highly skeptical of miracles, including those that constitute core Christian doctrines such as the Incarnation, the Virgin Birth, and the physical/bodily Resurrection of Jesus Christ. Likewise, they tend to question or outright reject the traditional belief that the Bible is supernaturally inspired and authoritative regarding all matters related to doctrine and practice. For liberals, the Bible is scientifically irrelevant and historically suspect, being an odd mix of actual history but also incorporating many fables, myths and legends. In contrast to traditionalists, liberals tend to regard biblical history as suspect unless it can be corroborated by outside secular and "objective" sources. In other words, the Bible is presumed guilty until proven innocent.

Liberal and secular scholars typically assign late dates to most of the books of the Old and New Testaments, and regard fulfilled prophecies in the biblical texts as either later additions to the texts or subjective speculations based on highly obscure and esoteric passages that were interpreted to advance a theological agenda. Skeptics often contend that the New Testament writers disingenuously interpreted the messianic prophecies of the Old Testament and manipulated the facts about Jesus' life and death in order to convince others that he was the Messiah, the Son of God.

In practice, liberal theologians, many of whom are professing Christians, often hold positions that are virtually indistinguishable from secular skeptics and agnostics. Typical of this mindset was Harold DeWolf (1905-86), a longtime theologian at Boston University and the author of *The Case for Theology in Liberal Perspectives* (1959). According to DeWolf, the Bible is not "the pure Word of God" but rather "a collection of intensely human documents" written by "obviously fallible human beings" that is full of contradictions and "distinctly sub-Christian" religious and moral teachings.

Most university schools of religion and mainline Protestant seminaries are predominately or exclusively liberal, which accounts for the fact that many mainline Protestant ministers and an increasing number of evangelical leaders question or outright reject many of the core beliefs of the historic Christian faith. The problem of liberal Bible scholars, theologians, seminary professors and ministers is one that Louis Markos addresses in *Apologetics for the 21st Century*:

> Liberal scholars begin not with an inductive search for truth but with an unsubstantiated prejudice against the supernatural.
>
> For nearly two centuries our modern culture has entrusted a matter of highest importance – whether the Bible is accurate and reliable – to a group of scholars who deny *a priori* the miraculous and prophetic claims around which the Bible is structured. [Louis Markos, *Apologetics for the 21st Century* (Crossway, 2010), p. 149.]

So if the Bible is not a reliable source of authority, where does one turn for the answers to the questions of life? Many liberals know intuitively that we cannot simply rely upon our own subjective feelings and emotions. Since all of us are limited in knowledge (including our own self-knowledge), there must be some authority outside ourselves that can generally be trusted. For many, science holds the key. Science is the authoritative repository for all knowledge, and all religious beliefs should be subject to current scientific explanations. Therefore, our interpretations of Scripture should be modified to conform to the prevailing views of history (i.e., a secularized understanding of history) and the dominant theories in the physical and social sciences. If the Bible is of any value at all, it must be reinterpreted in light of what we currently "know" about cosmology, micro-biology, evolutionary "science," anthropology, psychology, sociology, and human sexuality.

As the theologian Clark Pinnock observes, theological liberalism, in its ill-fated attempts to make Christianity relevant to the spirit of the times, undermines any authority that traditionally has been attributed to the Bible as God's written, infallible and eternal Word:

> In its view of biblical authority, liberal theology considers it important to insist that the Bible is a merely human text, written, copied, translated and interpreted by fallible people. It contains all manner of internal contradictions, moral blemishes, legend and saga, inaccuracies, and the like. It is a collection of intensely human documents and is not an authority beyond criticism or correction. To regard it as God's written Word is an idolatrous perversion of belief.... It is norms that no longer bind us. We are in a new historical situation, with a new awareness of our autonomy and responsibility to think things through for ourselves. No longer can we

appeal to the unquestioned authority of an inspired book....

Liberalism, in the search for relevance, deliberately adjusted the biblical message to the spirit of the times. [Quoted in "Three Views of the Bible in Contemporary Theology," in Jack Rogers, *Biblical Authority* (Word Books, 1977), pp. 51, 53.]

3. Neo-Orthodoxy.

Neo-orthodoxy is a carefully nuanced philosophy of the Bible that was developed by 20th century theologians such as **Karl Barth** (1886-1968) and **Emil Brunner** (1889-1966) who sought to salvage what they considered to be the spiritual essence of the Christian faith in light of the wholesale abandonment of traditional beliefs by theological liberals. As a more reverential view of Scripture than the liberal position, neo-orthodoxy seeks to preserve the inherent spiritual truth of the Bible even while it accepts much of the modernistic biblical criticism of the past 200 years.

Karl Barth

Neo-orthodoxy is expressly existentialist in orientation. Whereas traditional conservatives believe the Bible *is* God's written Word and liberals concede that the Bible *contains* God's written Word (to some extent or another), neo-orthodoxists contend that the Bible *becomes* God's Word as we encounter and interact with it. As Barth put it, "the Bible is not the Word of God; it *becomes* the Word of God to the believer as Christ is revealed through it."

In keeping with John 1:1, neo-orthodoxy emphasizes that the Word of God is a person – the eternal and living Lord Jesus Christ – not propositional truth gleaned from a book. In that sense the Bible is a medium of divine revelation, or as Brunner put it, "The Scriptures... are the primary witness to the revelation of God in Jesus Christ." But this does not mean that the Bible is objectively true or infallible. Rather, it is the product of human authors who were divinely-inspired (to some extent or another), but their writings may or may not be literally or historically true. According to Barth, the Bible contains "obvious contradictions," and its authors were common sinners "capable and actually guilty of error in their spoken and written word." So in effect, the Bible is an errant human book used by God as a witness to his divine Word, Jesus Christ.

However, according to the neo-orthodoxist, this is not so problematical as it may seem because these writings are spiritually true. Just as God has communicated to mankind throughout redemptive history, he now speaks to those who personally encounter Jesus through Scripture. But this is a purely subjective phenomenon, and it tends to relegate revelation to the personal experience and interpretation of each individual.

Neo-orthodoxists argue that the value of Scripture lies primarily in its ability to point one toward a life-changing encounter with the living Christ. However, the historical and doctrinal details of Scripture are relatively unimportant. Like liberals, neo-orthodoxists tend to accept the late dating for many biblical books, question the traditional authorship of many of the texts, and are generally skeptical regarding the historicity of Scripture. Therefore, when the Bible contradicts extra-biblical sources – or in cases in which there is no extra-biblical corroboration of historical events – neo-orthodoxists tend to assume that the Bible is erroneous. This same skepticism carries over into the realms of doctrine and morality. Neo-orthodoxists tend to give more weight to current scientific and social theories than is often warranted. In the mind of many neo-orthodoxists, our approach to Scripture should be adapted to conform to the dominant contemporary theories in history and the physical and social sciences.

The inherent problems with neo-orthodoxy are rather apparent. Although opposed to the secularizing trends of theological liberalism, neo-orthodoxists concede far too much in their attempts to preserve what they consider to be the intellectual credibility and the spiritual essence of the Christian faith. By minimizing the importance of biblical historicity, neo-orthodoxy can easily lead to an outright denial of biblical credibility. This view of Scripture is prone to a kind of smorgasbord approach to faith in which the individual believer becomes his/her own subjective authority in terms of discerning what is divinely-inspired and what should be believed. As Norman Geisler observes in *A General Introduction to the Bible*, the neo-orthodox position is that the Bible "in itself is not the Word of God: at best, the Bible only becomes the Word of God to the individual when he encounters Christ through it."[5] But subjective truth is valid only to the extent that it is based on a transcendent objective reality. So while it is true that Truth does us no good unless we personally accept it, it is also true that Truth doesn't become true merely because we happen to accept it.

---

[5] Norman L. Geisler and William E. Nix, *A General Introduction to the Bible* (Moody Publishers, 1986), p. 175.

What Is the Bible?

The Bible Is Not...

Before we address with more specificity what the Bible *is*, let us consider what it is *not*. Among the common misconceptions about the Bible, there are four in particular that Christians should avoid.

1. The Bible *is not* a book that was dictated verbatim by God to the prophets, chroniclers, scribes and apostles who wrote it down. Although there is much that is mysterious about the exact nature of divine inspiration (see Chapter 3: "Biblical Interpretation"), all reputable Bible scholars reject the "mechanical" or "dictation" theory of inspiration. This position was advocated by the influential Jewish philosopher Philo of Alexandria (c. 20 B.C. - 50 A.D.) who contended that the ancient prophets wrote in a spirit of ecstasy as the divine Spirit overpowered their mental faculties, but few other Jewish or Christian scholars ever accepted this view. In fact, Scripture itself indicates that divine inspiration was rarely a case of an author writing down verbatim a message that was conveyed through the audible voice of God.

2. The Bible *is not* a treatise on systematic theology. This is a concept that is particularly problematical, as many Christians seem to view the Bible as a kind of theological textbook. But in fact the Bible is not a formal and systematic study of theological doctrines that addresses and correlates all the pertinent questions and issues related to various topics into a grand unifying system. Written by some 40 authors over a period of 1500 years primarily in the context of their unique historical situations, the Bible was never intended to be a compendium on systematic theology. If it were, it is certainly a messy and confusing one, full of paradoxes, irony and ambiguities. Of course, there are doctrines that can be extracted from Scripture, and some books such as Romans and Galatians are explicitly theological. But for the most part the doctrines and spiritual principles that we derive from Scripture are conveyed in the context of real-life situations, as the Catholic scholar Albert Vanhoye, Secretary of the Pontifical Biblical Commission under Pope John Paul II, explains:

> The historical meaning of the text is important precisely because God has manifested himself in history. The Bible is not a collection of philosophical or theological treatises, nor does it present us with a set of eternal truths expressed in propositions. Instead, more than anything else, the Bible recounts the initiative of God to enter into relationship with human beings in our history. For this reason it is necessary to pay attention to the historical circumstances of the word of God and to use our knowledge of

the historical context to illuminate it. Only if we make this effort can we accurately transfer the word of God into contemporary life. [Peter Williamson, "Catholicism and the Bible: An Interview with Albert Vanhoye." *First Things* (June/July, 1997). http://www.firstthings.com/article/2008/08/004-catholicism -and-the-bible-an-inerview-with-albert-vanhoye-44]

Given this reality, it takes divine illumination as well as patient study and discernment on the part of the reader to discern the truths of Scripture. As Thomas Merton commented in his book, *Opening the Bible*, we can only begin to understand the profound insights of Scripture as our heart is spiritually transformed:

It is the very nature of the Bible to affront, perplex and astonish the human mind. Hence, the reader who opens the Bible must be prepared for disorientation, confusion, incomprehension, perhaps outrage. The Bible is one of the most unsatisfying books ever written – at least until the reader has come to terms with it in a very special way. [Thomas Merton, *Opening the Bible* (The Liturgical Press, 1970), p. 11]

3. The Bible *is not* a book of cryptic, esoteric messages, the truth of which is revealed only to select individuals endowed with special insight. Other than the apocalyptic literature of Scripture, God communicates to us through human authors in ways that normal human beings can readily understand. After all, the purpose of the Bible is to *reveal* truth, not *conceal* it. Each book was written to its audience in clear, common language, and even the allegories and archetypes contained in apocalyptic literature such as the Book of Revelation and sections of Daniel were written in a way that its initial audience would find intelligible. Contrary to the teachings of the gnostic heretics in early Christian history and some contemporary heretics today, there is no secret "Bible Code" that only those with special knowledge can discern.

4. The Bible *is not* a manual on spirituality. Although replete with divine revelations, historical references to God's interactions with humanity, and numerous instances of divine empowerment, the Bible actually says little about *how* one experiences God personally. Unlike the Vedas, the Upanishads, and much of Buddhist literature, the Bible is not a handbook on spiritual techniques intended to lead the practitioner to higher levels of consciousness and being. Instead, the Bible enjoins us to commune with God regularly through prayer, to meditate on his written Word, to follow his moral precepts, and to live a life of devoted and integrated discipleship. But we live by faith, not by rules and rituals and techniques, and in the course of living our lives, the Holy Spirit guides our thinking, our conversation and our actions.

[Note: This does not, however, imply that there is no value in practicing the traditional spiritual disciplines of the Christian faith. Indeed, those practices emphasized in Richard Foster's *Celebration of Discipline* and in the writings of Dallas Willard and others are the means by which we access divine grace, direction and empowerment in our lives and facilitate our spiritual maturation. But in keeping with the principle of Philippians 2:12 – "...continue to work out your salvation with fear and trembling, for it is God who works in you to will and to act according to his good purpose" – these spiritual disciples are for us to develop personally under the guidance of the Holy Spirit. The Bible prescribes no set program or methodology for leading us into a deeper communion and walk with God.]

The Bible Is...

Interestingly, the Bible says surprisingly little about itself, just as it makes little attempt to convince its readers of the existence of God. One rather obvious reason for this is that the Bible was a work-in-progress on the part of some 40 contributing authors over a period of about 1500 years. For much of that time there was no corpus of books that comprised "the Bible" as such, although by the time of Christ there was a recognized collection of ancient Hebrew texts known as the **Tanakh**[6] that devout Jews revered as divinely-inspired. These books, together with the apostolic writings of the 1st century, eventually coalesced into the Bible as we know it, although in fact the canonization process was not finalized until around the turn of the 5th century.

Writing in reference to the Tanakh, the apostle Paul affirms in II Timothy 3:15-16, "The holy Scriptures... are able to make you wise for salvation through faith in Christ Jesus. All Scripture is divinely inspired (i.e., 'God-breathed') and is useful for doctrine, reproof, correction, and instruction in righteousness." In II Peter 1:20-21 the apostle Peter writes, "Above all, you must understand that no prophecy of Scripture came about by the prophet's own interpretation. For prophecy never had its origin in the will of man, but men spoke from God as they were carried along by the Holy Spirit."

Significantly, later in this same epistle Peter attributes the same divine authority to Paul's writings as to the ancient Hebrew texts when he notes: "Bear

---

[6] **Tanakh** is an acronym for the three classifications of writings contained in the ancient Hebrew texts:

    (1) **Torah** – the Law (a.k.a. the Pentateuch, or the five books of Moses);
    (2) **Nevi'im** – the Prophets; and
    (3) **Ketuvim** – the "Writings."

in mind that our Lord's patience means salvation, just as our dear brother Paul also wrote you with the wisdom that God have him. He writes the same way in all his letters, speaking in them of these matters. His letters contain some things that are hard to understand, which ignorant and unstable people distort, as they do the other Scriptures, to their own destruction" (II Peter 3:15-16). And lest we overlook it, in Revelation 22:18-19 the apostle John issues a stern warning to those who would alter the words of his book – a condemnation that would make sense only if the author were writing under divine inspiration: "I warn everyone who hears the words of the prophecy of this book: If anyone adds anything to them, God will add to him the plagues described in this book. And if anyone takes words away from this book of prophecy, God will take away from him his share in the tree of life and in the holy city, which are described in this book."

Jesus repeatedly quoted the Tanakh as an infallible source of divine authority. For example, in Matthew 5:17 he declares, "Do not think that I have come to abolish the Law or the Prophets; I have not come to abolish them but to fulfill them." In the course of his temptation in the desert, Jesus repeatedly rebuked Satan by citing Old Testament principles. At the outset of his public ministry, he read a passage from Isaiah 61:1-2 in his hometown synagogue in Nazareth to validate his spiritual authority ("The Spirit of the Lord is on me..."), just as after his resurrection he explained the purpose of his life and crucifixion to the two disciples on the road to Emmaus by appealing to the ancient Hebrew Scriptures (ref. Luke 24:13-35). In fact, throughout the course of the New Testament Jesus and the apostolic writers appealed to the authority of the Old Testament some ninety times.

With minor variations, orthodox biblical scholars generally agree on the following nine points regarding the nature of Scripture:

1. The Bible is a collection of books of divine origin (or inspiration) but human authorship. As the written Word of God in the words of man, the Bible is the thoughts of God expressed through the common vocabularies and familiar idioms of its human authors who were products of their time and culture. This is an important principle to understand because God did not by-pass the mind of the prophets, the chroniclers and the apostles who wrote these books. Rather, the whole process was mysteriously superintended by the Holy Spirit.

Although some hyper-fundamentalists advocate a "dictation" or "mechanical" theory of inspiration, mainstream conservative scholars reject this view as an over-spiritualization of the process of divine inspiration that denies the human element in Scripture. Instead, conservatives argue for a more organic and synergistic understanding of the nature of biblical revelation.

2. The Bible is literature – ancient, sacred literature that contains narrative history, biographical sketches, genealogies, legal codes, poetry, proverbs, parables, letters, archetypes, hyperbole, moral instructions, doctrinal statements, and predictive prophecy. One of the basic keys to comprehending Scripture is to understand how to interpret different forms of literature. For example, one reads history and processes it differently than apocalyptic literature full of rich imagery. Some Scripture is meant to be taken literally, and some symbolically. But none should be read and interpreted *literalistically* – i.e., outside of its literary and historical context.[7]

In terms of literary genres, most of the Bible is narrative history. In fact, it is the ultimate metanarrative – the grand story that makes sense of all human history. Significantly, the Bible is also the only major religious writing that subjects itself to historical analysis. Written over a millennium-and-a-half, it provides a record of God's interaction with numerous individuals within the corporate community of ancient Israel – and then later in the personal lives of individual Christians and the corporate life of the early church – and how these groups and individuals responded in terms of their observations, interpretations and actions.

As the theologian George Eldon Ladd has written, "The uniqueness of the Christian religion rests in the mediation of revelation through historical events" – a theme borrowed from the Christian scholar Clement of Alexandria (c. 200), who described Holy Scripture as "the narration of a revelation which has been experienced in history... the story of the acts of God toward humanity, and of repeated divine interventions in history." As John N. Oswalt notes in *The Bible Among the Myths* (2009), the Bible is "the miraculously preserved account of the one God, YHWH, disclosing himself in unique events, persons, and experiences in time and space." More strikingly, as Ernest Loosley emphasizes in *When the Church Was Young*, the Bible is ultimately the product of "a great surging spiritual movement:"

> The literature [of the early Church] arose out of a situation. As the church developed, men wrote to speak to [specific] needs.... Neither the gospels nor the epistles can be really understood apart from the actual circumstances of the church's development. Simply to sit in one's study

---

[7] See chapter 4 – Biblical Hermeneutics: Basic Principles of Interpretation. For a useful basic primer in biblical hermeneutics, or the principles of interpretation, see Gordon D. Fee and Douglas Stuart, *How To Read the Bible for All Its Worth*. Third Edition (Zondervan, 2003).

and compare and analyze and dissect the documents is a very [inadequate] method of understanding the New Testament.... The church, and its literature, are the product of a great surging spiritual movement. It must be understood in relation to that movement. [Ernest Loosley, *When the Church Was Young* (Christian Books Publishing House, 1989), p. 32]

3. Compositionally, the Bible is unique. In terms of authorship, the Bible is a collection of 66 individual books written over a period of 1500 years by approximately 40 authors from a variety of backgrounds including prophets, chroniclers, priests, scholars, poets, kings, philosophers, peasants, apostles, and associates of apostles. The Bible was written in three languages. Originally, the Old Testament was composed predominantly in Hebrew, with about 1% of the text (mainly parts of Daniel and Ezra) in Aramaic, the common language of the Middle East from the time of the Assyrian Empire more than a half millennium before Christ. Conversely, most of the New Testament was written in common (*koine*) Greek, the international language at the time of Christ, augmented by a few Aramaic words and phrases.

4. Thematically, the Bible reveals a coherent and consistent story of redemption. The central message of the Bible addresses four issues: Creation, Fall, Redemption, and Restoration.

First, Genesis 1-2 provides an account of the phenomenon of Creation *ex nihilo* ("out of nothing") that corresponds remarkably to what we know as the Big Bang. The crowning glory of God's creation is humankind, the only creatures made in the *Imago Dei* ("Image of God").

Second, Genesis 3 relates the story of humanity's Fall into sin. Dissatisfied with their status as God's caretakers of the earth, Adam and Eve bought into Satan's lie, "You will be as gods," and chose to live independent of God. As a result, their Fall into sin broke their relationship with God, which has affected all of subsequent humanity in three ways: (1) It distorted their understanding of the nature and character of God; (2) it corrupted the divine image of God within them as they became selfish and rebellious; and (3) it alienated them from God and broke their spiritual relationship with him. According to the doctrine of Original Sin, we have inherited this sin nature from Adam and Eve that impairs our thinking, our emotions and our behavior. Therefore, like them, we suffer from the effects of the Fall: Morally, we became slaves to egoism and lost the ability to consistently discern good and evil; intellectually, our thinking became muddled and confused; psychologically, the Fall resulted in a plethora of mental disorders; socially, we rationalized the exploitation and abuse of others for our own selfish ends; and creatively, our imagination strayed further and further into the darker realms of mysticism and fantasy. In the first chapter of his Epistle to the Romans, the apostle Paul notes the pervasive consequences of the Fall:

> The wrath of God is being revealed from heaven against all the godlessness and wickedness of men who suppress the truth by their wickedness, since what may be known about God is plain to them, because God has made it plain to them. For since the creation of the world God's invisible qualities – his eternal power and divine nature – have been clearly seen, being understood from what has been made, so that men are without excuse.
>
> For although they knew God, they neither glorified him as God nor gave thanks to him, but their thinking became futile and their foolish hearts were darkened. Although they claimed to be wise, they became fools....
>
> Furthermore, since they did not think it worthwhile to retain the knowledge of God, he gave them over to a depraved mind, to do what ought not to be done. They have become filled with every kind of wickedness, evil, greed, and depravity.... Although they know God's righteous decree that those who do such things deserve death, they not only continue to do these very things but also approve of those who practice them. [Rom. 1:18*ff*]

Contrary to the claims of modern social scientists, the Bible asserts that mankind's basic problem is not political, social, economic, or psychological. It is spiritual. We are innately egoistic, selfish creatures who, in our natural state, are alienated from God. That being the case, we usurp the rightful place of God in our own lives – or as Satan promised Eve, "you will be like God" (Gen. 3:5).

Third, the rest of the Bible from Genesis 4 to Revelation is an extended narrative of God's efforts to reconcile humanity to himself. In his lovingkindness, God has taken the initiative to redeem rebellious humanity. This is the theme of the Old Testament, and the culmination of God's redemptive work is the Incarnation of his divine son, Jesus Christ, by whose sacrificial and atoning death for our sins we can be reconciled to God and experience an intimate relationship with him. As a result of Christ's redemptive work, we can experience liberation from sin and spiritual transformation, as Gordon Fee and Douglas Stuart explain in *How To Read the Bible Book By Book*:

Here is the heart of the story: A loving, redeeming God in his incarnation restored our lost vision of God, by his crucifixion and resurrection made possible our being restored to the image of God, and through the gift of the Holy Spirit became present with us in constant fellowship....

The genius of the biblical story is what it tells us about God himself, a God who sacrifices himself in death out of love for his enemies; a God who would rather experience the death we deserved than to be apart from the people he created for his pleasure; a God who himself bore our likeness, experienced our creatureliness, and carried our sins so that he might provide pardon and reconciliation; a God who would not let us go, but who would pursue us... so that he might restore us into joyful fellowship with himself. [Gordon D. Fee and Douglas Stuart, *How To Read the Bible Book by Book* (Zondervan, 2002), pp. 18-19.]

Fourth, the consummation of the biblical story is the revelation of God's plan for the Restoration of all things – the promise of eternal life for those who are his spiritual children and the creation of a New Heaven and a New Earth. This is the culmination of all history and theme of the Book of Revelation, the seeds of which extend all the way back in time to the Garden of Eden. It is also the reason for Jesus' Incarnation, as he proclaimed to Mary and Martha upon the death of their beloved brother, Lazarus: "I am the resurrection and the life. Anyone who believes in me will live, even though they die." – John 11:25.

As divinely-inspired metanarrative, the Bible can also be understood as the ultimate Myth – but not in the sense that it incorporates fictional fables and legends. Rather, as C. S. Lewis recognized, the Bible is the ultimate divinely-inspired Myth in that it sets forth the doctrines of Creation, the Fall of man into sin, and God's plan of Redemption for mankind within an historical metanarrative.[8] But unlike the fanciful mythology of antiquity, the Bible incorporates "true myth" – i.e., it actually happened. In the context of history, biblical narratives express divine truths in words, symbols, archetypes, and thought-forms that transcend the historicity of the accounts themselves. So in this sense, biblical stories can be understood as both historical and supra-historical or mythological. However, a word of caution is in order here: If we refer to the Bible as "myth" we must take care to define and explain exactly what principle we are conveying to assure that there is no misunderstanding. For some people, the concept of biblical narratives as "myth" carries great symbolic meaning. Others, however, find the concept confusing and difficult to grasp, in which case it is best not to use the term at all. After all, our purpose should be to clarify the truths of Scripture, not muddle or obscure them.

---

[8] See C. S. Lewis, *Mere Christianity* (HarperSanFrancisco, 1952, 1980), pp. 47-59.

5. The Bible is the only self-authenticating book ever written – as demonstrated by the numerous predictive prophecies that were fulfilled within its pages, culminating in the Resurrection of Jesus Christ, one of the best-attested events in ancient history. As primarily an historical book, the Bible is also subject to historical examination – unlike myths and fables or religious texts that are purely didactic or esoteric in nature. In addition, as stated earlier, the Bible sets forth a coherent, consistent and unified message that is remarkable given the fact that it was composed by multiple authors over more than a millennium. As discussed in the next chapter, these are integral factors in the church's acceptance of the Bible as a supernaturally-inspired source of divine authority, as Clark Pinnock notes in *Set Forth Your Case...*

> The unity of Scripture follows from the fact that God is the principal Author of it, and implies that the meaning of the parts agrees with the meaning of the whole, so that one passage sheds light upon another. The Bible is not simply a collection of assorted religious writings... it is a single book with a single Author, a perfect unity growing out of its integrating theme, Jesus Christ. [Clark Pinnock, *Set Forth Your Case: An Examination of Christianity's Credentials* (Moody Press, 1971).

6. The Bible is the divinely-inspired blueprint on which we base our faith and build our life. As the apostle Paul noted in his second epistle to his protégé Timothy: "From infancy you have known the holy Scriptures, which are able to make you wise for salvation through faith in Christ Jesus. All Scripture is inspired [i.e., "God-breathed"] and is useful for teaching, rebuking, correcting and training in righteousness" (II Tim. 3:15-16).

7. The Bible is existential revelations. Certainly, there are propositional truths set forth in Scripture. But for the most part the Bible deals with people's existential encounters with God – actual events and issues in their lives, and their responses to God – not abstract theology. That being the case, the moral instructions and doctrinal insights set forth in Scripture are mainly framed within the context of real life scenarios, as the New Testament scholar Luke Timothy Johnson observes:

> In the writings of the Bible – most directly and critically in the writings of the New Testament – we find the God-inspired reflections of the first Christians on their experience of God in Jesus, and the implications of that experience for their life together in the world. [Luke Timothy Johnson, *Faith's Freedom* (Augsburg Fortress Publishers, 1990), p. 11]

8. The Bible is progressive revelation. God's message is not static and locked in the past, but alive and vibrant and constantly unfolding, revealing new truths and insights from Genesis to Revelation. The message of the Bible culminates in the Incarnation, the ministry, the atoning death, and the Resurrection of Jesus Christ as presented in the Four Gospels. The rest of the New Testament reflects on the life and meaning of Christ and the outworking of the implications of the Gospel message.

9. The Bible is the written testimony to the Living Word of God, Jesus Christ, as proclaimed in the prologue of the Gospel of John:

In the beginning was the Word, and Word was with God, and the Word was God. He was with God in the beginning.

Through him all things were made; without him nothing was made that has been made. In him was life, and that life was the light of men....

The Word became flesh and made his dwelling among us. We have seen his glory, the glory of the One and Only, who came from the Father, full of grace and truth." [John 1:1ff]

As Martin Luther stated, the Bible is not *the* Word of God – it *contains* the Living Word of God, which is Jesus.[9] This is an important distinction. Nowhere in the Bible does it refer to itself as *"the* Word of God." As John 1 declares, the living Lord Jesus Christ is the Word of God, a point that C. S. Lewis emphasized when he observed, "It is Christ himself, not the Bible, who is the true word of God. The Bible, read in the right spirit and with the guidance of good teachers, will bring us to him." In the words of the church historian Hans von Campenhausen, Christianity is not "a religion of the Book" but rather "the religion of the Spirit and the living Christ."[10]

Scripture itself is not the "word of God," but through it we encounter the true and living Word of God, Jesus Christ. In this regard Karl Barth correctly noted that the Bible is the "Word of God" only in the secondary sense that it

---

[9] Luther's comment that the Bible is not *the* Word of God but "contains" the Word of God should be understood in context. Obviously, Luther was no theological liberal, nor did he doubt the historicity or doctrinal authority of the Bible. But sterile dogma is lifeless; what matters is that we *encounter* the living Word of God, the Lord Jesus Christ, and allow the indwelling Holy Spirit to transform our life.

[10] See Hans von Campenhausen, *Formation of the Christian Bible* (Fortress, 1972), pp. 62-66.

provides literary and historical documentation of the Living Word. Barth criticized conservative Christians for practicing what he called "Bibliolatry" – the worship of the Bible – while Emil Brunner charged that conservatives tend to treat the Bible as a "paper pope" in lieu of experiencing the revelation of the living Lord Jesus Christ personally. In this respect, their critique of modern evangelical Christianity was largely justified.

In his devotional book, *Opening the Bible*, the Trappist monk Thomas Merton cautioned against this tendency to substitute the written Word for the living Word:

> The fulness of the Bible is the personal encounter with Christ Jesus... He contains in himself all the questions and all the answers, all the hope and all the meanings, all the problems and all the solutions. To become utterly committed to this person... is to find the meaning of existence not by figuring it out but by living it as he did.
>
> The great question of the New Testament... is who is Christ and what does it mean to encounter him? All the rest follows. [Merton, *Opening the Bible*, p. 79]

Similarly, in *The Pursuit of God* A.W. Tozer noted that God is forever reaching out to communicate with mankind. Just as God has spoken in the past through the prophets, chroniclers and apostles, he still seeks to reveal his will and purpose to us today as we encounter him in Scripture and interact with him in prayer. Tozer reminds us that "God is not silent," but rather, "God is speaking. Not God *spoke*, but God *is speaking*."

> The Bible is the written Word of God, and because it is written it is confined and limited by the necessities of ink and paper and leather. The voice of God, however, is alive and free as the sovereign God is free. [As Jesus said,] "The words that I speak to you, they are spirit, and they are life" (John 6:63). The life is in the speaking words. God's word in the Bible can have power because it corresponds to God's word in the universe.
>
> I believe that much of our religious unbelief is due to a wrong conception of... the Scriptures. [For many Christians and non-Christians alike,] A silent God suddenly began to speak in a book and when the book was finished lapsed back into silence again forever. Now we read the book as the record of what God said when he was for a brief time in a speaking mood. With notions like that in our heads, how can we believe? The facts are that God is not silent, has never been silent. It is the nature of God to speak.... The Bible is the inevitable outcome of God's continuous speech.
>
> I think a new world will arise out of the religious mists when we approach our Bible with the idea that it is not only a book which was once spoken, but a book which is now speaking. [A. W. Tozer, *The Pursuit of God* (WingSpread Publishers, 1948), pp. 66-69, 77]

What Is the Bible?
Historical and Contemporary
Confessions of Faith

Roman Catholic Bibliology

In the mid-16th century, in response to challenges by Protestant reformers, Roman Catholic authorities were compelled to systematize over a thousand years of Church tradition, conciliar pronouncements and papal edicts into a comprehensive and consistent statement on theology and ecclesiology. The **Council of Trent** met three times over a period of 18 years from 1545-63, and in the process it affirmed three propositions in relation to the Church's position on the Bible. First, in contradistinction to the Protestant emphasis on *sola Scriptura*, the Council declared that the doctrinal, ecclesiastical and moral authority of the Church resides in two equally infallible sources of revelation: (1) Scripture, and (2) Church tradition as mediated through the magisterium – the pope and the bishops as "the successors of the apostles." As the Council stated it:

> In treating the canon of Scripture [the bishops] declare at the same time that in matters of faith and morals the tradition of the Church is, together with the Bible, the standard of supernatural revelation.... The Bible should be interpreted according to the unanimous testimony of the Fathers.

Second, the Council declared that the official Latin Vulgate translation of the Bible (including the Apocrypha) was to be regarded as the authoritative text. And third, the Church has the sole authority to interpret the Scriptures – thereby denying the need for new vernacular translations of the Bible as advocated by the Protestant reformers.

The pronouncements of the Council of Trent, with only slight modifications, have remained the Catholic Church's basic position on the Bible for the past 450 years. For example, **Rev. John O'Brien's "Catechism of the Bible,"** written in 1924 and periodically updated, reiterates the Church's traditional theory of Scripture:

> [The Roman Catholic] Church is the divinely appointed guardian of the writings divinely inspired by God, known as the Bible. This Holy Bible is like no other book, because no other book has God for its principal author. Nevertheless the Bible is not the foundation of the Church, but the Church is the foundation of the Bible. That is why Catholics need Mother Church

as the guardian and interpreter of the Bible. ["Foreword," in Rev. John O'Brien, "A Catechism of the Bible" (1924). Revised and enlarged by Fr. Jaime Pazat De Lys, 1997, 2003.]

Following the **Second Vatican Council** (1962-65), **Pope Paul VI** (r. 1963-78) endorsed the Catholic Church's most comprehensive statement on the Bible, "**Dogmatic Constitution on Divine Revelation**" (a.k.a. *Dei Verbum*). The following excerpts are taken from this extended 5,000-word document.

Preface. [F]ollowing in the footsteps of the Council of Trent and of the First Vatican Council, this present council wishes to set forth authentic doctrine on divine revelation and how it is handed on....

Chapter I: Revelation Itself. In His goodness and wisdom God chose to reveal Himself and to make known to us the hidden purpose of His will (see Eph. 1:9) by which through Christ, the Word made flesh, man might in the Holy Spirit have access to the Father and come to share in the divine nature (see Eph. 2:18; 2 Peter 1:4).... By this revelation then, the deepest truth about God and the salvation of man shines out for our sake in Christ, who is both the mediator and the fullness of all revelation....

[A]fter speaking in many and varied ways through the prophets, "now at last in these days God has spoken to us in His Son" (Heb. 1:1-2). For He sent His Son, the eternal Word, who enlightens all men, so that He might dwell among men and tell them of the innermost being of God (see John 1:1-18). Jesus Christ, therefore, the Word made flesh, was sent as "a man to men." He "speaks the words of God" (John 3;34), and completes the work of salvation which His Father gave Him to do (see John 5:36; John 17:4). To see Jesus is to see His Father (John 14:9). For this reason Jesus perfected revelation by fulfilling it through his whole work of making Himself present and manifesting Himself: through His words and deeds, His signs and wonders, but especially through His death and glorious resurrection from the dead and final sending of the Spirit of truth. Moreover He confirmed with divine testimony what revelation proclaimed, that God is with us to free us from the darkness of sin and death, and to raise us up to life eternal.

The Christian dispensation, therefore, as the new and definitive covenant, will never pass away and we now await no further new public revelation before the glorious manifestation of our Lord Jesus Christ (see 1 Tim. 6:14 and Tit. 2:13).

Through divine revelation, God chose to show forth and communicate Himself and the eternal decisions of His will regarding the salvation of men. That is to say, He chose to share with them those divine treasures whic totally transcend the understanding of the human mind.

As a sacred synod has affirmed, God, the beginning and end of all things, can be known with certainty from created reality by the light of human reason (see Rom. 1:20); but teaches that it is through His revelation that those religious truths which are by their nature accessible to human reason can be known by all men with ease, with solid certitude and with no trace of error, even in this present state of the human race.

Chapter II: Handing On Divine Revelation. In His gracious goodness, God has seen to it that what He had revealed for the salvation of all nations would abide perpetually in its full integrity and be handed on to all generations. Therefore Christ the Lord in whom the full revelation of the supreme God is brought to completion (see Cor. 1:20; 3:13; 4:6), commissioned the Apostles to preach to all men that Gospel which is the source of all saving truth and moral teaching, and to impart to them heavenly gifts. This Gospel had been promised in former times through the prophets, and Christ Himself had fulfilled it and promulgated it with His lips. This commission was faithfully fulfilled by the Apostles who, by their oral preaching, by example, and by observances handed on what they had received from the lips of Christ, from living with Him, and from what He did, or what they had learned through the prompting of the Holy Spirit. The commission was fulfilled, too, by those Apostles and apostolic men who under the inspiration of the same Holy Spirit committed the message of salvation to writing....

And so the apostolic preaching, which is expressed in a special way in the inspired books, was to be preserved by an unending succession of preachers until the end of time. Therefore the Apostles, handing on what they themselves had received, warn the faithful to hold fast to the traditions which they have learned either by word of mouth or by letter (see 2 Thess. 2:15), and to fight in defense of the faith handed on once and for all (see Jude 1:3). Now what was handed on by the Apostles includes everything which contributes toward the holiness of life and increase in faith of the peoples of God; and so the Church, in her teaching, life and worship, perpetuates and hands on to all generations all that she herself is, all that she believes.

This tradition which comes from the Apostles develops in the Church with the help of the Holy Spirit. For there is a growth in the understanding of the realities and the words which have been handed down.... For as the centuries succeed one another, the Church constantly moves forward toward the fullness of divine truth until the words of God reach their complete fulfillment in her....

Through the same tradition the Church's full canon of the sacred books is known, and the sacred writings themselves are more profoundly understood and unceasingly made active in her; and thus God, who spoke of old, uninterruptedly converses with the bride of His beloved Son; and the Holy Spirit, through whom the living voice of the Gospel resounds in the Church, and through her, in the world, leads unto all truth those who believe and makes the word of Christ dwell abundantly in them (see Col. 3:16).

Hence there exists a close connection and communication between sacred tradition and Sacred Scripture. For both of them, flowing from the same divine wellspring, in a certain way merge into a unity and tend toward the same end. For Sacred Scripture is the word of God inasmuch as it is consigned to writing under the inspiration of the divine Spirit, while sacred tradition takes the word of God entrusted by Christ the Lord and the Holy Spirit to the Apostles, and hands it on to their successors in its full purity, so that led by the light of the Spirit of truth, they may in proclaiming it preserve this word of God faithfully, explain it, and make it more widely known. Consequently it is not from Sacred Scripture alone that the Church draws her certainty about everything which has been revealed. Therefore both sacred tradition and Sacred Scripture are to be accepted and venerated with the same sense of loyalty and reverence.

Sacred tradition and Sacred Scripture form one sacred deposit of the word of God, committed to the Church. Holding fast to this deposit the entire holy people united with their shepherds remain always steadfast in the teaching of the Apostles... so that holding to, practicing and professing the heritage of the faith, it becomes on the part of the bishops and faithful a single common effort.

But the task of authentically interpreting the word of God, whether written or handed on, has been entrusted exclusively to the living teaching office of the Church, whose authority is exercised in the name of Jesus Christ. This teaching office is not above the word of God, but serves it, teaching only what has been handed on, listening to it devoutly, guarding it scrupulously and explaining it faithfully in accord with a divine commission and with the help of the Holy Spirit, it draws from this one deposit of faith everything which it presents for belief as divinely revealed.

It is clear, therefore, that sacred tradition, Sacred Scripture and the teaching authority of the Church, in accord with God's most wise design, are so linked and joined together that one cannot stand without the others, and that all together and each in its own way under the action of the one Holy Spirit contribute effectively to the salvation of souls.

Chapter III: Sacred Scripture, Its Inspiration and Divine Interpretation. Those divinely revealed realities which are contained and presented in Sacred Scripture have been committed to writing under the inspiration of the Holy Spirit. For holy mother Church, relying on the belief of the Apostles (see John 20:31; 2 Tim. 3:16; 2 Peter 1:19-20, 3:15-16), holds that the books of both the Old and New Testaments in their entirety, with all their parts, are sacred and canonical because written under the inspiration of the Holy Spirit, they have God as their author and have been handed on as such to the Church herself. In composing the sacred books,

God chose men and while employed by Him they made use of their powers and abilities, so that with Him acting in them and through them, they, as true authors, consigned to writing everything and only those things which He wanted.

Therefore, since everything asserted by the inspired authors or sacred writers must be held to be asserted by the Holy Spirit, it follows that the books of Scripture must be acknowledged as teaching solidly, faithfully and without error that truth which God wanted put into sacred writings for the sake of salvation. Therefore, "all Scripture is divinely inspired and has its use for teaching the truth and refuting error, for reformation of manners and discipline in right living, so that the man who belongs to God may be efficient and equipped for good work of every kind" (2 Tim. 3:16-17).

However, since God speaks in Sacred Scripture through men in human fashion, the interpreter of Sacred Scripture, in order to see clearly what God wanted to communicate to us, should carefully investigate what meaning the sacred writers really intended, and what God wanted to manifest by means of their words.

To search out the intention of the sacred writers, attention should be given, among other things, to "literary forms." For truth is set forth and expressed differently in texts which are variously historical, prophetic, poetic, or of other forms of discourse. The interpreter must investigate what meaning the sacred writer intended to express and actually expressed in particular circumstances by using contemporary literary forms in accordance with the situation of his own time and culture. For the correct understanding of what the sacred author wanted to assert, due attention must be paid to the customary and characteristic styles of feeling, speaking and narrating which prevailed at the time of the sacred writer, and to the patterns men normally employed at that period in their] everyday dealings with one another.

But, since Holy Scripture must be read and interpreted in the sacred spirit in which it was written, no less serious attention must be given to the content and unity of the whole of Scripture if the meaning of the sacred texts is to be correctly worked out. The living tradition of the whole Church must be taken into account along with the harmony which exists between elements of the faith. It is the task of exegetes to work according to these rules toward a better understanding and explanation of the meaning of Sacred Scripture, so that through preparatory study the judgment of the Church may mature. For all of what has been said about the way of interpreting Scripture is subject finally to the judgment of the Church, which carries out the divine commission and ministry of guarding and interpreting the word of God.

In Sacred Scripture, therefore, while the truth and holiness of God always remains intact, the marvelous "condescension" of eternal wisdom is clearly shown, "that we may learn the gentle kindness of God, which words cannot express, and how far He has gone in adapting His language with thoughtful concern for our weak human nature...."

Chapter IV: The Old Testament. In carefully planning and preparing the salvation of the whole human race the God of infinite love, by a special dispensation, chose for Himself a people to whom He would entrust His promises. First He entered into a covenant with Abraham (see Gen. 15:18) and, through Moses, with the people of Israel (see Ex. 24:8).... Then too, when God Himself spoke to them through the mouth of the prophets, Israel daily gained a deeper and clearer understanding of His ways and made them more widely known among the nations (see Ps. 21:29; 95:1-3; Is. 2:1-5; Jer. 3:17). The plan of salvation foretold by the sacred authors, recounted and explained by them, is found as the true word of God in the books of the Old Testament: these books, therefore, written under divine inspiration, remain permanently valuable. "For all that was written for our instruction, so that by steadfastness and the encouragement of the Scriptures we might have hope" (Rom. 15:4).

The principal purpose to which the plan of the old covenant was directed was to prepare for the coming of Christ, the redeemer of all and of the messianic kingdom, to announce this coming by prophecy (see Luke 24:44; John 5:39; 1 Peter 1:10), and to indicate its meaning through various types (see 1 Cor. 10:12). Now the books of the Old Testament, in accordance with the state of mankind before the time of salvation established by Christ, reveal to all men the knowledge of God and of man and the ways in which God, just and merciful, deals with men. These books, though they also contain some things which are incomplete and temporary, nevertheless show us true divine pedagogy.

These same books, then, give expression to a lively sense of God, contain a store of sublime teachings about God, sound wisdom about human life, and a wonderful treasury of prayers, and in them the mystery of our salvation is present in a hidden way. Christians should receive them with reverence....

[T]he books of the Old Testament with all their parts, caught up into the proclamation of the Gospel, acquire and show forth their full meaning in the New Testament (see Matt. 5:17; Luke 24:27; Rom. 16:25-26; 2 Cor. 14:16) and in turn shed light on it and explain it.

Chapter V: The New Testament. The word of God, which is the power of God for the salvation of all who believe (see Rom. 1:16), is set forth and shows its power in a most excellent way in the writings of the New Testament. For when the fullness of time arrived (see Gal. 4:4), the Word was made flesh and dwelt among us in His fullness of graces and truth (see John 1:14). Christ established the kingdom of God on earth, manifested His Father and Himself by deeds and words, and completed His work by His death, resurrection and glorious Ascension and by the sending of the Holy Spirit. Having been lifted up from the earth, He draws all men to Himself (see John 12:32), He who alone has the words of eternal life (see John 6:68). This mystery had not been manifested to other generations as it was now revealed to His holy Apostles and prophets in the Holy Spirit (see Eph. 3:4-6), so that they might preach the Gospel, stir up faith in Jesus, Christ and Lord, and gather together the Church. Now the writings of the New Testament stand as a perpetual and divine witness to these realities....

[A]mong all the Scriptures... the Gospels have a special preeminence, and rightly so, for they are the principal witness for the life and teaching of the incarnate Word, our savior.

The Church has always and everywhere held and continues to hold that the four Gospels are of apostolic origin. For what the Apostles preached in fulfillment of the commission of Christ, afterwards they themselves and apostolic men, under the inspiration of the divine Spirit, handed on to us in writing: the foundation of faith, namely, the fourfold Gospel, according to Matthew, Mark, Luke and John. Holy Mother Church has firmly and with absolute constancy held... that the four Gospels, whose historical character the Church unhesitatingly asserts, faithfully hand on what Jesus Christ, while living among men, really did and taught for their eternal salvation until the day He was taken up into heaven (see Acts 1:1.... For their intention in writing was that either from their own memory and recollections, or from the witness of those who "themselves from the beginning were eyewitnesses and ministers of the Word" we might know "the truth" concerning those matters about which we have been instructed (see Luke 1:2-4).

Besides the four Gospels, the canon of the New Testament also contains the epistles of St. Paul and other apostolic writings, composed under the inspiration of the Holy Spirit, by which, according to the wise plan of God, those matters which concern Christ the Lord are confirmed....

For the Lord Jesus was with His apostles as He had promised (see Matt. 28:20) and sent them the advocate Spirit who would lead them into the fullness of truth (see John 16:13).

Chapter VI: Sacred Scripture in the Life of the Church. The Church has always venerated the divine Scriptures just as she venerates the body of the Lord.... She has always maintained them, and continues to do so, together with sacred tradition, as the supreme rule of faith, since, as inspired by God and committed once and for all to writing, they impart the word of God Himself without change, and make the voice of the Holy Spirit resound in the words of the prophets and Apostles. Therefore, like the

Christian religion itself, all the preaching of the Church must be nourished and regulated by Sacred Scripture. For in the sacred books, the Father who is in heaven meets His children with great love and speaks with them; and the force and power in the word of God is so great that it stands as the support and energy of the Church, the strength of faith for her sons, the food of the soul, the pure and everlasting source of spiritual life. Consequently these words are perfectly applicable to Sacred Scripture: "For the word of God is living and active" (Heb. 4:12) and "it has power to build you up and give you your heritage among all those who are sanctified" (Acts 20:32; see 1 Thess. 2:13).

Easy access to Sacred Scripture should be provided for all the Christian faithful. That is why the Church from the very beginning accepted as her own that very ancient Greek translation of the Old Testament which is called the Septuagint; and she has always given a place of honor to other Eastern translations and Latin ones especially the Latin translation known as the Vulgate. But since the word of God should be accessible at all times, the Church by her authority and with maternal concern sees to it that suitable and correct translations are made into different languages, especially from the original texts of the sacred books. And should the opportunity arise and the Church authorities approve, if these translations are produced in cooperation with the separated brethren as well, all Christians will be able to use them....

Sacred theology rests on the written word of God, together with sacred tradition, as its primary and perpetual foundation. By scrutinizing in the light of faith all truth stored up in the mystery of Christ, theology is most powerfully strengthened and constantly rejuvenated by that word. For the Sacred Scriptures contain the word of God and since they are inspired, really are the word of God; and so the study of the sacred page is, as it were, the soul of sacred theology....

Therefore, all the clergy must hold fast to the Sacred Scriptures through diligent sacred reading and careful study, especially the priests of Christ and others, such as deacons and catechists who are legitimately active in the ministry of the word....

It devolves on sacred bishops "who have the apostolic teaching" to give the faithful entrusted to them suitable instruction in the right use of the divine books, especially the New Testament and above all the Gospels. This can be done through translations of the sacred texts, which are to be provided with the necessary and really adequate explanations so that the children of the Church may safely and profitably become conversant with the Sacred Scriptures and be penetrated with their spirit....

In this way, therefore, through the reading and study of the sacred books "the word of God may spread rapidly and be glorified" (2 Thess. 3:1) and the treasure of revelation, entrusted to the Church, may more and more fill the hearts of men. Just as the life of the Church is strengthened through more frequent celebration of the Eucharistic mystery, similarly we may hope for a new stimulus for the life of the Spirit from a growing reverence for the word of God, which "lasts forever" (Is. 40:8; see 1 Peter 1:23-25). [For the full text of the *Dei Verbum*, see http://www.vatican.va/archive/hist_councils/iivatican_council/documents/vat-ii_const_19651118_dei-verbum_en.html.]

Belgic Confession (1561)

During the Reformation era one of the first formalized Protestant statements on the Bible was the Belgic Confession of 1561. Influenced by a similar document written primarily by John Calvin two years earlier in France, the Belgic Confession sought to end the persecution of non-Catholics in the Low Countries by making the case that the Reformers were sincere and law-abiding citizens committed to only those doctrines that correlated to Holy Scripture. A copy of the statement was sent to King Philip II of Spain in which the signers affirmed that they were prepared to obey the government "in all things lawful," but declared that they would "offer their backs to stripes, their tongues to knives, their mouths to gags, and their whole bodies to fire, rather than deny the truth of God's Word." (In fact, the principle author of the confession, Guido de Brès, was captured and executed in 1567.) The Belgic Confession was adopted by the Reformed Church in the Netherlands in 1566 and adopted by the Synod of Dort in 1618-19. Thereafter, it was recognized as one of the "Three Forms of Unity" of the Reformed churches – along with the Heidelberg Confession (1563) and the Canons of Dort (1618-19) – to which all officials of the churches were required to subscribe.

In the document, the Belgic Confession devoted seven of its 37 articles specifically to the doctrine of the Bible, including the following:

Article 3: The Written Word of God. We confess that this Word of God was not sent nor delivered by the will of man, but that holy men of God spoke as they were moved by the Holy Spirit, as the Apostle Peter says (II Pet. 1:21); and that afterwards God, from a special care which He has for us and our salvation, commanded His servants, the prophets and apostles, to commit His revealed word to writing; and He Himself wrote with His own finger the two tables of the law. Therefore we call such writings holy and divine Scriptures.

Article 5: Whence the Holy Scriptures Derive Their Dignity and Authority. We receive all these books, and these only, as holy and canonical, for the regulation, foundation, and confirmation of our faith; believing without any doubt all things contained in them, not so much because the Church receives and approves them as such, but more especially because the Holy Spirit witnesses in our hearts that they are from God, and also because they carry the evidence thereof in themselves. For the very blind are able to perceive that the things foretold in them are being fulfilled.

Article 7: The Sufficiency of the Holy Scriptures to Be the Only Rule of Faith. We believe that those Holy Scriptures fully contain the will of God, and that whatsoever man ought to believe unto salvation is sufficiently taught therein. For since the whole manner of worship which God requires of us is written in them at large, it is unlawful for any one, though an apostle, to teach otherwise than we are now taught in the Holy Scriptures: but even if we, or an angel from heaven, as the Apostle Paul says (Gal. 1:8). For since it is forbidden to add to or take away anything from the Word of God (Deut. 12:32), it does thereby evidently appear that the doctrine thereof is most perfect and complete in all respects. Neither may we consider any writings of men, however holy these men may have been, of equal value with those divine Scriptures, nor ought we to consider custom, or the great multitude, or antiquity, or succession of times and persons, or councils, decrees or statutes, as of equal value with the truth of God, since the truth is above all.... Therefore we reject with all our hearts whatever does not agree with this infallible rule, as the apostles have taught us, saying, "Test the spirits, whether they are of God" (I Jn. 4:1). Likewise: "If anyone comes to you and does not bring this doctrine, do not receive him into your house" (II Jn. 1:10).

Westminster Confesson of Faith (1647)

In England, about 80 years after the Belgic Confession and some 30 years following the Council of Dort, the Westminister Confession of Faith (1647) was drafted by Anglican clergymen – primarily Puritans – to serve as the official statement of faith of the Church of England. In America, the Confession was revised in 1789 following the Revolution and the establishment of the United States, becoming the *de facto* doctrinal statement for most American Presbyterians for generations. Chapter 1 of the statement, entitled "Holy Scripture Is the Written Word of God," enumerates ten articles regarding the Bible:

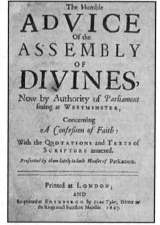

1. Our innate knowledge of God, the design, order and beauty of creation and God's sovereign purpose effected through history openly reveal his goodness, wisdom and strength. This natural revelation of God leaves all people without excuse should they not know, love and serve him. However, by itself this revelation is not sufficient to give the necessary knowledge of God and of his purpose leading to reconciliation with him. Consequently, it pleased the Lord to reveal himself using various historical events and methods.... The Lord put his revelation in written record, more effectively preserving and communicating his revealed truth. It provides a sure grounding... against our sinful disposition opposing God and against the evil intentions of Satan. Then God ceased revealing himself to his people as he had in previous ways. This made the written record of Holy Scripture absolutely necessary for the preservation of revealed truth.

2. [Article 2 includes a list of books that comprise the biblical canon, and concludes with the statement:] The Holy Spirit of God inspired these writings providing our only rule for faith and life.

3. The writings entitled The Apocrypha do not share in the Holy Spirit's inspiration. Thus, they are not included in the canon of Scripture.

4. The Bible, speaking with the authority of its author, merits our belief and obedience. Biblical authority for faith and life does not depend on human testimony nor on the witness of Christian institutions, but exclusively on God whose nature defines truth. We receive Holy Scripture because it is the Word of God.

5. ...We can be persuaded and assured of the infallible truth and godly source of the Bible through the Holy Spirit's testimony.

6. The entire purpose of God concerning all things necessary for his own glory, human salvation, faith and life style is expressly written in Scripture or may be reasonably concluded through careful and logical deduction from Scripture. Never may we add anything to the teaching of Scripture, whether pretending to be by revelation from the Holy Spirit or drawn from human traditions....

7. All Scripture is not easily interpreted nor clearly understood by each reader. Yet, everything we must know, believe and observe for salvation is understandably presented and taught somewhere in the Bible....

8. ...Both Testaments are authentic manuscripts being directly inspired by God and kept unadulterated and reliable through the centuries by his overseeing care. Consequently, the church must appeal to the Scriptures in all controversies about faith....

9. The Scripture provides its own infallible rule of interpretation. When a question arises,... it must be researched and understood from other texts speaking more clearly.

10. The Holy Spirit addressing us in the Scripture ultimately judges all controversies of faith, the decrees of church councils, opinions of ancient writers, al human teachings and privately held opinions. We resolve our differences with the judgment of him who judges all things.

Baptist Faith and Message (2000)

The Baptist Faith and Message, drafted in 2000 by the Southern Baptist Convention, includes a short paragraph on the church's doctrine of Scripture:

The Holy Bible was written by men divinely inspired and is God's revelation of Himself to man. It is a perfect treasure of divine instruction. It has God for its author, salvation for its end, and truth, without any mixture of error, for its matter. Therefore, all Scripture is totally true and trustworthy. It reveals the principles by which God judges us, and therefore is, and will remain to the end of the world, the true center of Christian union, and the supreme standard by which all human conduct, creeds, and religious opinions should be tried. All Scripture is a testimony to Christ, who is Himself the focus of divine revelation.

United Methodist Church Book of Discipline (2012)

According to the United Methodist Church Book of Discipline (United Methodist Publishing House, 2012)...

United Methodists share with other Christians the conviction that Scripture is the primary source and criterion for Christian doctrine. Through Scripture the living Christ meets us in the experience of redeeming grace. We are convinced that Jesus Christ is the living Word of God in our midst whom we trust in life and death. The biblical authors, illumined by the Holy Spirit, bear witness that in Christ the world is reconciled to God. The Bible bears authentic testimony to God's self-disclosure in the life, death, and resurrection of Jesus Christ as well as in God's work of creation, in the pilgrimage of Israel, and in the Holy Spirit's ongoing activity in human history.

As we open our minds and hearts to the Word of God through the words of human beings inspired by the Holy Spirit, faith is born and nourished, our understanding is deepened, and the possibilities for transforming the world become apparent to us.

The Bible is sacred canon for Christian people, formally acknowledged as such by historic ecumenical councils of the Church. Our doctrinal standards identify as canonical thirty-nine books of the Old Testament and the twenty-seven books of the New Testament.

Our standards affirm the Bible as the source of all that is "necessary" and "sufficient" unto salvation (Articles of Religion) and "is to be received through the Holy Spirit as the true rule and guide for faith and practice" (Confession of Faith)....

We interpret individual texts in light of their place in the Bible as a whole.

We are aided by scholarly inquiry and personal insight, under the guidance of the Holy Spirit. As we work with each text, we take into account what we have been able to learn about the original context and intention of that text. In this understanding we draw upon the careful historical, literary, and textual studies of recent years, which have enriched our understanding of the Bible.

Through this faithful reading of Scripture, we may come to know the truth of the biblical message in its bearing on our own lives and the life of the world. Thus, the Bible serves both as a source of our faith and as the basic criterion by which the truth and fidelity of any interpretation of faith is measured.

While we acknowledge the primacy of Scripture in theological reflection, our attempts to grasp its meaning always involve tradition, experience, and reason. Like Scripture, these may become creative vehicles of the Holy Spirit as they function within the Church. They quicken our faith, open our eyes to the wonder of God's love, and clarify our understanding.

The Wesleyan heritage, reflecting its origins in the catholic and reformed ethos of English Christianity, directs us to a self-conscious use of these three sources in interpreting Scripture and in formulating faith statements based on the biblical witness. These sources are, along with Scripture, indispensable to our theological task.

The close relationship of tradition, experience, and reason appears in the Bible itself. Scripture witnesses to a variety of diverse traditions, some of which reflect tensions in interpretation within the early Judeo-Christian heritage. However, these traditions are woven together in the Bible in a manner that expresses the fundamental unity of God's revelation as received and experienced by people in the diversity of their own lives....

Confession of Faith of the Evangelical Lutheran Church

Traditionally, the Augsburg Confession of 1530 has been the primary confession of faith of the Lutheran Church. However, none of the document's 28 Articles addressed the doctrine of the Bible directly. The **Confession of Faith of the Evangelical Lutheran Church** (ELCA), the largest Lutheran denomination in the United States, includes a brief statement on Scripture:

The proclamation of God's message to us as both Law and Gospel is the Word of God, revealing judgment and mercy through word and deed, beginning with the Word in creation, continuing in the history of Israel, and centering in all its fullness in the person and work of Jesus Christ.

The canonical Scriptures of the Old and New Testaments are the written Word of God. Inspired by God's Spirit speaking through their authors, they record and announce God's revelation centering in Jesus Christ. Through them God's Spirit speaks to us to create and sustain Christian faith and fellowship for service in the world.

This church accepts the canonical Scriptures of the Old and New Testaments as the inspired Word of God and the authoritative source and norm of its proclamation, faith, and life.

In addition, the ELCA's statement on "What We Believe/The Bible" includes this comment:

As Lutherans, ELCA members believe that the Bible is the written Word of God. It creates and nurtures faith through the work of the Holy Spirit and points us to Jesus Christ, the living Word and center of our faith. And in reading the Bible, we are invited into a relationship with God that both challenges us and promises us new life.

Mennonite Confession of Faith (1963)

Article II of the Mennonite Confession of Faith of 1963, a revision of the original 1527 Anabaptist statement, the Schleitheim Confession of Faith, puts forth a doctrine of Scripture in its section on "Divine Revelation:"

We believe that the God of creation and redemption has revealed Himself and His will for men in the Holy Scriptures, and supremely and finally in His incarnate Son, the Lord Jesus Christ. God's purpose in this revelation is the salvation of all men. Although God's power and deity are revealed in His creation, so that the nations are without excuse, this knowledge of Him cannot save men, for it cannot make Christ known. God revealed Himself in saving word and deed to Israel as recorded in the Old Testament; He fulfilled this revelation of Himself in the word and deed of Christ as recorded in the New Testament. We believe that all Scripture is given by the inspiration of God, that men moved by the Holy Spirit spoke from God. We accept the Scriptures as the authoritative Word of God, and through the Holy Spirit as the infallible Guide to lead men to faith in Christ and to guide them in the life of Christian discipleship.

Chicago Statement on Biblical Inerrancy (1978)

In 1978 the International Council on Biblical Inerrancy (ICBI) appointed a committee to draft a definitive statement on the Bible that would represent the position of conservative evangelicals. The resultant document, the Chicago Statement on Biblical Inerrancy, was signed by nearly 300 evangelical scholars and other leaders representing most major evangelical denominations and organizations. However, due to the statement's insistence upon the doctrines of inerrancy and verbal plenary inspiration, other notable evangelicals declined to endorse it. The statement's nineteen Articles of Affirmation and Denial include the following affirmations:

Article I: We affirm that the Holy Scriptures are to be received as the authoritative Word of God. We deny that the Scriptures receive their authority from the Church, tradition, or any other human source.

Article II: We affirm that the Scriptures are the supreme written norm by which God binds the conscience, and that the authority of the Church is subordinate to that of Scripture. We deny that Church creeds, councils, or declarations have authority greater than or equal to the authority of the Bible.

Article III: We affirm that the written Word in its entirety is revelation given by God. We deny that the Bible is merely a witness to revelation, or only becomes revelation in encounter, or depends on the responses of men for its validity.

Article IV: We affirm that God who made mankind in His image has used language as a means of revelation. We deny that human language is so limited by our creatureliness that it is rendered inadequate as a vehicle for divine revelation. We further deny that the corruption of human culture and language through sin has thwarted God's work of inspiration.

Article V: We affirm that God's revelation in the Holy Scriptures was progressive. We deny that later revelation, which may fulfill earlier revelation, ever corrects or contradicts it. We further deny that any normative revelation has been given since the completion of the New Testament writings.

Article VI: We affirm that the whole of Scripture and all its parts, down to the very words of the original, were given by divine inspiration.... [Note: This refers to the doctrine of "verbal plenary inspiration."]

Article VII: We affirm that inspiration was the work in which God by His Spirit, through human writers, gave us His Word. The origin of Scripture is divine. The mode of divine inspiration remains largely a mystery to us....

Article VIII: We affirm that God in His Work of inspiration utilized the distinctive personalities and literary styles of the writers whom He had chosen and prepared. We deny that God, in causing these writers to use the very words that He chose, overrode their personalities.

Article IX: We affirm that inspiration, though not conferring omniscience, guaranteed true and trustworthy utterance on all matters of which the Biblical authors were moved to speak and write. We deny that the finitude or fallenness of these writers, by necessity or otherwise, introduced distortion or falsehood into God's Word.

Article X: We affirm that inspiration, strictly speaking, applies only to the autographic text of Scripture [i.e., the original texts], which in the providence of God can be ascertained from available manuscripts with great accuracy. We further affirm that copies and translations of Scripture are the Word of God to the extent that they faithfully represent the original....

Article XI: We affirm that Scripture, having been given by divine inspiration, is infallible, so that... it is true and reliable in all the matters it addresses. We deny that it is possible for the Bible to be at the same time infallible and errant in its assertions. Infallibility and inerrancy may be distinguished, but not separated.

Article XII: We affirm that Scripture in its entirety is inerrant, being free from all falsehood, fraud, or deceit. We deny that Biblical infallibility and inerrancy are limited to spiritual, religious, or redemptive themes, exclusive of assertions in the field of history and science. We further deny that scientific hypotheses about earth history may properly be used to overturn the teaching of Scripture on creation and the flood.

Article XIII: We affirm the propriety of using inerrancy as a theological term with reference to the complete truthfulness of Scripture....

Article XIV: We affirm the unity and internal consistency of Scripture. We deny that alleged errors and discrepancies that have not yet been resolved vitiate the truth claims of the Bible.

Article XV: We affirm that the doctrine of inerrancy is grounded in the teaching of the Bible about inspiration....

Article XVI: We affirm that the doctrine of inerrancy has been integral to the Church's faith throughout its history. We deny that inerrancy is a doctrine invented by Scholastic Protestantism, or is a reactionary position postulated in response to negative higher criticism.

Article XVII: We affirm that the Holy Spirit bears witness to the Scriptures, assuring believers of the truthfulness of God's written Word. We deny that this witness of the Holy Spirit operates in isolation from or against Scripture.

Article XVIII: We affirm that the text of Scripture is to be interpreted by grammatico-historical exegesis, taking account of its literary forms and devices, and that Scripture is to interpret Scripture....

Article XIX: We affirm that a confession of the full authority, infallibility, and inerrancy of Scripture is vital to a sound understanding of the whole of the Christian faith.... We deny that such confession is necessary for salvation. However, we further deny that inerrancy can be rejected without grave consequences, both to the individual and to the Church.

The Summa: What Is the Bible?

As these and other statements of faith declare, the Bible, although it rarely comments on its own credibility and authority, matter-of-factly posits itself as the written expression of God's eternal Word. This is to be expected from a book that from Genesis to Revelation purports to be the product of divine revelation and an infallible guide along the path of spiritual salvation. As the written testimonial to the message and mission of the incarnate Son of God, it embodies the words of eternal life. This is why we can return time and time again to the same passages in Scripture for inspiration and guidance while never exhausting the implications of its truths. Like an ever-flowing river from which we can drink our fill, Scripture is always fresh and spiritually revitalizing. If having encountered Scripture we sometimes come away still feeling parched and unfulfilled, this is a reflection not on Scripture but on the state of our soul. As Jesus declared in his dialogue with the woman at the well in Sychar:

> Jesus said, "Everyone who drinks from the water [of this well] will be thirsty again, but whoever drinks the water I give him will never thirst. Indeed, the water I give him will become in him a spring of water welling up to eternal life." [John 4:13-14]

In light of the foregoing statements of faith, what then can we conclude about the Bible? What exactly *is* it? At the outset of this chapter I posed the question, "If asked to explain, 'What is the Bible?' without resorting to the familiar cliche', 'The Bible is the Word of God,' what exactly would you say?"

In summary, perhaps the best, most succinct definition might be as follows: **The Bible is the revelation of God's will and purpose for mankind in the context of history and in relation to four doctrinal themes: Creation, Fall, Redemption, and Restoration.**

To reiterate a seminal point from the Introduction, the Bible is unique. Unlike any other book ever written, there is life in its words because it testifies to the Living Word of God, the Lord Jesus Christ. This is why we are continually drawn to it, rereading it and absorbing it as we are illuminated, inspired, and convicted by the truth of its message. In this regard the Bible is certainly a book to be studied for its historical value as well as its doctrinal and moral principles. But more essentially, the Bible is a book to be *absorbed* as we encounter in the text our Creator, our Sustainer, and our Savior.

2
The Philosophy of the Bible
Components of a Biblical Worldview

The Bible as Philosophy

From Genesis to Revelation, the Bible puts forth a rational philosophical and theological explanation of reality that is coherent, consistent and comprehensive. In that respect, it encompasses the totality of reality and addresses the salient perennial issues of life. Many students of the Bible begin to realize this as they delve deeper into Scripture and start to absorb not only its metanarrative and doctrinal principles but also its underlying philosophy. As we mature in our understanding of Scripture we come to realize that the Bible addresses more than just the four cardinal theological themes of Creation, Fall, Redemption and Restoration. Undergirding these core doctrines, biblical revelation has a substructure – a particular worldview from which its unique philosophy and theology are derived.

Prior to the Enlightenment, Western societies, influenced by nearly a millennium-and-a-half of state-sponsored Christendom, generally held a consensus worldview. Despite individual ethnic and national distinctives, most Europeans, British and Americans agreed on certain philosophical and theological foundational principles that conditioned their understanding of God, human nature, morality and ethics, social relationships, and reality in general. As James Sire notes in his classic study of worldviews, *The Universe Next Door*, "The apostles of absurdity [i.e., Hume, Feuerbach, Nietzsche, Marx, Freud, *at al.*] were yet to arrive."[1]

The primary differences that divided Westerners came in the realm of religion and involved two issues in particular:

---

[1] James W. Sire, *The Universe Next Door: A Basic Worldview Catalogue*. Fourth Edition (IVP Academic, 1976, 2004), p. 25.

1. Ecclesiology – the principles of church structure and government. Roman Catholicism was built on a monarchical episcopate with an elaborate supporting hierarchy, answerable to the pope and the ecclesiastical magisterium. Anglicans (and later Methodists) held to an episcopal form of church government that included an ecclesiastical hierarchy of regional bishops who supervised individual churches, while Presbyterians adopted a representative government based on an eldership model. Baptist, Congregational and Anabaptist churches were governed democratically with each individual church being, at least in theory, autonomous.

2. Soteriology – the doctrine of spiritual salvation. The Roman Catholic Church held a sacramentalist view wherein salvific grace was dispensed via the Church through its teachings and sacraments. By contrast, Protestants understood salvation to be by grace alone (*sola gracia*) through faith in Jesus Christ (*sola fide*). The Anabaptist view was salvation by grace alone through faith as manifest by living in accord with the teachings of Jesus.

Theoretically, most Westerners derived their understanding of morality and ethics from the Bible. Common and civil law, based at least in part on biblical morals and ethics and principles of social justice, set the parameters of civic life – although in reality this was carried out very inconsistently and imperfectly. But for the past 250 years there has been a steady erosion in the cultural and moral consensus of the past under a constant barrage of anti-Christian *isms* – everything from Enlightenment rationalism and deism to theological liberalism, secularism, naturalism, scientism, Darwinism, Marxism, Freudianism, existentialism, and postmodernism. The deterioration process accelerated following the two great wars of the 20th century, and the collapse has become particularly apparent since the 1960s as traditional biblically-influenced values have been replaced by secular humanism, radical individualism, materialism and hedonism. The result has been social chaos, cultural disintegration, and a dysfunctional society that is spiraling dangerously out of control.

Basic Tenets of a Worldview

What Is a Worldview?

"I believe in Christianity as I believe that the sun has risen;
not only because I see it, but because by it I see everything else."
– C. S. Lewis, "Is Theology Poetry?"

In the above quote, C. S. Lewis was describing his basic worldview – the lens through which he viewed and processed all of reality, including that of his own existence. In essence, Christianity is a personal spiritual relationship with God through faith in Jesus Christ. Of course, Christianity is also a religion with its distinctive literature, doctrines, institutions, traditions, and modes of worship – although only in a secondary or supplemental sense. But what many Christians fail to understand is that the Bible also presents a coherent, consistent and comprehensive worldview that encompasses the total universe of reality. This is a wholistic and integrated system of thought through which we process not only theology but philosophy, morality, science, history, and the arts. As A. W. Tozer noted in his classic, *The Pursuit of God*, the moment we resolve to follow God regardless of the cost, we acquire "a new viewpoint" on everything about this life.

One of the best introductions to the concept of worldviews is James W. Sire's *The Universe Next Door*. In his book, Sire observes that few people have a carefully constructed theology, and even fewer have a well-reasoned and consistent philosophy of life, but everyone has a general worldview in terms of how they perceive the world to be structured and how it functions. No one is purely objective, no one lives values-free, and no one experiences life without processing what he/she observes through a particular reality grid. For example, the left-wing theoreticians Jung Min Choi and John W. Murphy concede in their book, *The Politics and Philosophy of Political Correctness*, that "any apparent absence of values" is an illusion, and that everything has a worldview context that "should be understood to represent particular claims rather than a vacuum." The point is that everyone has a worldview – a general conception of reality – although for most people their worldview is strictly subconscious.

So what is a worldview? As James Sire defines the term:

A worldview is a... fundamental orientation that can be expressed as a story or in a set of presuppositions (assumptions which may be true, partially true or entirely false) which we hold (consciously or subconsciously, consistently or inconsistently) about the basic constitution of reality, and that provides the foundation on which we live. [James Sire, *The Universe Next Door*, p. 17.]

Essentially, a worldview is a philosophical (and by extension, theological) matrix by which we make sense out of life. As the futurist Alvin Toffler put it, "Every person carries in his head a mental model of the world, a subjective representation of external reality."[2] In another of his books, *Naming the Elephant*, James Sire describes a worldview as "the fundamental orientation of one's heart" that encapsulates the deepest desires, hopes, feelings and beliefs of our intellect, emotions, and will. As the theologian James Orr conceptualized it, our worldview comes from "deep within the constitution of our human nature"[4] and involves our intellect, our emotions and our will.

[2] The first philosopher to introduce the concept of "worldviews" was Immanuel Kant, who used the term *weltanschauung* to denote a set of basic beliefs that underlie all human thought and action.

In the 1890s the theologian James Orr adapted the concept to a Christian context in *The Christian View of God and the World*. About the same time, Abraham Kuyper, a Dutch theologian and statesman, emphasized that the Christian faith incorporates "three fundamental relations of human existence: our relation to God, to man, and to the world." Kuyper also related the worldview concept to culture, and argued that a Christian worldview illuminates all areas of life from politics to science and the arts.

In the 1950s the philosopher Herman Dooyeweerd argued that worldviews are not so much philosophical as *pretheoretical* [or presuppositional] matters of faith and commitment. For him, theory and practice are products of the heart and will more than the intellect.

For an in-depth analysis of worldviews from a Christian perspective, see...
- Arthur F. Holmes, *Contours of a World View* (Eerdmans, 1983); and
- David Naugle, *Worldview: The History of a Concept* (Eerdmans, 2002).

Why Do Worldviews Matter?

Simply stated, our worldview is our interpretive framework for making sense out of the world. Experience tells us that people can look at the same data and derive totally opposite conclusions based on their respective worldview differences. Consider this simplistic example:

GODISNOWHERE

A Christian with a theistic worldview will interpret this message to say, "God is now here," while an atheist with a naturalistic worldview will assume that it says, "God is nowhere." The difference in how one interprets this and all other data that we receive and process in life depends upon one's worldview perspective. However, it should be emphasized that the fact that people view things differently and disagree about fundamental realities does not mean there is no objective, absolute truth about these realities. It is simply a matter that some people are more perceptive of truth and receptive to it than others.

In today's culture it is imperative that Christians understand the concept of worldviews. Contemporary America is the most religiously diverse nation in the world. Beginning in the mid-1800s the traditional Protestant monopoly on American religious life was broken by the mass immigration of Roman Catholics from Germany and Ireland, and later from other southern and eastern European nations. In addition, America became a haven for Orthodox Christians and Jews in the decades surrounding the turn of the 20th century. Despite their religious differences, thoughtful and committed Christians (whether Protestant, Catholic or Orthodox) and religious Jews shared a similar worldview based on fundamental biblical principles which set them apart from devotees of other religions and those with a more secular orientation: nominal Protestants, merely cultural Catholic and Orthodox "Christians," non-religious and liberal Reformed Jews, atheists, agnostics, "free-thinkers," *et al.* But throughout the 20th century as secularists gained more status, prominence, power and influence in American life and our cultural institutions, by the 1960s it was evident that the generic Christian consensus of the past was long gone

Today, a multiplicity of worldviews, philosophies, religions and "spiritualities" compete in the public marketplace of ideas – everything from Islam and Eastern religions such as Hinduism and Buddhism to Scientology and the New Age movement. In that respect, our situation today is remarkably similar to the pluralistic culture in which the early church operated, which makes the apostle Paul's counsel to the Colossian Christians all the more relevant when he wrote: "Make certain that no one seduces you through hollow and deceptive philosophies which depend on human tradition and the principles of this world rather than on Christ" (Col. 2:8).

In particular, there are four reasons why Christians should be familiar with the concept of worldviews:

(1) To understand that the Bible presents a worldview – an interpretive framework for understanding all of reality – that contrasts sharply with that of other alternative worldviews.

(2) To understand how alternative worldviews developed historically, and the distinctive beliefs, values and practical ramifications of these worldviews.

(3) To increase our own self-awareness and self-understanding. As James Sire writes, "Our worldview generally lies so deeply embedded in our subconscious that unless we have reflected long and hard, we are unaware of what it is. Therefore, to discover one's worldview... is a significant step toward self-awareness, self-knowledge and self-understanding."[3]

(4) To help equip us to better understand and communicate more effectively with others – both those who share our own worldview as well as those who do not. As Sire notes, "To be fully conscious intellectually," it is essential that we be aware not only of our own worldview but that of others.[4] This is particularly relevant and essential given the diverse multi-cultural society in which we live.

Components of a Worldview

A worldview is a general interpretive framework for processing and making sense of the realities we encounter in this life. As such, it provides a grid by which we receive and evaluate truth. But what is truth? **Simply stated, truth is that which corresponds to reality**. So the popular relativistic claim that there *is* no (absolute) truth is tantamount to claiming that there is no (absolute) reality, which all sane people know intuitively to be absurd. That being the case, our worldview will influence (consistently or not, and consciously or not) our philosophy of life, our understanding of who and what we are, our views of God and religion, and even how we look at social and political issues.

All of philosophy is divided into two basic fields of study: **ontology** and **epistemology**. Ontology (or **metaphysics**) deals with the nature of being – in other words, the reality of what exists. Epistemology is the study of knowing – i.e., how

---

[3] Sire, *The Universe Next Door*, p. 19.

[4] Ibid., p. 11.

we can know or understand the reality of what exists. All worldviews attempt to address the basic ontological and epistemological questions of life.

Four Ontological Issues

(1) Prime reality: What is the ultimate, eternal, self-existent and self-sufficient reality?

(2) Origins: Why is there something rather than nothing, and what is the source of everything that exists?

(3) The human condition: What is humanity in nature and essence?

(4) Destiny: What happens when a person dies?

Three Epistemological Issues

(5) The basis for knowledge: How can we know anything at all?

(6) Morality: Are good and evil objective realities – and if so, how do we know what is right and wrong?

(7) Meaning: What (if anything) is the purpose of human life?

For the most part, these seven questions can be reduced to four perennial issues of life as they affect us personally.

The Perennial Issues of Life

(1) Identity: Who am I?

(2) Origin: Where did I come from?

(3) Meaning: What am I doing here (or, What *should* I be doing here)?

(4) Destiny: Where am I going?

Although a worldview is not a religion, there is a close connection between the two. As the church historian Martin Marty observes, every religion serves two functions: First, it offers a message of personal salvation – i.e., how does one get right with God (or get in tune with the Cosmic Order)? Second, it serves as a lens for interpreting the world.

The Validity of a Worldview

For a worldview to be credible, it must provide reasonable and plausible answers to the basic questions of life. Therefore, a valid worldview must be comprehensive. It must provide satisfactory answers – or at least, *better* answers – to the perennial issues of life than any alternative worldview. Second, a valid worldview must be coherent and consistent. It cannot be internally disjointed or riddled with contradictions. As James Sire explains, the crucial questions to ask of a worldview are:

- How does it explain the fact that human beings think but think inconsistently, love but also hate, are creative but also destructive, wise but often foolish?
- What explains our longing for truth and personal fulfillment? What does it matter?
- Why is pleasure rarely enough to satisfy us?

A valid worldview must be livable and practicable. It cannot deny the realities of life, as in the Eastern pantheistic doctrine of *maya* ("All that we observe and experience in this life is an illusion") or the secular humanistic notion that human beings are innately good. As Ronald Nash comments in his book, *Life's Ultimate Questions*, a worldview must correspond to reality and be verifiable in "the laboratory of life" – in everyday living. In other words, "Can people who profess [a particular] worldview live consistently in harmony with the system they profess?" This is simply another way of saying that for a worldview to be valid, it must be *true*: it must correspond to reality.

This is true for the Christian theistic worldview just as it is for any other. If the Christian worldview is true, it must be comprehensive, coherent, consistent, and livable. This is why the whole "sacred v. secular" dichotomy is so absurd, as A. W. Tozer noted in his book, *The Pursuit of God*:

> One of the greatest hindrances to internal peace which the Christian encounters is the common habit of dividing up lives into two areas – the sacred and the secular. As these areas are conceived to exist apart from each other and to be morally and spiritually incompatible [not to mention, intellectually incompatible]... our inner lives tend to break up so that we live a divided instead of a unified life....
>
> This is the old sacred-secular antithesis. Most Christians are caught up in its trap. They cannot get a satisfactory adjustment between the claims of the two worlds. They try to walk a tightrope between two kingdoms and they find no peace in either....
>
> I believe this state of affairs to be wholly unnecessary.... the dilemma is not real. It is a creature of misunderstanding. The sacred-secular antithesis has no foundation in the New Testament....
>
> The Lord Jesus Christ is our perfect example, and he knew no divided life. [A. W. Tozer, *The Pursuit of God* (WingSpread Publishers, 1948), pp. 111*ff*.]

For the follower of Christ, all of life is holy, and everything should be received as a manifestation of God's grace. One effective way of doing this is by practicing the traditional Christian spiritual disciplines.[5] In doing so, we learn to transform every common thought and every common act into a

---

[5] See Richard J. Foster, *Celebration of Discipline* (HarperSanFrancisco, 1978, 1998).

sacrament, and in effect we fulfill Jesus' admonition to "pray without ceasing." This requires focused intentionality and mental effort, but in keeping with Paul's exhortation in Romans 12:1, we allow the Holy Spirit to transform our heart by the renewing of our mind.

Three Basic Options

In *The Universe Next Door* James Sire describes the component principles of a Christian theistic worldview, and then proceeds to compare and contrast Christian theism with seven alternative worldviews: deism, naturalism, nihilism, existentialism, pantheistic monism, the New Age, and postmodernism. Sire's treatment of the subject is illuminating, and I highly recommend it. However, in essence there are only three basic worldviews from which all others are derived.

1. Naturalism is an atheistic and materialistic worldview based on the belief that we live in a chaotic and purposeless universe in which matter is eternal, all physical laws arranged themselves naturalistically, life began as a result of a combination of natural chemical reactions that remain undiscovered, and all life forms (including human beings) are the product of random evolutionary processes over billions of years. Naturalists believe there is no God or Intelligent Designer of the universe, and that all is ultimately meaningless. When we die, we simply cease to exist as living and sentient beings.

In such a materialistic system, of course, there is no objective basis for morality since all that exists simply *is*. There are no good and bad chemicals, no good and bad atoms, and no good and bad organisms. Therefore, categories of right and wrong are merely subjective assessments that human beings manufacture according to their own preferences and needs.

2. Pantheistic monism holds that there is a mysterious Life Force that pervades all of nature and holds everything together. All that exists is part of this mystical force, including human beings. Therefore, as the line from the Beatles' song, "I Am the Walrus," puts it: *"I am he as you are he as you are me and we are all together."* So whereas naturalism teaches that all is material and there is no supernatural or transcendent God, pantheism in its Eastern (Hinduistic) manifestations declares that the physical world is *maya* – an illusion – and that everything is "god" or "godness" (including you and me). According to this belief system, the goal and purpose in life is to transcend the physical/material realm and achieve mystical oneness with Ultimate Reality as we are absorbed into Brahman, the Universal Soul, at which point we cease to exist as individual sentient beings.

Ironically, just as naturalism has no basis for morality, neither does pantheism. If all that exists is God, then there is no anti-God. Therefore, in keeping with the doctrine of non-duality, all that exists is good, which eliminates the very concept of evil.

3. Theism declares that an infinite and transcendent God created the universe and sustains it by his power and will. God is the only eternal reality, and by him and through him all things exist. God created human beings in his image, and as such we have a purpose and goal in life, as articulated in the Westminster Shorter Catechism: "Man's chief end is to glorify God, and to enjoy him forever." Furthermore, God is Goodness and the essence of all morality. Therefore, distinctions between good and evil are not subjective illusions or human constructs, but instead reflect cosmic realities.

In his book, *What Is Religion and of What Does Its Essence Consist?*, Leo Tolstoy commented on these three worldview options, and the inextricable relationship between our worldview and how we live our lives.

> Men in general, having defined their position in the world in one way or another, unavoidably and naturally act according to this definition (which is sometimes not even a definition but a vague consciousness). Thus, for instance, a person who has defined his position in the world as being a member of God's chosen people, who in order to enjoy God's protection must fulfil his demands, will live in such a way as to fulfill these demands. Another person who has defined his position in such a way that he believes he has passed, and is passing through, various forms of existence and that the deterioration or improvement of his future more or less depends on his actions, will be guided in life by this definition. The behaviour of a third person, who has defined his position as that of an incidental combination of atoms in which a consciousness has been temporarily ignited but which is bound to be extinguished forever, will differ from the two above-mentioned. The conduct of these people will be completely different. [Cited in Leo Tolstoy, *A Confession and Other Religious Writings* (Penguin Classics, 1987), pp. 97-98.]

Human beings either work their way through life mindfully and intentionally, or else they drift along mindlessly and aimlessly. So long as we live, we will live either an examined or an unexamined life, and as Socrates warned 2400 years ago, "The unexamined life is not worth living." This is the value in reflecting upon the component features of a Christian theistic worldview. It clarifies and sharpens our understanding of what it means to be a true follower of Jesus Christ, or what Francis Schaeffer called "the Lordship of Jesus Christ over the whole of life."

Basic Tenets of Christian Theism

"God Is..." – The Character and Attributes of God

As stated previously, all of philosophy is divided into two broad areas: ontology (metaphysics) and epistemology. Ontology is the foundation of all worldviews and, as Aristotle explained, it is "the first philosophy." This is quite sensible when we think about it for the simple reason that, logically, ontology precedes epistemology because if nothing exists then there is nothing to be known. Therefore, in defining Prime Reality, we begin with the Ultimate Being: God.

As the medieval philosopher and theologian Thomas Aquinas (1225-74) observed, finite human beings can only conceive of the infinite God analogically, and although we can know something about God through his creation (general revelation) and his revealed Word (special revelation), some aspects of his character and nature are beyond our capacity to comprehend. This is why Scripture employs figurative and even anthropomorphic language in which, as Aquinas noted, spiritual truths are taught in relation to material things. This is an essential principle to keep in mind as we consider the character and attributes of God.

According to the Bible, God is the **Ultimate Being** and the sole **Self-existent Reality**. This is the philosophical and theological principle of **aseity** (Latin: *aseite*) which denotes that God exists in and of himself and is wholly self-sufficient. God is also the great **Uncaused Cause** – the fundamental necessary Being for all that exists. As such, he is the **Creator** and the **Sustainer** of all matter, space, time, and energy, which he brought into existence *ex nihilo* ("out of nothing"). Numerous Scripture passages attest to these divine characteristics:

- Genesis 1:1 – "In the beginning God created the heavens and the earth."
- Exodus 3:14 – "I AM THAT I AM."
- Psalm 90:2 – "... from everlasting to everlasting you are God."
- John 1:1, 3 – "In the beginning was the Word,... and the Word was God.... Through him all things were made."
- John 5:26 – "For as the Father has life in himself, so he has granted the Son also to have life in himself."
- Acts 17:25, 28 – "[God] gives everyone life and breath and everything else.... For in him we live and move and have our being."
- Romans 11:36 – "For from him and through him and for him are all things."
- Colossians 1:16 – "For by him all things were created."

- I Timothy 1:17 – "Now to the King eternal, immortal, invisible, the only God, be honor and glory forever and ever."
- I Timothy 6:15-16 – "God, the blessed and only Ruler, the King of kings and Lord of lords, who alone is immortal and who lives in unapproachable light, whom no one has seen or can see. To him be honor and might forever."
- Hebrews 2:10 – "... God, for whom and through whom everything exists...."
- Rev. 1:8 – "'I am the Alpha and the Omega,' says the Lord God, 'who is, and who was, and who is to come, the Almighty.'"
- Revelation 4:11 – "You are worthy, our Lord and God, to receive glory and honor and power, for you created all things, and by your will they were created and have their being."

As many of these verses imply, God is **Eternal and Infinite**, the only self-existent and unlimited Being who is not only the Ultimate Reality but the Primordial Reality. God is also absolute **Perfection** who, in terms of his descriptive features and defining characteristics, is the Ultimate Standard for all that is True, Good, and Beautiful.

God is the one and only true God – the doctrine of **monotheism**. Deuteronomy 6:4 declares, "Hear, O Israel: The Lord our God, the Lord is one." Logically, there can be only one God because in order to be God, he must personify Perfection. There could not be two (or more) separate beings who have all the perfections of God because each one would have to differ from the other(s) qualitatively. But if that were true, one or both (or others) would be less than total Perfection – in which case, that one (or others) would not be God.

God is **Personal** – not an impersonal cosmic energy force. In ancient times Plato idealized God as an impersonal principle – "The Good." Likewise, the Romans conceived of "the gods" collectively as "Fate." But in Scripture God reveals himself in personal terms as YHWH (a name that Jews refer to as the "sacred Tetragrammaton"), and he communicates his will and purpose to mankind (see Chapter 3). God has personality – self-consciousness and self-determination – and in the Bible we are told that God thinks and acts and has a will. (Ref. II Timothy 2:19; Jeremiah 29:11; I John 2:17; Exodus 3:13-14; and Ephesians 1:11.) Most astonishingly, the Bible also declares that God is knowable and One to whom we can personally relate.

Logically, it is impossible that God is impersonal. Matter and consciousness are distinct, and personhood is more complex than any other manifestation of creation. Conscious entities do not and cannot emerge from unconscious and strictly material processes. As the philosopher John Searle comments, "The leading problem in the biological sciences is the problem of explaining how neurobiological processes cause conscious experiences." Just as an effect cannot be greater than its cause, the creation cannot be greater (or more complex) than its Creator. Therefore, personhood cannot derive from an impersonal force. Furthermore, only persons make conscious choices – such as, for example, the choice to create!

The Bible teaches the profound mystery that God is not only Personal and One but Triune in nature. Although one in essence, God exists in three Persons – the doctrine of the **Trinity** ("Tri-Unity" – "Three in One"). Therefore, God has a communal and relational nature. One of the most common names for God in the ancient Hebrew texts is Elohim, which is plural, and the doctrine of the Trinity is implied in the Hebrew Scriptures. For example, Genesis 1:26 declares, "Let us make man in *our* own image, and in Genesis 3:22 we read, "And the Lord God said, 'Man has now become like *one of us*, knowing good and evil.'" Likewise, Genesis 11:7 states, "[The Lord said], 'Let *us* go down and confuse their language so they will not understand each other.'"

However, the concept of the Trinity was not apparent until the coming of Jesus Christ and the revelation of the New Testament Scriptures. Early Christians acknowledged the reality of the Trinity, and the doctrine was formalized at the Council of Nicaea in 325 A.D. when the term used to define the relationship between God the Father, the Son, and the Holy Spirit was *homoousios* – of the same nature. God exists as one in essence and three in personhood – i.e., one What and three Whos. Scripture teaches that God is One (Deut. 6:4), the Father is God (John 6:27), the Son is God (John 1:1), and the Holy Spirit is God (Acts 5:3-4).[6]

God is **Spirit**. Although the Bible often uses anthropomorphic language to describe God and his characteristics, God is in fact immaterial and non-corporeal. (Ref. John 4:24; Luke 24:39; I Timothy 1:17; and Colossians 1:15.)

---

[6] There are numerous inferences in the New Testament to the Trinity and the co-equal relationship between the Father, Son, and Holy Spirit, including the following:

- Matt. 3:13-17; Mark 1:9-11; Luke 3:21-22; and John 1:29-34.
- Matthew 28:19-20.
- John 1:1-14.
- John 8:58.
- John 10:25-33.
- John 14:6-17.
- John 16:5-16.
- John 20:28.
- Acts 1:7-8.

- Acts 5:3-4.
- Romans 10:9-13.
- II Corinthians 3:17.
- Philippians 2:5-11.
- Colossians 1:15-20.
- Colossians 2:9.
- Titus 2:13.
- Hebrews 1:3.
- II Peter 1:1-2.
- I John 5:20.

God is **Transcendent**. God is not of the cosmos, but over and above it. In contrast to ancient Mesopotamian mythology, God was not created out of the (presumably eternal) earth, but is Wholly Other. Correspondingly, God is **holy** – i.e., ontologically and existentially separate and distinct from his creation.

God is **Immanent**. God is ontologically distinct from his creation but also integrally involved in it. There is nowhere in the universe that God is not present, and God inhabits those who have a personal relationship with him through the indwelling presence of the Holy Spirit. As Jesus taught, "The Kingdom of God is within you" (Luke 17:21), and as he instructed his disciples, "I will ask the Father, and he will give you another Counselor to be with you forever – the Spirit of truth... [and] when he, the Spirit of truth, comes, he will guide you into all truth" (John 14:15-16; 16:13). This is particularly significant because only Christian theism holds that God is both transcendent *and* immanent. Deism holds that God is separate from the world, while pantheism declares that God *is* the world and everything in it.

God is **Omniscient** – i.e., all-knowing. Having created us, God is the ultimate source of all knowledge and intelligence, and he is conscious of our every thought, word and action. (Ref. Psalm 139; Psalm 147:5; Hebrews 4:13; and Isaiah 46:10.)

God is **Omnipresent**. Although God transcends his creation, his presence is everywhere in the universe.

God is **Omnipotent** and **Sovereign**. God is all-powerful, and nothing is beyond God's control and authority. (Ref. Revelation 19:6; Ephesians 1:19-21; and Isaiah 46:10.)

God is **Immutable** – i.e., unchanging. To change, God would either have to progress or regress, improve or deteriorate, expand or contract, which is metaphysically impossible for an absolute and perfect Being. In Scripture, God identifies himself as the great "I AM," and in Malachi 3:6 he declares, "I the Lord do not change." Jesus emphasized this attribute of God when he proclaimed in John 8:58, "Before Abraham was born, I AM."

God is **Inscrutable**. God is beyond our capacity to fully understand, which is a characteristic one would expect from an infinite Being. As Job finally realized after his extended dialogue with God, "Surely I spoke of things I did not understand, things too wonderful for me to know" (Job 42:1-6). This is the truth that God conveyed through the prophet Isaiah who wrote, "'For my thoughts are not your thoughts, neither are your ways my ways,' says the Lord. 'As the heavens are higher than the earth, so are my ways higher than your ways and my thoughts than your thoughts'" (Isaiah 55:8-9).

God is **Goodness**. As James Sire observes in *The Universe Next Door*, "This is the prime statement about God's character."[7] It is vitally important to distinguish between God being "good" and God being "Goodness." In his essay, "The Poison of Subjectivism," C. S. Lewis emphasizes the point that "God is not merely good, but goodness." In other words, God is not accountable, nor are his actions accountable, to some higher standard of "good." God is himself Goodness by which all things are judged. As John 1:5 declares, "God is light; in him is no darkness at all." As such, God's character is the source and the standard for all morality and ethics. In his chapter on Judaism in *The World's Religions*, author Houston Smith observes, "The supreme achievement of Jewish thought was in the character it ascribed to God. Unlike the gods of other cultures, YHWH was neither amoral nor indifferent toward humanity, but a God of justice, righteousness and lovingkindness."[8]

Finally, God is **Love**: There is hope for humanity because God is not indifferent toward his creation. As I John 4:16 declares, "God is love," and in John 3:16 we read, "For God so loved the world that he gave his only begotten Son" as a sacrifice for our sins. In this context we should note that God is love even before he created the present universe. As a sacred Trinity, it is God's nature to be the personification of love.

The Nature of the Cosmos

According to the tenets of Christian theism, **God created the cosmos to operate with a uniformity of cause-and-effect in an open system**. God created the physical/material universe out of nothing – not out of himself in accord with the philosophy of pantheism. Furthermore, God is not the product of an eternal universe, contrary to the creation myths of ancient Mesopotamia.

As the creative product and expression of a rational God, the universe is orderly, not random and chaotic, and it operates according to natural physical laws of cause and effect. However, in contrast to naturalistic and materialistic presumptions, the cosmos operates within an open system. God created natural physical laws to govern the normal functions of the cosmos, but God can

---

[7] Sire, *The Universe Next Door*, p. 28.

[8] Houston Smith, *The World's Religions* (HarperSanFrancisco, 1958, 1991), p. 275. Smith is correct that the God who revealed himself to Moses and subsequent Hebrew prophets stands in stark contrast to the imaginary deities of other ancient religions, but it should be noted that he is wrong in assuming that this understanding of God was simply the product of "Jewish thought." In fact, as Scripture declares, this awareness of God was the result of divine revelation, not human imagination.

intervene supernaturally to supervene the natural order of things. Christians also believe that God can (and does) intervene in the lives of individuals, as the apologist Ron Rhodes explains:

> It is important to keep in mind... that the laws of nature are merely observations of uniformity or constancy in nature. They are not forces that *initiate* action. They simply describe the way nature behaves when its course is not affected by a superior power.... When a miracle occurs, then, the laws of nature are not violated, but are rather superseded by a higher (supernatural) manifestation of the will of God. [Ron Rhodes, *Answering the Objections of Atheists, Agnostics & Skeptics* (Harvest House, 2006), p. 65.]

Regarding the phenomenon of divine intervention and the suspension of the natural order, it is important to note that miracles are *not irrational* but rather *supra-rational*. There is nothing irrational about an omnipotent Creator who is capable of overriding the natural physical laws that he himself put into place if and when he so chooses to do so. Without that power and ability, he would not by definition be God because he would be subject to a higher natural law.

The Bible teaches that human existence is not deterministic, and that we possess considerable freedom of choice within certain human limitations. We are not robots, and our choices have consequences. As such, we can be channels through whom God works. God created humanity to have fellowship with him and to share his love, which requires a certain degree of free-will on our part. As James Sire explains in *The Universe Next Door*:

> The [cosmos] is open, and that means it is not programmed. God is constantly involved in the unfolding pattern of the ongoing operation of the universe. And so are we human beings! The course of the world's operation is open to reordering by either....
>
> If the universe were not orderly, our choices would have no effect. If events were pre-determined, our decisions would have no significance. [Sire, *The Universe Next Door*, pp. 30, 31]

The Christian theistic view of the universe has two significant implications: First, contrary to the pantheistic worldview, the Bible teaches that the physical universe is real, not an illusion, and furthermore it is not innately evil. As C. S. Lewis noted in *Mere Christianity*, "God never meant man to be a purely spiritual creature. He likes matter. He invented it."[9] Second, contrary to atheistic naturalism, Scripture teaches that the cosmos is rational, orderly and purposeful rather than random, chaotic and meaningless. Throughout Scripture the message is not only proclaimed but demonstrated repeatedly: all of creation reflects the glory of God, and is therefore rational, orderly and purposeful.

---

[9] C. S. Lewis, *Mere Christianity* (HarperSanFrancisco, 1952, 1980), p. 64.

The Human Condition

There are two aspects of our human nature and the human condition to be considered. First, the good news: **Human beings have been created in the Imago Dei** – the Image of God. As Genesis 1:26-27 recounts the creation of man, God declares, "Let us make man in our image." We are a special creation, not the random by-products of blind naturalistic evolutionary forces.

Old Testament scholars explain that in the context of the ancient Near East, the concept of the "Image of God" suggests that man has been commissioned to act as God's representative agent on Earth. Therefore, in order to function in this capacity, man possesses certain delegated properties. Like God, we have personality – a phenomenon that entails five attributes:

(1) We have **self-consciousness** and self-awareness – an innate sense of self.

(2) We have **self-determination** – the capacity (within certain limitations) to think and act independently and to exercise free will. Nothing in this life is deterministic, and each of us is responsible in terms of how we choose to respond to life's situations.

(3) We have **intelligence** – the capacity to acquire knowledge and to think rationally, critically and creatively. Being made in God's image, we can express ourselves in complex, abstract language. We are aware of the past and present, and we can anticipate the future. As imaginative and creative beings, we can express ourselves through art, crafts, music, literature, science, and technological inventions.

(4) We have a sense of **moral consciousness**, the innate capacity for discerning right and wrong, good and evil.

(5) We are, in a sense, **spiritual beings** with an innate sense of God-consciousness. Contrary to the teachings of pantheism, we are *not* divine, but contrary to the presuppositions of naturalism, we are more than purely physical/material beings. We have an eternal soul that is our true essence and an innate sense of God-consciousness that John Calvin referred to as the *sensus divinitatis*. As the famous line attributed to C. S. Lewis puts it, "You do not *have* a soul. You *are* a soul. You *have* a body."

These five properties are unique to our soul, not to our hominid body. In that respect it does not matter so much how we got our body since the crucial element that makes us human is our soul.[10]

---

[10] That being said, I find the popular theory that human beings evolved from lower life-forms to be highly problematic. Not only is theistic evolution (or evolutionary creationism) difficult to reconcile with biblical theology and a high view of Scripture, but there is no conclusive scientific evidence for such a presumption.

The second aspect of our human nature is bad news, although fortunately it need not be terminal: **The Fall has seriously corrupted human nature and the *Imago Dei* – but God has provided a path to redemption**. Human nature is neither totally good nor totally bad, but a complex and curious mix phenomenon. As such, human beings are capable of great acts of kindness, compassion, altruism and even self-sacrifice, but also extreme narcissism, selfishness, insensitivity, jealousy, hatred, and gross savagery and brutality.

In this regard, it is important to note that the Calvinistic doctrine of "total depravity" relates to the fact that our nature has been corrupted in every respect, but not that human beings are totally incapable of any goodness at all. Perhaps a better term would be "innate depravity." But as John Wesley propagated in his doctrine of prevenient grace, humankind, although seriously flawed and spiritually sick unto death, still retains some residual spark of the *Imago Dei* that distinguishes us from the rest of God's creatures.

Human beings were created with a degree of free will. This is a unique capacity that sets us apart from the rest of the animal kingdom that operate on the bases of instinct and impulse alone. The original sin was the choice by Adam and Eve to intentionally defy God's will. Dissatisfied with their status as stewards of God's creation, they sought to usurp his place as the lords over creation. Yielding to the serpent's temptation, they committed the ultimate act of rebellion in return for Satan's promise, "You will be like God" (Gen. 3:5).

As a result, everything about our human nature, including our perceptions of truth and reality, has been tainted by the effects of the Fall: it distorted our understanding of the nature and character of God; it corrupted the divine image of God within us as we became selfish, rebellious, and alienated from God; and it broke our relationship with God. In the process, humanity lost the divine presence. (This reality is as true for babies as for adults. As Augustine once quipped, if babies do no harm it is not for lack of will but simply for lack of strength!)

According to the doctrine of Original Sin, we inherited a sin nature from Adam and Eve, and like them we suffer through all of life from the effects of this condition. Our humanity is flawed and our thinking and behavior are impaired. As James Sire comments, "In this manner people... have attempted to set themselves up as autonomous beings," and they choose to act "as if they had an existence independent from God." The results are comprehensive: intellectually, our thinking is muddled and confused; morally, we need divine insight to discern good and evil; socially, we take advantage of others and use them for our own selfish ends; and creatively, as Sire notes, "Our imagination became separated from reality; imagination became illusion, and artists who created gods in their own image led humanity further and further from its origin."[11]

Our condition is desperate, yet most people prefer to live in an illusion rather than honestly confront their situation. Enshrouded in the fog of our own egoism, as the Christian philosopher J. Budzisweski observes, "Reality poses a constant problem for fallen man."[12] In Romans 1:18*ff*, the apostle Paul writes perceptively of the pervasive consequences of the Fall.

> The wrath of God is being revealed from heaven against all the godlessness and wickedness of men who suppress the truth by their wickedness, since what may be known about God is plain to them, because God has made it plain to them. For since the creation of the world God's invisible qualities – his eternal power and divine nature – have been clearly seen, being understood from what has been made, so that men are without excuse.
>
> For although they knew God, they neither glorified him as God nor gave thanks to him, but their thinking became futile and their foolish hearts were darkened. Although they claimed to be wise, they became fools....
>
> Furthermore, since they did not think it worthwhile to retain the knowledge of God, he gave them over to a depraved mind, to do what ought not to be done. They have become filled with every kind of wickedness, evil, greed, and depravity... Although they know God's righteous decree that those who do such things deserve death, they not only continue to do these very things but also approve of those who practice them. [Rom. 1:18*ff*]

[NOTE: Not all Christian thinkers have accepted this view of Original Sin and the Fall. Irenaeus (c. 130-202) believed that Adam and Eve were not created perfect but with the capacity to grow and develop in the image of God, and that the Fall disrupted this progress. Clement of Alexandria (c. 150-215) doubted that we receive our sin nature from Adam, arguing instead that Adam symbolizes what happens to each of us when we individually rebel against God. So in effect, each person recreates the Fall for him/herself.]

A fundamental teaching of Christian theism is that mankind's basic problem is not social, economic, political, or even psychological, but spiritual. God has initiated our reconciliation, and the Bible is the narration of God's involvement in human affairs over centuries to restore humankind to himself. First in the Old Testament with the Jewish nation, and again in the New Testament with

---

[11] James Sire, *The Universe Next Door*, p. 39.

[12] J. Budziszewski, *What We Can't Not Know* (Spence Publishing Company, 2003), p. 206.

the church, God has chosen a people to bear his image and demonstrate to the world God's gracious gift of salvation. Just as Adam and Eve were not forced to sin, we can choose how we respond to God's grace. But for those who honestly acknowledge their condition and accept God's terms, he forgives their sin and reconciles them to himself. Although our basic human nature remains the same, we take on a new nature through the indwelling presence of the Holy Spirit.

Theistic Epistemology

Being made in the image of an omniscient God, we are capable of being at least partially-knowing. Most importantly, we can know (at least to some extent) both the creation and the Creator. As James Sire explains, "Knowledge is possible because there is something to be known (God's creation) and someone to know (God, and human beings made in his image)." This simple truth is the foundation for all Christian theistic epistemology.

God reveals himself through two means: general and special revelation. Regarding **general revelation**, Psalm 19:1-2 states that "All creation declares God's handiwork and glory," and in Romans 1:18-22, as cited above, the apostle Paul writes that since the creation of the world, God has revealed "his eternal power and divine nature" to all people through the wonders of the physical world. More explicitly, God also reveals himself through **special revelation** in four ways:

(1) Through the Ten Commandments and the Torah – the Hebrew law.

(2) Through the testimony of the ancient Hebrew prophets.

(3) Through Jesus Christ – as we are informed in Hebrews 1:1-2: "In the past God spoke to our forefathers through the prophets at many times and in many ways, but in these last days he has spoken to us by his Son... through whom he created the universe. The Son is the radiance of God's glory and the exact representation of his being, sustaining all things by his powerful word."

Jesus Christ is God's ultimate special revelation. In his incarnate state, Jesus demonstrated what God is like more fully than any other form of divine expression. Accordingly, as the French philosopher Blaise Pascal commented, God has revealed evidence of himself that is sufficiently clear to those with open hearts and minds, but sufficiently vague so as not to force those whose hearts and minds are closed to him. Yet within the souls of even those who resist the Spirit of God, there is a yearning for transcendence. In Pascal's words, "There is a God-shaped vacuum in the heart of every man"which only the indwelling Spirit of God can fill – or as Augustine put it, "Our hearts are restless till they rest in thee." James Sire explains this longing for transcendence this way:

> God satisfies our longing for interpersonal relationship, by being... the end to our search for knowledge, by being... our refuge from all fear, by being in his holiness the righteous ground in our quest for justice, by being in his infinite love the cause of our hope of salvation, by being in his infinite creativity both the source of our creative imagination and the ultimate beauty we seek to reflect as we ourselves create. [James Sire, *The Universe Next Door*, pp. 32*ff*]

(4) Through the inspired writings of the New Testament in their testimony to the salvation available by grace through faith in Jesus Christ.

The Basis of Morality and Ethics

Morality and ethics are not abstractions extrapolated from ethereal concepts. Rather, they derive from the nature and character of God. It is the person of the infinite and perfect God who is the standard of right and wrong. Therefore, morality and ethics are absolute, not relative.

Like modern secular humanists, ancient Greek sophists contended that "Man is the measure of all things." In other words, we individually and independently decide what is right and wrong for ourselves. In countering their subjectivism, Socrates encouraged his followers to "Know thyself" – i.e., realize that you are merely a man, not a god. But while disputing the sophists' contention that morality is relative and subjective, all that Socrates could proclaim was that there was some Absolute Ideal for Goodness to which we are accountable. But operating within a pagan culture and ignorant of the revelations of the Hebrew Scriptures, Socrates was unable to say whether this Absolute Ideal was personal or impersonal.

The Bible declares that God is the measure of all things – including all that is right and good – and that God has revealed his standard through both general and special revelation. An integral aspect of general revelation is **natural (moral) law** – the precept that, although flawed, human nature is not utterly incapable of understanding right and wrong. As cited previously, the apostle Paul argued in the prologue to his Epistle to the Romans that this concept of natural law is innate to every individual. As such, it is universal and undeniable. All societies hold that some values and actions are objectively right and others wrong, and although different cultures often disagree on specifics, this is usually the difference between applications rather than principles.

God also reveals his moral standards through special revelation as conveyed in the Bible and confirmed by the internal witness of the Holy Spirit. As believers in Christ who are spiritually regenerated and transformed through the renewing of our mind (Rom. 12:1-2), our calling is to grow progressively Christlike throughout our life as we are illuminated and empowered by the indwelling presence of the Holy Spirit. This is the spiritual phenomenon of the New Birth, and it is a theme that Paul emphasizes in many of his writings as he expounds upon the process of conversion in passages such as I Corinthians 15:

> So it is written: "The first man Adam became a living being," the last Adam [Jesus] a life-giving spirit. The spiritual did not come first, but the natural, and after that the spiritual. The first man was of the dust of the earth, the second man from heaven. As was the earthly man, so are those who are of the earth; and as is the man from heaven, so also are those who are of heaven. And just as we have borne the likeness of the earthly man, so shall we bear the likeness of the man from heaven. [I Cor 15:45-49]

Moral discernment is integral to what it means to be made "in the image (or likeness) of God." In our modern secular culture, "tolerance" is often extolled as the highest of all virtues, and any kind of value judgments are regarded as arrogant and insensitive. But in fact Jesus taught that we *should* be judgmental – at least in terms of exercising wisdom and discernment regarding matters of right and wrong. Immediately after declaring, "Do not judge, or you too will be judged" (Matt. 7:1-6), Jesus warned his followers to "Watch out for false prophets" – i.e., wolves dressed in sheep's clothing (Matt. 7:15-20) – an admonition that requires prudent discernment. The problem, as Jesus later addressed, is that we tend to judge others unjustly or hypocritically (ref. John 7:24). But discernment is absolutely essential in this life. From point of fact, all laws are intolerant and judgmental in the sense that they prohibit certain actions that are deemed offensive, dangerous, inappropriate, or blatantly evil. Furthermore, those who criticize Christians as intolerant and judgmental are guilty themselves of being intolerant and judgmental when it comes to Christian values and practices. What matters is the *basis* on which we judge. For the Christian, our standard of authority is the Bible and the universal principles derived from natural law. For many non-Christians, the final arbiter of right and wrong is their own conscience and feelings, or the opinions of "experts" in various fields of the social sciences, or whatever seems to be socially acceptable. But as the Christian philosopher Vishal Mangalwadi comments in *The Book That Made Your World: How the Bible Created the Soul of Western Civilization*, value judgments are not only inevitable but essential. Commenting on the conventional wisdom in his homeland of India, he writes:

My intellectual environment [in India] told me that we make a mistake every time we made a value judgment. But those who said we shouldn't judge kept judging those who judged. That showed that making value judgments is an integral, inescapable part of who we are as human beings. [Vishal Mangalwadi, *The Book That Made Your World: How the Bible Created the Soul of Western Civilization* (Thomas Nelson, 2011), p. 51.]

Because **God is love**, it is the character and nature of God himself that is the essence of morality and ethics. And because God is love...

- He created humanity with a capacity to have a relationship with him;
- He became incarnate in human form and lived a "normal" human life in order to exemplify the character and nature of God;
- He sacrificed his life as an atonement for our sins; and
- He rose from the dead to demonstrate what our eternal destiny in God will be.

In *How To Read the Bible Book by Book*, authors Gordon Fee and Douglas Stuart comment on the extent of the breadth and depth of God's love as recounted in Scripture:

Here is the heart of the [biblical] story: A loving, redeeming God in his incarnation restored our lost vision of God, by his crucifixion and resurrection made possible our being restored to the image of God, and through the gift of the Holy Spirit became present with us in constant fellowship....

The genius of the biblical story is what it tells us about God himself, a God who sacrifices himself in death out of love for his enemies; a God who would rather experience the death we deserved than to be apart from the people he created for his pleasure; a God who himself bore our likeness, experienced our creatureliness, and carried our sins so that he might provide pardon and reconciliation; a God who would not let us go, but who would pursue us... so that he might restore us into joyful fellowship with himself. [Gordon D. Fee and Douglas Stuart, *How To Read the Bible Book by Book* (Zondervan, 2002), p. 18-19]

And because God is love – and because love by nature is a voluntary commitment of one's will – he does not force himself upon us but "wants all to be saved and to come to a knowledge of the truth" (I Tim. 2:4).

Finally, Scripture also declares that **God is just**. But unlike human justice that is based on the principle that people get what they (supposedly) deserve – i.e., "bad" people are punished while "good" people are rewarded – divine justice is fundamentally different. In the case of divine justice we get not so much what we *deserve* as what we *choose*. For those who submit to the Lordship of Jesus Christ, God imputes righteousness to them. As the apostle John wrote,

"To all who received him – to those who believed in his name – he gave the right to become children of God" (John 1:12). Based on our decision for Christ, God declares us "righteous" and rewards us with eternal life. Those who reject Christ remain imprisoned in their sin and, by their own choice, inherit eternal separation from the presence of God.

Philosophy of History

The Bible sets forth a view of history that was unique in ancient times. In contrast to the idea that the world is eternal and that history is cyclical, Scripture teaches that **history is linear and teleological**. Human history began at a particular point in the past, and it is moving toward a destination (or goal).

History is, as John Calvin declared, "the theater of God's glory," but it is anything but clear and simple. In fact, being the product of human choices, it is exceedingly messy and complicated, and the meaning of history is often shrouded in mystery. As James Sire comments, "The actions of people – as confusing and chaotic as they appear – are nonetheless part of a meaningful sequence that has a beginning and an end." This is the message of the Bible from Genesis to Revelation. In the end all of creation will be restored, and "Every knee shall bow, and every tongue confess, that Jesus Christ is Lord" (Phil. 2:10-11). But in the meantime history can certainly appear, especially to non-Christians, as little more than a random, purposeless and chaotic bloody mess.

Human Destiny

The Bible declares that human beings will live eternally in a conscious state of existence. This is in contrast to the beliefs of other worldviews such as atheistic naturalism, which holds to an annihilationist view of human destiny, or Eastern pantheism, which teaches reincarnation and the eventual extinction of the individual soul. Conversely, Scripture affirms that those who have accepted God's gift of spiritual salvation through belief in Jesus Christ will live eternally in the presence of God in Heaven.

- John 14:6 – "I am the way, the truth, and the life. No one comes to the Father except through me."
- Acts 4:12 – "Salvation is found in no one else, for there is no other name under heaven given to men by which we must be saved."
- I Timothy 2:5 – "For there is one God and one mediator between God and humanity, the man Christ Jesus."

- John 1:12 – "To those who received [the Word – i.e., Christ], to those who believed in his name, he gave the right to become children of God.

Correspondingly, those who reject God's gift of salvation will exist eternally apart from God in Hell.

- Prov. 11:21 – "Be sure of this: The wicked will not go unpunished."
- Psalm 37:20 – "The wicked will perish."
- Jesus' warning to the Pharisees: "Woe to you,... you hypocrites!... You snakes! You brood of vipers! How will you escape being condemned to hell?" (Matt. 23:25, 33).
- Apostle Paul: "God is just... He will punish those who do not know God and do not obey the gospel of our Lord Jesus. They will be punished with everlasting destruction and shut out from the presence of the Lord" (II Thess. 1:6*ff*).
- See Luke 16 – the parable of the rich man and Lazarus.
- The Final Judgment: The separation of the sheep and goats. As Jesus declared, "Then [God] will say to those on his left: 'Depart from me, you who are cursed, into eternal fire prepared for the devil and his angels'" (Matt. 25:41).

In a sense, the afterlife is where our deepest desires and wishes are fulfilled. Those who submit to God's will get what they want: eternal life with him in Heaven. Likewise, those who reject God get what they want: eternal separation from his presence. As G. K. Chesterton described it, Hell is "a monument to human freedom – or as C. S. Lewis wrote in The Great Divorce, "There are only two kinds of people in the end: those who say to God, 'Thy will be done,' and those to whom God says in the end, '*Thy* will be done.'"[13] In Hell, there is no love and therefore no restrictions on one's selfishness. Those who go there get to do their own thing forever apart from the moral law of God. So in a very real sense, Hell is a manifestation of divine justice and the recognition that our choices here on earth have consequences.

Without Heaven and Hell, human existence here on earth would have no ultimate meaning, and justice would have no reality. Many people who live selfish lives and who exploit and abuse others prosper in this life. Conversely, many who try to live upright, honorable and godly lives suffer. There is often little justice in this realm of reality, but the Bible teaches that there will be perfect justice in the afterlife.

---

[13] C. S. Lewis, *The Great Divorce* (HarperSanFrancisco, 1946, 1973), p.75.

Christianity as Religion and Spirituality

What Is Christianity? People commonly use the term "Christianity" in four different ways.

1. Christianity as a cultural tradition associated with Western (and American) civilization. In *The Closing of the American Mind*, Alan Bloom, a conservative Jewish professor of education at the University of Chicago, wrote endearingly of the Bible as the unifying metanarrative undergirding all of Western civilization:

> In the United States, practically speaking, the Bible was the only common culture, one that united the simple and the sophisticated, rich and poor, young and old, and – as the very model for a vision of the order of the whole of things, as well as the key to the rest of Western art, the greatest works of which were in one way or another responsive to the Bible – provided access to the seriousness of books. With its gradual and inevitable disappearance, the very idea of such a total book and the possibility and necessity of world-explanation [re: "worldview analysis"] is disappearing. And fathers and mothers have lost the idea that the highest aspiration they might have for their children is for them to be wise – as priests, prophets or philosophers are wise. Specialized competence and success are all that they can imagine. Contrary to what is commonly thought, without the book even the idea of the whole is lost. [Alan Bloom, *The Closing of the American Mind* (Simon & Schuster, 1987), p. 58.]

In a sense, Bloom was correct that the Bible, as the repository of "Judeo-Christian" heritage, morality and ethics, served for centuries as a kind of cultural glue. But knowledgeable Christians understand that although the Christian faith has certainly had a discernible *influence* on Western civilization, to equate the Kingdom of God with Western culture is ultimately blasphemous.

2. Christianity as religion – with its own unique literature, doctrines, institutions, traditions, rituals, etc. This is the sense in which scholars will often note that "Christianity is the largest religion in the world with over 1 billion followers." In fact, there *are* religious aspects of the Christian faith, although Christianity is not in essence a formal religion.

3. Christianity as a spiritual relationship with God through faith in Jesus Christ. Jesus Christ declared himself to be "the Way, the Truth, and the Life," and true Christians are those who have been spiritually regenerated ("born again") by divine grace through faith in Jesus Christ. This is the true essence of Christianity – a living spiritual relationship with God through the internal presence of the Holy Spirit. (For a distinction between the spiritual and religious dimensions of the Christian faith, see the chart on page 95.)

4. Christianity as a worldview. As discussed previously in this chapter, Christianity is a coherent, consistent and comprehensive belief system that incorporates a biblical view of ontology and epistemology. Ontologically, Christianity is founded on biblical teachings regarding the nature and character of God; God's purpose behind creation; the nature and character of humanity; and our human destiny. Epistemologically, Christianity sets forth a theory of knowledge based on the *imago Dei* that allows individuals to know God and his will and purpose for mankind via general revelation in nature and special revelation through the Bible and the internal witness of the Holy Spirit.

As with the religious definition, one might hold generally to a biblical worldview without in fact being a true Christian – i.e., without having a living spiritual relationship with God. But suffice it to say that all conscientious Christians should strive to align their values, their beliefs, their actions and their lifestyle in keeping with the principles of a comprehensive biblical worldview.

The Religious Dimension. The religious dimension of Christianity emphasizes the doctrinal, organizational, and practical aspects of the Christian faith. Religion is an organized system that includes a general worldview, a body of literature, doctrines, institutions, rituals, traditions, modes of worship, and other means of expressing our belief in God and the salvific mission of Jesus Christ. Religion is important, but it is neither the most important thing nor even the real thing. There is no life in religion *per se*. In fact, by focusing exclusively on the religious aspects, we can totally miss the essence – the real life – of the Christian faith. As John Bunyan commented in *Pilgrim's Progress*, "It is possible to learn all about... the Bible and never be affected by it in one's soul. Great knowledge is not enough." Throughout Christian history many have warned against the excessive preoccupation with religion to the exclusion of the spiritual/relational aspects of the faith. Commenting on the state of evangelical Christianity in the mid-20th century, A. W. Tozer observed how the focus on programs and methods and institutional issues can obscure the true reality of the faith.

> Every age has its own characteristics. Right now we are in an age of religious complexity. The simplicity which is in Christ is rarely found among us. In its stead are programs, methods, organizations, and a world of nervous activities which occupy time and attention but can never satisfy the longing of the hearer. The shallowness of our inner experience, the hollowness of our worship and that servile imitation of the world which marks our promotional methods all testify that we, in this day, know God only imperfectly, and the peace of God scarcely at all. [A. W. Tozer, *The Pursuit of God* (WingSpread Publishers, 1948), p. 17]

The Spiritual/Relational Dimension. Christian spirituality is the heart and soul (or the life-blood) of the Christian religion. Religion is organizational and external, whereas spirituality is organic – it personalizes and internalizes the search for God. Christian spirituality is more than simply theological and doctrinal; it is incarnational and existential.

In essence, Christianity is about a living relationship with God through faith in Jesus Christ. It is the active presence of God in the world, historically incarnate in Jesus Christ and presently alive in the hearts of Christians in the person of the Holy Spirit. In the truest sense, a Christian is one whose heart and mind are in the process of being transformed by the power of the Holy Spirit. This is the very essence of true Christian faith, as Tozer commented:

> The presence of God is the central fact of Christianity....
>
> Being made in [God's] image we have within us the capacity to know him....
>
> We have almost forgotten that God is a person and, as such, can be cultivated as any person can....
>
> The moment the Spirit has quickened us to life in regeneration our whole being senses its kinship to God and leaps up in joyous recognition. That is the New Birth without which we cannot see the kingdom of God. It is, however, not an end but an inception, for now begins the glorious pursuit. [Tozer, *The Pursuit of God*, p. 14, 13, 14]

Despite the checkered history of the Christian religious tradition, the real work of the true church of Christ has continued unabated throughout the centuries in the transmission of a great spiritual tradition, as F. F. Bruce notes in his history of the early church, *The Spreading Flame:*

> The real history of Christianity is the history of a great spiritual tradition. The only true apostolic succession is the lives of [committed believers]. Clement of Alexandria compared the church to a great river, receiving effluent from all sides. The great river sometimes flows like a raging torrent through a narrow channel; sometimes it spreads out like a flood; sometimes it divides into several streams; and sometimes, for a time, it seems to have been driven underground. But [through it all], the Holy Spirit has never left himself without witness. [W.R. Inge, *Things New and Old* (1933), p. 57ff – quoted in F.F. Bruce, *The Spreading Flame* (Wm. B. Eerdmans Publishing Company, (1958), p. 161.]

In a world in which most people are trying to escape reality through money, power, status, materialism, sex, drugs, art and/or entertainment, the church should be the one place that confronts people with the reality of their spiritual condition and grounds them in the reality of God. This is innately a spiritual mission, not a religious one. The purpose of the Christian religion – its institutions, doctrines, practices, traditions, and modes of worship – is to facilitate the nourishment and cultivation of our soul to the end that we become progressively Christ-like. That is the process of discipleship and sanctification, and that should be the primary goal of every church and every individual believer.

In summary, the following chart highlights the fundamental distinctions between the religious and the spiritual dimensions of the Christian faith.

Two Dimensions of Christianity

The **Religious** Dimension	The **Spiritual** Dimension
The visible organized/institutional church.	The invisible church of all believers in Christ who have been spiritually converted.
The "body" of religious faith: church doctrines, practices, traditions, institutions, etc.	The "soul" of religious faith: personal and direct communion with God.
The "wineskin."	The "new wine."
The mother board and circuitry that connect the believer to the power source.	The power source (the energy, or the electrical current) that animates the life of the believer.
Emphasis on theology and orthodoxy: knowing about and understanding God.	Emphasis on discipleship and orthopraxy: living in the presence of God and guided by the Holy Spirit.
Historically: At times, the religious dimension has nurtured personal spiritual growth and generally enriched society and culture. At other times, the Christian religion has been imperialistic and oppressive and a bastion of hypocrisy, greed, and corruption.	Historically: At times, the spiritual dimension has been in accord with mainstream Christian religion. At other times, the spiritual dimension has been at odds with the religious system and has functioned as a kind of spiritual protest and dissent from the visible, institutional church.

3
Biblical Inspiration

Part 1:
Revelation, Inspiration and Illumination

Theopneustia

Christians believe that the divine inspiration of the Bible is a reality, but there is no question that it is also a mystery. Although the term is commonly and casually used by Christians, in fact the church has never articulated a clear, precise, or comprehensive definition of inspiration. In II Timothy 3:16 the apostle Paul uses the expression *theopneustia* ("God-breathed") in reference to the phenomenon of supernatural inspiration. Similarly, the apostle Peter writes in II Peter 1:19-21 that no prophecy came by way of the prophet's own initiative or as a result of his own interpretation, but rather, "holy men... spoke as they were *moved* by the Holy Spirit."[1] These are oft-quoted verses, but rarely do Christians ponder the deeper implications of their meaning.

Regarding his own teaching and writings, Paul informed the Galatians, "I want you to know, brothers, that the Gospel I preached is not something that anyone made up. I did not receive it from any man, nor was I taught it; rather, I received it by revelation from Jesus Christ" (Galatians 1:11). Similarly, John declares in Revelation 1:9, "I, John,... was in the Spirit on the Lord's day, and heard behind me a great voice, as a trumpet...." – followed by a series of vivid visions and prophetic messages. As the Christian scholar Origen (c. 185-254) put it, "The sacred books are not the works of men... [but] were written by inspiration of the Holy Spirit at the will of the Father of All, through Jesus Christ."

---

[1] In Acts 27:15, Luke uses the same Greek word to describe how Paul's ship was "driven along" by a mighty wind during his trip from Caesarea to Rome.

97

But what exactly is "inspiration," and what are the phrases "God-breathed" or "moved by the Holy Spirit" supposed to mean? The apologist Josh McDowell offers a concise definition:

Inspiration can be defined as the mysterious process by which God worked through human writers, employing their individual personalities and styles to produce divinely authoritative writings. [Josh McDowell, *New Evidence That Demands a Verdict* (Thomas Nelson Publishers, 1999), p. 334.]

Note that McDowell acknowledges that the whole process is "mysterious." In other words, it is a supra-rational phenomenon that transcends human reason. No one understands exactly *how* the process of inspiration works, or how an infallible Bible could be produced by fallible men. But nonetheless, there are good reasons to believe that God *did* in fact inspire the biblical authors, and that while it is true that "To err is human," the Bible is not merely a human book.

The Transmission Process

In the New Testament Epistle to the Hebrews we read, "In the past God spoke to our forefathers through the prophets at many times and in various ways" (Heb. 1:1). Although Scripture is vague exactly how most of these revelations were conveyed to the prophets, chroniclers and psalmists who wrote them down, this esoteric knowledge was apparently transmitted via six means.

1. An audible voice. In several instances Scripture tells us that God spoke audibly to various men, and in other cases angelic messengers communicated God's message directly as in the following scenarios:

- Genesis 18-19 – Three angels appeared to Abraham and Lot, warning them of God's impending judgment upon the towns of Sodom and Gomorrah.
- Exodus 3:1 - 4:17 – God spoke to Moses in the midst of a burning bush and commissioned him to liberate the Hebrews from bondage in Egypt.
- Exodus 19-31 – God conversed with Moses on Mount Sinai and dictated the Ten Commandments and the Mosaic Law.
- Exodus 34:27 – God commanded Moses, "Write these words...."
- Leviticus 1:1 – "The Lord called to Moses and spoke to him from the Tent of Meeting."
- Numbers 1-2 – "The Lord spoke to Moses in the Tent of Meeting in the Desert of Sinai...."
- Numbers 12:1-9 – God rebuked Aaron and Miriam for criticizing their brother Moses and informed them, "When a prophet of the Lord is

among you, I reveal myself to him in visions, I speak to him in dreams. But this is not true of my servant Moses... With him I speak face to face."

- Joshua 1:1 – "After the death of Moses the servant of the Lord, the Lord said to Joshua son of Nun...."
- In Job 38 - 42 God carried on an extensive dialogue with Job.
- In I Samuel 3:4 God spoke audibly to the young boy Samuel.

2. A mental impression. In most instances God seems to have "spoken" to the prophets through the inner voice of their conscience. On numerous occasions Scripture records that "the word of the Lord" came to an oracle, commanding him to speak or write. In most cases it is never quite clear whether this admonition came by way of an audible voice or a mental impression, but it seems likely that it was usually via the latter means:

- Exodus 19 - 31 – In the passage cited above in which Moses received the Ten Commandments and the Mosaic Law, it is possible that God imparted this revelation intuitively rather than audibly.
- Isaiah 8:1 – "The Lord said to me, 'Take a large piece of parchment and write on it....'"
- Isaiah 30:8 – "Go now, write it on a tablet in their presence and inscribe it on a scroll...."
- Jeremiah 1:1*ff* – "The words of Jeremiah son of Hilkiah.... The word of the Lord came to him in the thirteenth year of the reign of Josiah son of Amon king of Judah, and through the reign of Jehoiakim son of Josiah king of Judah, down to the fifth month of the eleventh year of Zedekiah son of Josiah king of Judah, when the people of Jerusalem went into exile.

  "The word of the Lord came to me, saying, 'Before I formed you in the womb I knew you; before you were born I set you apart; I appointed you as a prophet to the nations'....

  "Then the Lord reached out his hand and touched my mouth and said to me, 'Now, I have put my words in your mouth. See, today I appoint you over nations and kingdoms to uproot and tear down, to destroy and overthrow, to build and to plant.'

  "The word of the Lord came to me: 'What do you see, Jeremiah?'"
- Jeremiah 36:27-28 – "[T]he word of the Lord came to Jeremiah: 'Take another scroll, and once again write on it....'"
- Ezekiel 1:3 – "The word of the Lord came directly to Ezekiel the priest.... and the Lord's hand was on him there."

- Hosea 1:1-2 – "The word of the Lord that came to Hosea soon of Beeri.... When the Lord first spoke to Hosea, He said this to him...."
- Joel 1:1 – "The word of the Lord that came to Joel son of Pethuel...."
- Jonah 1:1 – "The word of the Lord came to Jonah son of Amittai: 'Get up! Go to the great city of Nineveh and preach against it, because their wickedness has confronted Me."
- Zephaniah 1:1 – "The word of the Lord that came to Zephaniah son of Cushi..."
- Haggai 1:1 – "In the second year of King Darius, on the first day of the six month, the word of the Lord came through Haggai the prophet to Zerubbabel son of Shealtiel, the governor of Judah, and to Joshua son of Jehozadek, the high priest."
- Zechariah 1:1 – "In the eighth month, in the second year of Darius, the word of the Lord came to the prophet Zechariah son of Berchiah, son of Iddo...."
- Malachi 1:1 – "An oracle: The word of the Lord to Israel through Malachi...."

Scripture is clear that this means of divine communication was not restricted to the Old Testament alone:

- Acts 8:26*ff* – An angel of the Lord spoke to Philip and directed him to the place where he would encounter the Ethiopian eunuch.
- Revelation 1:9 – "I, John,... was in the Spirit on the Lord's day, and heard behind me a great voice, as a trumpet...."

3. Dreams and/or visions. There are many references in the Old Testament to divine revelations via dreams and/or ecstatic visions:

- Genesis 37:1-11 – The prophetic dreams of Joseph.
- Numbers 12:6 – "[The Lord said to Aaron and Miriam], 'Listen to my words: When a prophet of the Lord is among you, I reveal myself to him in visions, I speak to him in dreams.'"
- Isaiah 1:1 – "The vision concerning Judah and Jerusalem that Isaiah son of Amoz saw during the reigns of Uzziah, Jotham, Ahaz and Hezekiah, kings of Judah."
- Ezekiel 1:1 – "In the thirtieth year [note: probably the thirtieth year of his life], in the fourth month on the fifth day, while I was among the [Jewish] exiles... the heavens were opened and I saw visions of God."
- Daniel 7: 1 – "In the first year of Belshazzar king of Babylon, Daniel had a dream, and visions passed through his mind as he was lying on his bed. He wrote down the substance of his dream."

- Obadiah 1:1 – "The vision of Obadiah. This is what the Lord God has said about Edom...."
- Micah 1:1 – "The word of the Lord came to Micah the Moreshite – what he saw regarding Samaria and Jerusalem in the days of Jotham, Ahaz, and Hezekiah, kings of Judah."
- Nahum 1:1 – "The oracle concerning Nineveh. The book of the vision of Nahum the Elkoshite."
- Habakkuk 1:1-4; 2:2 – "The oracle that Habakkuk the prophet saw. 'How long, Lord, must I call for help and You do not listen, or cry out to You about violence, and You do not save? Why do You force me to look at injustice? Why do You tolerate wrongdoing?...

  "The Lord answered me: 'Write this vision; clearly inscribe it on tablets so one may easily read it.'"

Similarly, the New Testament records several instances of supernaturally-inspired dreams and visions, including...

- Acts 10:1*ff*– Peter's vision in which "he saw heaven opened" and a sheet containing all kinds of animals and birds descending to earth, representing the fact that the Kingdom of God included all ethnic and nationality groups.
- II Corinthians 12:1*ff* – Paul relates his experiences of "visions and revelations," including one in which he was "caught up to paradise" and "heard inexpressible things, things that man is not permitted to tell."
- Revelation 1:9*ff*– "I, John,... was in the Spirit on the Lord's day, and heard behind me a great voice, as a trumpet....

  "I turned around to see the voice that was speaking to me. And when I turned I saw seven golden lampstands, and among the lampstands was someone 'like a son of man'....

  "When I saw him, I fell at his feet as though dead. Then he placed his right hand on me and said... 'Write, therefore, what you have seen, what is now and what will take place later....'"

  [Note: Interestingly, John's Apocalypse is the only book in the New Testament that specifically claims to be a direct revelation from God.]

4. **Previous prophetic writings.** Some prophetic pronouncements came as a result of the prophet being inspired by his predecessors.

- Daniel 9:2 – God spoke to Daniel through the writings of Jeremiah (cf. Jer 25:11).
- Ezra 1:1 – Ezra acknowledged the prophetic authority of Jeremiah's writings.

- Ezra 5:1 – Ezra acknowledged the authority of Haggai and Zechariah's writings.
- Nehemiah 9:30 – Nehemiah acknowledged that God's Spirit had inspired the former prophets.
- Zechariah 7:12 – Zecharaiah spoke of "the law and the words which the Lord had sent by his Spirit through the former prophets."

5. Spirit-led research. In some cases biblical writers accessed previous (non-biblical) texts for some of their historical information. Throughout the Old Testament various prophets and chroniclers reference more than a dozen books and annals that have been lost down through the ages from which they derived some of their information. For example:

- *Book of the Wars of the Lord*, cited in Numbers 21:14;
- *Book of Jashar*, cited in Joshua 10:13 and II Samuel 1:18;
- *Book of the Annals of Solomon*, cited in I Kings 11:41;
- *History of the Kings of Israel*, cited in I Kings 14:19;
- *History of the Kings of Judah*, cited in II Kings 23:28;
- "The book of the kings of Israel," "the book of the kings of Judah," and "the book of the annals of King David," cited in I Chronicles 27:24;
- "The records of Samuel the seer," "the records of Nathan the prophet," and "the records of Gad the seer," cited in I Chronicles 29:29;
- "The prophecy of Ahijah the Shilonite" and "the visions of Iddo the seer," cited in II Chronicles 9:29; and
- "The records of Shemiah the prophet," cited in II Chronicles 12:15.

6. The life of Jesus Christ. In the New Testament the focus of revelation is on the person of Jesus Christ and the meaning of his life. As the author of the Epistle to the Hebrews states, "God, who at various times and in various ways spoke in times past to the fathers by the prophets, has in these last days spoken to us by His Son" (Heb. 1:1-2). This is the culmination of all Old Testament messianic prophecies and the basis of authority for all that we read in the New Testament.

The gospel accounts of the life of Christ are either eyewitness recollections as in the case of Matthew and John or narratives based on primary sources such as in Mark and Luke. According to Papias, an early 2nd century church leader, the Gospel According to Mark was written based on the recollections of the apostle Peter. Luke, in the prologue to his gospel, relates that his information was compiled from interviews with "original eyewitnesses and servants" of Christ whom he "carefully investigated" in order to assure their accuracy.

Luke 1:1-4: Many have undertaken to compile a narrative about the events that have been fulfilled among us, just as the original eyewitnesses and servants of the word handed them down to us. It also seemed good to me, since I have carefully investigated everything from the very first, to write to you an orderly account... so that you may know the certainty of the things about which you have been instructed.

The fact that the Old Testament writers relied upon previous historical accounts that apparently were not divinely-inspired, and that Luke compiled his gospel (at least in part) using standard historical methods, only confirms the mystical nature of supernatural revelation. Written by at least 40 authors over some 1500 years, and in some cases relying upon sources that were not divinely-inspired, nevertheless the end product was one that was superintended by the Holy Spirit in such a way as to present a unified and consistent theme. Most remarkably, and most inexplicably, the Spirit of God animates and quickens the words and the message of the Bible with the power to transform lives not only intellectually and morally but spiritually.

Beyond the four gospels, the epistles of Paul, Peter, John, James and Jude offer additional insights into the meaning of Christ's life, atoning death and resurrection. Furthermore, the apostle Paul makes it clear that the spirit of revelation that inspired the ancient Hebrew prophets was still at work among the apostles of his generation, as he notes in Ephesians 3:2*ff*:

Surely you have heard about the administration of God's grace that was given to me for you, that is, the mystery made known to me by revelation, as I have already written briefly. In reading this, then, you will be able to understand my insight into the mystery of Christ, which was not made know to people in other [previous] generations as it has now been revealed by the Spirit to God's holy apostles and prophets.

The Uniqueness of Biblical Revelation

Inspiration as Revelation. The concept of "**inspiration**" is derived from the Latin *inspirare*, meaning "to breathe upon or into something." In the most general sense, inspiration may be defined as "the stimulation of the mind and/or emotions to a high level of activity or feeling."[2] But most Christians sense that there is a difference between the kind of inspiration that animated the prophets, psalmists, chroniclers and apostles who wrote the Bible, and that which motivates an artist to conceptualize and produce a work of art, a songwriter to compose a song, an author to research and write a book, a pastor to prepare and preach a sermon, or a Christian to offer up a prayer. A broad generic term such as "inspiration" tends to blur the distinction between these various manifestations of inspiration. But what exactly *is* the difference?

The Bible is clear that the Holy Spirit will inspire the thoughts and actions of Christians until Christ returns, as Jesus himself taught in John 16:13 when he informed his disciples, "But when he, the Spirit of truth, comes, he will guide you into all truth." Undoubtedly, this has been the case throughout Christian history, and it continues today. As we pray for divine guidance and open our heart and mind to God, the Holy Spirit animates our sensibilities and stimulates our will. When a sincere and dedicated pastor sits down in his office to prepare a sermon, studying and praying and ruminating on what to say, there is a sense in which the end product, the sermon, has been "inspired." Likewise, this same phenomenon often occurs whenever a heartfelt prayer is offered up to God either privately or publicly, or when a Christian witnesses for Christ in the context of a private conversation or in a public setting. Similarly, when a Christian author researches and writes a book, or when a Christian songwriter composes a song, such efforts might very well be considered inspired.

As mentioned earlier, Paul regarded his preaching and writing to be "by revelation from Jesus Christ" (Galatians 1:11) in the same sense that John declared that his visions and pronouncements in Revelation were received while "in the Spirit" (Rev. 1:9). But other early Christian writings also claimed to be the product of divine inspiration. Clement of Rome (c. 95) reminded his readers that Paul's epistles to the Corinthians were written "with true inspiration," but he also maintained that his own letter was written "through the Holy Spirit" (ref. *I Clem. 47:3* and *63:2*). The author of *II Clement* (early 2nd century) also apparently believed that *I Clement* was inspired as he cites *I Clem. 23:3-4* with the words, "for the prophetic word also says..." (*II Clem. 11:2*), a

---

[2] Ref. *Webster's II New Riverside University Dictionary* (Riverside Publishing Company, 1984, 1994), p. 632.

phrase usually reserved for inspired writings. Similarly, in his *Epistle to the Philadelphians* (c. 112) Ignatius declares that "I spoke with a great voice – with God's own voice..." and that "the Spirit was preaching and saying this [through me]" (*Phld. 7:1-2*). The author of the *Epistle of Barnabas* even introduces a passage from an apocryphal book, *II Enoch*, with the words, "for the Scripture says..." (*Barn. 16:5*). Two centuries later, Gregory of Nyssa (c. 330-95) claimed that Basil's (330-79) commentary on the Genesis creation story was inspired. In fact, Gregory even thought that Basil's account surpassed that of Moses himself in terms of its beauty, complexity and form, calling it "an exposition given by inspiration of God."[3]

However, most Christians believe that these examples of inspiration are qualitatively different than what we encounter in Scripture, which is why *I Clement*, the *Epistle of Barnabas*, *The Shepherd* of Hermas, and other post-apostolic Christian writings were eventually judged as unworthy of canonization. It is not that these works are untrue. Indeed, there is much truth and wisdom in them. But they are not *wholly true*. Similarly, no pastor or author or songwriter today produces a work that is inerrant or infallible. The Holy Spirit may very well inspire our efforts, but he also works within the parameters of our mind, our character, and the knowledge, insight and wisdom we have accumulated in our life. Furthermore, we understand that we can never fully transcend our human limitations, and that any insights and truths that we convey are simply our interpretations of the truth that we encounter in Scripture. Unlike the prophets and apostles who were uniquely inspired by the Holy Spirit, none of us serves as a medium for any new propositional truth. At best, we merely seek to understand and apply the truths that God has already revealed in his written Word. In contrast to *theopneustia*, biblical inspiration that was "breathed-out" by the Spirit of God, all other manifestations of "inspiration" are emanations of truth that we receive via nature or that emerge from within our own soul.

Divine inspiration is a spiritual reality, but it is nonetheless a mysterious phenomenon. If we think of it as a process by which God communicates truth to and through human beings, then we must distinguish between the kind of inspiration we encounter in Scripture and anything we might sense or conceptualize as a result of our own human nature and experience. This is why it is helpful to think of biblical inspiration in terms of "**revelation**" (Latin: *revelare*; Greek: *apocalyptein*), a term meaning "to unveil." In contrast to inspiration that comes from within, revelation is qualitatively different. It is a

---

[3] Cited in Bruce M. Metzger, *The Canon of the New Testament: Its Origin, Development, and Significance* (Oxford University Press, 1987), p. 256.

transcendent form of inspiration that the biblical writers received from outside themselves.[4]

As discussed previously, in his great love God has communicated truth to mankind through two means: **general revelation** and **special revelation**.[5] In the case of general revelation, these are truths available to all people through their natural senses and reasoning capacity. Having been made in the image of God, we have an innate sense of God consciousness and moral consciousness, as well as a mind that is capable of perceiving reality and thinking rationally. As Romans 1-2 declares, everyone, regardless of their culture or the time period in which they live, has an sense of moral consciousness – what philosophers refer to as **natural law**. Therefore all are accountable before God.[6]

But although general revelation can reveal certain truths about the natural world and the human condition, we need special revelation in order to understand God's specific will and purpose for our lives. The Bible is just that – God's special revelation in written form. Special revelation is the impartation of truth, insight and wisdom that transcends normal human thought, reason and imagination. This is why Paul writes in Galatians 1:11, "I want you to know, brothers, that the gospel I preached is not something that man made up. I did not receive it from any man, nor was I taught it; rather, I received it by revelation from Jesus Christ." In other words, revelation is a process of divine disclosure rather than human discovery.

As Origen explained, "The sacred books are not the works of men... [but] were written by inspiration of the Holy Spirit at the will of the Father of All, through Jesus Christ." It was in this context that the Church Fathers regarded the ancient Jewish Scriptures and the apostolic Christian writings as the "rule of faith"– the authoritative standard by which we judge all truth-claims, including all extra-biblical claims of divine inspiration. It is also the standard by which we judge ourselves. In *The Book That Made Your World*, Vishal Mangalwadi observes that in contrast to literature that we interpret, "revelation

---

[4] Many biblical scholars and theologians reject the belief that the Bible was uniquely inspired, just as they challenge the concept of a closed canon of Scripture. Naturally, all liberal scholars contest this view, but so do others who are more theologically-moderate. Reference Lee Martin McDonald, *The Biblical Canon: Its Origin, Transmission, and Authority* (Hendrickson Publishers, 2007), pp. 416*ff.*

[5] For more on general and special revelation, see the Index.

[6] For more on natural law, see the Index. The fact that people often ignore and violate these moral impulses doesn't negate the fact that we have an innate sense of right and wrong, although our moral sensitivities can certainly become desensitized through intentional and habitual violation of the moral law.

interprets and evaluates *us*. It stands above us, judges us, and calls us back to moral and ethical sanity." Repeatedly throughout their history the Jews rebelled against God and degenerated into unbelief and immorality. Their holy Scriptures, however, "remained a transcendent standard that promoted self-criticism and reform," which over time rendered the Jewish nation "a blessing to the world."[7]

Biblical revelation is also unique in that it is not only doctrinally and morally authoritative but infallible. Other manifestations of inspiration, being expressions of human thought and imagination, are simply interpretations of the ultimate truths of God. The Bible, however, is different in the sense that it is the product of a concursive process of divine revelation and human illumination in which the Holy Spirit worked symbiotically and synergistically in accord with the mind of the writers. In this respect, we judge extra-biblical inspiration as "true" to the extent that it corresponds to the ultimate standard – the truths we encounter in Scripture.

Having distinguished between "inspiration" in the general sense of the word and "revelation" as it comes to us via Scripture, there is still the challenge of conveying exactly how revelation was transmitted and received. The problem with all attempts to explain this phenomenon is that our mind is simply inadequate in terms of understanding such a profound spiritual mystery and how it occurred. All that we can do is marvel at its results. Perhaps this is analogous to attempting to describe in words a majestic landscape, a beatific painting, or a soul-stirring piece of music. All such descriptions pale by comparison to the real thing. There is simply no substitute for encountering existentially the phenomenon itself.

Inspiration as Illumination. All other forms of inspiration, even those derived explicitly from the truths of the Bible or implicitly from general revelation, are products of human intelligence and imagination. They may be animated by the Holy Spirit, but they are not revelation in the sense that they convey any new spiritual or moral truths. Therefore, when a pastor is inspired to preach a sermon, an author is inspired to write a book, or a composer is inspired to write a song, he is not unveiling new truth. At best, he is merely expressing his understanding (or his interpretation) of the truths he has gleaned from God's revelation in Scripture or in nature. This kind of inspiration is best characterized as "illumination" – insights that clarify or provide practical application to the truths we encounter in the Bible and the natural world,

---

[7] Vishal Mangalwadi, *The Book That Made Your World: How the Bible Created the Soul of Western Civilization* (Thomas Nelson Publishing, 2011), p. 53.

including those truths related to human nature. Any human product – whether a sermon, a book, a movie, a song, or anything else – is only "inspired" in the sense that it accurately reflects the truth, the goodness, and the beauty of Scripture and/or the realities of the world in which we live.

[We should note, however, that for a work of art to be "inspired" it does not necessarily need to be positive and uplifting, nor must it glorify God explicitly. It must only shed light on the realities of life and the condition of the human soul. It is in this context that we do well to distinguish between two kinds of "art": that which accurately depicts the realities of life, including the effects and consequences of sin; and that which glorifies gratuitous violence and mindless depravity, narcissism, materialism and hedonism. The former is true art, and as such it can be disturbing but also profoundly insightful and even redemptive. Conversely, the latter is crass, salacious, exploitative, degrading, dehumanizing, and worthless. So while it is true that "art needs no justification," this is true only of true art. It is patently untrue of human expressions that distort or ridicule truth, goodness and beauty.]

Inspiration via Nature. So what about literature, lectures, speeches, movies, music, and other intellectual and artistic expressions that do *not* reflect the True, the Good and/or the Beautiful? What about intellectual, literary and artistic expressions that glorify and promote depravity? Are such endeavors not "inspired" even if they are the products of great minds and creative geniuses?

I think not, and I would argue that such works are not the product of "inspiration" at all. They are merely the manifestations of human nature – those impulses and motivations that operate upon and within our mind. Having been made in the image of God, human beings are endowed with intelligence and creativity. However, due to the noetic effects of the Fall, we can misuse our mind, our talents and our imagination in ways that are quite destructive. When Karl Marx wrote *The Communist Manifesto*, when Rudolf Bultmann devoted his academic career to "demythologizing" Christianity, when Madonna recorded "Like a Virgin," when Dan Jinks produced the movie, *American Beauty*, or when Richard Dawkins wrote *The God Delusion*, it would be blasphemous to dignify such endeavors as "inspired." Undoubtedly, they are the products of human intelligence, creativity and motivation, but they are nonetheless the results of warped and perverted minds. Far from being "inspired" in the true sense, they were merely expressions of the dark side of human nature.

This is not to imply that non-Christians are incapable of producing worthy works of art and scholarship. Oftentimes, non-Christians are motivated by the same natural law principles derived from general revelation that inspire

Christians – not only ideals related to truth, goodness and beauty in general but specific insights related to justice, honor, civility, compassion, generosity, humanitarianism, and even self-sacrifice. But just as moral-based Platonic and Stoic philosophy shed some light on natural law and the human condition, it took Jesus Christ, the pure "Light of the World," to illuminate our understanding regarding God's perfect will for humanity.

Two Pathways of Inspiration. The following graphic illustrates the difference between inspiration via divine illumination in contrast to the kind of inspiration that comes from purely natural means. We have emphasized that God imparts truth to mankind through two means, special and general revelation. Christians have access to both of these manifestations of reality, and as we grow in faith, knowledge and wisdom our heart and mind are illuminated as we acquire greater insight from the truths we access through Scripture and nature. No longer confined by the values and thought-patterns of this world, we are transformed spiritually and intellectually to the extent that we discern with increasing clarity God's good and perfect will for our life (ref. Romans 12:2).

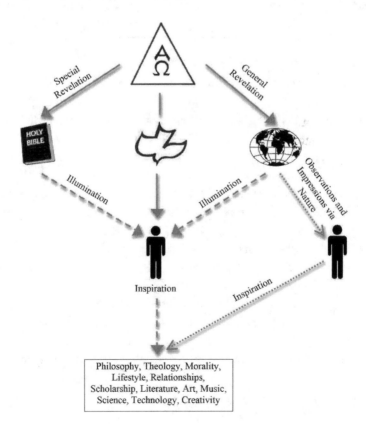

As a result, the Holy Spirit inspires how we think and relate to the full range of issues in life – everything from theology and morality to politics, lifestyles, personal relationships, literature, art, science, technology, and all other forms of human expression.

For the non-Christian, however, the situation is radically different. Cut off from God's special revelation via the Bible and the indwelling presence and illumination of the Holy Spirit, the only source of truth and reality that the non-believer has is what can be gleaned through nature alone. This can, of course, provide *some* intellectual and moral insight, which is why non-Christians can make formidable contributions in terms of human thought and creativity. But natural means alone are insufficient when it comes to providing the kind of specific Truth necessary to fulfill God's ultimate purpose and calling for our life. The non-Christian is limited by his/her own nature and the insights and impressions one can glean through general revelation. In no way does this render non-Christians totally incapable of thinking clearly and morally about many (or even most) of the great issues of life, but it does restrict their understanding of the Source as well as the organic inter-connectivity of all that is reflective of ultimate reality.

Does the Bible Teach Biblicism?

Some Christians assume that the Bible alone is the repository of all truth – a concept known as "biblicism" – but obviously this is fallacious. The Bible is not a textbook on mathematics, science, world geography or psychology, yet there is truth in these and other specialized fields of knowledge that are not only useful in life but positively essential. In Romans 1-2 the apostle Paul argues that we can access truth through natural means via general revelation. This incorporates two features: (1) The knowledge gleaned through a careful observation and study of the physical world as evidence of divine creation; and (2) our innate sense of reason and the principles of a universal moral law that God has instilled within us as a result of being created in his image. Therefore, there is much we can learn through general revelation outside the more specific special revelation that we encounter in Scripture.

Even Augustine, who had a profound respect for the holy Scriptures, denied that the Bible alone is our sole medium of divine revelation. It does, however, provide unique insight into what matters most in life: our relationship to God. And for this, general revelation is insufficient. We need the special revelation that God has imparted only through Scripture via the words of his chosen prophets, psalmists, chroniclers and apostles.

The Principle of Accommodation

The principle of revelation does not necessitate that God communicate truth in scholarly, technical or scientific language. Many biblical scholars emphasize the principle of accommodation – that God condescended to adapt his truth in Scripture in accord to our human ways of thinking and speaking. In so doing, God's greatness was manifest in that he could communicate his will and purpose despite human weaknesses and limitations. In *A General Introduction to the Bible*, Norman Geisler explains the issue this way:

> The Bible is written for the common men of every generation, and it therefore uses their common, everyday language. The use of observational, nonscientific language is not *un*scientific, it is merely *pre*scientific. The Scriptures were recorded in *ancient* times by ancient standards, and it would be anachronistic to superimpose *modern* scientific standards upon them....
>
> Just because God condescends to man's level to communicate his truth to them does not mean he has to compromise his truth in doing so. Adaptation to human limitations does not necessitate accommodation to human error....
>
> The biblical view of inspiration does not assert that prophets and apostles were infallible, nor that in their own learning they were exempt from limitations imposed by their cultures. What it asserts, rather, is that the writers did not teach the doubtful views of the cultures in which they lived. [Norman L. Geisler, and William E. Nix, *A General Introduction to the Bible* (Moody Publishers, 1968, 1986), pp. 57, 62.]

Origen understood the human component in Scripture and rejected any idea of mechanical inspiration. He acknowledged that New Testament writers such as Paul sometimes expressed their own opinions, and that they could err when speaking on their own authority. Likewise, he realized that divine revelation did not consist of the human words themselves but in the transcendent meaning of the ideas being expressed. In other words, God's revelation to mankind "accommodated" itself to human understanding. God conveyed truth in simple ways so that humanity could understand his message and be saved.

This is a principle that most Bible scholars have upheld. For example, John Calvin emphasized this point in his commentary on Genesis. In Calvin's words:

> Moses wrote in popular style things which, without instruction, all ordinary persons, endued with common sense, are able to understand.... Had [Moses] spoken of things generally unknown, the uneducated might have pleased in excuse that such subjects were beyond their capacity. [John Calvin, *The First Book of Moses Called Genesis*. Commentary on Genesis 1:15-16]

Seven Views on Biblical Inspiration

Historically, there have been seven discernible views regarding the nature of biblical inspiration. Several of these are sub-Christian positions, but over the centuries most orthodox Christians have held either to the "verbal/plenary" or the "conceptual" view of inspiration.

1. Mechanical inspiration. This view holds that God essentially dictated the Bible in its entirety, and that the original authors were little more than stenographers who recorded his words. In effect, God by-passed the mind of the individual writers. Advocates of this view hold to the theory of verbal/plenary inspiration in the sense that God dictated all the words of Scripture. Therefore, the Bible is inerrant in terms of its historical reliability and infallible regarding its doctrinal and moral pronouncements. Proponents of mechanical inspiration tend to interpret Scripture literalistically (i.e., without regard to literary style or authorial intent), and some reject the principle of progressive revelation.

This view is problematical, to say the least. With some exceptions (see the examples cited previously), Scripture itself does not support the mechanical theory. Presumably, a dictated text would be totally consistent in style and vocabulary and display none of the diversity of literary styles and human characteristics that we find in the 66 books of the Bible. In over-spiritualizing the phenomenon of revelation, this view is essentially a docetic concept that largely eliminates the human and organic elements involved in the process.

2. Verbal/plenary inspiration. This theory advocates that God inspired the writing of Scripture in such a way that he guided the very words used by the original authors, and that all the words used by the original writers were equally inspired. However, God did not dictate the words of Scripture (except on rare occasions when biblical authors indicate as such), nor did he by-pass the personalities of the original authors who wrote using the literary styles, thought-forms, vocabulary, idioms and expressions common to their time and culture. Nonetheless, the Holy Spirit guided the authors in such a way that their writing was both verbally and fully inspired – the process that the Princeton theologian B. B. Warfield (1851-1921) referred to as "concursus." Therefore, the original manuscripts are infallible in terms of their doctrinal and moral pronouncements and inerrant in terms of their historical, geographical and scientific accuracy.

Many proponents of verbal/plenary inspiration draw a distinction between a literal interpretation of Scripture versus one that is literal*istic*. In other words, a sensible interpretation of the text must consider the author's intent and the hermeneutical principles applicable to the literary style of a particular book or passage. (See Chapter 4, "Biblical Hermeneutics: Basic Principles of

Interpretation.") While holding that the Old Testament is as fully inspired as the New Testament, most advocates of this view accept the principle of progressive revelation and believe the Old Testament must be interpreted in light of the New Covenant.

3. Conceptual inspiration. This view shares most of the tenets of the verbal/plenary position, but allows for more human expression. The Bible is God's unique revelation to mankind. In specific instances some of Scripture was actually dictated verbally by God, and there are other cases in which biblical authors clearly expressed their own views (such as I Corinthians 7:12*ff* and the Old Testament book of Ecclesiastes). But generally speaking, the truths of the Bible are revealed to the authors in keeping with the principle of *theopneustia*, and the authors conveyed these truths using the vocabulary, literary styles, thought-forms, idioms and expressions common to their time and culture.

Conceptualists believe that all Scripture is divinely-inspired and infallible in terms of its historical and scientific reliability and its doctrinal and moral truths. The Bible should be interpreted literally (but not literal*istically*) in light of the author's intent and the hermeneutical principles applicable to the literary style of a particular book or passage. Furthermore, in keeping with the principle of progressive revelation the Old Testament should be interpreted in light of the revelations of the New Testament.

More than those who hold to the verbal/plenary view, conceptualists emphasize that Scripture is the revealed truths of God expressed in the authors' own distinctive vocabularies and styles. This principle is self-evident, for example, when one considers that any translation of the biblical texts from the original language into another language (whether ancient or modern) is, in a sense, a functional equivalency rather than a strict word-for-word rendering. (See Chapter 4.) But of course there are seminal concepts in Scripture that depend upon key theological terminology – precise words, terms and phrases that convey essential Christian doctrines – and conceptualists readily concede that in such cases the Holy Spirit supernaturally impressed upon the mind of the original authors the very words they wrote. A similar case might be made for subsequent translators who, through prayer, careful study, and an earnest desire to render as true and accurate a translation as possible, were guided in terms of the precise words they chose.

4. Partial inspiration. This is the view of most theological liberals (see pages 34-36), and it holds that while certain passages and concepts in Scripture have been (or might have been) divinely-inspired, other parts are merely the ideas of man and reflect the mentality, the beliefs, the cultural prejudices and the superstitions of their time. In general, the Old Testament is regarded as historically suspect, and in some instances it is doctrinally and morally questionable if not "sub-Christian" – such as the genocide carried out against the Canaanites and the "imprecatory psalms" such as Psalms 69, 109, 137, etc. In fact, this view is itself sub-Christian. The tendency is to assume that the Bible is suspect if it offends modern sensibilities or unless its historicity can be validated by outside secular sources. There is often an implicit anti-supernatural bias in this perspective as well. The inclination is to concede far too much to the current wordviews and theories that prevail in the physical and social sciences and the humanistic values of our contemporary culture when assessing the historicity, the scientific veracity, and the doctrinal and moral pronouncements of Scripture.

5. Neo-orthodox view. As conceptualized and promoted after World War I by theologians such as Karl Barth and Emil Brunner (see pages 36-37), the neo-orthodox view was a reaction against modernistic liberal theology. While upholding the divine inspiration of Scripture, neo-orthodoxy discounts the historical or scientific factuality of the Bible. As an existentialist orientation, neo-orthodoxy contends that although the Bible communicates truth, this truth is ultimately realized only to the extent to which the reader subjectively recognizes and responds affirmatively to it. So the Bible is divinely-inspired, but only in the sense that it is a channel through which divine inspiration flows. Therefore, the implication is that while the Bible is (or can be) subjectively true, its inherent objective truthfulness is irrelevant.

6. Deistic view. There is a personal God who created the universe and allowed for life to exist, but this God is purely transcendent and does not involve himself in human history or the lives of individuals. In his book, *The Bible Among the Myths*, John Oswalt writes, "Revelation assumes that this world is not self-explanatory and that some communication from beyond it is necessary to explain it." Deists reject this notion and claim that all that can be known of God comes via general revelation in nature and by virtue of the *Imago Dei* – the image of God as expressed in the rational capacity of the human mind. Therefore, special revelation is unnecessary, it has never happened, and the Bible, although an impressive literary work, is merely the product of human thinking and imagination.

As with the liberal view, deists regard Bible "history" as a mix of real-life events, legend and mythology. Furthermore, biblical doctrinal and moral teachings, although expressing some profound truths and insights, are nonetheless tainted by the beliefs, biases, ignorance and superstitions of its ancient authors.

7. Naturalistic view. An atheistic and skeptical view of Scripture that holds that the Bible is just another ancient religious text of purely human origins. As such, it expresses the beliefs, biases, ignorance and superstitions of ancient Middle Easterners. The Bible is scientifically irrelevant, and in terms of historical validity, it is a confusing mix of real history, legend and mythology. Furthermore, it is in no sense binding on modern men and women as it represents a pre-modern view of morality, ethics, and human psychology that is grossly out-dated.

Part 2:
Why Should We Believe the Bible
Is Divinely-Inspired?

The Fundamental Question

Three of the foundational tenets of the Christian faith are (1) the existence of God; (2) the reality of absolute Truth based on the nature and character of God; and (3) the revealed Truth of God as recorded in the Bible. For Christians, the Bible is (or should be) our ultimate source of authority for what we believe and how we live our lives. But when we read the Bible or hear it referred to as "the (written) Word of God," how do we know that it was divinely-inspired? How many sermons have you ever heard, or how many books have you read, that offer plausible and convincing reasons for why we should take the Bible seriously as an infallible source of spiritual and moral authority? Ironically, there are scores of Bible study courses and programs, many of which are quite in-depth and comprehensive, yet few address this fundamental question.

Simply studying the Bible without a thoughtful and defensible philosophy of the Bible is like trying to build a castle in the clouds. There is no solid foundation. Everything depends upon one's own subjective faith or perhaps one's own personal experiences. But nonbelievers want to know – and certainly, Christians should want to know – *why* it is reasonable to have faith and confidence in the Bible as the divinely-inspired written Word of God. When studying the Bible without a well-considered philosophy of the Bible, it is easy to become fixated on specific stories, principles, or even individual verses to the extent that we miss the overall purpose and message of Scripture. Historically, this has been the root of many misunderstandings and even some prominent heresies.

In the following pages I set forth three "bad" reasons and five good reasons for believing that the Bible was "God-breathed" and therefore historically reliable and doctrinally and morally authoritative. It is important to keep in mind, however, that the Bible does not make the Christian faith true. The message and meaning of Christ's life, death and resurrection would be true whether or not the Bible was ever written. But there are good and compelling reasons to believe that the Bible does indeed accurately record God's interactions in human history and his purpose for mankind.

Three "Bad" Arguments

In their efforts to defend the integrity of the Bible, Christians often resort to arguments that are, to say the least, unconvincing. The following are three commonly-used "bad" arguments for making the case for the divine inspiration of Scripture. These arguments are "bad" not necessarily because they are fallacious, but simply because no thoughtful spiritual seeker or skeptic would accept them as being in any way persuasive. These arguments might, however, be effective when used to supplement the "Five Good Arguments" that follow.

1. The Argument from Authority

The basic argument from authority goes something like this: "I believe the Bible is divinely-inspired and authoritative because that's what my pastor (or church or denomination) teaches." For example, in the Roman Catholic Church's "Catechism of the Bible," the question is asked, "What proof have we that the Bible is inspired?" – to which the answer is, "The Catholic Church, which is infallible, teaches us so."[8] This may be a convincing argument for some Catholics, but suffice it to say that it is not going to convince a serious non-Catholic skeptic or spiritual seeker. (Apparently, if recent religious surveys are correct, this argument doesn't even convince many Catholics.)

These sources of authority may be correct, but nonetheless this is a poor argument. After all, what matters are the factual and rational reasons for believing in the supernatural inspiration of the Bible, not who or what authority claims that it is. Furthermore, there are many acknowledged "authorities" – liberal pastors, priests, Bible scholars, seminary professors, etc. – who argue that the Bible is *not* in fact divinely-inspired and authoritative. So unless we want to get into a protracted battle of competing authorities, this argument is not a compelling reason for accepting the authority of Scripture.

2. The "Spiritual" Argument

We have all heard Christians say things such as, "I know the Bible is true because I feel it in my heart," or "I know the Bible is the Word of God because it has changed my life," or "I believe in the Bible because God's Spirit bears witness with my spirit that it is true." Perhaps you have said something similar to this yourself.

---

[8] Rev. John O'Brien, "A Catechism of the Bible." Lesson 2: Inspiration of the Bible (1924). Revised by Fr. Jaime Pazat De Lys, 1997, 2003. In fact, Christian philosophers and theologians, including great Catholic thinkers such as Thomas Aquinas, have long recognized that the argument from authority is the weakest of all arguments.

Now all of this may be true, but we should understand that such affirmations sound like merely subjective personal opinions to nonbelievers. We might think that testimonials such as these have a strong impact on skeptics, but in fact they are quite unconvincing. After all, this kind of "spiritual" argument can be dismissed as simply an emotional response that we have to reading the Bible. Furthermore, devotees of other religions and cults often claim the same thing: they get a "warm feeling" when they read their favorite religious texts.

Many things in life, including interacting with various kinds of literature, stir people's emotions and evoke strong sentiments. Like the argument from authority, the claim that one's spiritual life, one's values and priorities have been profoundly transformed by reading and studying the Bible might well be true. However, such arguments are personal and subjective (although not *purely* subjective – there *can be* an objective reality behind such claims). But we should understand, both for our own sake and that of others, that there are other reasons for believing in the Bible that are more convincing because they are essentially factual, rational and objective rather than subjective and emotional.

3. The Self-Referential Argument

Logically, the argument that "the Bible is true because it says it is" is rather obviously fallacious. There are good reasons to believe the Bible is true, but self-referential arguments are inherently weak. It would be as if I said, "You can believe what I say because I can assure you that what I say is true." This may in fact be true, but it is nonetheless a flawed argument. As the Christian philosopher William Lane Craig explains:

> It would be circular reasoning if we were to try to *show* that the gospel is true on the basis of the Scriptures, since the Scriptures are a written expression of the gospel. Thus, while one can use the Scriptures as historical documentary evidence, one cannot, without begging the question, use them as God's Word to argue for the truth of God's Word. [Cited in Steven B. Cowan, *Five Views on Apologetics* (Zondervan Publishing House, 2000), p. 315.]

In various Scripture passages the claim is made that the writings of the ancient prophets and chroniclers that constitute the *Tanakh* were divinely-inspired. As cited previously, in II Timothy 3:16 the apostle Paul writes that "all Scripture is inspired by God and is useful for teaching, for rebuking, for correction, and for training in righteousness." In John 5:39 Jesus is quoted as saying, "You study the Scriptures thoroughly because you think in them you possess eternal life, and it is these same Scriptures that testify about me." This is the theme that is emphasized in the Epistle to the Hebrews as the author writes, "In the past God spoke to our forefathers through the prophets in many times and in various ways, but in these last days he has spoken to us by his Son" (Hebrews 1:1).

These statements are all true, but philosophically none of them offer convincing *reasons* to believe. Of course, no one should doubt that there is spiritual power in the words and message of Scripture that when animated by the Holy Spirit can be convincing in themselves. But here we are making the case that philosophically, self-referential arguments employ circular logic – just as if you were to ask me, "Why should I trust you," and I replied, "Because I'm trustworthy!" Not a particularly persuasive argument, is it?

Also consider that other religious texts claim to be true. For example, the very first verse of the Quran, just following the introductory *Shahada* ("There is no God but Allah, and Muhammad is the Messenger of Allah"), declares, "This Book is not to be doubted." But of course, the Quran *should* be doubted: it is a false text that constantly contradicts the Bible. So the fact that the Quran assures us that it is true is no reason necessarily to believe that it is true indeed.

Five Good Arguments

1. The Bible Is Historically and Scientifically Reliable

John Calvin wrote that it is "great folly" to attempt to demonstrate the inspiration and authority of the Bible to non-believers since this is a reality that "cannot be known without faith." As a corollary, he added that the inspiration and authority of Scripture is self-evident to all who have received the gift of faith. As he put it, "The Holy Spirit is... like a guarantee which confirms in our hearts the certainty of the divine truth."

Calvin was certainly correct that we can never "prove" definitively that the Bible was divinely-inspired. So why should we even believe that it was?[9] In fact, there are several reasons. First, we can build a circumstantial case for the supernatural inspiration of Scripture by showing that the Bible is historically reliable. Written by approximately 40 authors over nearly 1500 years, it offers

---

[9] In actuality, we can "prove" very little in this life. Virtually everything we believe we do so on the basis of reasonable faith – i.e., on the basis of experience, reason and probabilities. For example, you cannot prove that you're experiencing reality as you read this chapter – you might be dreaming, or perhaps this is all just an illusion (or even a nightmare!). But in all probability it is real, and in all likelihood you are in fact having a real existential experience as you immerse yourself in this scintillating book!

a reliable chronicle of Hebrew and early Christian history. No book has been more studied, scrutinized and critiqued over the centuries, yet the historical reliability of the Bible is astonishingly accurate, as Louis Markos notes in his book, *Apologetics for the 21ˢᵗ Century*:

> In order to substantiate the basic claims of Christ and the essential doctrines of Christianity, the apologist need not prove the inspiration or inerrancy of the Bible; he need only show the Bible to be reliable in its account of Jewish and Christian history. [Louis Markos, *Apologetics for the 21ˢᵗ Century* (Crossway, 2010), p. 146.]

This is a point that cannot be over-emphasized. Generally-speaking, ancient "historians" were not interested so much in relating truth as in promoting a particular agenda. History for them was almost exclusively a literary art, not a social science, and in that regard they often functioned more as propagandists or polemicists than reliable chroniclers. Not that they were always averse to the truth or totally incapable of recording straight facts – they often did, but usually when it served their purposes. Otherwise, they had few qualms about twisting and embellishing the facts, omitting crucial information, and incorporating popular superstitions and fables into their narratives. As the acknowledged "father of history," the Greek historian Herodotus (484-424 BC), informed his readers, history should be primarily entertaining.

In stark contrast to this mentality is the history we encounter in Scripture, which appears to be scrupulously (and sometimes excruciatingly) honest, unsanitized and unvarnished. Unlike the ultra-nationalistic pagan chronicles and the common panegyric idolatry of great leaders, biblical history is written from a higher, more objective perspective that often offers scathing critiques of Israel, God's "chosen people," and even revered characters such as Abraham, Moses, David, and other national heroes. This same objectivity is carried through into the New Testament in its realistic depictions of Jesus' disciples along with the problem of hypocrites and schismatics in the early church.

It is important to note here that historical accuracy isn't in any way a conclusive argument for the divine inspiration of the Bible. Keep in mind that we are building a cumulative case for why it is reasonable to believe the Bible was supernaturally inspired. Nonetheless, we can reasonably assume that *if* the Bible were divinely-inspired, it would be historically reliable. And that is precisely what we have. The Bible is certainly a book of faith, but it is a faith grounded in actual historical events. In the case of the New Testament, if it were some other ancient text it would be regarded by all serious and honest scholars as probably the most reliable historical text of the ancient world. As for the Old Testament, the strongest argument for its historical reliability is the fact that Christ often testified to its historicity and authority. Certainly, this alone should be sufficient for Christians to accept it as holy Scripture. But of course nonbelievers will demand more evidence, in which case we must remind them that this is only one of several reasons to believe the Bible is a unique book that was supernaturally-inspired.

Along with history, archaeology also confirms the historical reliability of the Bible. There has never been an archaeological discovery that disproved a biblical statement, and according to the renowned Jewish archaeologist, Nelson Glueck, "It may be stated categorically that no archaeological discovery has ever controverted a biblical reference. Scores of archaeological findings have been made which confirm in clear outline or exact detail historical statements in the Bible. And, by the same token, proper evaluation of biblical descriptions has often led to amazing discoveries."[10] Similarly, the *New York Times* review of Werner Keller's *The Bible As History* (Hodder & Stoughton, 1965) declared categorically, "No archaeological discovery has ever been made that contradicts or controverts historical statements in Scripture." Likewise, archaeologist John McRay is quoted in Lee Strobel's *The Case for Christ* as affirming, "Archaeology has not produced anything that is unequivocally a contradiction in the Bible."[11]

Over the past 150 years critics have repeatedly charged the Bible with errors, only to be proven wrong. As the Oxford historian A. H. Sayce observed:

> Time after time the... assertions of a skeptical criticism have been disproved by archaeological discovery, events and personages that were confidently pronounced to be mythical have been shown to be historical, and the older writers have turned out to have been better acquainted with what they were describing than the modern critic who has flouted them. [Quoted in McDowell, *New Evidence That Demands a Verdict*, p. 415.]

However, as means for accessing the truth of the past, history and archaeology have their limitations. History and archaeology can confirm many names, dates, locations, and actual events in the Bible, but they cannot prove that Jesus, Paul, or any other biblical character said or did anything in particular that is attributed to them. Furthermore, history and archaeology cannot prove what is most important about Jesus – the *meaning* of his life – nor can they prove the existence of God or the spiritual truth of the Bible. Just as the archaeologist Heinrich Schliemann's discovery of the ancient city of Troy

---

[10] Nelson Glueck, *Rivers in the Desert* (Farrar, Strous and Cudahy, 1959), p. 136.

[11] Lee Strobel, *The Case for Christ* (Zondervan, 1998), p. 100.

For an exhaustive study of biblical archaeology and its confirmation of many historical figures and events, see *The New International Version Archaeology Study Bible* (Zondervan, 2005).

does not verify that *The Iliad* is necessarily true, no historical or archaeological evidence for the life of Christ or any other biblical story can verify the specific details or the meaning of these narratives. Historical and archaeological confirmations can only demonstrate that the biblical accounts *could be* true. Stated otherwise: **What history and archaeology can show is that there are no good reasons to necessarily doubt the biblical narratives.**

Regarding the scientific accuracy of the Bible, astrophysicist Hugh Ross has written extensively on this subject, particularly in *Why the Universe Is the Way It Is* (BakerBooks, 2007). Not only does the Bible support modern cosmology (including an instantaneous creation and the constant expansion of the universe), but it did so more than 3,000 years ago in stark contrast to all other ancient cosmological theories and long before Moses and other writers of the texts would have known the truth about such phenomena. Indeed, the Bible describes features of the universe that would not be discovered until recent times. This knowledge is only explicable in terms of supernatural revelation.

2. The Resurrection of Jesus Christ [12]

The Christian faith is rooted in history. As the late-2nd century Christian scholar Clement of Alexandria observed, "The Bible is the narration of a revelation which has been experienced in history; it is the story of the acts of God toward humanity, and of repeated divine interventions in history." In recent times, George Eldon Ladd stated it this way: "The uniqueness of the Christian religion rests in the mediation of revelation through historical events."

Christianity is different than other religions in that its unique truth claims are testable – or in other words, it is subject to falsifiability. **The Christian faith is not a subjective leap of faith, and its core message can be verified on the basis of historical evidence – in particular, the evidence for the historicity of the resurrection of Jesus Christ.**

---

[12] For comprehensive studies of the historicity of the resurrection, see Michael R. Licona, *The Resurrection of Jesus: A New Historiographical Approach* (IVP Academic, 2010), and N. T. Wright, *The Resurrection of the Son of God* (Fortress Press, 20013).

As the New Testament scholar Luke Timothy Johnson argues, "The matter is one of simple logic: for an effect, we need a necessary and sufficient cause," and the entire early history of Christianity can only be explained in light of the phenomenon of the resurrection. See Luke Timothy Johnson, *The Real Jesus* (HarperOne, 1997), pp.136, 139.

Johnson notes that "Christianity begins with Jesus' followers experiencing Jesus after his death in a radically new way. Christianity is a religion of personal encounter with God, and resurrection faith is the birth of Christianity." See Luke Timothy Johnson, *The Writings of the New Testament* (Fortress Press, 1986), p. 101.

The resurrection is the cornerstone of the Christian faith, and it is the linchpin that holds the whole Christian belief system together. If the resurrection is true, then all the rest of Christianity makes sense. As the Anglican cleric N. T. Wright argues in *The Resurrection of the Son of God*, "Without the resurrection, there is a gaping hole in first century history that nothing else can plug.... [But] once [we] grant that Jesus really was raised... all the pieces of the historical jigsaw puzzle of early Christianity fall into place."[13] Similarly, the Yale historian Jaroslav Pelikan puts the centrality of the resurrection in its proper place when he stresses, "If Christ is risen, then nothing else matters. And if Christ is not risen, then nothing else matters."[14]

In I Corinthians 15:1ff, the apostle Paul emphasizes that Christ's resurrection was the cornerstone of the faith – without which the Christian faith is "useless" and "futile."

> Now, brothers, I want to remind you of the gospel I preached to you, which you received and on which you have taken your stand. By this gospel you are saved, if you hold firmly to the word I preached to you....
>
> For what I received I passed on to you as of first importance that Christ died for our sins according to the Scriptures, that he was buried, that he was raised on the third day according to the Scriptures, that he appeared to Peter, and then to the Twelve. After that, he appeared to more than 500 of the brothers at the same time, most of whom are still living....
>
> This is what we preach, and this is what you believed.
>
> But if it is preached that Christ has been raised from the dead, how can some of you say that there is no resurrection of the dead?
>
> If there is no resurrection of the dead, then not even Christ has been raised. And if Christ has not been raised, our preaching is useless and so is your faith. More than that, we are found to be false witnesses about God, for we have testified about God that he raised Christ from the dead .... And if Christ has not been raised, your faith is futile.

Furthermore, in I Peter 1:16 the apostle Peter reminds his readers that Christ's resurrection was not a legend or a myth but a real historical event that he and others actually witnessed: "We did not follow cleverly invented stories when we told you about the power and coming of our Lord Jesus Christ, but we were eyewitnesses of his majesty." In Lee Strobel's *Case for Christ*, Gary Habermas emphasizes this point: "The earliest Christians didn't just endorse Jesus' teachings; they were convinced they had seen him alive after his crucifixion. *That's* what changed their lives and started the church."[15]

---

[13] http://www.christianity.co.nz/res-4.htm.

[14] Yale Department of History Newsletter, cited at http://jaroslavpelikan.blogspot.com.

[15] Quoted in Strobel, *The Case for Christ*, p. 235.

Similarly, New Testament scholar Ben Witherington argues that the historical significance of the resurrection cannot be exaggerated:

> Whether Christianity stands or falls depends on certain historical facts.... Among these facts that are most crucial to Christian faith is the fact of Jesus' resurrection from the dead. The Christian faith is not mere faith in faith – but   rather a belief about the significance of certain historical events....
>
> The resurrection demonstrates that there is a power in the universe greater than death – namely, the life-giving power of God. This power means not merely that God is capable of creating new life from scratch, but that he is able to re-create life which has died. The resurrection means that God, not death, has the last word about human ends and destiny.... From this point of view, the resurrection of Jesus is the most important event in all of human history....
>
> With regularity I am confronted with students who ask why it matters that this or that event happened as long as they find their own personal faith experiences to be satisfying and transforming. The answer is that if we retreat into pure subjectivity, then there is no objective criterion by which we may determine the difference between a heartwarming experience sent by God and mere heartburn, between things that are good for us and things that merely feel good.
>
> 'Resurrection Lite,' or the resurrection as pure metaphor... was not what the earliest Christians believed in.... They had an interest in historical reality, especially the historical reality of Jesus and his resurrection. ["Resurrection Redux," in Paul Copan, ed., *Will the Real Jesus Please Stand Up?* (Baker Books, 1998), p. 138, 140.]

The fact that the early church believed in the physical bodily resurrection of Jesus Christ is one of the best-attested facts of ancient history. So what accounts for their belief in this phenomenal event? For centuries skeptics have tried desperately to refute the historicity of the resurrection by putting forth various alternative theories:

- The gospel accounts of the resurrection are contradictory.
- There is insufficient evidence to believe that Jesus actually rose from the dead.
- It isn't necessary to believe that Jesus actually rose physically from the grave; what matters is the spiritual symbolism surrounding the concept of the resurrection.
- Pagan mystery religions included similar resurrection myths and legends.
- Jesus didn't rise from the dead; his body was stolen from the tomb either by his followers, by Jewish religious leaders, or by the Roman authorities.

- The "swoon theory" – Jesus never actually died on the cross, and he was resuscitated while in the tomb and subsequently escaped.
- The hallucination theory – Jesus' followers only imagined that they had seen him after his burial.
- The whole story of Jesus' resurrection was a legend that early Christians concocted to claim that he was the Messiah and the Son of God.
- The whole concept of resurrection is unscientific and reflects a premodern mentality.

A careful examination of these alternative hypotheses shows that each of them is seriously flawed. Furthermore, none explain how and why a pseudo-resurrection or a purely symbolic resurrection could have animated the early followers of Christ and led to an explosion of belief in Christ as the divine Son of God. As the New Testament scholar Luke Timothy Johnson comments:

> When all is considered, the only sensible explanation for the genesis and subsequent growth of the Christian faith is that God raised Jesus from the dead, thereby validating his life and ministry including Jesus' claim to be the divine Savior of humanity. In addition, not only does the resurrection lend ultimate credibility to Christ's claims concerning his own messianic mission, but it also lends credence to belief in the divine inspiration of Scripture. [Johnson, *The Writings of the New Testament*, p. 98.]

3. A Unified and Progressive Theme

The Bible, written over a millennium-and-a-half by some forty authors, is consistent from beginning to end in terms of four key elements:

(1) **A unified theme.** From Genesis to Revelation, the Bible reveals a progressive unfolding of God's plan for humanity from Creation and Fall to Redemption and Restoration. This is particularly impressive because no individual or group of scholars or religious authorities put the Bible together or edited the final version to assure that it presented a standardized message. The various books were added to the collection over centuries as they were written by the prophets, the chroniclers and the apostles, and they were preserved because they were revered as inspired Scripture.

(2) **The nature of Ultimate Reality** in the personhood, the nature and the character of God.

(3) **The human condition.** In Scripture we encounter a consistent and realistic appraisal of the paradox of human nature as having been created in the *Imago Dei* (the Image of God) and yet existing as fallen, egocentric sinners.

(4) **The solution to mankind's problem** – as summarized succinctly in Habakkuk 2:4 in the Old Testament and Romans 1:17 in the New Testament: "The righteous shall live by faith."

4. A Rational and Plausible Worldview That is Coherent, Consistent, and Comprehensive

Many Christians spend a lifetime studying the Bible, and some even progress on to become knowledgeable and astute amateur or professional theologians. But few Christians ever seriously ponder the Bible philosophically. This is a problem because, when it comes to understanding the Bible, the tendency among many Christians is to miss the proverbial forest (i.e., the general worldview set forth in Scripture) for the trees (particular stories, principles, theological doctrines, and practical exhortations). Yet it cannot be overemphasized that underlying the theology of the Bible is a fundamental philosophy of life. And once we grasp this, the divine inspiration of Scripture becomes all the more apparent.

As discussed at length in Chapter 2, the Bible offers a particular worldview that sets it dramatically apart from all other belief systems. The following is a succinct summary of the key components of the biblical worldview that strongly suggests divine inspiration.

First, a biblical worldview is **coherent** – i.e., it is orderly and rational in terms of its explanation of reality as we perceive it and experience it in life. In other words, the worldview set forth in the Bible is sensible. This is not to deny that there are theological doctrines in Scripture that are *supra-rational* – i.e., above and beyond mere human understanding such as the doctrines of the Trinity, the deity of Christ, the Incarnation, the Atonement and the Resurrection. But although supra-rational mysteries, none of these is philosophically *illogical* or *irrational*.

Second, a biblical wordview is **consistent**. Of all the core doctrines that Christians hold, none are inherently contradictory. (Note: This would include the doctrines of the Trinity and the dual nature of Christ.)

Third, a biblical worldview is **comprehensive**. The Bible sets forth rational explanations for what philosophers call the perennial issues of life, including:

- **The origins of the universe**. Unlike all other ancient religions and philosophies that taught an eternal universe, the Bible is the only ancient text that affirms that the universe had a beginning – the doctrine of *creatio ex nihilo* (creation out of nothing). Obviously, something (or someone) has to be eternal, and there are only two options: either matter or a

Supernatural Being. It makes no sense to argue that matter is eternal: Where did it come from, where did the laws of physics come from, and how did matter arrange itself into its present forms? It is more sensible to believe in a personal, eternal and omnipotent Grand Designer as presented in the Bible than to imagine that lifeless and impersonal matter is responsible for all that exists.

- **The origins of life**. Only the Bible offers a plausible explanation for the appearance of life on earth and human life in particular. Otherwise, it is impossible that non-living matter could spontaneously produce life for the simple reason that non-living matter has no *potential* to produce life. Life-producing energy has to be added from the outside by an omnipotent and omniscient Intelligent Designer. As C. S. Lewis argues in *Mere Christianity*, only a Superior Being such as the God of the Bible has the potential to bring into existence complex beings such as ourselves.

- **The realities of human nature**. Being made in the *Imago Dei*, human beings have attributes such as consciousness, self-awareness, self-determination, intelligence, creativity, and a sense of morality. That being the case, why do humans often behave so badly – like predatory animals? The answer, according to Scripture, is due to the deleterious effects of the Fall that corrupted every aspect of our human nature:
  - It distorted our understanding of the nature and character of God;
  - It corrupted the divine image of God within us and rendered us selfish, rebellious, and alienated from God; and
  - It broke our relationship with God.

As James Sire writes in his classic study of alternative worldviews, *The Universe Next Door*, "In this manner people ... have attempted to set themselves up as autonomous beings.... They chose to act as if they had an existence independent from God." The result is that intellectually, our thinking became muddled and confused; morally, we lost the ability to discern good and evil; socially, we take advantage of others and use them for our own selfish ends; and creatively, our imagination became separated from reality – or as Sire puts it, "imagination became illusion, and artists who created gods in their own image led humanity further and further from its origin."[16] This is essentially why, as the Christian philosopher J. Budziszewski comments, "Reality poses a constant problem for fallen man."[17]

---

[16] Sire, *The Universe Next Door*, pp. 38*ff.*

[17] J. Budziszewski, *What We Can't Not Know* (Spence Publishing Co., 2003), p. 206.

So while we are capable of great acts of love, compassion and self-sacrifice, Scripture constantly reminds us that we are also prone to great selfishness, jealousy, bitterness, cruelty and brutality.

- **The essence of morality.** Materialistic elements such as atoms, molecules and cells are not conscious entities, nor do they have a sense of right and wrong. This is true for atoms, molecules and cells individually, and it is also true when they unite to form more complex physical properties. But if matter is all that is real, how is it that we carry within us an innate sense of good and evil? Obviously, there must exist a metaphysical (non-material) realm of reality. Our moral sensibilities are totally inexplicable from a purely naturalistic and materialistic worldview perspective, but are immanently understandable if we have been created in the image of a God who is the source and the personification of goodness and morality.

- **A sense of purpose and meaning.** As in the case for morality, there is no reason to think that purely materialistic elements would have a sense of purpose and meaning in life. Such elements merely exist physically, not consciously, and they possess no metaphysical properties. Yet we as human beings do indeed have an innate sense of purpose and meaning. The Bible offers the reason: we have been made in the image of a purposeful God and imbued with a soul. We have been made for spiritual union with God, and as Augustine declared some 1600 years ago: "O God, you made us for yourself, and our hearts will never find peace until they rest in you."

- **The longing for eternal life.** C. S. Lewis deftly observed, "If we find ourselves with a desire that nothing in this world can satisfy, the most probable explanation is that we were made for another world. If none of my earthly pleasures satisfy it, that does not prove that the universe is a fraud. Probably earthly pleasures were never meant to satisfy it, but only to arouse it, to suggest [or hint at] the real thing."[18] God has set eternity in our hearts (Ecclesiastes 3:11), and our deepest longing is to become "partakers of the divine nature" and experience eternal life (II Peter 1:4). This is our ultimate hope, and given that the Bible can be trusted in what it reveals about the origins of the universe, the origins of life, and the realities of human nature, it is sensible to believe that it also can be trusted when it comes to the realities of our ultimate destiny in the next realm of reality.

---

[18] C. S. Lewis, *Mere Christianity* (HarperSanFrancisco, 1952, 1980), pp. 136*ff.*

5. Fulfilled Biblical Prophecy

Throughout the New Testament the apostles appealed to two arguments from the life of Jesus to validate his messianic claim: (1) His miraculous resurrection; and (2) his fulfillment of ancient messianic prophecies. But there is considerable misunderstanding surrounding this whole issue of biblical prophecy, and because it is a key component in biblical apologetics we should have a firm grasp of it. The Bible uses the word "prophecy" in two senses:

- **Forthtelling** – proclaiming God's message in the present; and
- **Foretelling** – i.e., predictive prophecy of things yet to come.

Most Bible prophecy falls into the first category. In fact, less than 5% of Old Testament prophecy relates to the New Covenant age, less than 2% is specifically messianic in nature, and less than 1% concerns events yet to come.[19] Some prophecies are certainly futuristic, but most address current conditions with the intention of exhorting, confronting and warning the immediate audience to repent and get their lives in order. Berkeley Mickelsen emphasizes this point in his classic work on biblical hermeneutics, *Interpreting the Bible*:

> Hence the message of the prophet was meant to induce holy living and a spontaneous, loving obedience to God. To differentiate the various elements in the message, to see what stretched out far beyond the original hearers, is proper as long as the totality of the message is not lost sight of in the process. But to lose sight of the original hearers and to focus our attention on what may tickle the fancy of the curious-minded in the present day is to lose sight of the very reason for the message. This results in a tragic distortion of the purpose behind prophecy....
>
> Prophecy was not given to satisfy man's curiosity about the future. When interpreters force prophecy to function in this way, prophecy is being turned aside from its real purpose. [A. Berkeley Mickelsen, *Interpreting the Bible* (Wm. B. Eerdmans Publishing Company, 1963), p. 288.]

Nonetheless, when it comes to predictive prophecy, the Bible is unique. Many passages in Scripture are proleptic – i.e., they anticipate and address things yet to be fulfilled. Speaking through the prophet Isaiah, God declares, "I am YHWH, that is my name.... The past events have indeed happened. Now I declare new events; I announce them to you before they occur.... I AM the first and I AM the last. There is no God but me. Who, like me, can announce the future?" [Is. 42:8-9; 44:6-7] **No other religious writings, ancient or modern, include predictive prophecies such as we find in the Bible, which is a powerful testimony to the fact that it was supernaturally inspired.**

---

[19] See Gordon D. Fee and Douglas Stuart, *How To Read the Bible for All Its Worth*. Third Edition (Zondervan, 1981, 2002), p. 182.

Certainly, the coming of Christ opened up a new understanding of the ancient Hebrew Scriptures that had previously been veiled. As the theologian Hans von Campenhausen observed, the Old Testament is "the book of a history which leads to Christ and indeed points toward him, and without him cannot itself be understood."[20] In Revelation 19:10 we read that "the testimony of Jesus is the spirit of prophecy," and on numerous occasions Jesus cited various prophecies to validate his life and ministry:

- Luke 4:20-21 – At the outset of his ministry, Jesus read from Isaiah 61 in his hometown synagogue in Nazareth. "Then he closed the book, and gave it back to the attendant and sat down. And the eyes of all who were in the synagogue were fixed on Him. And He began to say to them, 'Today this Scripture was fulfilled in your hearing.'"
- Matt. 5:17 – "Do not think that I came to destroy the Law or the Prophets. I did not come to destroy but to fulfill."
- John 5:39*ff* – "You study the Scriptures because you think in them you possess eternal life, and it is these same Scriptures that testify about me. But you are not willing to come to Me that you may have life. For if you believed Moses, you would believe Me; for he wrote about Me."
- Luke 24:27 – "And beginning at Moses and all the Prophets, He expounded to them in all the Scriptures the things concerning Himself."
- Matt. 26:56 - "But all this was done that the Scriptures of the prophets might be fulfilled."
- Luke 24:44 – "Then [Jesus] said to [his disciples], 'These are the words which I spoke to you while I was still with you, that all things must be fulfilled which were written in the Law of Moses and the Prophets and the Psalms concerning Me.'"

Biblical authority rests in part on scores of prophecies fulfilled by Jesus' birth, ministry, death and resurrection, including:

- Micah 5:2-4, which indicates that the Messiah would be born in Bethlehem.
- Isaiah 52:13 - 53:12, which speaks of the coming suffering Servant (cf. Acts 8:30-35; I Peter 2:23).
- Jesus' triumphal entry into Jerusalem, as prophesied in Zechariah 9:9.
- Jesus' burial in a rich man's grave, in keeping with the prediction of Isaiah 53:9.
- Malachi 3:1-5, which refers to a coming messenger who will carry out the work that only God can do.

---

[20] Hans von Campenhausen, *The Formation of the Christian Bible* (E.T., 1972), p. 333.

The Problem... and the Solution. However, there is a problem that has to be reconciled regarding the messianic prophecies related to Jesus. If we look at the historical context for many of these attributions, we find that they often referred to specific people or events in ancient Hebrew history, not to a coming Messiah. For example:

- Matthew 2:15 attributes Hosea 11:1 to Jesus – *"Out of Egypt I called my son"* – but in fact Hosea was referring to Exodus 4:22 where YHWH calls Israel his "firstborn son."

- Matthew attributes Isaiah 7:14 to Mary – *"Behold, the alman [maiden, or virgin] shall conceive and give birth to a son, and will call him Immanuel."* But this prophecy was addressed to King Ahaz of Judah, and the context indicates that this child would be born in Ahaz's day and would be a sign to the king and the people of Judah that God would protect them from an invasion by the Northern Kingdom of Israel and its ally, Syria. The child, whom many scholars identify as Isaiah's son, Maher-Shalal-Hash-Baz (Isa. 8:3), would be called "Immanuel" because he would be a sign to the people of Judah that God was with them. Of course, Isaiah's wife wasn't a virgin when she gave birth to their son, but presumably she was a virgin (or a young maiden) at the time Isaiah wrote the prophecy.

- Matthew 2:17 cites Jeremiah 31:15 as the basis for Herod's slaughter of the innocents in Bethlehem when Jesus was an infant: "A voice was heard in Ramah, a lament with bitter weeping – Rachel weeping for her children, refusing to be comforted for her children because they are no more." However, the original context for this verse related to the Babylonian Exile.

- In Matthew 15:7-8 Jesus quoted Isaiah 29:13 in his condemnation of Jewish leaders: "You hypocrites! Isaiah was right when he prophesied about you: 'These people honor me with their lips, but their hearts are far from me.'" But the historical context of this verse had nothing to do with a future Messiah, and Jesus was simply drawing a comparison between apostate Jews in the time of Isaiah and those of his own day.

- During his crucifixion (Matthew 27:47) Jesus recited the first line of Psalm 22: "My God, my God, why have you forsaken me?" But this cry of anguish was originally uttered by David, who in the midst of his own suffering felt abandoned by God as he was being mocked and pursued by his enemies. Similar feelings were also expressed by Job in the crucible of his sufferings.

So the question is: Did Jesus actually "fulfill" these prophecies – and if so, in what sense? Critics, including Jewish scholars, charge that the early Christian writers merely mined the Old Testament for anything they could find that they then attributed to Jesus to make the case that he was the Messiah.

This controversy centers around a basic misunderstanding of what the New Testament writers meant when they declared that Jesus "fulfilled" certain predictive prophecies that were written centuries earlier. What they meant was this: Jesus, along with the writers of the New Testament, interpreted the ancient texts Christocentrically in the sense that all previous Scripture anticipated the coming of the Messiah – from Genesis 3:15 on ("I will put hostility between you [Satan] and the woman, and between your seed and her seed; he will strike your head, and you will strike his heel"). Therefore, in keeping with the principle of progressive revelation, they understood Jesus to be the fulfillment of the ancient Scriptures *typologically or analogically.* In other words, Jesus was the ultimate personification, representation, completion, and/or the perfection of various historical events, concepts, images and personages that were recorded in the ancient Scriptures. This is what the apostle Paul refers to in Ephesians 3:3*ff* when he writes of the great "mystery made known to me by revelation... which was not made known to people in other generations as it has now been revealed by the Spirit to God's holy apostles and prophets."

As Berkeley Mickelsen notes in *Interpreting the Bible,* "The New Testament does not simply add additional facets to the Old Testament concept of God and his people; it *transforms* the whole concept." For example:

- Israel was intended to be a light to the nations (Isaiah 42:6), while Jesus proclaimed himself "the light of the world" (John 8:12).
- Alluding to the manna that God provided to the Israelites during the Exodus, Jesus referred to himself "the living bread" and "the bread of life" (John 6:48-51).
- In the ancient Scriptures YHWH was depicted as the shepherd of his people (Psalm 23:1; Ezekiel 34:15); similarly, Jesus described himself as "the good shepherd" (John 10:11-16; Mark 14:27).
- Jesus' temptation in the desert lasted 40 days, symbolizing Israel's 40 years of testing in the wilderness during the Exodus.
- Jesus selected twelve disciples as symbolic of a new movement of God that replaced the twelve tribes of Israel.

The great medieval philosopher/theologian Thomas Aquinas (1225-74) addressed this broader understanding of prophecy in the preface to his *Commentary on Psalms* when he noted:

> Prophecies are sometimes uttered about the things which existed at the time in question, but are not uttered primarily with reference to them, but in so far as these are a figure of things to come. Therefore the Holy Spirit has provided that, when such prophecies are uttered, some details should be inserted which go beyond the actual thing done, so that the mind [of a later reader] may be raised to the thing signified. [Quoted in F. F. Bruce, *The Canon of Scripture*, p. 319.]

In most instances the term "fulfillment" in the New Testament doesn't mean the consummation of a prediction. In fact, in most cases ancient prophets were not knowingly or intentionally writing predictive prophecy. Paul Copan explains the issue this way:

> The Greek word for "fulfill" (*pleroo*) means something much broader than "the completion of a prediction." In fact, most instances of the word "fulfill" do not imply prediction at all. Fulfillment is part of the very fabric of the New Testament, which sees Jesus and his work bringing to fruition the significance of the entire Old Testament....
>
> [F]ulfillment has the sense of embodying, bringing to completion, or perfecting. [Paul Copan, *That's Just Your Interpretation* (Baker Books, 2001), p. 191.]

For example, in Matthew 5:17, when Jesus says that he came to "fulfill" the Law and the Prophets, the implication is that he was the personification of the ultimate intention of the Law by completing the symbolic meaning of the sacrificial system, the priesthood, the Sabbatical laws, the Year of Jubilee, and other sacred traditions.

Likewise, in Matthew 27:46 Jesus "fulfills" (or embodies) the suffering that David wrote about in Psalm 22. But whereas David was writing metaphorically of his suffering, many of his allusions were fulfilled literally and historically in the crucifixion of Christ:

- Psalm 22:7-8 – "Everyone who sees me mocks me; they sneer and shake their heads: 'He relies on the Lord; let Him rescue him; let the Lord deliver him, since He takes pleasure in him.
- Psalm 22:16 – "All my bones are disjointed."
- Psalm 22:16-18 – "For dogs have surrounded me; a gang of evildoers has closed in on me; they pierced my hands and my feet. I can count all my bones; people look and stare at me. They divided my garments among them, and they cast lots for my clothing."

Particularly significant was Jesus' fulfillment of the prophecy concerning his resurrection that David composed in Psalm 16:9-10 – "Therefore my heart is glad and my tongue rejoices my body also will rest secure, because you will not abandon me to the grave, nor will you let your Holy One see decay." (Cf. Acts 2:22-36.)

Therefore, throughout the New Testament the writers declare that Jesus embodies, symbolizes, completes, or perfects certain Old Testament themes or personages. This was the point of Augustine's oft-quoted statement, "the Old Testament revealed in the New, the New veiled in the Old." In his book, *Jesus and the Old Testament*, R. T. France explains the fuller significance of Jesus' messianic mission:

> Jesus uses *persons* in the Old Testament as types of himself (David, Solomon, Elijah, Elisha, Isaiah, Jonah) or of John the Baptist (Elijah); he refers to Old Testament *institutions* as types of himself and his work (the priesthood and the covenant); he sees in the *experiences* of Israel foreshadowings of his own; he finds the *hopes* of Israel fulfilled in himself and his disciples and sees his disciples as assuming the *status* of Israel; in Israel's *deliverance* by God he sees a type of the gathering of men into his church, while the *disasters* of Israel are foreshadowings of the imminent punishment of those who reject him, whose *unbelief* is prefigured in that of the wicked Israel. [R. T. France, *Jesus and the Old Testament* (InterVarsity Press, 1977), pp. 38-39.]

The accusation that early Christians plundered the Old Testament texts in a desperate attempt to prove that Jesus was the fulfillment of earlier prophecies misrepresents what actually happened. In fact, the element of predictive prophecy is one of the most unique features of the Bible, and it is a compelling reason why we should regard the Bible as supernaturally-inspired. But Christians should be prudent and discerning in their utilization of biblical prophecy as evidence for the truth of Scripture. This is an issue that is commonly misunderstood, and we should be wise in how we present this argument. Otherwise, it can backfire on us.

Our first task in interpreting prophetic passages is to consider the primary historical reference of the author, and then consider the extent to which various visions and oracles can be related to later situations. But we should also be cautious in terms of how we interpret the Bible in general, holding to the principles of sound hermeneutics as discussed in the next chapter. Otherwise, we will have the tendency to interpret Scripture in cavalier and bizarre ways that actually detract from its inherent integrity.

The Summa

Christians have traditionally affirmed that the Bible is the product of divine inspiration, but most never seriously consider the implications of what this means. In this chapter I sought to draw a clear distinction between the kind of unique inspiration or "revelation" that produced the biblical texts in contrast to the natural impulses that motivate human beings to conceptualize and produce great works of intellectual, scholarly and artistic merit. How was biblical revelation communicated, to what extent is it authoritative, and why should we regard it as qualitatively superior to the kind of "inspiration" that results in the composition and recording of great music, the writing of a scholarly treatise, or the development of new technology?

With the Bible subjected to a constant barrage of criticism in our culture today, Christians need to be knowledgeable, well-prepared and wise when it comes to explaining why we believe the Bible was supernaturally inspired. This is imperative because the Bible is our ultimate authority for what we believe about the things that matter most: the existence and nature of God, our understanding of the human condition, our purpose and meaning in life, issues related to right and wrong, and our ultimate destiny. The Bible sets forth the one and only way by which we can be reconciled to God, and it alone offers the true and unadulterated "words of life." As the apostle Peter proclaimed in II Peter 1:3-4:

> [God's] divine power has given us everything we need for life and godliness through our knowledge of [Christ] who called us by his own glory and goodness. Through these he has given us his very great and precious promises, so that through them you may participate in the divine nature and escape the corruption in the world caused by evil desires.

In summary, there are five good reasons that cumulatively offer a compelling case for why belief in the divine inspiration of Scripture is justifiable:

1. The Bible is historically reliable.
2. The resurrection of Jesus Christ is one of the best-attested events in ancient history.
3. Written over a period of 1500 years by some 40 authors, the Bible sets forth a consistent and progressive theme and message.
4. The Bible offers a rational and plausible worldview that is coherent, consistent and comprehensive, and one that provides realistic answers to the perennial issues of life.
5. The phenomenon of fulfilled prophecy makes the Bible unique among all religious texts.

Supplemental to these reasons are three "bad" (i.e., unconvincing) arguments that Christians often use:

> 1. **The argument from authority.**
> 2. **The "spiritual" argument.**
> 3. **The self-referential argument.**

As discussed earlier, the latter three arguments are "bad" not necessarily because they are fallacious or erroneous, but only in the sense that they are inherently subjective or self-referential. The Bible *does* in fact claim to be true – and there are good reasons to believe that it is – but self-referential arguments are inherently weak. Likewise, some authorities (Bible scholars, church leaders, church traditions, etc.) are indeed reliable, but unfortunately others are not. And of course the argument based on a changed life can certainly be a powerful one, but only if we have earned the trust and respect of those with whom we are sharing our faith. Otherwise, they might dismiss our personal testimony as purely subjective and unconvincing. After all, followers of other religions and cults have testimonies, too. So unless we want to descend into a battle over whose personal testimony is better or more persuasive, we are well-advised to base our arguments for the divine inspiration and authority of Scripture on more solid and objective grounds.

Finally, John Wesley is not usually regarded as one of Christianity's premier apologists, but his argument on behalf of the divine inspiration of the Bible is concise and compelling. As Wesley framed the issue:

> The Bible must be the invention either of good men or angels, bad men or devils, or of God.
>
> It could not be the invention of good men or angels; for they neither would nor could make a book, and tell lies all the time they were writing it, saying 'Thus saith the Lord,' when it was their own invention.
>
> It could not be the invention of bad men or devils; for they would not make a book which commands all duty, forbids all sin, and condemns their souls to hell for all eternity.
>
> Therefore, I draw this conclusion, that the Bible must be given by divine inspiration. [Cited in Norman L. Geisler, *A General Introduction to the Bible* (Moody Press, 1968, 1986), p. 199.]

4

Biblical Hermeneutics
Basic Principles of Interpretation

Those who are familiar with the Bible understand that it is not a treatise on systematic theology. Obviously, the Bible contains theology – insights into the character and nature of God – just as it includes many theologically-derived doctrines, teachings, principles, anecdotes and examples. But for the most part biblical theology is presented either implicitly in the context of God's active involvement through history in the lives of individuals, the nation of Israel and the church, or sometimes explicitly in the context of real-life circumstances and scenarios as in the ministry and teachings of Jesus and the various epistles of the New Testament.

As discussed in previous chapters, the Bible is the written Word of God set forth in the words of man. In their introduction to biblical hermeneutics, *How To Read the Bible for All Its Worth*, authors Gordon Fee and Douglas Stuart note that "In speaking through real persons, in a variety of circumstances over a 1500-year period, God's Word was expressed in the vocabulary and thought patterns of those persons and conditioned by the culture of those times."[1] Contrary to the old myth that the New Testament was written in a special "spiritual" (or "Holy Ghost") language, modern scholarship has demonstrated that in fact it was written in the common (*koine*) Greek of the time. Fortunately, most of Scripture is straightforward and easily understandable. But some books and passages are not, which presents a challenge. We are 2,000 or more years removed from their time, and our culture is drastically different than that of the biblical authors. This makes it imperative that we understand the elemental and essential precepts related to **biblical hermeneutics – the study of the basic principles of biblical interpretation**.

---

[1] Gordon Fee and Douglas Stuart, *How To Read the Bible for All Its Worth*. Third Edition (Zondervan, 2003), p. 23.

In the process of communicating his Word to humanity over many centuries, God used various forms of literary expression:

- Narrative history;
- Genealogies;
- Law codes;
- Poetry and proverbs;
- Prophetic oracles;
- Parables;
- Biographical vignettes;
- Letters; and
- Prophetic/apocalyptic visions.

Each of these literary forms carries with it certain common sense guidelines for interpretation that are essential for gleaning the true meaning of the text.

Biblical Interpretation

Christians understand that the Holy Spirit is not only the Spirit of divine revelation who inspired the writing of Scripture but also the Spirit of illumination who enlightens our understanding of the text. The writing of Scripture was only the first phase of the process; the ultimate goal was (and is) the comprehension and application of the truths of Scripture in the heart and mind of the reader. The mysterious process of *theopneustia* (the "inbreathing" of the Holy Spirit – ref. II Tim. 3:16) is as essential in reading and interpreting the Bible as it was in the writing of the text itself. This is in keeping with Jesus' promise in John 14:26: "But the Counselor, the Holy Spirit, whom the Father will send in my name, will teach you all things and remind you of everything I have said to you." Implicit in Jesus' words was the assumption that his followers would have the capacity not only to accurately recall his teachings but also properly interpret and apply them to their life situation.

As commonly practiced, biblical interpretation is a two-step process that involves both exegesis and hermeneutics. Simply stated, **exegesis is what the text *says* – or what it originally *meant* in its original language and context. Hermeneutics deals with what the text *means* to us today.** In his classic work on hermeneutics, *Interpreting the Bible*, Berkeley Mickelsen explains this process by drawing a distinction between exegesis and hermeneutics (or in his words, "exegesis" and "exposition"):

> Everyone who interprets a passage of the Bible stands in a *present* time while he examines a document that comes form a *past* time. He must discover what each statement meant to the original speaker or writer, and

to the original hearers or readers, in *their* own present time. Then he must
convey this message to his contemporaries....
There are two steps involved. First, we must discover the meaning of
the expression or statement in the past. Then we must drive this meaning
home to our present society with the same impact it had when it was
originally written.... Correct interpretation demands both sound exegesis
and valid exposition. [Berkeley Mickelson, *Interpreting the Bible* (William B.
Eerdmans Publishing Company, 1963), pp. 55, 56.]

Exegesis. As stated above, exegesis (Greek: "to draw meaning out of")
focuses on what the text *says* – i.e., the best and clearest translation of the text
from the original language. **Inherent in exegesis is the study of the original
intent of a text, or what it meant when it was written to its original
audience.** Logically, exegesis should be our first consideration when we study
a biblical book or passage, and as we delve into a particular text we want to
to consider the following factors:

- **The author.** Who wrote this book, and what do we know about him?
- **The date.** When was the book written?
- **The audience.** To whom was the book written?
- **The literary genre.** What kind of literature is this? As listed above, the
  Bible includes various forms of communication – everything from
  narrative history to poetry. Therefore, to maximize our understanding of
  a particular text, it is preferable that we use a Bible translation that is
  formatted to accommodate different literary forms, including paragraphs
  for most standard text and proper indentations for poetry. Different
  literary forms and expressions should be interpreted according to certain
  principles that are applicable to their respective genres.
- **The historical and cultural context.** The Bible is the revelation of God's
  message to mankind within a broad 1500-year swath of human history.
  Because every book has its own historical setting and other distinctives,
  each is conditioned by the time and culture in which it was written. It is
  often insufficient to simply quote Scripture without considering to whom
  the text was written and the circumstances surrounding the passage.
  Biblical interpretation requires that we understand the Scriptures in this
  historical setting. As Gordon Fee and Douglas Stuart explain in *How To
  Read the Bible for All Its Worth*, "The Bible is not a series of propositions
  and imperatives.... Rather, [God] chose to speak his eternal truths within
  the particular circumstances and events of human history."[2]

---

[2] Fee and Stuart, *How To Read the Bible for All Its Worth*, p. 22.

Since the text of the Bible is set in an historical and cultural context that is unfamiliar to modern readers, it is important that we understand as much as possible about the customs and lifestyles of ancient Israel and the surrounding cultures. Most newer Bible translations include prefatory comments that address the pertinent historical and cultural issues of each book. Otherwise, it is helpful to consult a Bible dictionary, a Bible handbook, a Bible atlas, and a reputable commentary. In addition, I would recommend that anyone involved in serious Bible study read two books by Gordon Fee and Douglas Stuart: *How To Read the Bible for All Its Worth* and *How To Read the Bible Book by Book*.

- **The purpose of the book**. Why was it written, and what is the author's main point(s)?

The first step in exegesis, of course, is to start with a good standard translation of the Bible (see the following section on "Bible Translations"). Then, before beginning a detailed study of a book or a particular passage, read through the book in its entirety to get an overview of it. As you do, note the natural divisions in the book, and highlight any recurring or key words, phrases or themes. Learn to read and think paragraphically – i.e., what is the main point of this particular section? And lastly, after reading, studying and praying through the text, consult a reliable commentary for additional insight. A systematic approach such as this will maximize both your enjoyment and your understanding of the text.

Note: Exegesis is in contrast to **eisegesis** (Greek: "to read meaning into"), the normal human tendency to impose meaning on a text to suit one's own preconceived assumptions or agenda. We are often guilty of practicing eisegesis when we search the Bible for proof texts to confirm what we want to find, or to validate what we already believe or something we already intend to do. Rather than allow God's written Word to speak to us with full power and conviction, we prefer to be the arbiter of its message and meaning.

Hermeneutics. Whereas exegesis focuses on what the text *meant* to the original audience, hermeneutics (Greek: *hermeneuo*, "to interpret or explain") deals with what the text *means* to us today. **Hermeneutics is the art and discipline of interpreting and applying the biblical text within the context of a commitment to wholistic discipleship**. Considering its literary genre, its historical and cultural context, its theme, and the author's intent, what is the message and the meaning of the text in the context of our current condition?

Hermeneutics depends upon proper exegesis since we can only interpret the text hermeneutically to the extent that we understand it exegetically. Due to our human limitations and fallibility, this can pose quite a challenge. Therefore, when it comes to hermeneutics three regulating principles should be considered.

First, since a text can never mean (to us) what it never meant (to the original audience), it stands to reason that the essential meaning of it for us is what God intended when he originally inspired it. A text may have a different *significance* or *application* for readers today, but it cannot have a different *meaning*. Hermeneutics addresses questions such as, How is this text relevant to me? and What does this text require of me? In this regard, we should be mindful that the purpose of hermeneutics, as Paul wrote in II Timothy 2:15, is so that we can "correctly discern [and apply] the word of truth."

Second, we must strive to check our biases and presuppositions when encountering Scripture. Everyone approaches the Bible with various *a priori* assumptions, preferences and prejudices, and we tend to read and interpret Scripture in the light (or more correctly, in the darkness) of these factors. But integral to spiritual maturity is the recognition of these presuppositions and a determination not to allow them to unduly influence and distort our understanding of the biblical text. It is our unconscious presuppositions that are potentially harmful, and our theology and morality must derive from an honest exegesis of Scripture, not vice versa. Otherwise, we become practitioners of eisegesis who use Scripture to justify any preconceived biases, preferences and assumptions that we find comfortable and reassuring. No one ever attains perfect objectivity, but we should always strive to read, interpret and apply Scripture as honestly as possible.

Third, common sense should be a guiding principle. The Bible is not a mysterious book full of esoteric secrets that only certain "enlightened" people can understand, nor is the goal of hermeneutics to come up with a new and novel insight that no one has previously discovered. Unique interpretations are almost always the product of pride and a false sense of spiritual superiority. This was the fundamental fallacy of Gnosticism, one of the original heresies in Christian history, as well as countless other frauds and pseudo-Christian cults throughout the ages. But the aim of sound hermeneutics is simply to glean the plain meaning of the text, and as Fee and Stuart note, "the most important ingredient one brings to this task is enlightened common sense." Even in the case of apocalyptic writings full of rich symbolism, the Bible was written in language that the original audience would have understood.

Hermeneutics is a dedicated search for biblical truth, and as such it should be a regular spiritual discipline in the life of every committed Christian. Even the Pharisees of Jesus' day conscientiously studied the ancient Torah, as Jesus commented in John 5:39: "You diligently study the Scriptures because you think that by them you possess eternal life. These are the Scriptures that testify about me." Later, in his final words to his disciples just prior to his arrest and crucifixion, Jesus informed them, "[W]hen he, the Spirit of truth, comes, he will guide you into all truth" (John 16:13). In Acts 17:11 we read that "the Bereans were of more noble character than the Thessalonians, for they received the [Gospel] message with great eagerness and examined the Scriptures every day to see if what Paul said was true." Years later, in his second epistle to Timothy, Paul exhorts his young protégé to minister diligently in order to earn the respect of those whom he shepherds as "a workman who does not need to be ashamed and who correctly handles the word of truth" (II Tim. 2:15).

Hermeneutics should guide our understanding and application of biblical truths both individually and corporately. In the latter context, it should be practiced in a spirit of love and humility. After all, the primary purpose of Bible study is not necessarily to correct others and straighten out their theology, but to encourage them to develop a love for Scripture and, ultimately, a deep love relationship with the God of Scripture. In this regard, and as we apply hermeneutics in a corporate setting, we should be mindful that when it comes to issues other than the clear core doctrines of Scripture, we must maintain a spirit of humility. After all, as inconceivable as it might seem, we could be wrong!

The Hermeneutical Process:
From Exegesis to Application

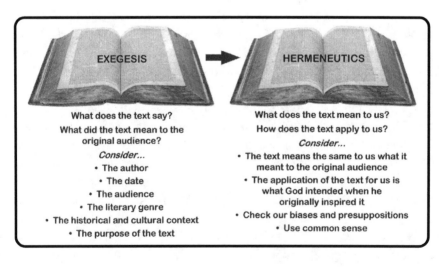

EXEGESIS	HERMENEUTICS
What does the text say?	What does the text mean to us?
What did the text mean to the original audience?	How does the text apply to us?
Consider...	*Consider...*
• The author	• The text means the same to us what it meant to the original audience
• The date	• The application of the text for us is what God intended when he originally inspired it
• The audience	
• The literary genre	
• The historical and cultural context	• Check our biases and presuppositions
• The purpose of the text	• Use common sense

Problems In Hermeneutics

Biblical hermeneutics can be problematic. As mentioned above, most everyone has a tendency to practice eisegesis rather than exegesis when it suits their purpose. We all prefer to process and understand Scripture in keeping with our own life experiences, our own cultural and moral values, our own priorities, and our own presuppositions. In other words, we would all prefer that the Bible conform to our own way of thinking. But this is, of course, a tendency we should constantly resist.

An associated problem is related to our own subjectivity or lack of consistency when it comes to interpreting certain passages. As Gordon Fee and Douglas Stuart note:

> Hermeneutical difficulties... are all related to one thing – our lack of consistency. Without necessarily intending to, we bring our theological heritage, our ecclesiastical traditions, our cultural norms, or our existential concerns to the epistles as we read them. And this results in all kinds of selectivity or "getting around" certain texts. [Fee and Stuart, *How To Read the Bible For All Its Worth*, p. 72.]

Throughout history Christians (and pseudo-Christians) have claimed scriptural support for every imaginable heresy and practice – from early Arianism and Pelagianism to modern Mormonism and the Prosperity Gospel, and from strict asceticism and priestly celibacy to snake handling and baptizing for the dead. So when we encounter Scripture, how do we discern what to believe and how to live?

One of our most difficult challenges relates to cultural relativism. As we read Scripture, which pronouncements should be regarded as concessions to 1st century culture, and which are doctrinal, moral or ethical principles that are transcultural and applicable to us today?

To reiterate a basic principle of biblical hermeneutics: A text can never mean (to us) what it never could have meant (to the original audience) when it was written. Three examples should suffice. First, in Jesus' encounter with the rich young man (ref. Matt. 19:23; Mark 10:24; and Luke 18:24), he warns him, "It is hard to enter the kingdom of God! Indeed, it is easier for a camel to go through the eye of a needle than for the rich to enter the kingdom of God." Oftentimes, expositors will explain that this was a reference to a low and narrow gate in Jerusalem called "the Needle's Eye" in which a camel would have to bend down low and unload any baggage it was carrying in order to squeeze through (much as a man might have to bow his head and squeeze through on his hands and knees). The problem is that there is no evidence that such a gate existed. In fact, the earliest known reference to the "Needle's Eye" gate comes from an 11th century commentary by a Greek cleric, Theophylact. So the point of Jesus' words is not that it is *hard* for a camel to go through the eye of a needle. On the contrary, it is *impossible*! Likewise, it is impossible for one who trusts in riches to enter the kingdom of God. It takes a supernatural miracle – which is why Jesus concludes by saying, "But all things are possible with God."

A second example comes from III John 2 in which the author writes, "Dear friend, I pray that you may enjoy good health and that all may go well with you, even as your soul is getting along well." This is a favorite verse among the "Word of Faith" Prosperity Gospel preachers who insist that good health (and wealth) should be normative for those who are called to enjoy an "abundant life." But this is an absurd distortion of what the text means. This is simply a friendly salutation in which John is expressing the hope that his friend Gaius is as healthy physically as he is spiritually. To take this verse out of context and use it as a proof text for some grandiose and unbiblical doctrine of health and wealth is the epitome of eisegesis.

A third example is I Corinthians 13:10 in which Paul writes, "When the perfect comes, the imperfect will pass away." Various attempts have been made through the centuries to claim that Paul was referring to the completion of the New Testament canon, which renders the imperfect (various "charismatic" gifts such as prophecy, tongues, miracles, etc.) unnecessary. But this interpretation is nonsensical. Paul's readers had no concept of a New Testament, and the Holy Spirit would not have inspired him to write something incomprehensible to his target audience.

In his book, *The Canon of Scripture*, F. F. Bruce cautions that some passages in Scripture had a meaning for the early church that are obscure to us today, such as the apostle Paul's reference in I Cor. 15:29 to Christians in Corinth being "baptized for the dead." Conversely, other passages may be even more relevant for contemporary Christians than for the original audience due to changing circumstances over time. However, as Bruce notes, "the interpretation of Scripture, even if it accrues at compound interest from generation to generation, cannot get more out of Scripture than is there already."[3]

Whenever we share circumstances that directly relate to that of the Christians in the 1st century, God's Word to us is the same as it was to them. The challenge is to do our exegesis well so that we can determine if the two situations are in fact comparable. This principle applies to any overt theological/doctrinal statements that we encounter in Scripture as well as to

---

[3] F. F. Bruce, *The Canon of Scripture* (InterVarsity Press, 1988), p. 320.

any moral pronouncements that are clearly articulated such as the sins listed in Romans 1:29-30; I Corinthians 5:11 and 6:9-10; and II Timothy 3:2-4.

But what about passages that address 1st century cultural issues that have little if any direct relation today? For example, what about the issue in I Corinthians 8-10 related to attending feasts at pagan temples and eating food sacrificed to idols? Is there a basic principle we might glean from this passage that transcends culture and time? If so, then we are wise to heed the biblical teaching as relevant and applicable to us today.

In this particular passage Paul forbids participating in pagan temple meals because they involve demonic rituals. The application for us is that Christians should avoid involvement in any form of activity related to the Occult or that sanctions false religions. Perhaps a contemporary application of the principle might pertain to Halloween celebrations, a perennial controversy among Christians. Another application might relate to whether Christians should eat in a Hooter's restaurant. Given that there are always other options for dining out, why would a conscientious Christian want to patronize an establishment that was founded to exploit the sexuality of its waitresses in order to profiteer off the lust of its male (or female) customers?

In this passage Paul directly addresses the issue of eating food that has been sacrificed to idols. While he makes it clear that such idols are merely pagan superstitions and that there is nothing unclean about such food *per se*, the operative principle is the law of *agape* (love): Certain things are not wrong in themselves, but in particular situations they may send the wrong message to nonbelievers or damage the fragile faith of less mature Christian brothers and sisters. In such cases, the more mature or "liberated" Christian should not flaunt his/her freedom out of respect for those who are "weaker." However, Paul also makes it clear that the offended person should refrain from judging others for doing something that he/she chooses not to do.

One of the most common contemporary controversies related to this principle is the issue of Christians consuming alcohol. Some Christians are offended that fellow believers choose to drink wine or beer, but in most cases this is a cultural issue, not a moral one. Scripture is clear that Jesus drank wine (ref. John 2:1-10; Luke 7:33-34), and in I Timothy 5:23 Paul even advises young Timothy to "Stop drinking only water, and use a little wine because of your stomach and your frequent illnesses." Indeed, in the Bible wine often symbolizes God's blessing, prosperity, and the enjoyment of life. But of course it becomes a moral rather than strictly a cultural issue in the case of over-indulgence. Those who cannot drink responsibly or have addiction issues should avoid any kind of alcohol like the proverbial plague, in keeping with I

Timothy 3:3, 8; Ephesians 5:18; Titus 1:7, 2:3; and I Peter 4:3. But nowhere in the New Testament is moderate drinking condemned. Yet as in the case of eating food sacrificed to idols, the law of *agape* should prevail. There might very well be scenarios in which a Christian should forego drinking while in the presence of someone who has a problem with alcoholism out of respect for that person's physical and spiritual health. In such cases, empathy and sensitivity toward others should always trump our own personal preferences.

Unlike cultural traditions, moral issues transcend time and are relevant to all ages and cultures. For example, indifference toward others, exploitation of others, lack of personal discipline, jealousy, dishonesty, greed, indulgence, drunkenness, sex outside of marriage and adultery are never excusable. The standards for Christian discipleship are high, and Jesus came not to abolish the Old Testament moral law but to fulfill it. In fact, Jesus calls us to a much higher standard of morality and ethics than even the Mosaic Law prescribed. His teachings extend beyond mere outward behavior into the realm of internal motives. Jesus makes it clear that we will be judged not only for what we say and do, but on the basis of the intent of our heart. As Thomas Merton notes in *Opening the Bible*, there is no place in the Kingdom of God for apathy, passivity or anything less than total commitment:

> It would be entirely wrong, a complete misunderstanding of the Bible, to interpret [it] in a very shallow way, as liberal Christianity might do, asserting that the ultimate fruit of the New Testament is merely a kind of bland religious indifference which tolerates any and every kind of conduct provided there is "good will" and "you don't hurt others".... Jesus was not mild and tolerant but extremely demanding. [Thomas Merton, *Opening the Bible* (The Liturgical Press, 1970), p. 87]

Regarding issues on which the New Testament is ambiguous, we must avoid treating them as absolute imperatives. For example, practices such as foot-washing, head coverings for women, and women's roles in ministry and church leadership have always been controversial. Obviously, if the New Testament was crystal clear on such matters it would be simple to distinguish between cultural concessions and moral and spiritual imperatives.

In this regard it is important to keep in mind that some passages are so difficult (if not impossible) to understand because, frankly, they were not written to us – at least, not directly. They addressed social conventions in a culture long ago and far away, and one that was in many ways drastically different than our own. So we should accept the fact that we may never fully understand certain vague and problematical texts. But that which is essential – and that which transcends time and culture – God has communicated clearly and unequivocally. And with that we must be content. There are limitations to what we can comprehend, which should serve as a constant reminder that one of the greatest of all virtues is humility – a realistic understanding of who we are and our limitations. But even in those cases where we cannot know everything, we can still understand *something* when we learn to distinguish between...

- What is clear, and what we know for certain;
- What is unclear, and what the various options are for understanding the meaning of the text (in which a good Bible handbook or commentary will list the possible options, citing the pros and cons of each interpretation); and
- What is unclear, and what we may never know for certain.

The first step in seeking to understand a problematical passage is exegetical: what was being communicated to the original audience *back then and there*. Second is hermeneutics: what is the meaning of this passage *here and now*. A systematic and methodical approach to hermeneutics will not resolve all the controversies or answer all our questions related to the interpretation and application of Scripture, but it will certainly reduce them to a minimum and greatly enrich our insight and understanding of the biblical text.

Hermeneutical Authority

When we encounter difficult passages and are uncertain of their meaning or application, where do we turn for authoritative answers? Historically, Christians have held three positions.

1. Roman Catholics and Eastern Orthodox Christians look to Church tradition, Church authorities and Church councils, which they believe have been supernaturally inspired throughout history and are therefore infallible in their pronouncements.

2. Protestants have traditionally emphasized *sola scriptura*, the doctrine that Scripture alone is our ultimate source of authority on all matters that it addresses. Since we are each accountable before God for what we believe and how we live, it is imperative that we become biblically literate and responsive to the internal guidance of the Holy Spirit. But although Protestantism has traditionally emphasized the individual interpretation of Scripture, in reality most simply follow the lead of their denomination, their pastor, or other acknowledged "experts."

3. The Anabaptist position is also based on the principle of *sola scriptura*, but it discourages private interpretation in favor of a community consensus approach to hermeneutics. This is simply a concession to the realities of human nature. As essentially self-centered creatures, we are capable of believing (and practicing) most anything that we can rationalize as being in our own best interest. Therefore, at least in theory, the local church as a covenantal community checks the egoistic impulses and personal agendas of each individual. As Job 34:4 counsels, "Let us discern for ourselves what is right; let us learn together what is good." The assumption is that hermeneutics is best done by the church coming together to discern "the mind of Christ." Individual interpretations should be submitted to the counsel and authority of the church in general. Unique interpretations stem from self-pride, a false sense of superior spirituality, or the need to protect a cherished bias, and are therefore often self-serving and erroneous.

Five Schools of Interpretation

Our approach to hermeneutics should be based on sensible and realistic principles that we can systematically and consistently apply to any biblical text. When seeking to properly interpret a particular book or passage, there are four fundamental components to be considered:

(1) The literary genre of the text;
(2) The unique linguistic and grammatical characteristics of the text;
(3) The historical, cultural and socio/political context of the text; and
(4) The author's intent.

A careful consideration of these four components should mitigate any novel and bizarre misinterpretations that we might be inclined to hold. Throughout history the church has had to deal with numerous heresies, all of which were based at least in part on flawed interpretations of Scripture. Some aberrant theologies and practices derive from a rigid literalistic view of Scripture, while others emanate from a highly subjectivized misreading of the biblical texts. Both of these extremes lead to serious misunderstandings and misapplications of Scripture as they fail to adequately account for these four component factors that constitute a sound and sensible hermeneutic.

The following is a brief description of five basic schools of interpretation. Any biblical text should first and foremost be evaluated and interpreted according to its plain and literal meaning in accord with the four factors listed above. This is the foundation of the historical/grammatical (or literary/ contextual) method, which traditionally has been the basis for Protestant and Anabaptist hermeneutics for the past 500 years. In contrast, Protestant fundamentalism has often been characterized by rigid literalism, while the Holiness and Pentecostal movements have been influenced (to a greater or lesser extent) by illuminism and an allegorical approach to Scripture. For the most part, modern mainline liberal Protestantism is the product of the historical/critical method. Historically, the Eastern Orthodox Church has promoted the allegorical approach to hermeneutics. As noted below, factions within the Roman Catholic Church have utilized all five of these methods through the centuries, but the Church has never officially sanctioned any particular hermeneutical methodology.

1. The Historical/Grammatical Method.

Perhaps a more descriptive term for this approach would be the **literary/contextual** method. This view holds that there is a single original meaning of each text that should inform our understanding and application of the text, and that this primary meaning is derived from the four factors that comprise a rational, responsible and credible interpretation of all Scripture: (1) Literary genre; (2) the text's linguistic and grammatical characteristics; (3) the text's historical and cultural context; and (4) authorial intent. In addition, this method incorporates **the correspondence view of Scripture** – the principle that "Scripture interprets Scripture" – which often aids in clarifying our understanding of problematic passages.

The goal of the historical/grammatical method is to discern the plain meaning of the text – first, as the original author would have intended and the original audience would have understood, and secondly, its meaning for us today. As such, this method lends itself to a three-step inductive approach to Bible study: (1) An examination of the text based on the four factors above; (2) a rational interpretation of the text; and (3) a common sense application of the text to determine its practical significance for the reader. This is in contrast to the "reader-response method," a subjective approach that focuses on how the text is perceived by the reader rather than the original intention of the author.

The Bible includes several literary genres such as narratives, histories, prophecies, apocalyptic writings, poetry, psalms, and letters (epistles). Each genre has its own set of interpretive rules that apply to it, and within each genre the authors employ different literary forms and techniques such as straight narrative prose, symbolic and allegorical language, metaphors, similes, hyperbole, etc. Meaning is derived from the text based on a familiarity with the languages in which the text was written and by an understanding of the history, geography, laws, culture and social customs that influenced the authors. **Ultimately, however, it should be emphasized that a clear understanding of Scripture is a process of illumination in which the Holy Spirit reveals the true meaning and purpose of the text to those who earnestly seek it. In that respect, biblical hermeneutics is a spiritual discipline. As Athanasius wrote,**

"One cannot possibly understand the teaching of the [prophets and apostles] unless one has a pure mind and is trying to imitate their life."

Historically, many early Christian scholars and Bible commentators adhered to the historical/grammatical hermeneutical method, including Clement of Rome, Theophilus of Antioch, John Chrysostom, and Theodoret. Augustine of Hippo interpreted Scripture according to this method, although he also supplemented it with subjective allegorical speculations in a misguided attempt to explicate the deeper "spiritual meaning" of the text. Jerome also advocated this method, but like Augustine he allowed himself in his commentaries on Scripture to be carried away into the realm of speculative allegorizing.

The historical/grammatical method does not necessarily exclude an allegorical or illuminist interpretation if the clear meaning of a passage indicates that it be interpreted in that light. However, the historical/grammatical method does require that we interpret Scripture in keeping with the plain and literal meaning of the text according to the aforementioned principle: *a text can never mean (to us) what it never originally meant (to the original audience).* So we should be mindful that any other meaning that we might attribute to a text – including any other "deeper spiritual" meaning that we might ascribe to it – is subjective and speculative, and should be held tentatively at best.

Regarding apocalyptic literature such as the Book of Revelation, symbolic language, cryptic allusions and mystical imagery are inherent to the genre itself. Therefore, the historical/grammatical method acknowledges that linguistic features such as archetypes, allegories, metaphors and hyperbole are integral to a "literal" or "plain" reading of the text. Similarly, this principle applies to the Genesis creation account in which the use of phenomenological and observational language is interwoven into the narrative.

Texts that share a common literary genre should normally be interpreted in the same way. In *How To Read the Bible for All Its Worth*, Gordon Fee and Douglas Stuart devote separate chapters to the hermeneutical principles applicable to the various literary genres of Scripture: the Old Testament narratives; the Mosaic law; the prophets; the psalms; the wisdom literature; the gospels; Jesus' parables; the Acts of the Apostles; the epistles; and the Apocalypse. As the authors remind the reader, the key to sound hermeneutics is the application of enlightened common sense. But nonetheless, their treatment of the subject, written in clear and nontechnical language for a general audience, is perhaps the best introduction to hermeneutics currently in print.

Interestingly, the Protestant Reformation began when scholars such as Luther and Calvin rejected the Roman Catholic preoccupation with the allegorical or mystical approach to biblical hermeneutics and reestablished the primacy of the historical/grammatical method, as Berkeley Mickelsen explains:

> [Luther] abandoned the fourfold interpretation of the medieval period and stressed the single fundamental [i.e., historical/grammatical] meaning. The complexity of multiple meanings had brought only a confused babel to the simple believer. Luther's new emphasis led to a greater clarity of Scripture....
>
> Luther also balanced the literal or grammatical sense with the spiritual depth of meaning.... Allegory for Luther had no depth. It consisted of "monkey tricks" to show the ingenuity of the exegete. Luther knew that for genuine depth of spiritual meaning, we must experience the illumination of the Holy Spirit. [Mickelsen, *Interpreting the Bible*, p. 38.]

This approach to hermeneutics, along with the Reformers' emphasis on *sola scriptura*, established a solid theological foundation for the Reformation and forever changed Christian history.

2. Literalism.

Literalism is an orientation that interprets the biblical text literalistically and word-for-word regardless of its literary genre, historical context, unique linguistic and grammatical characteristics, or authorial intent. **It is important to differentiate between a literal interpretation of Scripture and literal*ism*.** When we read and interpret the Bible literally, we take into account the four factors discussed above. Literalism does not. This issue often surfaces in the context of how we should properly interpret the Genesis creation narrative and whether the text requires that we believe that God created everything in six literal 24-hour days. Likewise, the apocalyptic prophecies we encounter in Daniel and Revelation also present insurmountable problems for those who insist on interpreting these passages literalistically.

In the time of Christ many Jewish scholars insisted upon a literalistic interpretation of the Old Testament. This was a major factor in why they rejected Jesus of Nazareth as the Messiah – he did not fit their preconceived profile of who and what the Messiah should be. In contrast to Jewish literalism, the early Christians interpreted the Old Testament contextually, although as noted below, some also employed the allegorical/spiritual approach in their commentaries on certain Old Testament passages.

Just as the liberal historical/critical method of interpretation undermines the authority of Scripture, literalism jeopardizes its credibility. In the same way that he excoriated theological liberalism, C. S. Lewis had little patience for those who interpret the Bible literalistically. Lewis regarded literalists as intellectual simpletons, and in *Mere Christianity* he advised that if such people "cannot understand books written for grown-ups, they should not talk about them." For example, he noted, the scriptural imagery related to Heaven (harps, crowns, gold, etc.) "is, of course, a merely symbolical attempt to express the inexpressible." So musical instruments are mentioned because music inspires feelings of "ecstasy and infinity," crowns suggest that we will reign with God eternally, and gold represents the splendor and preciousness of Heaven. But for Lewis, "People who take these symbols [literalistically] might as well think that when Christ told us to be like doves, He meant that we were to lay eggs."[4]

3. Illuminism.

An individualistic (and sometimes mystical) approach to interpreting Scripture, this view tends to overlook the text's literary and historical context and authorial intent. Rather than focusing on the plain meaning of the *logos*, God's general word and message that we encounter in Scripture, illuminists are primarily concerned with discovering a *rhema* – a specific word (or spiritual revelation) from God regarding the course of their own personal life.

There are two rather obvious problems with this approach to Scripture. For one, illluminism fosters spiritual pride – a kind of Christianized Gnosticism in which the reader senses that he/she is privy to special knowledge and wisdom above and beyond that of most people (including most other Christians). Secondly, illuminism tends to promote a self-centered and subjective orientation to reading the Bible in which one assumes that everything in it is a direct word from God to him/her personally. As Fee and Stuart caution:

> The Bible *is* a great resource. It contains all that a Christian really needs in terms of guidance from God. But this does not mean that each individual narrative is somehow to be understood as a direct word from God for each of us separately.... Perhaps the single most useful bit of caution we can give you about reading and learning from [biblical] narratives is this:... No Bible narrative was written specifically about you.
> [Fee and Stuart, *How To Read the Bible for All Its Worth*, p. 103.]

This approach to hermeneutics, which its advocates usually consider to be more "spiritual" than a simple literal reading of the text, is a favorite among Word of Faith preachers. This factor alone should be reason enough for alarm, for as Fee and Stuart observe, "If you take things out of context enough, you can make almost any part of Scripture say anything you want it to."[5]

---

[4] C. S. Lewis, *Mere Christianity* (HarperSanFrancisco, 1952, 1980), p. 137.

[5] Fee and Stuart, *How To Read the Bible for All Its Worth*, p. 103.

4. Allegorical Interpretation.

The allegorical approach is based on the presupposition that the Bible has various levels of meaning, and that the ultimate goal should be to ascertain the deeper "spiritual" significance of the text beyond the literal, surface-level narrative itself. In other words, the allegorical method interprets the historical narratives and precepts of Scripture as superficial expressions of deeper spiritual truths. In that sense, the Old Testament and even the gospels and the apostolic writings of the New Testament serve ultimately as analogies and typologies for the true meaning of the text. As Lee Martin McDonald explains, "The multilayered meanings of a biblical text, often discovered through allegorical exegesis, emphasized that the text had fluidity and adaptability."[6] This meant that Scripture should be probed for deeper meanings, which was conducive to a variety of interpretations and commentaries.

The allegorical method of interpretation is sometimes used in Scripture itself, although only as a supplement to the primary meaning of a text. For example, in Galatians 4:22ff Paul cites the story of Hagar and Sarah to illustrate a spiritual principle:

> For it is written that Abraham had two sons, one by the slave woman [Hagar] and the other by the free woman [Sarah]. His son by the slave woman was born in the ordinary way; but his son by the free woman was born as the result of a promise.
>
> These things may be taken figuratively, for the women represent two covenants. One covenant is from Mount Sinai and bears children who are to be slaves: This is Hagar. Now Hagar stands for Mount Sinai in Arabia and corresponds to the present city of Jerusalem, because she is in slavery with her children. But the Jerusalem that is from above is free, and she is our mother....
>
> Now you, brothers, like Isaac, are children of promise. At that time the son born in the ordinary way persecuted the son born by the power of the Spirit. It is the same now. But what does the Scripture say? 'Get rid of the slave woman and her son, for the slave woman's son will never share in the inheritance with the free woman's son.' Therefore, brothers, we are not children of the slave woman, but of the free woman. [Galatians 4:22-31]

Similarly, in I Corinthians 10:4 Paul recounts the stories in Exodus 17:1-7 and Numbers 20:1-13 wherein Moses and the Israelites received fresh water from rocks in the desert as symbolic of an encounter with Christ, noting that "they drank from the spiritual rock that accompanied them, and that rock was Christ." But of course this is to be taken allegorically. Paul is not suggesting that

---

[6] Lee Martin McDonald, *The Biblical Canon* (Hendrickson Publishers, 2007), p. 403.

Christ actually appeared to Moses and the Israelites in the form of a water-filled boulder, nor do the original texts indicate that these were anything but ordinary rocks.

The question then arises: If the New Testament writers sometimes interpreted the Old Testament texts in allegorical terms, isn't this a perfectly acceptable method of interpretation? But as we discussed in Chapter 3, there is a qualitative difference between the insights of the biblical authors and our own comprehension of divine truth. Unlike Paul and other New Testament writers, we are not channels of direct divine revelation. At best, the Holy Spirit can illuminate our understanding of the truths of Scripture, but we lack their unique insights into the deeper meaning of the historical texts. This is why it is essential that we derive our hermeneutics primarily on the basis of the historical/ grammatical method lest we misinterpret and misrepresent what the text actually means. As Berkeley Mickelsen cautions in *Interpreting the Bible*, "Allegorizing tells the observer clearly what the interpreter is thinking but it tells nothing about what the biblical writer was saying."[7]

Unfortunately, many Jewish and Christian Bible scholars, theologians and church leaders have advocated the allegorical method of interpretation over the centuries. In the ancient world, allegorization was often considered to be the most respectful way to interpret a sacred text. Among Jewish scholars one of the most influential allegorists was the 1st century philosopher, Philo of Alexandria, but it also became the popular approach to hermeneutics used by heretical groups such as the Gnostics. Ironically, this method was also a central feature in the hermeneutics of Church Fathers such as Justin Martyr, Irenaeus, Clement of Alexandria, Origen, and the author of the *Epistle of Barnabas*. Predicated on their belief that the contents of both the Old and New Testament were verbally-inspired and fully historical, they interpreted many of the stories in the ancient Hebrew Scriptures Christocentrically – i.e., as symbolic allegories that were fulfilled in the life of Jesus. Likewise, they often interpreted New Testament teachings in a similar way.

Origen once remarked that allegorizing Scripture was the method that "intelligent" scholars employed, and as an example he advocated a threefold theory of hermeneutics that paralleled Paul's trichotomous view of human nature in I Thessalonians 5:23 incorporating the body, soul and spirit. Similarly, Origen theorized that there were three levels of Scripture: (1) The surface (literal) level; (2) the human relational (soulish) level; and (3) the spiritual level – the latter two of which required considerable allegorizing. However, it is

---

[7] Mickelsen, *Interpreting the Bible*, p. 32.

important to note that Origen could only justify this approach to hermeneutics on the basis of his belief that Scripture was unquestionably the inspired written Word of God. Therefore, he concluded that spiritual allegorization was the ultimate testimony to the majesty and higher truth of Scripture.

Nonetheless, the allegorization of Scripture can lead to some truly bizarre interpretations. For example, in the *Epistle of Barnabas* (c. 120 A.D.) the author explains the Mosaic dietary law prohibiting the eating of pork this way:

> Therefore it is not God's commandment that they [literally] should not eat [pork], but Moses spoke in the spirit.... For this reason, then, he mentions the 'pig': Do not associate, he is saying, with... men who are like pigs. That is, men who forget their Lord when they are well off... just as when the pig is feeding it ignores its keeper.... [*Epistle of Barnabas* 10.]

Regarding the prohibition on eating birds of prey – eagles, hawks, vultures, etc. – *Barnabas* contends that this is a warning against associating with men "who do not know how to procure their own food by honest labor" but who "plunder the possessions of others." Likewise, when Moses forbids the consumption of sea creatures that do not have fins and scales, this means that the Israelites are to avoid "impious" men who skulk around in the murky depths of society. As for rabbits, they are prohibited because they represent the sexually immoral and "corrupters of boys," while hyenas are sexual perverts that "annually change their sex." (*Barnabas* apparently thought they were hermaphrodites). And if that is not weird enough, the prohibition on eating weasels is a warning against indulging in oral sex – those who "commit wickedness with the mouth," including "impure women who commit iniquity with the mouth." To further clarify the issue, *Barnabas* adds, "For this animal conceives by the mouth [i.e., it copulates via the mouth]."

Conversely, Israelites are allowed to eat "every split-hoofed and cud-chewing animal." According to *Barnabas*, the meaning here is that animals that eat fodder are aware of who feeds them, and they are "content." Therefore, the Hebrews are to associate with people who resemble cud-chewing cattle – those who "fear the Lord," who "proclaim the Lord's righteous ordinances and keep them," and who "ruminate" on the word of the Lord [apparently while eating]. "And what does the 'split-hoofed' mean? That the righteous man both walks in this world and anticipates the holy age to come." Furthermore, in case anyone has any reservations regarding *Barnabas*' interpretation of this passage, he assures the reader, "We are speaking as the Lord desired. This is why he circumcised our ears and hearts, so that we might understand these things."[8]

---

[8] *Epistle of Barnabas* 10.

For obvious reasons, this approach to hermeneutics exasperated other early Christian scholars who saw it as unduly subjective and open-ended. In his work, *Prescription Against Heretics*, Tertullian (c. 160-225) observed that there was no common ground when arguing doctrine with allegorists, whether they be Christians or heretics, because they could always extract from Scripture any meaning they preferred regardless of the plain sense of the text.

As mentioned earlier, Augustine held that Scripture should be interpreted primarily according to its plain and literal meaning, yet throughout his career he made extensive use of allegory. Due to his influence, this established an unfortunate precedent, and during the medieval period Roman Catholic scholars including even Thomas Aquinas postulated a fourfold approach to hermeneutics that addressed the literal meaning of a text along with an allegorical, a moral, and an anagogical (mystical) interpretation. The result was that Scripture could be interpreted with few if any regulating guidelines.

The question sometimes is raised: But what about apocalyptic literature that contains cryptic imagery, symbolism, archetypes, metaphors, hyperbole, etc.? Doesn't this require that we interpret such texts allegorically? Of course allegory is an integral aspect of such literature, but this is acknowledged within the interpretive guidelines that govern the historical/ grammatical method. As with illuminism, the allegorical approach may serve a legitimate purpose in the context of teaching and exhortation, but it should never function as one's primary interpretive position. At best, it is purely supplemental to the plain and primary meaning of the text.[9]

5. The Historical/Critical Method.

In contrast to all four of the preceding hermeneutical methodologies, which despite their differences are predicated on a high view of Scripture and biblical authority, the historical/critical method is based on modernistic assumptions that question (or outright reject) the divine inspiration of the Bible. Since the mid-1700s many scholars and theologians have adopted a theologically liberal approach to Scripture based on the philosophical principles of "**historical criticism**" (a.k.a. "higher criticism"). Initially influenced by biblical textual criticism (see Chapter 7), historical criticism emerged in the 18th century as an effort to reinterpret the content and message of the Bible in keeping with more rationalistic and scientific presuppositions, and in contrast to the faith-based orientation of traditional hermeneutics. Over the past 200 years historical

---

[9] For a critique of the history and influence of allegorical hermeneutics, see Mickelsen, *Interpreting the Bible*, pp. 28*ff.* For a commentary on the hermeneutics of Thomas Aquinas, see Peter Kreeft, *A Summa of the Summa* (Ignatius Press, 1990), pp. 48-50.

criticism has been refined into various sub-methodologies such as **source criticism, form criticism, redaction criticism, tradition criticism,** and **canonical criticism.** Conservative Christians should understand that there is nothing fundamentally fallacious or heretical about historical criticism per se. Indeed, these areas of study can shed considerable light on the origins, the authorship, the dating, and the cultural context of Scripture. If the Bible is indeed reliable and true, it can stand up to intense scrutiny – provided it is judged fairly by reasonable standards of literary criticism. However, there are two problems in the way modern historical criticism is often applied to the Bible:

(1) Much of historical criticism is based on naturalistic (i.e., anti-supernaturalistic) premises and unwarranted skepticism regarding traditional views of Scripture; and

(2) Bible critics often apply different (and unrealistically high) standards of verification for the Bible in contrast to any other ancient literature. ancient literature.

Therefore, historical criticism can degenerate into the kind of **radical revisionism** as practiced by biblical deconstructionists such as Adolf von Harnack, Rudolf Bultmann, Jurgen Habermas, Hermann Dettering, Bart Ehrman, and the fringe scholars of the infamous Jesus Seminar. Operating on rationalistic and naturalistic presuppositions that began with the 17th century philosopher Baruch Spinoza, radical critics approach the Bible with an *a priori* bias against its divine inspiration. As a result, they argue that nothing in the Bible should be accepted at face value unless it can be confirmed by secular historical sources or if it conforms to current conventional thinking in the humanities, the social sciences, and/or the physical sciences. So for instance, any allusions in Scripture to miracles are automatically dismissed as illusions.

Liberal theology either questions or outright rejects the divine inspiration of the Bible and its historical reliability, including the traditional authorship and dating of many of its books. Core doctrines of the historic Christian faith are also either dismissed or reinterpreted such as the Trinity, the deity of Christ, the Incarnation and the Virgin Birth, Christ's atoning death on the cross, and the Resurrection of Jesus Christ. Theological liberalism also regards many biblically-based moral precepts – particularly those related to sexual morality – as antiquated and passe. As George Eldon Ladd observed, theological liberalism undermines not only the historicity and ethics of the Bible but the core message of Scripture: God's redemption of mankind through the ages.

If one's view of history is such that he cannot acknowledge a divine plan
of salvation unfolding in historical events, then he cannot accept the
witness of the Bible.... [T]he historical-critical method denies the role of
transcendence in the history of Jesus as well as in the Bible as a whole,
not as a result of scientific study of the evidences, but because of its
philosophical presuppositions about the nature of history. [Quoted in Harold
Lindsell, *The Battle for the Bible* (Zondervan, 1976), p. 82.]

In contrast to the high view of Scripture that is integral to the
historical/grammatical method, the historical/critical method generally
approaches the Bible as merely another ancient religious text of human origin.
As with biblical textual criticism, the various sub-methodologies of historical
criticism can be beneficial apologetically when applied by honest scholars in
defense of the Bible. But as C. S. Lewis famously quipped, "Education without
values, as useful as it is, seems rather to make man a more clever devil."
Modern theological liberalism is just that: the concoction of clever devils who
have destroyed many people's faith in the Bible on purely spurious grounds.

Bible Translations

The sixty-six books that comprise the Bible were written over a period of
about 1500 years by some forty authors in three languages. Virtually all of the
Old Testament was in Hebrew with the exception of half of Daniel and two
passages in Ezra that were written in Aramaic, the official language of the old
Assyrian Empire and the common language of Western Asia from the 8th
century B.C. to the time of Christ. The New Testament was written in Greek,
the acknowledged international language in the 1st century A.D., but it also
includes a few Aramaic words and expressions.

The question is often asked, "How can we trust that the original biblical
texts were accurately preserved and transmitted through the centuries?" This is
the field of scholarship known as biblical textual criticism, which I address in
detail in Chapter 7. For our present purposes, suffice it to say that there *are*
compelling reasons to believe that the Bible has in fact been accurately
preserved and transmitted through the ages, which makes accurate translations
not only possible but highly likely when carried out by intellectually honest
scholars who are highly-trained experts in the ancient languages.

Nonetheless, translating the Bible into modern languages such as English
is as much an art as a science. As such, it presents some interesting challenges
due to all the nuances and eccentric idiomatic expressions inherent in various
languages and the vast differences between the culture of the ancient Middle
East in which the Bible was written and modern societies such as contemporary

America. In that regard, a fundamental underlying issue in biblical translation is a philosophical one:

- Should the biblical text be translated as *literally* (i.e., word-for-word) as possible from the original language into the receptor language? or

- Should the translator seek to express the essential *meaning* of the text as accurately as possible even if it necessitates changing the syntax and grammatical structure of a sentence or paragraph and substituting more descriptive words or phrases from the receptor language for the purpose of greater clarity?

In general, how one understands these questions determines one's preferences when it comes to various Bible translations. For example, consider the King James Version (KJV) and the New King James Version (NKJV) of the Bible. For some 350 years the KJV was the most prominent and influential English-language translation. Unfortunately, despite its often eloquent (but sometimes turgid) Shakespearean prose it was a fundamentally flawed translation, as Fee and Stuart comment:

> The KJV for a long time was the most widely used translation in the world; it is also a classic expression of the English language... However, for the New Testament, the only Greek text available to the 1611 translators was based on late manuscripts which had accumulated the mistakes of over a thousand years of copying. Few of these mistakes... make any difference to us doctrinally, but they often do make a difference in the meaning of certain specific texts. Recognizing that the English of the KJV was no longer a living language... it was decided by some to 'update' the KJV by ridding it of its 'archaic' way of speaking. But in so doing, the NKJV revisers eliminated the best feature of the KJV (its marvelous expression of the English language) and kept the worst (its flawed text).
>
> This is why for study you should use almost any modern translation rather than the KJV or the NKJV. [Fee and Stuart, *How To Read the Bible for All Its Worth*, p. 40.]

Presently, there are more than 30 different English language translations of the Bible, all of which can be placed on a continuum between one of the following categories.

Formal equivalence. A literal (often word-for-word) translation, this approach attempts to keep as close as possible to the "form" of the original Hebrew or Greek in terms of both words and grammar. But this can be problematical in terms of clarity when translating from one (archaic) language into another (modern) language. For instance, some Hebrew and Greek words have various shades or ranges of meaning that are difficult to convey in English.

Furthermore, it is virtually impossible to accurately convey certain subtleties such as idiomatic expressions and plays on words when translating from one language to another.

Archaic language such as one encounters in the King James Version of the Bible is also a problem. Several examples should suffice. In the KJV and the Revised Standard Version translations of Gen. 31:35, Rachel informs her father, Laban, that "the manner of women is upon me" – a reference to her monthly period. In several verses in the KJV we are told that a man "knew" his wife (or another woman) – an oblique euphemism for sexual intercourse (re. Gen. 4:1; 4:25; etc.). The KJV translation of II Sam. 13:14 informs us that Amnon "forced [his stepsister Tamar] and lay with her" – i.e., he raped her. In the New Testament the KJV translates the Greek word *sarx* as "the flesh" both as a reference to Christ's human body (as in Rom.1:3 and John 1:14 – "the Word was made flesh, and dwelt among us") and as a confusing synonym for our sinful human nature (ref. Rom. 7:5; 8:1; Gal. 3:3; 5:17; 6:8, II Cor. 7:1; I Pet. 4:2; I John 2:16; etc.). As a child reading and memorizing the 23rd Psalm in the KJV, I recall being perplexed by the apparent counterintuitive meaning of the first line: "The Lord is my shepherd, I shall not want." I assumed it couldn't possibly mean what it appeared to say (Why would David write that he did not want the Lord as his shepherd?), yet I found it puzzling to say the least.

Most modern translations, even those that seek to retain an essential formal equivalency, recognize the inherent problems associated with this approach. This is why, for instance, the committee charged with updating the Revised Standard Version adopted as its guiding principle the axiom, "As literal as possible, as free as necessary."

Functional (or **dynamic**) **equivalence.** This approach attempts to keep the true and full meaning of the original Hebrew or Greek text, including key theological terminology, while using language and syntax that are familiar to modern English. For example, many recent translations have replaced gender-exclusive terms such as "men" or "brothers" with more inclusive words such as "all" or "everyone" or "brothers and sisters" when the reference is clearly to collective humanity. This is not a concession to "political correctness" so much as it accurately expresses the original intention of the original author. Where these translations appropriately draw the line, of course, is in their use of male terminology and male pronouns in reference to the deity, in which case gender-inclusive language would be theologically inappropriate.

This approach to Bible translation is nothing new. In fact, the "Bible" of the early church – and the sacred Scriptures that Jesus quoted from and commented upon – was the Septuagint, the 2nd century B.C. Greek translation that was itself a thought-for-thought rather than a word-for-word rendering of the ancient Hebrew text. (See Chapter 5: Biblical Canonicity.) This approach to Scripture is retained throughout the New Testament as well as in the citations and commentaries of the early Church Fathers.

Free translation (or **paraphrase**). The goal of a paraphrase is to translate the concepts or principles from one language to another without undue regard for substituting the exact equivalent words for the original. Of course, paraphrases aim to remain true to the intent and spirit of the original text, but often they sound excessively colloquial and even slangy, which can detract from the gravity and solemn dignity of the written Word of God.

Regarding one's personal preferences for devotional reading and study, I would suggest considering the following points:

- The best translation is one that remains as faithful as possible to the original text while conveying the truths of Scripture as clearly as possible in modern language. In other words, opt for a translation that avoids the extremes of rigid literalism and a breezy paraphrase.

- Choose a translation that you consider to be the most readable, understandable and inspiring, and use it consistently in your own personal Bible reading and devotionals. Also, use this translation when you endeavor to memorize Scripture.

- For more concentrated Bible study, there are several options including the various Thompson Chain-References Bibles and the popular Life Application Bibles. In addition, there are several specialty study Bibles such as the Holman Apologetics Study Bible, the Zondervan NIV Archaeological Study Bible, and The Narrated Bible in Chronological Order published by Harvest House.

Bible Translations

Formal Equivalence (Literal word-for-word)	Functional Equivalent (Dynamic Equivalent)	Paraphrase (Free)
KJV NKJV NASB NRSV ESV	NIV TNIV NAB GNB	JB NLT LB TM

KJV	King James Version	TNIV	Today's New International Version
NKJV	New King James Version	NAB	New American Bible
NASB	New American Standard Bible	GNB	Good News Bible
	(Updated)	JB	Jerusalem Bible
NRSV	New Revised Standard Version	NLT	New Living Translation
ESV	English Standard Version	LB	Living Bible
NIV	New International Version	TM	The Message

5
Biblical Canonicity

Introduction

Without the Bible, the Christian faith would be an amorphous mix of traditions, beliefs and practices lacking any clear vision, mission or parameters. But when formulating a thoughtful philosophy of the Bible and pondering the ramifications of it as God's inspired written word, a seminal consideration is one that is rarely considered: What exactly constitutes the Bible? This is the issue of canonicity – the parameters of the biblical text – and it addresses three basic questions:

- Why were certain books included in the Bible and others excluded, and what were the criteria used in making this determination?
- Who made the decisions regarding which books to include? and
- When was the biblical canon finalized?

As used in biblical studies, the term "canon" refers to those writings that were determined to constitute divinely-inspired "Scripture." The Greek word **kanon** denotes a "rule" or "standard," and as used by early Christian scholars and church leaders the term referred to both correct orthodoxy (theological doctrines) and orthopraxy (practical behavior). In other words, as originally conceived the Christian canon was the fixed and authoritative "rule of faith"(*regula fidei*) that was passed on by Christ to the apostles and then disseminated among the various Christian communities of faith – first by oral transmission but soon in written form by the various apostolic authors. Eventually, as used by Athanasius of Alexandria (c. 297-373) and other Christian scholars and clerics, the canon came to be associated with a set collection of authoritative books – the idea of a closed canon of Scripture.[1] As the Roman Catholic philosopher/theologian Thomas Aquinas would note

---

[1] With this in mind, it is technically anachronistic to refer to a biblical canon that included a set list of both Old and New Testament Scriptures prior to the 4th century A.D. However, a case can be made that church leaders, under the guidance of the Holy

centuries later, "canonical Scripture alone is the rule of faith."

The primary function of the biblical canon was to provide a philosophical, theological and historical explanation for what it meant to be a member of the Kingdom of God under the New Covenant established by Christ, and to serve as the primary source of inspiration and guidance for the church (the *ekklessia*), the physical manifestation of the Body of Christ in this world. The history of canonization was a 350-year-long deliberative process that was complicated and sometimes contentious. Nonetheless, as we look back in retrospect it is apparent that church leaders were guided by the Holy Spirit to the point that they eventually reached a sensible consensus – or more accurately, a providential consensus. Over a period of several generations the books that were accorded canonical status conclusively demonstrated their divine authority.

As Lee Martin McDonald notes in *The Biblical Canon: Its Origin, Transmission, and Authority*, "The primary function of a canon is to aid the community of faith in its own self-definition (who we are) and to offer guidelines for living (what we are to do)."[2] Similarly, in his classic study, *The Canon of Scripture*, F. F. Bruce makes a crucial point regarding canonization that is often overlooked, and although his comments pertain primarily to the writings of the New Testament, the general principle applies to the Bible as a whole:

> The suggestion is made from time to time that the canon of scripture might be augmented by the inclusion of other 'inspirational' literature, ancient or modern, from a wider cultural spectrum. **But this betrays a failure to appreciate what the canon actually is. It is not an anthology of inspired or inspiring literature.** If one were considering a collection of writings suitable for reading in church, the suggestion might be more relevant. When a sermon is read in church, the congregation is often treated to what is, in intention at least, inspirational literature; the same may be said of prayers which are read from the prayerbook or of hymns which are sung from the hymnbook. **But when the limits of the canon are under consideration, the chief concern is to get as close as possible to the source of the Christian faith....**
>
> **In the canon of Scripture we have the foundation documents of Christianity, the charter of the church, the title-deeds of faith. For no other literature can such a claim be made....** In the words of Scripture

---

Spirit, had been moving toward the canonization of Scripture since at least the turn of the 2nd century.

[2] Lee Martin McDonald, *The Biblical Canon: Its Origin, Transmission and Authority* (Hendrickson Publishers, 2007), p. 64.

the voice of the Spirit of God continues to be heard. Repeatedly new spiritual movements have been launched by the rediscovery of the living power which resides in the canon of Scripture.... [F. F. Bruce, *The Canon of Scripture* (InterVarsity Press, 1988), pp. 282-83.]

As in all areas of biblical studies and Christian history, canonicity has been a controversial issue. In keeping with a foundational premise of postmodernism, a popular myth holds that the biblical canon was the result of a power struggle between various factions within Judaism and Christianity to define and control the parameters of orthodoxy. But in fact the books that were eventually included and excluded were chosen on the basis of the accepted criteria for canonicity.

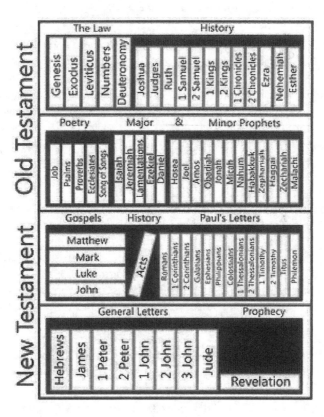

Part 1:
The Old Testament

The Traditional Boundaries

No one knows when the canon of Hebrew Scriptures was first formulated, but by at least the 1st century B.C. there was a general consensus on most of its books. Regarding the preservation of the ancient Hebrew prophetic writings, Lee Martin McDonald makes the case that the motivation for such a concerted effort extended back centuries to the events surrounding the destruction of Jerusalem in 586 B.C. and the subsequent Babylonian Captivity. As he explains:

> After Israel had lost everything in terms of its national identity – especially its temple and cultus – in the terrible destruction of 586 BCE, what was it that enabled the Jewish people to continue their identity? Why not like many other nations before them and after them simply merge with other nations and become extinct as a people with a separate identity who served Yahweh? Merger with and assimilation into other nations and cultures, with the consequent loss of separate national identity, would have been the most natural course of action,... but instead the nation of Israel was reborn. What was it that kept them alive as a nation when all of the things that identified them as a nation had been taken away – their land, sovereignty, rulership, temple, cultus, and language?...
>
> [O]nly something indestructible, commonly available, adaptable, and portable could keep this people from extinction. The only thing that fits this description... was a *story* that could be transported to Babylon and adapted to the new circumstances of the nation in captivity.... [D]uring the exile a remnant remembered the witness of the prophets who had predicted accurately what would happen to the nation. As these individuals realized that the prophets had told the truth regarding the fate and story of Israel, they realized that the message of the judgmental prophets before the exile also had a story that could offer them hope and allow them to survive the terrible judgments currently inflicted upon them. [McDonald, *The Biblical Canon*, pp. 65-66.]

Unlike other nations that attributed the destruction of their cities, temples and armies to other more powerful gods, the Jews were convinced that their defeats were the result of their own sinfulness and lack of fidelity to the one true God. It was within this context that the words of the prophets were remembered. At the time when the prophets warned of impending destruction, they were dismissed not only as unpatriotic lunatics but often subjected to brutal persecution. But now it was apparent that they had spoken for God, and what they foretold had come to pass. Therefore, they were accorded renewed respect, and their writings were revered as the very words of God – a tradition that extended into the time of Jesus.

Historically, Jews referred to these ancient writings as the **Tanakh** – an acronym derived from three traditional categories of Hebrew sacred literature. As these Scriptures were eventually canonized, the composition of these categories incorporated...

(1) The Torah (the Law, or the Penteteuch), comprising the five books of Moses: Genesis, Exodus, Leviticus, Numbers, and Deuteronomy.

(2) The Nevi'im (the Prophets): Joshua, Judges, Samuel, Kings, Isaiah, Jeremiah, Ezekiel, Hosea, Joel, Amos, Obadiah, Jonah, Micah, Nahum, Habbakuk, Zephaniah, Haggai, Zechariah, and Malachi.

(3) The Ketuvim (the Writings): Psalms, Proverbs, Job, Songs of Songs, Ruth, Lamentations, Ecclesiastes, Esther, Daniel, Ezra-Nehemiah, and Chronicles.

According to the Jewish historian **Josephus** (c. 37-100 A.D.), following the siege of Jerusalem in 70 A.D. the Roman general Titus presented to him as a gift the "sacred books" confiscated from the Temple. Apparently, these were the books that were approved for reading in synagogue services, and twenty years later, writing to a mainstream Hellenistic audience, Josephus explained the uniqueness of these ancient Hebrew texts:

> We [the Jews] do not have vast numbers of discordant and conflicting books [as do the Gentiles], but only twenty-two, containing the record of all time, and justly deemed divine. Of these, five are the books of Moses, containing the Law and the tradition of human history up to his own death. This period covers nearly three thousand years. From the death of Moses to the time of Artaxerxes... the prophets who followed Moses have written down in thirteen books the things that were done in their days. The remaining four books contain hymns to God and principles of life.
> [Josephus, *Against Apion* I:37-40]

The above quotation from Josephus is often cited as evidence for a set Jewish canon by the 1st century A.D. But while there was always unanimity on the "five books of Moses," the identity of the other 17 books is more problematic. It is often considered that rabbinical scholars regarded I and II Samuel as a single volume, as they did I and II Kings and I and II Chronicles. Likewise, it is possible that they considered Ezra and Nehemiah as one book, and that they regarded Ruth as an appendix to Judges and Lamentations as an appendix to Jeremiah. Still, it is difficult to account for the remaining 22 books of the Old Testament even if all the minor prophets (Hosea through Malachi) are conflated into a single volume. If we conclude that the "four books of hymns to God and principles of life" refers to Psalms, Proverbs, Ecclesiastes, and Song of Songs, we are still left with Joshua, Esther, Job, and the major prophets – Isaiah, Jeremiah, Ezekiel, and Daniel.

Therefore, although some scholars point to Josephus' statement as evidence of a fixed canon of Jewish Scriptures in the 1st century A.D., in lieu of more specific information one can only speculate as to how he managed to fit all 39 books of the Christian Old Testament (or all 24 books of the Jewish Tanakh) into a 22-volume canon. Some think that Josephus' canon might have reflected the views of the Pharisaic school of Hillel of his day, but this is also only speculative.[3] Certainly, the evidence from the Dead Sea Scrolls discovered in the late 1940s at Qumran indicates that a variety of texts in the 1st century were revered by at least some Jewish sects, which further calls into question the argument for a fixed canon.

Several decades prior to Josephus the Jewish scholar, **Philo of Alexandria** (c. 20 B.C.-50 A.D.), also commented on the ancient Scriptures. But like Josephus, Philo never identified specifically which books he regarded as sacred, noting only the special status accorded "the laws, inspired oracles given through the prophets, hymns and other books by which knowledge and piety may be increased and brought to perfection" – presumably a reference to the Pentateuch, the "major" and "minor" prophets, and the books of wisdom and poetry.[4] To reiterate, it is highly probable that a corpus of ancient writings was accepted by devout Jews and Christians in the 1st century A.D. that corresponds closely to what became the Jewish Tanakh and the Christian Old Testament. But prior to the early 2nd century A.D. Jewish scholars produced no known list of books that specifically identifies which texts were accepted as sacred Scripture, and there were probably a dozen or more tangential books and supplemental writings that were revered by at least some scholars and sects.

---

[3] By the 1st century A.D. there were two major rabbinical schools associated with Pharisaic Judaism, **Beth Shammai** and **Beth Hillel**. Shammaites were radical fundamentalists who followed the teachings of Shammai Ha-zaken (fl. 15 B.C. - 15 A.D.), a Jerusalem rabbi who advocated strict adherence to the Torah and the "Traditions of the Elders." Shammaites were noted for their harsh, legalistic approach to religion and the law, and during the time of Christ they were the dominant Pharisaic school. Hillelites were followers of another popular rabbi, Hillel (fl. 15 B.C. - 15 A.D.), who was renowned as a liberal and tolerant man. Hillel's grandson was Gamaliel – the apostle Paul's mentor.

[4] Ref. Philo, *On the Contemplative Life* 25.

Interestingly, though, there does appear to have been a general belief among Jewish scholars, both before and after Christ, that the "spirit of prophecy" had departed from Israel after the time of the last prophet, Malachi, circa 400 B.C. This assumption was based on a couple of references in *I Maccabbees*, but it was probably a venerable oral tradition as well.

- *I Maccabees 9:27* – "So there was great distress in Israel, such as had not been since the time that prophets ceased to appear among them."
- *I Macc. 14:41* – "The Jews and their priests resolved that Simon [Maccabeus] should be their leader and high priest forever, until a trustworthy prophet should arise."
- Josephus: "From Artaxerxes [c. 464-24 BC] until our time everything has been recorded but has not been deemed worthy of like credit with what preceded, because the exact succession of the prophets ceased.... For though so much time has passed, no one has dared to add, subtract, or change anything in them, but it is inborn in Jews from birth to regard the Scriptures as the ordinances of God, to live in them, and, if need be, to die for them gladly." [*Against Apion*, I:38-41]
- The Babylonian Talmud (c. 550): "Our rabbis taught: After the latter prophets Haggai, Zechariah, and Malachi, the Holy Spirit departed from Israel."

Therefore, books written after the era of the prophets might be valued for their wisdom or historical insights, but it is doubtful that they were regarded as divinely-inspired in the sense of the earlier writings.

The Collection Process

There is no historical record of when Jewish scribes first began systematically collecting and preserving their holy books, but undoubtedly it must have been many centuries before Christ. Many biblical scholars speculate that the process began with the Torah in the late 6th century B.C. in the years following the Babylonian Captivity. Later, perhaps in the late 3rd century B.C., there were systematic efforts to collect and preserve the corpus of texts that comprise the Nevi'im (the Prophets), followed by the Ketuvim (the Writings) in the 1st century B.C. However, this is mostly conjecture in lieu of any historical records detailing the process. Furthermore, the fact that in the 3rd century B.C. only the Torah was translated into Greek calls into question the scriptural status of the Neviim and the Ketuvim at the time. (See the following section on the Septuagint.)

Some scholars believe that the first reference to a collection of prophetic writings is in Daniel 9:2, when Daniel found Jeremiah's prophecy regarding the duration of Jerusalem's desolation (Jer. 25:11-12) "in the Scriptures." *I Maccabees 1:56ff* relates the account of how the Syrian tyrant Antiochus IV "Epiphanes" (r. 215-164 B.C.) ordered the destruction of "the books of the law" – the holy Scriptures of the Jews, while *II Maccabees 2:13* states that Nehemiah "founded a library and collected the books about the kings and prophets, and the writings of David." *II Macc. 2:14-15* also informs us that following the Maccabean Revolt (167-160 B.C.), the Jewish leader Judas Maccabeas "collected all the books that had been lost on account of the war... and they are in our possession."

As mentioned previously, following the destruction of Jerusalem in 70 A.D. the Roman general Titus presented Josephus with the sacred scrolls taken from the Temple. Despite their theological differences, Pharisees and Sadducees seemed to have recognized most of the same books as authoritative. When Josephus noted that the Sadducees "admit no observance at all apart from the laws," he did not mean the Torah to the exclusion of the Prophets and the Writings, but the written Law (contained in the Torah) in contrast to the oral law tradition.[5] Interestingly, this corpus of books corresponds closely to many of the ancient manuscripts found among the Dead Sea Scrolls of the Qumran community, which included all the books in the Tanakh other than Esther. This is particularly significant because it indicates that the Essenes, a radical ultra-orthodox separatist sect that despised the mainstream Jewish religious establishment, nonetheless revered essentially the same books as the Pharisees

---

[5] Josephus, *Antiquities* 18:16; 13:297.

and Sadducees. (The heterodox Samaritans, on the other hand, accepted only the Pentateuch as divine Scripture.) And of course we know from the Four Gospels and the rest of the New Testament that Jesus and the apostles also held the same books sacred as the Jewish establishment. So while they disagreed on many points of interpretation, both traditional Jews and Christians essentially agreed on the composition and the authority of the ancient Scriptures.

Regarding the exact parameters of Hebrew sacred literature, there apparently was some debate between the two rival Pharisaic schools, Beth Hillel and Beth Shammai, concerning the divine inspiration of some of these books. For instance, the Shammaites were skeptical of Ecclesiastes because, they declared, its philosophy reflected the wisdom of Solomon rather than of God, and they cited several passages that they considered problematical:

- Eccl. 1:3 – "What does man gain from all his labor at which he toils under the sun?" – was criticized for denying the value of studying the Torah.
- Eccl. 9:3b – "Follow the ways of your heart and whatever your eyes see" contradicts God's command to follow his law rather than one's own desires.
- Eccl. 2:24 – "A man can do nothing better than to eat and drink and find satisfaction in his work."

In addition, they pointed out an apparent contradiction in Eccl. 4:2 and 9:4:

- Eccl. 4:2 – "And I declared that the dead, who had already died, are happier than the living, who are still alive."
- Eccl. 9:4 – "Anyone who is among the living has hope – even a live dog is better off than a dead lion!"

Some ancient scribes and rabbis were also skeptical of other books. In particular, Esther was controversial because there is no mention of the name of God in the book. Similarly, Song of Songs does not contain the name of God, and some regarded its subject content as too sexual and therefore insufficiently holy. Proverbs also caused some consternation due to the fact that it seems to contradict itself – particularly Prov. 26:4-5: "Do not answer a fool according to his folly, or you will be like him yourself. Answer a fool according to his folly, or he will be wise in his own eyes." It should be noted, however, that these debates concerned only books in the traditional Jewish canon. So far as we know, none of the apocryphal books (see the section below) or other writings of a more recent vintage were ever considered for inclusion in the Jewish canon.

The Septuagint (LXX)

Some time in the 3rd century B.C. Jewish scholars in Alexandria, Egypt translated the Torah into Greek – a version known as the Septuagint (LXX). The project was probably motivated by practical considerations: reading the Torah was essential to synagogue worship, yet many Jews of the Diaspora no longer spoke Hebrew. So the Torah was first translated into Greek, and then at various times over the next century or two the rest of the Tanakh followed.

A legend associated with the development of the Septuagint was recorded in the **Letter of Aristeas** (a.k.a. Letter to Philocrates), traditionally dated to the 2nd century B.C. In his correspondence Aristeas, apparently a Hellenistic Jew, relates the story that King Ptolemy II Philadelphus of Egypt (r. 285-246 B.C.) wanted to develop the largest library in the world, whereupon he commissioned Demetrius, the chief librarian of the Alexandrian Museum, to collect all the volumes of the classical writers, including the ancient Hebrew texts. According to ancient sources the project was phenomenally successful, and by the mid-to-late 3rd century B.C. the library had amassed half a million scrolls.

In the process Demetrius supervised the translation of the ancient Hebrew Scriptures into Greek. According to the Letter of Aristeas, seventy (or seventy-two?) Jewish scholars were brought to Alexandria to translate the Torah. Working collaboratively, they finished their work in seventy-two days.

Historians suspect that at least some elements of Aristeas' account are purely legendary. It seems clear that his purpose was to make the case that the ancient Jewish religion and its revered texts were of divine origin, and to demonstrate the superiority of the Greek Septuagint over any other version of the Hebrew Bible. Based on anachronisms in the text of the letter, most scholars regard it as a forgery that was written some time in the mid-2nd century B.C. As the Princeton biblical scholar Bruce Metzger comments, "Most scholars who have analyzed the letter have concluded that the author cannot have been the man he represented himself to be but was a Jew who wrote a fictitious account in order to enhance the importance of the Hebrew Scriptures by suggesting that a pagan king had recognized their significance and therefore arranged for their translation into Greek."[6]

Over time the legend of the Septuagint's origins became more embellished. In his *Life of Moses*, Philo of Alexandria claimed that the high priest in Jerusalem selected six scholars from each of the twelve tribes of Israel, and that they worked independently and produced identical versions of the Pentateuch "as though it were dictated to each by an invisible prompter."[7] Josephus, in his

---

[6] Bruce M. Metzger, *The Bible in Translation* (Baker Academic, 2001), p. 15.

multi-volume *Antiquities of the Jews*, repeated Philo's account of the origin of the Septuagint, only to have later Christian writers claim that the seventy scholars produced identical copies of the entire Tanakh along with the books of the Apocrypha.

In addition to the ancient Tanakh, Jewish scholars also translated other intertestamental Jewish religious literature into Greek – most of which were originally written in Hebrew but including some that were composed in Greek. These books, sometimes referred to as the "**Septuagintal plus**," would later be designated by Christian scholars as the **Apocrypha** or the **Deuterocanonical** books. (See the following section, "The Apocrypha.") Along with these intertestamental books, the Septuagint included expanded versions of Esther and Daniel and an additional Psalm 151. However, other recent Jewish texts such as *I Enoch* and the *Book of Jubilees* were never included in the Septuagint.

In the time of Jesus the Septuagint was regarded as the Holy Scriptures of Greek-speaking Jews both inside and outside of Palestine. Fragments of the Septuagint have also been found among the manuscripts of the exclusivistic Essene community near the Dead Sea along with Jewish apocalyptic works including *I Enoch* and *Jubilees*.

In some respects the Septuagint functioned as the "Bible" of the early church. The New Testament writers, when referring to the ancient Jewish Scriptures, usually cited the Septuagint, as did the early Church Fathers.[8] As such, the Septuagint became synonymous with the "Greek Old Testament." Christian writers read and cited the Septuagint as authoritative in the same way as the ancient Scriptures written in Hebrew, and some even called it "inspired." The sequential order of books in the Septuagint also became the pattern for later Christian Bibles – Orthodox, Roman Catholic and Protestant versions. In fact, Christians so revered the Septuagint and used it so effectively for evangelistic purposes in the first hundred years of church history that Jews came to reject it by the mid-2nd century.

However, it should be noted that New Testament references to Old Testament passages sometimes varied from the Septuagint text. Some were closer to the Hebrew construction, while others were loose paraphrases. As F.

---

[7] Philo, *Life of Moses* II:57.

[8] According to Lee Martin McDonald, "[M]ore than 90 percent of the quotations [in the New Testament] from the Old Testament come from the Greek Bible." He adds, "The pervasive agreement between New Testament citations and the Greek Jewish Scriptures is a formidable argument that by and large the New Testament writers were working primarily from Greek versions of the Scriptures." See McDonald, *The Biblical Canon*, pp. xvii, 238.

F. Bruce comments in *The Canon of Scripture*, "It looks at times as if the New Testament writers enjoyed liberty to select a form of Old Testament text which promoted their immediate purpose in quoting it; certainly they did not regard any one form of text as sacrosanct."[9]

Jamnia

According to the Talmud, in the aftermath of the Zealot Revolt (66-73 A.D.) and the destruction of Jerusalem and the Temple, a new center for the Jewish religion was established at Jamnia [Hebrew: Jabneh or Yavne], south of Joppa, where it became the home base for a reconstituted Sanhedrin and the rabbinical school of **Beth ha-Midrash**. The foremost religious authority at Jamnia was **Rabbi Yohanan ben Zakkai**, one of Jerusalem's most influential Pharisees at the time of the Zealot Revolt. According to legend, Zakkai sought to escape from Jerusalem during the Roman siege. With hundreds dying every day, he arranged to have his friends carry him inside a coffin past the guards at the gate, and once outside the walls, he emerged from the box and managed to gain an audience with Titus. Using a loose allegorical interpretation of Isaiah 10:34 – "Lebanon shall fall to a mighty one" – he convinced the Roman general that the prophecy foretold that the Temple (constructed from Lebanese cedar) would fall to Vespasian, Titus' father and the new emperor in Rome.

Roman authorities permitted Zakkai to establish an academy for the study of the Jewish law and religion, and over the next decades the Pharisaic rabbis and scholars at Jamnia set about reconstructing Jewish religious life. In the process they defined orthodox Judaism from that time to the present. Students were subjected to a regimented study curriculum, after which they were officially ordained and commissioned as "rabbis." At the time, their efforts were seen as merely an interval between the destruction of the former Temple and the construction of a new one in the future – an expectation that was never fulfilled.

In 1871 Heinrich Graetz, a Prussian Jewish historian, popularized the theory that the scholars at Jamnia established the canon of the ancient Hebrew Scriptures in the years following the Zealot Revolt. Graetz relied in part on comments in the **Mishnah** (compiled circa 200-220 A.D.) that alluded to discussions or debates between Beth Hillel and Beth Shammai over the status of some of the more controversial books of the Ketuvim such as Ecclesiastes, Esther, Song of Songs, and Proverbs. Based on this reference, Graetz concluded

---

[9] Bruce, *The Canon of Scripture*, p. 285.

that a "**Council of Jamnia**" had debated the authenticity of the ancient writings and settled on a fixed canon of sacred Scriptures. Significantly, Jewish scholars rejected the Septuagint along with the intertestamental Hebrew and Greek writings that constituted the Apocrypha. They also charged that the Septuagint mistranslated some Hebrew texts, motivated at least in part by their desire to distinguish their version of the ancient Scriptures (later called the **Masoretic Text**) from that which Christians used. In particular, they disputed the Septuagint translation of prophetic passages such as Isaiah 7:14 – "Behold, a virgin [Greek: *parthenos*] shall conceive and bear a son...." In Greek, *parthenos* refers specifically to "virgin," whereas the ancient Hebrew term, *almah,* simply means a "young maiden" (and normally a virgin).

The rabbinical rejection of the Septuagint was in contrast to the views of earlier scholars such as Philo and Josephus who accepted the Greek version of the Hebrew Scriptures as divinely-inspired in the same sense as the original Hebrew texts. The controversy between Jewish and Christian scholars over the accuracy of the Septuagint continued throughout the 2nd and 3rd centuries, fueled in part by Christian scholars such as Justin Martyr who appeared to regard the Septuagint as the *only* reliable text of the ancient Scriptures. In his *Dialogue with Trypho* (c. 150), Justin charged that Jewish scribes altered some Hebrew texts to render them less Christological, but his friend, a learned Jew named Trypho, remained unconvinced by the Christian interpretation of the ancient prophecies.

The Hebrew Canon

The debate over the parameters of the Hebrew canon was far from settled at Jamnia, and in fact it continued over the next three centuries. Around the year 200 the influential Rabbi Simeon ben Menasia continued to argue that Ecclesiastes should be excluded from the sacred Scriptures because, in his opinion, it reflected purely human wisdom. A century-and-a-half later Rabbi Tahum of Neway was still bothered by what he regarded as contradictions in Ecclesiastes. In addition, various rabbis were still questioning the divine inspiration of Esther in the late 300s.

Heinrich Graetz's view of the Council of Jamnia became the prevailing scholarly consensus for much of the 20th century, but few historians still hold to it. In his 1983 article, "The Council of Jamnia and the Old Testament Canon," Robert C. Newman provided a modern assessment of Graetz's theory:

> A basic feature of most liberal theories of the Old Testament canon is an alleged council held at Jamnia about AD 90 which is supposed to have canonized or at least finalized the Writings or Hagiographa.... In this

paper... the Talmudic evidence for such a council is surveyed. It is concluded that there is no real evidence for such a council nor for any binding canonical decisions at that time. Instead there appears to have existed a consensus on the content of the Old Testament in the first century AD which was already ancient at that time.... It appears that a general consensus already existed regarding the extent of the category called Scripture. [Robert C. Newman, "The Council of Jamnia and the Old Testament Canon" 1983). http://www.ibri.org/RRs/RR013/13 jamnia.html]

There is little doubt that the majority of the Old Testament canon was accepted without question by the time of Christ. A few books remained a matter of controversy, in particular Esther, Ecclesiastes, and perhaps Lamentations. But otherwise, as Newman noted, there appears to have been a general consensus. Many evangelical scholars such as F. F. Bruce contend that the widespread acceptance of these books was probably a three-stage process:

A common, and not unreasonable, account of the formation of the Old Testament canon is that it took shape in three stages, corresponding to the three divisions of the Hebrew Bible. The Law was first canonized (early in the period after the return from the Babylonian exile), the Prophets next (late in the third century BC). When these two collections were closed, everything else that was recognized as holy scripture had to go into the third division, the Writings, which remained open until the end of the first century AD....

Later prophets recognized the divine authority underlying the ministry of earlier prophets (cf Jer. 7:25; Ezek. 38:17), but the idea of collecting the oracles of a succession of prophets did not occur at once. Zechariah the prophet refers to "the former prophets" (Zech. 1:4; 7:7), meaning those who prophesied before the [Babylonian] exile, but he does not imply that their words have been published as a collection. Such a collection did come into being in the following centuries, but by what agency must be a matter of speculation. [Bruce, The Canon of Scripture, pp. 36, 37.]

Although we will never know the specifics of canon formation, neither are we totally clueless regarding the process. From within the Tanakh itself we have evidence that it probably happened over a period of several centuries. Second Chronicles 17:9 informs us that early in the reign of King Jehoshaphat of Judah (r. 873-849), he sent court officials and priests throughout the land to read and teach "the Book of the Law of YHWH." According to II Kings 22:8 and II Chronicles 34:14, two centuries later, during the reign of King Josiah of Judah (r. 641-609 B.C.), the High Priest Hilkiah discovered "the Book of the Law of YHWH that had been given through Moses" while renovating the Temple (ref.

Joshua 1:8 and 8:34). But as in the foregoing instance, whether "the Book of the Law" refers to the entire Pentateuch of Moses or only a copy of the book of Exodus, Leviticus and/or Deuteronomy is uncertain.

The earliest specific reference to a collection of books comes in Daniel 9:2, when Daniel found Jeremiah's prophecy regarding the duration of Jerusalem's desolations (Jer. 25:11*ff*) among "the books." According to Josephus, in the century following the Babylonian Captivity (c. 605-537 B.C.), Nehemiah "founded a library and collected the books about the kings and prophets, and the writings of David." A few years later, Ezra the priest assembled the residents of Jerusalem together where he read aloud "the Book of the Law of Moses" from daybreak till noon, as recorded in Nehemiah 8:1*ff.* Three centuries after that, *II Macc. 2:13ff* records that Judas Maccabeus "collected all the books that had been lost on account of the war which had come upon us [i.e., the Maccabean Revolt of 167-160 B.C.], and they are in our possession." Furthermore, *II Macc. 15:9* states that Judas Maccabeus, prior to a major battle, encouraged his troops "from the law and the prophets."

In all likelihood, the sacred scrolls of the Jews were housed in the Holy Place in the Temple, and as mentioned previously, following the Roman destruction of Jerusalem in 70 A.D. Titus presented copies of "the sacred books" to Josephus.

Jesus, the Apostles, and the Old Testament

Regarding the authorship and dates of the ancient Hebrew texts, we have only ancient traditions, none of which are verifiable. Nor do we know the extent to which the texts were changed prior to the time of Christ. We have, of course, manuscripts and fragments of the ancient Hebrew texts in the Dead Sea Scrolls, along with extensive citations from the Septuagint and the ancient Hebrew Scriptures in the apostolic writings of the New Testament and the early Church Fathers. But intellectual honesty requires that we acknowledge that there is no conceivable way that we can ever reconstruct the original text of Genesis, Psalms, Isaiah, or any other Old Testament book with absolute certainty.

Once we understand this reality, it often leads to the question, "Then why should we take the Old Testament seriously – either historically or theologically? After all, we have no idea to what extent the original manuscripts were altered over the centuries in the transmission process." This is a valid question, and the most direct answer is simply, "Because Jesus did." As John Warwick Montgomery has stated, "Christ's attitude toward the Old Testament was one of total trust."[10] Jesus directly quoted from or alluded to 23 of the 39 books in the Old Testament, and he endorsed the divine inspiration of the Hebrew Scriptures without reservation.[11] So unless we want to assume that (1) God is incapable of preserving accurately the essential message of these texts through the centuries, and (2) Jesus was ignorant regarding the essential credibility of these writings, then there is no compelling reason to doubt the integrity of the texts as they have come down to us. Jesus accepted them, and this factor alone should be sufficient.[12]

Of course, simply citing an earlier source does not imply that one necessarily considers it to be true, authoritative and inspired – either in part or in full. For example, in Acts 17:28 Paul quotes the ancient Greek poet Epimenides and the opening lines from Aratus' *Phaenomena* in his comments at the Areopagus, but no one should assume that Paul regarded these writers as divinely inspired. He simply uses something they wrote to illustrate a particular truth. So context is everything, which is why in the New Testament Jesus and the apostolic writers often preface their quotations from the Hebrew Scriptures with the words "it is written" or "as the Scripture says."

In the New Testament the ancient Scriptures are often called "the Law and the Prophets," as Jesus referred to them in Matthew 7:12. From the beginning of his public ministry to his ascension, Jesus based his Messianic legitimacy on the fulfillment of various ancient prophecies. At the outset of his ministry Jesus read from the scroll of Isaiah in his hometown synagogue in Nazareth regarding

---

[10] Cited in Harold Lindsell, *The Battle for the Bible* (Zondervan, 1976), p. 44.

[11] See McDonald, *The Biblical Canon*, p. 193. This is particularly impressive when we consider that relatively little of what Jesus taught is actually recorded in the Four Gospels, as John 21:25 notes. So it is certainly possible that Jesus referenced additional books over the course of his ministry.

Three Old Testament books are never mentioned in the New Testament: Esther, Judges and Ruth. This does not imply, of course, that Jesus and the apostles rejected these books as Scripture. They simply were not directly relevant to any particular themes emphasized in the New Testament. However, the status of Esther *was* controversial, as discussed throughout this chapter.

[12] Devout Jews also accepted the received texts as divinely-inspired Scripture, and they based not only their understanding of history but also their moral and doctrinal precepts and their entire way of life on the credibility of these writings. One can assume that they also had supreme confidence in the integrity of these texts and would have taken great care to preserve and transmit them accurately from generation-to-generation.

the coming Messiah, after which he declared, "Today this Scripture is fulfilled in your hearing" (Luke 4:16-30). Three years later, following his resurrection, Jesus appeared to his disciples and reminded them, "This is what I told you while I was still with you: Everything must be fulfilled that is written about me in the Law of Moses, the Prophets and the Psalms." Then, we read, "he opened their minds so they could understand the Scriptures" (Luke 24:44*ff*).

Even many liberal scholars concede that Jesus regarded the Old Testament writings as sacred. In his book, *Jesus and the Word*, the theologian Rudolph Bultmann stated categorically that "Jesus agreed always with the scribes of his time in accepting without question the authority of the (Old Testament) Law.... Jesus did not attack the Law but assumed its authority."[13] The Harvard Divinity School professor H. J. Cadbury concluded that "Jesus held to the common Jewish view of an infallible Bible,"[14] a position that Adolph von Harnack also affirmed. Similarly, F. C. Grant of Union Theological Seminary, like Bultmann, Cadbury and Harnack a critic of the Bible, agreed that Jesus was in the mainstream of Jewish religious thought regarding his view of the Old Testament. As Grant stated it:

> The passage quoted [II Tim. 3:16 – "All Scripture is God-breathed..."] is the most explicit statement of the doctrine of biblical inspiration to be found in the New Testament. But its view of inspiration is not more advanced than that of any other part of the volume.... Everywhere it is taken for granted that what is written in Scripture [i.e., the Old Testament] is the work of divine inspiration, and is therefore trustworthy, infallible, and inerrant.... What is described or related in the Old Testament is unquestionably true. No New Testament writer would dream of questioning a statement contained in the Old Testament, though the exact manner or mode of its inspiration is nowhere explicitly stated. [Frederick C. Grant, *An Introduction to New Testament Thought* (Abingdon, 1950), p. 75.]

The apostolic writings of the New Testament repeatedly emphasized the supernatural prophetic quality of the ancient writings and interpreted them Christocentrically. As F. F. Bruce has noted, "That the Old Testament prophecies were 'mysteries' whose solution awaited their fulfilment in New Testament age was axiomatic in the early church."[15] For example:

- Throughout the Gospel of Matthew the author cites numerous ancient Hebrew prophecies fulfilled in the life of Jesus (ref. Matt. 2:3-6, 15, 17, 23; 4:14; 8:17; 12:17; 21:4; 26:54, 56; and 27:9).

---

[13] Rudolph Bultmann, *Jesus and the Word* (Scribner's, 1934), p. 61.

[14] Cited in Lindsell, *The Battle for the Bible,* p. 43.

[15] Bruce, *The Canon of Scripture,* p. 59.

- In John 5:39 Jesus rebukes his Jewish opponents with these words: "You diligently study the Scriptures because you think that by them you possess eternal life; [but] these are the Scriptures that testify about me."
- Using the prophetic passage from Isaiah 53, Philip the evangelist shared the gospel of Jesus Christ with the Ethiopian eunuch (ref. Acts 8:30-35).
- In Acts 10:43, in his testimony before Cornelius, Peter declared that "all the prophets testify about him [Jesus Christ]."
- In Romans 1:1-3 the apostle Paul writes that the "gospel of God" was revealed "through his prophets in the Holy Scriptures regarding his Son... Jesus Christ our Lord."
- In his second epistle to Timothy, Paul declares in reference to the Old Testament writings, "All Scripture is God-breathed and is useful for teaching, rebuking, correcting and training in righteousness, so that the man of God may be thoroughly equipped for every good work" (II Tim. 3:16-17).
- Paul reminds his readers in Ephesians 3:2-5 – "Surely you have heard about the administration of God's grace that was given to me for you, that is, the mystery made known to me by revelation, as I have already written briefly. In reading this, then, you will be able to understand my insight into the mystery of Christ, which was not made known to men in other generations as it has now been revealed by the Spirit to God's holy apostles and prophets."
- In the prologue to the Epistle to the Hebrews the writer declares, "In the past God spoke to our forefathers through the prophets at many times and in various ways, but in these last days he has spoken to us by his Son...." (Heb. 1:1-2).
- In I Peter 1:10-12 the apostle Peter writes that the prophets of old "searched intently... trying to find out the time and circumstances to which the Spirit of Christ in them was pointing when he predicted the sufferings of Christ and the glories that would follow."
- Peter writes in II Peter 1:19*ff,* "[W]e have the word of the prophets made more certain, and you will do well to pay attention to it, as to a light shining in a dark place, until the day dawns and the morning star rises in your hearts. Above all, you must understand that no prophecy of Scripture came about by the prophet's own interpretation. For prophecy never had its origin in the will of man, but men spoke from God as they were carried along by the Holy Spirit."

The Apocrypha

In its literal sense, the term "apocrypha" means "the things that are hidden." As applied to Jewish intertestamental literature and the biblical canon, the term "Apocrypha" is a misnomer as it refers to more than a dozen books or supplements to books that postdate the Old Testament. Although highly regarded by Jewish scholars and religious leaders for their historical and/or moral value, these writings were considered supplemental rather than scriptural. However, due to their inclusion in the Septuagint, many Christian scholars and church leaders in the first four centuries A.D. accepted at least some of these writings as authentic Scripture. During the Reformation era, however, Protestant leaders such as Luther and Calvin rejected the Apocrypha while Roman Catholic authorities approved these writings as "**deuterocanonical**" – i.e., "later additions to the canon" – in contrast to the "**protocanonical**" books that comprised the ancient Hebrew Tanakh.

Among the various Christian denominations that recognize the apocryphal writings as Scripture, there is no standardized list. However, since the time of Jerome and the publication of the Latin Vulgate edition of the Bible, the Roman Catholic canon has remained fairly constant. The Bibles of the various Orthodox denominations include all of the texts in the Catholic Apocrypha along with a few other books and additions, as indicated below.

In terms of literary genres, the Apocrypha is composed of books and supplements that can be divided into 8 categories. Texts marked † are included in the Roman Catholic Bible, while ‡ indicates that a text is accepted as deuterocanonical by one or more of the various Orthodox denominations.

(1) Historical.

- *I Esdras* ‡ – A history of the restoration of the Jews to Palestine after the Babylonian exile. The book correlates to II Chron. 35:1 to Nehemiah 8:13, although the author also includes some legendary material.
- *I Maccabees* (c. 100 B.C.) †‡ – Historically, this is the most valuable book in the Apocrypha. *I Maccabees* relates the exploits of the Jewish patriot Mattathias and his sons in their struggles against Syria to

establish an independent Jewish state. The book was probably written
shortly after the death of the Hasmonean king John Hyrcanus I in
104 B.C. The most objectionable aspect of the book is its effusive
praise of the Romans and their system of government, which later
Jews would despise.

(2) Polemical history.

- *II Maccabees* (1ˢᵗ century B.C.) ✝✝ – Not a sequel to I Maccabees, but
  a parallel account of the Maccabean Revolt that incorporates more
  legendary features.

(3) Historical fiction.

- *Tobit* (c. 200 B.C.) ✝✝ – Although purportedly historical, *Tobit* is
  essentially a romantic novel, set in Nineveh and Pharisaic in tone,
  that extols piety and faithfulness to YHWH. The book incorporates
  three popular folktales, including the tale of the Grateful Dead, and
  implies that alms-giving atones for one's sins.
- *Judith* (late-2ⁿᵈ century B.C.?) ✝✝ – A fictitious Pharisaic novel in
  which the beautiful heroine, Judith, saves Israel by defeating an
  Assyrian army that is marching on Jerusalem.
- **Additions to Daniel** (1ˢᵗ century BC):
  - **"Susanna"** (1ˢᵗ century B.C.) ✝✝ – A legendary story added to
    Daniel as a 13th chapter.
  - **"Bel and the Dragon"** ✝✝ – A legendary story set during
    Daniel's lifetime and added as a 14th chapter.
  - **"Prayer of Azariah"** and the **"Song of the Three Jews"** (c.
    100 B.C.?) ✝✝ – An extended passage and antiphonal hymn
    that follows Daniel 3:23 in Roman Catholic and Eastern
    Orthodox Bibles. The passage features the prayer of Azariah
    (a.k.a. Abednego – see Daniel 1:6-7) while he and his two
    young Jewish companions were cast into the fiery furnace, a
    brief account of an angel who preserved them while in the
    furnace (whom Christian scholars later interpreted as a
    theophany of the Son of God), and the hymn of praise they
    sang when delivered from the flames. The passage does not
    appear in the Hebrew/Aramaic text of Daniel.
- *III Maccabees* (1ˢᵗ century B.C.) ✝ – A misnomer, the book has nothing
  to do with the Maccabees or their revolt against the Seleucid Empire
  as described in *I-II Maccabees*. Rather, it relates three stories of the
  persecution of the Jews under Ptolemy IV Philopator (222–205 B.C.)

several decades before the Maccabean uprising, including the dramatic account of Jews being herded into the hippodrome near Alexandria to be trampled to death by intoxicated elephants. Although parts of the story are fictitious, some elements are probably based on real incidents.

(4) Legendary.

- *Jubilees* – The book of *Jubilees* claims to present an authoritative "history of the division of the days of the Law, of the events of the years, the year-weeks, and the jubilees of the world" as revealed by angels to Moses while he was on Mount Sinai for forty days and nights. The chronology given in *Jubilees* is based on multiples of seven: the "Jubilees" are periods of 49 years, seven "year-weeks," into which the entire history of creation and of Israel is divided. *Jubilees* covers many of the same themes as Genesis, but often with additional detail. For example, the book narrates the appearance of angels on the first day of creation and the story of how a group of fallen angels mated with mortal females, giving rise to the race of giants identified as the Nephilim (ref. Gen. 6:1-4). Approximately 15 copies of *Jubilees* were found in various caves at Qumran, which indicates that it was highly revered by the Essene sect and perhaps regarded as sacred Scripture.

(5) Wisdom literature.

- *Wisdom of Solomon* (c. 40 B.C.?) ✝✝ – One of most respected apocryphal books, *Wisdom of Solomon* was written to warn Jews against religious apostasy, materialism and idolatry. Although written in the tradition of Solomonic wisdom literature, few ancient scholars ever attributed the book to the historical Solomon.
- *Wisdom of Jesus ben Sirach* (*Ecclesiasticus*, c. 180 B.C.?) ✝✝ – Similar in theme to the ethical teachings in the book of Proverbs, *Sirach* is attributed to the Jewish scribe Shimon ben Yeshua ben Eliezer ben Sira of Jerusalem.
- *IV Maccabees* ✝ – A recount of the persecution of Jews under Antiochus IV Epiphanes (r. 175-164 B.C.) as drawn from *II Maccabees*, and Stoic-influenced philosophical reflections on these incidents. The author portrays martyrdom as bringing atonement for the past sins of the Jews.

(6) Devotional.

- **"Prayer of Manasseh"** (2nd century B.C.) ✝✝ – Purportedly, the prayer of the wicked King Manasseh of Judah while a captive of the Assyrians (ref. II Chron. 33:1-19). Traditionally, the prayer has been placed at the end of II Chronicles.

- **Additions to Esther** (c.100 B.C.) ✝✝ – Long prayers attributed to Esther and Mordecai; probably conceived to compensate for the lack of mention of the name of God in the book of Esther.

- **Psalm 151** ✝ – Excluded from virtually all Hebrew manuscripts of the Psalter, *Psalm 151* contains 7 verses in which David celebrates his selection by YHWH as the "leader of his people and ruler over the people of his covenant."

- *Psalms of Solomon* (1st century B.C.) – A collection of 18 songs that includes a celebration of the coming Messiah who will conquer the heathen world "by the word of his mouth." The book implies that Roman general Pompey's conquest of Jerusalem in 63 B.C. was divine punishment for the sins of the Jewish Hasmonean dynasty.

(7) Prophecy.

- *Baruch* (late 2nd century B.C.) ✝✝ – Although purportedly authored by Baruch ben Neriah, Jeremiah's scribe (c. 582 B.C.), some scholars propose that it was probably written during or shortly after the period of the Maccabees. In the Latin Vulgate and many other versions, the **"Letter of Jeremiah"** ✝✝ is appended to the end of *Baruch* as a sixth chapter. *Baruch* 1:1,14: "And these are the words... which Baruch... wrote in Babylonia.... And when [the Jewish exiles] heard it they wept, and fasted, and prayed before the Lord."

(8) Apocalyptic.

- *II Esdras* (date unknown) ✝ – Seven apocalyptic visions utilizing symbolic language and numbers, strange creatures, and angelic visitations. Martin Luther found the book so exasperating that he tossed it into the Elbe River.

- *I Enoch* (c. 300 B.C. - 1 A.D.?) – A collection of apocalypses written by several authors addressing issues such as the origin of evil, the creation and destiny of angels, the nature of Gehenna and Paradise, and the pre-existent Messiah. The first section describes the fall of the Watchers, the angels who fathered the *Nephilim* (ref. Gen. 6:1-4), while the remainder of the book describes Enoch's visits to heaven in the form of travels, visions and dreams, and his revelations. Most scholars believe the various sections of the books were originally independent works composed at different times, and that they were later redacted into what became *I Enoch*. The New Testament epistle of Jude quotes a "prophecy" from *I Enoch*, implying that at least some early Christians considered the book to be authoritative and perhaps even scriptural. The earliest complete copy of the book is preserved in an Ethiopic translation that includes references to the Messiah as the Son of Man. (Most scholars believe these references have been redacted.) *Enoch* was regarded as Scripture by some early Christian scholars including Justin Martyr, Tertullian, Clement of Alexandria, and the author of the *Epistle of Barnabas*, and parts of the book were preserved on 12 manuscripts that have been found among the Dead Sea Scrolls.

The Old Testament, the Apocrypha, and the Canonization Process

Historically, the only "Bible" that the early church had until the apostolic Christian writings began to be circulated and collected by various churches was the Septuagint. The post-apostolic Christian community accepted these writings as historically accurate and doctrinally and morally authoritative. They also regarded them as holy Scripture which, when properly interpreted, had the power to transform lives.

An example of how an encounter with Scripture could radically change one's life comes from the testimony of the 2nd century Christian scholar Tatian in his *Address to the Greeks* (c. 170). After reading Greek philosophy and investigating the various mystery cults, Tatian noted the profound difference between these writings and what he encountered in the ancient Hebrew Scriptures:

> [R]etiring by myself, I sought how I might be able to discover the truth. And while I was giving my most earnest attention to the matter, I happened to encounter certain 'barbaric' [i.e., non-Greek] writings, too old to be compared with the opinions of the Greeks and too divine to be compared with their error. I found myself convinced by these writings because of the unpretentious cast of the language, the authentic character of the writers, the foreknowledge displayed of future events, the excellent quality of the precepts, and the declaration of the government and of the universe as centered in one Being. And my soul being taught by God, I understood that the pagan writings led to condemnation, whereas these put an end to the slavery that is in the world, and rescue us from many rulers and tyrants. These writings do not indeed give us something which we had not

received before but rather something which we had indeed received but were prevented by error from making our own. [Tatian, *Address to the Greeks* XXIX.]

As the New Covenant people of God, the church considered itself to be the spiritual heir of ancient Israel. Therefore, Christians venerated the Hebrew Scriptures just as Jesus and pious Jews had always revered these books. However, there were questions regarding the exact parameters of the Old Testament as some scholars, both Jewish and Christian, were less than convinced that books such as Esther and Ecclesiastes should be accepted as holy Scripture. Likewise, the status of the Apocrypha was somewhat controversial, and it took more than three centuries before the church reached a general consensus on a set canon of the Old Testament.

As mentioned previously, most apocryphal books were part of the Septuagint. In fact, fragments of five of these texts have been found among the Dead Sea Scrolls: *Wisdom of Sirach, Tobit*, the "Letter of Jeremiah," *I Enoch*, and *Jubilees*. There is no indication that Philo of Alexandria, Josephus, nor any of the major Jewish rabbinical schools of the 1st century A.D. regarded these books as Scripture *per se*, and they were always on the periphery and never at the core of the Jews' corpus of sacred literature. Nonetheless, due to their inclusion in the Septuagint, most Christian scholars apparently accepted at least some of these writings as legitimate Scripture. In fact, there are far more references in the writings of the Ante-Nicene Church Fathers (scholars and influential clerics who lived and wrote prior to the Nicene Council of 325 A.D.) to books such as the *Wisdom of Solomon, Wisdom of Sirach, Judith, Tobit, II Esdras, II Maccabees*, and even *I Enoch* than to Ruth, Ezra, Nehemiah, Lamentations, Obadiah, Micah, or Haggai.[16]

The New Testament specifically cites two apocryphal books. In Hebrews 11:35 the author refers to an incident recorded in *II Maccabees*, and Jude 14 quotes from *I Enoch* 1:9:

- **Hebrews 11:35-38** – In the past, many righteous men and women "were tortured and refused to be released, so that they might gain a better resurrection." These were people of whom "the world was not worthy."
- *II Macc. 6:18-7:4* relates the stories of righteous Jews who suffered excruciating torture rather than forsake their faith.
- **Jude 14** – "Enoch, the seventh from Adam, prophesied about these men: 'See, the Lord is coming with thousands upon thousands of his holy ones

---

[16] See McDonald, *The Biblical Canon*, p. 221.

to judge everyone, and to convict all the ungodly of all the ungodly acts they have done in the ungodly way...."

- *I Enoch 1:9* – "And behold! He cometh with ten thousands of His holy ones to execute judgement upon all, and to destroy all the ungodly: And to convict all flesh of all the works of their ungodliness which they have committed, and of all the hard things which ungodly sinners have spoken against Him."

In addition to these two examples, there are numerous other parallels and allusions to apocryphal writings throughout the New Testament such as in the following examples:

- **Rom. 1:18-32** – "The wrath of God is being revealed from heaven against all the godlessness and wickedness of men who suppress the truth by their wickedness, since what may be known about God is plain to them, because God has made it plain to them. For since the creation of the world God's invisible qualities – his eternal power and divine nature – have been clearly seen, being understood from what has been made, so that men are without excuse.

  "For although they knew God, they neither glorified him as God nor gave thanks to him, but their thinking became futile and their foolish hearts were darkened. Although they claimed to be wise, they became fools and exchanged the glory of the immortal God for images made to look like mortal man and birds and animals and reptiles.

  "Therefore, God gave them over in the sinful desires of their hearts to sexual impurity for the degrading of their bodies with one another. They exchanged the truth of God for a lie, and worshiped and served created things rather than the Creator....

  "Because of this, God gave them over to shameful lusts. Even their women exchanged natural relations for unnatural ones. In the same way the men also abandoned natural relations with women and were inflamed with lust for one another. Men committed indecent acts with other men, and received in themselves the due penalty for their perversion.

  "Furthermore, since they did not think it worthwhile to retain the knowledge of God, he gave them over to a depraved mind, to do what ought not to be done. They have become filled with every kind of wickedness, evil, greed, and depravity. They are full of envy, murder, strife, deceit and malice. They are gossips, slanderers, God-haters, insolent, arrogant and boastful; they invent ways of doing evil; they disobey their parents; they are senseless, faithless, heartless, ruthless. Although they know God's righteous decree that those who do such things deserve death, they not only continue to do these things but also approve of those who practice them."

- **Wisdom of Solomon 13:5-10; 14:22-30** – "For from the greatness and beauty of created things comes a corresponding perception of their Creator. Yet these people are little to be blamed, for perhaps they go astray while seeking God and desiring to find him. For while they live among his works, they keep searching, and they trust in what they see, because the things that are seen are beautiful. Yet again, not even they are to be excused; for if they had the power to know so much that they could investigate the world, how did they fail to find sooner the Lord of these things? But miserable, with their hopes set on dead things, are those who give the name 'gods' to the works of human hands....

  "Then it was not enough for [pagan idolaters] to err about the knowledge of God, but though living in great strife due to ignorance, they call such great evils peace. For whether they kill children in their initiations, or celebrate secret mysteries, or hold frenzied revels with strange customs, they no longer keep either their lives or their marriages pure, but they either treacherously kill one another, or grieve one another by adultery, and all is a raging riot of blood and murder, theft and deceit, corruption, faithlessness, tumult, perjury, confusion over what is good, forgetfulness of favors, defiling souls, sexual perversion, disorder in marriages, adultery, and debauchery. For the worship of idols not to be named is the beginning and cause and end of every evil. For their worshipers either rave in exultation, or prophesy lies, or live unrighteously, or readily commit perjury; for because they trust in lifeless idols they swear wicked oaths and expect to suffer no harm. But just penalties will overtake them on two counts: because they thought wrongly about God in devoting themselves to idols, and because in deceit they swore unrighteously through contempt for holiness. For it is not the power of the things by which people swear, but the just penalty for those who sin, that always pursues the transgression of the unrighteous."

- **II Cor. 5:1,4** – "Now we know that if the earthly tent we live in is destroyed, we have a building from God, an eternal home in heaven not built by human hands.... For while we are in this tent, we groan and are burdened...."

- *Wisdom of Solomon 9:13-15* – "For who can learn the counsel of God? Or who can discern what the Lord wills? For the reasoning of mortals is worthless, and our designs are likely to fail; for the perishable body weighs down the soul, and this earthy tent burdens the thoughtful mind."

- **James 1:19 and 13** – "My dear brothers, take note of this: Everyone should be quick to listen, slow to speak, and slow to anger...

   "When tempted, no one should say, 'God is tempting me.' For God cannot be tempted by evil, nor does he tempt anyone."

- *Wisdom of Sirach 5:11* and *15:11-12* – "Be quick to hear, but deliberate in answering....

   "Do not say, 'It was the Lord's doing that I fell away;' for he does not do what he hates. Do not say, 'It was he who led me astray;' for he has no need of the sinful. The Lord hates all abominations; such things are not loved by those who fear him."

- **II Peter 2:4 and 3:6** indicate an awareness of *I Enoch*.

- **I Cor. 2:9** – "No eye has seen, no ear has heard, no mind has conceived what God has prepared for those who love him" – appears to cite either the *Ascension of Isaiah 11:34* or the lost *Apocalypse of Elijah* derived from Isaiah 64:3.[17]

There are several quotations in the New Testament taken from earlier writings that are unknown to us, but which are cited as if they were holy Scripture.

- **Matt. 2:23** – "So was fulfilled what was said through the prophets: 'He shall be called a Nazarene.'"

- **John 7:38** – "Whoever believes in me, as the Scripture has said, streams of living water will flow from within him."

- **I Cor. 2:9** – "However, it is written, 'No eye has seen, nor ear has heard, no mind has conceived what God has prepared for those who love him....'" (Some Church Fathers thought this quote came from the *Secrets of Elijah* or the *Apocalypse of Elijah*, but there is no way to substantiate this.)

- **Eph. 5:14** – "This is why it is said, 'Awake, o sleeper, and rise from the dead, and Christ will shine on you.'"

---

[17] For other examples, see "Appendix D: New Testament Citations of and Allusions to Apocryphal and Pseudepigraphical Writings" in McDonald, *The Biblical Canon*, pp. 452-64.

- **II Timothy 3:8** – "Just as Jannes and Jambres opposed Moses...." These names, in various forms, appear in several Jewish writings, but most postdate the time of Paul. The earliest known reference is to "Yahaneh and his brother" in the *Book of the Covenant of Damascus*, circa 100 B.C.
- **James 4:5** – "Or do you think Scripture says without reason that the spirit he caused to live in us envies intensely?"

Because they revered the ancient Hebrew Scriptures as divinely inspired, Christian scholars and church leaders considered it vital to distinguish between three classifications of writings:

(1) Books that were worthy of canonical status;

(2) Books that were efficacious but supplemental to the sacred texts; and

(3) Books that were purely legendary and mythical in nature.

In reality, this proved to be a particularly messy and complicated process as it related to the Apocrypha.

Versions of the Old Latin translations of the Bible that predated the Latin Vulgate included the books in the later Roman Catholic Apocrypha, along with others such as *I* and *II Esdras*. Likewise, many of the Ante-Nicene Church Fathers quoted from these books and implied that they were authoritative Scripture, including Clement of Rome, Polycarp, Irenaeus, Tertullian, Clement of Alexandria, Cyprian, and the authors of the *Epistle of Barnabas* and the *Didache*.[18] In the 4th century many church leaders in the Greek-speaking East (including Eusebius, Athansius, Cyril of Jerusalem, and Gregory of Nazianzus) distinguished between the books in the traditional Hebrew canon and the Apocrypha, while in the Latin West most clerics and scholars tended to integrate these writings into the Old Testament corpus.

The status and authority of the Apocrypha had always been controversial. The 1st century A.D. Alexandrian Jewish scholar **Philo** quoted and commented extensively from the Tanakh but never from the Apocrypha. Likewise, **Josephus** excluded the Apocrypha from his list of sacred books.[19] Furthermore, there is no indication that the Pharisaic Jewish scholars at Jamnia ever accepted these texts as divinely-inspired. Among other factors, it was often noted that none of these intertestamental writings includes the common authoritative declaration of the ancient prophets, "Thus saith the Lord."

---

[18] See Bruce M. Metzger and Roland E. Murphy, eds., *The New Oxford Annotated Apocrypha* (Oxford University Press, 1991), pp. iii*ff.* Also ref. McDonald, *The Biblical Canon*, pp. 196-98.

[19] Josephus, *Against Apion*. I:8.

The first-known church leader to establish a set list of sacred Hebrew texts was **Melito** (d. 180), the bishop of Sardis. (He might also have been the first to refer to this collection of books as the "Old Covenant" or "Old Testament.") Melito may have been motivated to do this by the fact that Jewish scholars were debating the limits of their Scriptures in the 2nd century. Apparently, their lack of consensus on the issue prompted him to travel "to the east" (probably Judea) some time around the year 175 to research the matter. As the church historian Eusebius later recounted Melito's testimony:

> Accordingly, when I went East and came to the place where these things were preached and done, I learned accurately the books of the Old Covenant, and send them to you as written below. Their names are as follows: Of Moses, five books: Genesis, Exodus, Numbers, Leviticus, Deuteronomy; Jesus Nave [Joshua]; Judges, Ruth; of Kings, four books [I and II Samuel and I and II Kings]; of Chronicles, two; the Psalms of David, the Proverbs of Solomon, *Wisdom*; also, Ecclesiastes, Song of Songs, Job; of Prophets, Isaiah, Jeremiah; of the twelve [minor] prophets, one book; Daniel, Ezekiel, Esdras [Ezra/Nehemiah]. From which also I have made the extracts, dividing them into six books. [Eusebius, *Ecclesiastical History* IV.26.13-14.]

Many scholars suppose that Melito probably regarded Lamentations as an appendage to Jeremiah, but conspicuously absent from his list was the book of Esther. He also omitted all the writings of the Apocrypha other than *"Wisdom"* – either a reference to *Wisdom of Solomon* or *Wisdom of ben Sirach* (*Ecclesiasticus*).

Despite Melito's efforts to establish the parameters of the Old Testament, subsequent Christian scholars over the next two centuries expressed various opinions regarding the scope of sacred literature – few of which were identical. **Tertullian** (c. 160-225) never articulated a set list of books, but he seems to have accepted the Septuagint (including the "Septuagintal plus") as authoritative Scripture. He considered the *Wisdom of Solomon* to be of Solomonic authorship, "The Song of the Three Hebrews" and the story of "Bel and the Dragon" to be credible additions to Daniel, and the "Letter of Jeremiah" to be authentically Jeremiah's. Unlike most scholars, Tertullian even regarded obscure and generally discredited writings such as *I Enoch*, the *Apocalypse of Ezra*, and the *Sibylline Oracles* as legitimate. In his comments on *I Enoch* he acknowledged that "the Scripture of *Enoch*... is not received by some [Christian scholars] because it is not admitted into the Jewish canon," but he speculated that this was because "they did not think that, having been published before the deluge, it could have safely survived that world wide calamity [i.e., Noah's flood]."[20]

---

[20] Quoted in McDonald, *The Biblical Canon*, p. 106.

[Note: Tertullian was a notorious misogynist – even by ancient history standards – and in his treatise *On Women's Dress* he cited *I Enoch 8:1* as the source for his contention that Azaz'el, leader of the fallen angels, first introduced women to bracelets, ornamentation, eye-shadow, "the beautifying of eyelids," hair-dying, and jewelry in general.]

F. F. Bruce comments that Tertullian was representative of all the Western (Latin-speaking) church leaders before the time of Jerome in that "the Bible which they used [i.e., the Septuagint] provided them with no means of distinguishing those parts which belonged to the Hebrew canon from those which were found only in the Septuagint."[21]

A generation after Tertullian, **Origen** (c. 185-254), the greatest Greek biblical scholar of antiquity, compiled a list of Old Testament books. Like Josephus, Origen was intent on preserving the twenty-two book tradition, and he drew a sharp distinction between the Apocrypha and the ancient Hebrew Scriptures. But even at that, he often referred to the Apocrypha and even cited other works outside the Septuagint. Like some other Christian scholars, Origen was prone to fudge a bit in his approach to the canon. In contrast to Melito, he included Esther in his list, but he also incorporated the apocryphal "Letter of Jeremiah" into the text of Jeremiah. After concluding his remarks with the comment, "These are the twenty-two books according to the Hebrews," he added: "Outside of these are the books of Maccabees."

In his dialogues with Jewish scholars Origen adhered to the narrower Jewish canon that excluded the Apocrypha, noting that "In discussions with the Jews, we do not bring forward what is not contained in their copies, but use in common with them the [books] which they recognize." However, in his *Homily on Numbers* he recommended that Christians read, in addition to the books of the Old Testament, apocryphal works such as *Judith*, *Tobit*, and the *Wisdom of Solomon*. (Origen also counseled Christians to avoid Numbers and Leviticus – probably because he considered them insufficiently inspirational.) His opinion of some marginal books changed over the years. For example, early in his career, like his predecessor Clement of Alexandria, he accepted *I Enoch* as the work of the antediluvian patriarch, but he later doubted its authenticity.[22]

A half-century after Origen the **Clermont List** (*Codex Claromontanus*) of sacred books was compiled in Alexandria around the year 300. The Old Testament portion of the list followed the Septuagint order and included not only *I* and *II Maccabees* but also *IV Maccabees*. A few decades later the scholar/

---

[21] Bruce, *The Canon of Scripture*, p. 87.

[22] See McDonald, *The Biblical Canon*, pp. 177, 202.

bishop **Hilary of Poitiers** (c. 310-367) essentially followed Origen's list, but he added *Tobit* and *Judith* to make a twenty-four-book canon. He also combined the "Epistle of Jeremiah" and Lamentations with the book of Jeremiah.

In his annual Festal letter of 367, Bishop **Athanasius** of Alexandria (c. 297-373) was the first to use the term *kanon* specifically in reference to a list of books. Athanasius' twenty-two-book canon corresponded closely to that of Origen except that he excluded Esther and included *Baruch* and the "Letter of Jeremiah" in a single book with Jeremiah and Lamentations. Some scholars suspect that he probably also integrated the Greek additions to Daniel and Esther into those books as well. Following his list of Old Testament texts, he commented on the status of the Apocrypha:

> But for the sake of greater accuracy I must... add this: there are other books outside these, which are not indeed included in the canon, but have been appointed from the time of the fathers to be read to those who are recent converts to our company and wish to be instructed in the word of true religion. These are the *Wisdom of Solomon*, the *Wisdom of Sirach* [*Ecclesiasticus*], Esther, *Judith*, and *Tobit*. [Cited in Bruce, *The Canon of Scripture*, p. 79.]

Curiously, Athanasius did not mention two of the most popular apocryphal books, *I* and *II Maccabees*, and he concluded his comments on the Old and New Testament canons with the stern warning, "Let no one add to these nor take anything from them."

About this same time **Cyril** (c. 313-86), the bishop of Jerusalem, also drafted a canonical list of twenty-two books that corresponded to that of Origen in which he integrated Lamentations, the "Letter of Jeremiah" and *Baruch* into the book of Jeremiah. Also like Origen, Cyril omitted the book of Esther from his canon, as did **Gregory of Nazianus** (c. 330-90) a few years later. Meanwhile, **Epiphanius** (c. 315-403), the bishop of Salamis, catalogued a twenty-two book canon identical to that of the current Protestant Old Testament canon, but he also held a high opinion of *Wisdom of Solomon* and *Wisdom of Sirach*, which he called "helpful and useful" while acknowledging that they were not included in the "recognized" Scriptures."

In *An Exposition on the [Apostles] Creed*, **Rufinus of Aquileia** (345-410) delineated the "canonical" books of the Hebrew Bible from what he called the "ecclesiastical" books of the Apocrypha.

> But it should be known that there are also other books which our fathers call not Canonical but Ecclesiastical: that is to say, *Wisdom*, called the *Wisdom of Solomon*, and another *Wisdom*, called the *Wisdom of the Son of Sirach*, which last-mentioned the Latins called by the general title

Ecclesiasticus, designating not the author of the book, but the character
of the writing. To the same class belong the Book of *Tobit*, and the Book
of *Judith*, and the Books of the Maccabees." [Ibid., p. 224.]

Beginning in 382 **Jerome** (340-420) translated the ancient Jewish and
Christian writings into a new version of the Bible, the Latin Vulgate, which was
to become the standard Roman Catholic Bible for the next 1500 years. Until he
produced his version of the Old Testament, previous Old Latin texts had been
direct renderings of the Septuagint. Jerome originally intended to follow the
traditional Hebrew canon and exclude the Apocrypha altogether. However, his
skepticism regarding the scriptural status of these writings was not shared by
many other Christian scholars at the time, and at the insistence of **Bishop
Damasus** of Rome (r. 366-84) and the renowned scholar, Augustine, he
consented to translate many of these intertestamenal writings. While he added
a codicil to the effect that these books were never regarded as part of the canon
and should not be used in the formulation of doctrine, Jerome also conceded
that books such as *Wisdom of Solomon, Wisdom of Sirach, Judith* and *Tobit*
contained wisdom that rendered them appropriate for reading in the context of
Christian worship. Oddly, he failed to mention the book of *Baruch*, and he
noted that Jewish scholars had always dismissed the additions to Daniel as
"fables." As for the book of Esther, he included it in the non-canonical
Apocrypha section.

Interestingly, the four great extant majuscule (or uncial) codices of the
Greek Bible from the 4th and 5th centuries incorporated some apocryphal texts
into the Old Testament without any distinction between these books and the
rest of the Hebrew canon – all of which suggests that Christian scholars and
church leaders were still undecided regarding the precise parameters of the Old
Testament even at this late a time:

* **Codex Sinaiticus** (c. 350) includes *Tobit, Judith, I- IV Maccabees, Wisdom
  of Solomon*, and *Wisdom of Sirach* (*Ecclesiasticus*).
* **Codex Vaticanus** (c. 350) includes *Wisdom of Sirach* (*Ecclesiasticus*),
  Judith, Tobit, Baruch, and the "Letter of Jeremiah." (Inexplicably, the
  books of *Maccabees* are absent.)
* **Codex Alexandrinus** (c. 425) includes *Baruch, Tobit, Judith, I-IV
  Maccabees, Wisdom of Solomon, Wisdom of Sirach, Psalms of Solomon*, and
  the "Letter of Jeremiah."
* **Codex Ephraemi** (5th century) contains *Wisdom of Solomon* and *Wisdom
  of Sirach*.

Augustine (354-430), the influential bishop of Hippo in North Africa and the most outstanding scholar of his era, strongly endorsed the Apocrypha. His biblical canon included Esther, *Wisdom of Solomon*, *Wisdom of Sirach*, *Tobit*, *Judith*, *Baruch*, the "Letter of Jeremiah," *I-II Maccabees*, the additions to Daniel, Esther, and the additions to Esther. Under his influence the **Synod of Hippo** (393) and the **Councils of Carthage** (397 and 419) officially approved these books in their canonical pronouncements. Likewise, in 405 **Pope Innocent I** (r. 401-17) endorsed this same list, and for the next 1100 years there was little dispute regarding the status of the Apocrypha. Throughout the medieval era the Roman Catholic Church generally regarded these writings as part of Scripture. Occasionally, fastidious scholars such as Pope Gregory the Great (r. 590-604) or Hugh of St. Victor (c. 1096-1141) might question their legitimacy, but on the whole they were given a pass, as F. F. Bruce comments:

> So far as the Old Testament was concerned, [the status of the Apocrypha]... was a matter of interest only to a minority. For purposes of devotion or edification, why make any distinction between Esther and *Judith*, or between Proverbs and *Wisdom [of Solomon]*?
>
> It became customary to add to copies of the Latin Bible a few books which Jerome had not even included among those which where to be read 'for the edification of the people,' notably *III* and *IV Esdras* and the *Prayer of Manasseh*....
>
> Throughout the following centuries most users of the Bible made no distinction between the apocryphal books and the others; all were handed down as part of the Vulgate. [Ibid., pp. 98-99.]

Part of this lack of discrimination regarding the status of the Apocrypha stems from the fact that during the medieval period the allegorical method of interpretation was commonly applied to Scripture (see Chapter 4).

Understandably, those who were concerned primarily with the devotional, inspirational or "spiritual" meaning of the text had relatively little interest in the historicity of these books.

In 1383 **John Wycliffe**, the renowned "Morning Star of the Reformation," included the Apocrypha in his English translation of the Bible (other than *II Esdras*), although in his Prologue to the Old Testament he distinguished between these books and those of the traditional Hebrew canon. Regarding the additions to Esther and Daniel, Wycliffe and his associates noted Jerome's remarks concerning these accretions.

The Reformation Era Debate

During the Reformation era controversy over the doctrine of *sola scriptura*, Protestants considered it imperative to distinguish between books that were doctrinally authoritative and those that were not. In fact, some Catholic scholars such as Cardinal Thomas Cajetan questioned the divine inspiration of the Apocrypha. Despite the fact that many early Christian scholars had regarded these books as "profitable reading," some doubted their legitimacy on the basis of three factors.

- Skepticism on the part of Jewish scholars regarding the divine inspiration and authority of these books. As mentioned previously, none of these books contain predictive prophecy or any "Thus saith the Lord" pronouncements. For example, *I Maccabees 9:27* states, "So there was great distress in Israel, such as had not been since the time that prophets ceased to appear among them."

- Doctrinal problems. For example, *II Maccabees 12:43-45* implies that prayers and "atonement" should be made for the dead "so that they might be delivered from their sin."

- Historical and geographical inaccuracies. Some narratives in apocryphal accounts are clearly fictitious and/or mythical. For example, *II Esdras 6:42* implies that most of the earth's surface is land: "On the third day you commanded the waters to be gathered together in a seventh part of the earth; six you dried up and kept so that some of them might be planted and cultivated and be of service before you."

In 1520 **Andreas Bodenstein** (a.k.a. Karlstadt), a colleague of Martin Luther at Wittenberg University, published a treatise in which he separated the canonical books of the Hebrew Old Testament from the Apocrypha. Bodenstein then distinguished between certain apocryphal books which he deemed "outside the Hebrew canon" yet "holy writings" – *Wisdom, Ecclesiasticus, Judith, Tobit,* and *I* and *II Maccabees* – and the more "controverted" and fanciful writings of the Apocrypha.

The first Bible to segregate the apocryphal books from the others was a Dutch Bible published by **Jacob van Liesveldt** in 1526. Following the Old Testament book of Malachi, the publisher set apart a separate section entitled, "The books which are not in the canon, that is to say, which one does not find among the Jews in the Hebrew." About the same time the Swiss reformer **Ulrich Zwingli**, in his Zurich Bible (1524-29), excluded the Apocrypha altogether and published these books in a separate volume. In 1530 Zwingli's colleague, **Johann Oecolampadius**, summed up the view of many Protestants when he wrote, "We do not despise *Judith, Tobit, Ecclesiasticus, Baruch*, the last two books of *Esdras*, the three books of *Maccabees*, the Additions to Daniel; but we do not allow them divine authority with the others."[23] In his German translation of the Old Testament (1534), **Martin Luther** relegated the Apocrypha to an appendix entitled: "The Apocrypha: Books which are not to be held equal to holy scripture, but are useful and good to read."

Meanwhile, the history of Bible translation in England, being directly influenced and often controlled by political factors, was unsettled for decades. The brilliant scholar **William Tyndale** was martyred in 1536 before he finished translating the Old Testament, but in all likelihood he would have followed Luther's precedent and segregated the Apocrypha from the traditional Hebrew canon. **Miles Coverdale's** English Bible of 1535 followed the trend by the Continental Protestant reformers and placed the Apocrypha after the Old Testament, separated by a title page reading,

William Tyndale

"Apocripha." Likewise, so did the **Matthew's Bible** of 1537, which was essentially an officially approved version of Tyndale's translation. Thirty years later, the **Bishop's Bible** of 1568 added the Apocrypha in a section following the Old Testament with no introductory commentary.

The Church of England adopted a compromise position on the Apocrypha. Readings from the Apocrypha were incorporated into the lectionary attached to the Book of Common Prayer from 1549 onward, and passages from these books were included in the liturgy. However, Article VI of the Thirty-nine Articles of Religion (1562) contained a list of books "necessary to salvation" that excluded the Apocrypha, followed by a separate section of "other Books the Church doth read for example of life and instruction of manners; but yet doth it not apply them to establish any doctrine." (Readings from the Apocrypha are included in most modern lectionaries in the Anglican Communion, based on the Revised Common Lectionary.)

Puritans were more critical of these books than mainstream Anglicans due to their association with Roman Catholicism. The **Geneva Bible** of 1560 included the Apocrypha in a section following the Old Testament along with an explanatory paragraph that commended them for their historical value and

---

[23] Quoted in Metzger and Murphy, eds., *The New Oxford Annotated Apocrypha*, p. vii.

"for the instruction of godly manners," but cautioned against citing them in doctrinal matters except so far that their teachings were confirmed by canonical books. However, a later edition of the Geneva Bible published in 1599 excluded the Apocrypha altogether, which began a trend among more conservative Protestants.

The **Authorized (King James) Bible** of 1611, being essentially a revision of the Bishops' Bible, continued the tradition of featuring the Apocrypha in a separate section. In addition to the Catholic deuterocanical books and additions, the KJV included *I Esdras* (Vulgate *III Esdras*), *II Esdras* (Vulgate *IV Esdras*), and the "Prayer of Manasses." It was also during this time that the Archbishop of Canterbury outlawed the printing and selling of Bibles without the Apocrypha on penalty of one year's imprisonment, but the controversy remained far from resolved. In 1644, in the midst of the

English Civil War, the Puritan-controlled Long Parliament turned the tables and outlawed the reading of the Apocrypha in church services. Three years later the Westminster Assembly of Divines produced the **Westminster Confession of Faith**. In Chapter 1, Article, 2, the document listed the books that constitute "the Holy Scripture, or the Word of God written," followed by a paragraph that stated, "The Books commonly called Apocrypha, not being of divine inspiration, are no part of the canon of Scripture; and therefore are of no authority in the Church of God, nor to be any otherwise approved, or made use of, than other human writings." By the mid-1600s most versions of the King James Bible omitted the disputed books, although with the Restoration of the Stuart monarchy in 1660 the lectionary readings from the Apocrypha were restored in Anglican church services.

The first Bible published in America was **John Eliot's "Indian Bible"** (1661-63), in which he translated the Geneva Bible into the Algonquin language. Being a staunch Puritan, Eliot excluded the Apocrypha. In 1782, with the Revolution having cut off the supply of Bibles to America, **Robert Aitken**, a Philadelphia printer, petitioned the U.S. Congress to authorize a new edition of the Bible. The Aitken Bible was reviewed and approved by Congress, after which the *Journals of Congress* recorded:

> Resolved. That the United States in Congress assembled highly approve the pious and laudable undertaking of Mr. Aitkin, as subservient to the interest of religion as well as an influence of the progress of arts in this

country and being satisfied from the above report, they recommend this edition of the bible to the inhabitants of the United States and hereby authorize him to publish this recommendation.

In keeping with the sensibilities of most American Protestants, Aitken omitted the Apocrypha from his edition of the Bible, as did most all subsequent American Protestant Bibles.

Traditionally, of course, Roman Catholics have viewed these books as "deuterocanonical" and therefore part of the Bible. In 1546, in response to the Protestant criticism of the Apocrypha, the **Council of Trent** (1545-63) officially accorded full canonical status to these books, ignoring Jerome's distinction between the books of the traditional Hebrew canon and those that were to be read only "for the edification of the people." In their decree the Catholic prelates pronounced an anathema upon anyone who "does not accept as sacred and canonical the aforesaid books in their entirety... as they have been accustomed to be read in the Catholic Church and as they are contained in the old Latin Vulgate Edition." Inexplicably, the Council did not accord canonical status to the "Prayer of Manasseh" and *I - II Esdras* despite the fact that these books had been included in some manuscripts of the Latin Vulgate.

Like the Catholic Church, the various Eastern Orthodox Churches have also accepted these books as deuterocanonical, but only in the sense that they are secondary in terms of authority to the rest of the Old Testament. The canonical status of these texts had been accepted for more than a millennium by Orthodox Christians, but it wasn't until 1642 and 1672 that Orthodox synods at Jassy (Iasi) and Jerusalem officially recognized the Deuterocanon as "genuine parts of Scripture." In addition to the seven books included in the Roman Catholic Bible – *Tobit, Judith, Wisdom of Solomon; Wisdom of Jesus ben Sira, Baruch*, and *I - II Maccabees* – the Eastern Orthodox canon includes *III Maccabees* and *I Esdras*. *Baruch* is divided from the "Letter of Jeremiah," making a total of 49 Old Testament books in contrast to the Protestant 39-book canon. Other texts included in various Orthodox Bibles include *Psalm 151* and the "Prayer of Manasses," which, as in Catholic Bibles, are integrated into the Old Testament rather than printed in a separate section. In addition, two other books are included as an appendix: *IV Maccabees* and *II Esdras*. However, it should be emphasized that most Orthodox scholars continue to regard these writings as a lower level of authority than the "protocanonical" texts of the traditional Hebrew Bible.

Part 2:
The New Testament

The Living Word

The Christian faith was founded not on a book of sacred writings but on a person – the living Word of God, Jesus Christ – and the Gospel message as propagated by his apostles. The ancient Hebrew Scriptures were revered because they bore witness prophetically to Christ, while the writings of the apostles and their associates gained scriptural status due to their accurate testimony to his life and teachings. So in a sense, the original Christian "canon" (the standard of faith) was Jesus himself.

Just as the impetus on the part of devout Jews to collect and preserve their sacred writings was rooted in their historical circumstances, likewise there are parallels concerning the emergence of the New Testament canon of Scripture. The early Jesus movement was animated by the testimony of those who had known Jesus and witnessed his resurrection from the dead. This story, along with the illumination and empowerment that came through the internal presence of the Holy Spirit, was what gave the early Christian communities their identity and their mission.

Initially, the Jesus story spread orally in the preaching and teaching of the apostles, but within a few decades it was expressed in various literary forms – gospels,[24] history, epistles, and apocalyptic literature. By the turn of the 2nd century there were already attempts to collect and preserve many of these key writings, but the process was undoubtedly hampered by the belief that many (or most?) Christians held at the time that Christ's return was imminent. There was also considerable disagreement among influential Christian scholars regarding the apostolic status of some early writings, so the process of recognizing a Christian canon of Scripture was a deliberative (and sometimes contentious) one that was not finalized until the late 3rd or early 4th century.

---

[24] The term "gospel" (Greek: *euangelion*) literally meant "good news" – such as the "good news" about Jesus Christ. In the 2nd century it came to be applied to a genre of literature – the written accounts of the life and teachings of Jesus based on the memoirs of eyewitnesses.

The Skeptics' Theory

In his book, *Lost Christianities* (2003), the New Testament scholar Bart Ehrman of the University of North Carolina (Chapel Hill) puts forth the common argument by skeptics regarding the authorship and veracity of the New Testament writings. According to Ehrman, "The Gospels that came to be included in the New Testament were all written anonymously," and it was generations later that they were finally assigned to "their reputed authors," Matthew, Mark, Luke, and John. However, he charges, none of these books "contains a first-person narrative... or claims to be written by an eyewitness or companion of an eyewitness."[25]

Contentions such as these have floated around for centuries, and they contradict the testimonies of the New Testament writers themselves who claim that they were either eyewitnesses to the ministry of Jesus or privy to information passed on by eyewitnesses. In the prologue to his gospel account, Luke writes...

> Many have undertaken to draw up an account of the things that have been fulfilled among us, just as they were handed down to us by those who from the first were eyewitnesses.... Therefore, since I myself have carefully investigated everything from the beginning, it seemed good also to me to write an orderly account... so that you may know the certainty of the things that have been taught (Luke 1:1-4).

Luke may have relied upon previous written accounts of Jesus' life, along with personal interviews of those who knew Jesus, in order to construct a more accurate account of Jesus' life and ministry. Other New Testament writers wrote based on their own firsthand experiences, as the apostle Peter reminded his readers in II Peter 1:16 when he declared, "We did not follow cleverly invented stories when we told you about the power and coming of our Lord Jesus Christ, but we were eyewitnesses of his majesty." Regarding the Gospel According to Mark, we are informed in *The Expositions of the Oracles of the Lord* (c. 120s) by the early church chronicler **Papias** that Mark obtained his information about Jesus based on Peter's recollections. As the church historian Eusebius later recounted Papias' testimony:

> And [John] the presbyter said this: "Mark, having become the interpreter of Peter, wrote down accurately whatever he remembered. It was not, however, in exact order that he related the sayings or deeds of Christ. For he [Mark] neither heard the Lord nor followed him. But later, as I said, he accompanied Peter, who adapted his teachings to the needs [of his

---

[25] Bart D. Ehrman, *Lost Christianities* (Oxford University Press, 2003), pp. 3, 235.

hearers], but with no intention of giving a regular narrative of the Lord's sayings. Whereof Mark made no mistake in thus writing some things as he remembered them. For he took special care not to omit anything he had heard, and not to put anything fictitious into the statements." [Cited in Alexander Roberts and James Donaldson, eds., *Ante-Nicene Fathers*, Vol. 1 (Hendrickson, 1994), p. 154.]

Similarly, in the epilogue to his gospel the apostle John indicates that he (and his literary colleagues) wrote of the life of Christ based on his personal experience as a disciple of the Lord (ref. John 21:20-25). As for Matthew, Christian tradition associates him with Levi, the tax collector whom Jesus called to be his disciple. If this is accurate, then it is almost certain that he was literate and therefore capable of writing the gospel account that is attributed to him.

Motives for the Compilation of a New Testament Canon

In the first several decades of the Christian movement there was no impetus to identify and collect a corpus of Christian writings for two reasons: (1) Most Christians believed that the *Parousia*, the Second Coming of Christ, was imminent; and (2) the oral tradition of passing along information about the life and teachings of Christ was adequate so long as the apostles and other eyewitnesses to Jesus' ministry were still alive. But eventually the eyewitnesses died out and Christ had not yet returned. Therefore, later generations of Christian scholars and church leaders felt the need to identify the authentic apostolic writings, distinguish them from all the other works being produced by Christian authors, and collect them into a well-defined corpus of books that Christians could trust as accurate and authoritative. In effect, there were four compelling motives for the compilation of a New Testament canon of Scripture.

1. To preserve an accurate account of the life and teachings of Jesus.

For most of the 1st century the oral transmission of the Gospel was given preeminence over the written texts of the New Testament. However, with the passing of the apostolic generation 40 or so years after Jesus' death and resurrection, more attention was given to the written texts. A new generation of Christians needed an accurate account of Jesus' life and teachings just as devout Jews had always valued the ancient chronicles detailing their national history and the written pronouncements of their prophets. For Christians, this necessitated a new written testament (Latin: *testamentum*) and an exposition of God's new covenant with mankind as mediated through the atoning death and resurrection of Jesus Christ. Practically-speaking, the apostles understood that a strictly oral transmission of the Jesus story had strict limitations, although as New Testament scholar John Wenham comments, for many years the oral and written traditions about Christ circulated together among the churches:

> Textual criticism bears out the gradualness of growth of the idea of canonicity, since the great majority of significant textual variants date back to the first two centuries, which suggests that much of the copying in the early days was done without a belief in the sanctity of the very wording of the books as the oracles of God.
>
> These factors account for the paucity of references to the gospels [in other New Testament writings] as manuals of instruction and show that in practice reliance was placed for a long time on oral instruction rather than on written texts. Only gradually did confidence in the process of oral transmission wane and the superiority of written apostolic traditions establish itself.
>
> From circa 40-160 written and oral tradition circulated side by side. The special authority of the written, being less subject to change, was recognized [only] as the apostolic era passed away. [John Wenham, *Redating Matthew, Mark and Luke* (InterVarsity Press, 1992), p.222; 217]

As time goes by memories fade, and as the generation that witnessed the ministry of Jesus died off, it made the writing and preservation of accurate accounts of his life and teachings all the more necessary. As F. F. Bruce explains, "The perpetuation of the words and deeds of Jesus could not be entrusted indefinitely to oral tradition." Therefore, "It was both desirable and inevitable that the oral tradition should be committed to writing if it was not to be lost."[26] Christianity is an historically-based belief system centered around a real historical character who lived, died, and rose from the dead in Palestine around the year 33 A.D. Therefore, the written accounts of Christ's life by those who knew him personally (or by close associates of those who knew him) were invaluable sources of information for those who put their faith and trust in him as their Lord and Savior. Church historian Cyril Richardson emphasizes this point in his anthology of early Christian writings:

> [T]he corruptions to which the oral tradition was subject soon necessitated the writing of Christian books; and as the living witnesses to Christ and the apostles passed away, these books took on a new significance. They came to be read in worship, and by AD 150 they had gained the authority that had once belonged exclusively to the Old Testament. [Cyril B. Richardson, *Early Christian Fathers* (Collier Books, 1970), pp. 21-22.]

---

[26] Bruce, *The Canon of Scripture*, pp. 118, 119.

As a result, by the mid-2nd century three or four of the gospel accounts of Jesus' life were circulating as a collection, and in 165 the scholar **Tatian** (c. 120-185) compiled the *Diatessaron*, a paraphrased chronological harmony of the Four Gospels. Likewise, from the early 2nd century Paul's letters circulated together, a practice that probably started among some churches much earlier. In Colossians 4:16 Paul encouraged the churches of Colossae and Laodicea to exchange letters that they had received from him, and in all likelihood this kind of inter-correspondence between churches became normative. Churches probably made copies of each letter to pass on and retained the original for themselves. So for example, when Clement of Rome wrote to the church of Corinth in the year 95 he cited passages from several of Paul's epistles including Romans, I and II Corinthians, Galatians, Ephesians, Philippians, and Titus, in addition to the Epistle to the Hebrews. As noted in Chapter 5, the oldest surviving copy of a Pauline corpus is the Chester Beatty manuscript p46 (c. 200) that includes portions of Romans, I and II Corinthians, Galatians, Ephesians, Philippians, Colossians, I Thessalonians, Hebrews, and possibly Philemon.

Throughout the 2nd and 3rd centuries various spurious "gospels" were being written and circulated, all of which were pseudonymous and named for famous apostles and other luminaries in the early church. These "apocryphal gospels" – the *Acts of Peter*, the *Apocalypse* (or *Revelation*) *of Peter*, the *Acts of Paul (including the Acts of Paul and Thecla)* the *Protoevangelium of James*, and others – qualify essentially as Christian fiction, and most orthodox church leaders dismissed them as inauthentic and inconsequential at best. Although most scholars believe there are probably kernels of truth in at least some of these writings, and that they might have preserved some authentic sayings of Christ derived from the oral tradition that were never incorporated into the Four Gospels, their contributions to our understanding of Jesus and early Christian history are negligible. By introducing fanciful tales and speculations into the Christ story, they obscured the clear truth and accuracy of the legitimate accounts of the life and teachings of Jesus. This made it all the more imperative that church leaders draw a clear distinction between these pseudo-gospels and those authored by Christ's apostles and their associates.

A common question that surfaces in relation to the gospels and other New Testament writings is: Did the apostles realize they were writing "Scripture?" Just as Jesus gave his disciples authority to preach the Gospel (Mark 3:14-15; Matt. 10:14, 20), likewise their writings carried special authority. Several passages infer that at least some of the New Testament writers were cognizant of this fact.

- In Luke 1:1-4 the author claims to be passing on an accurate account of Jesus' life and the apostolic tradition. In his prologue he claims that the traditions incorporated into his gospel have been "delivered" to him by those "who from the beginning were eyewitnesses and ministers of the word" – a clear reference to the apostles. The implication is that Luke doesn't see himself primarily as a biographer or a historian but as a writer of Scripture.

- In the apostle Paul's first epistle, I Thessalonians, he is unequivocal regarding his own authority as an apostle of Jesus Christ as he writes, "[W]hen you received the word of God, which you heard from us, you accepted it not as the word of men but as it actually is, the word of God" (I Thes. 2:13). In his use of the phrase, "the word of God," Paul is referring to the authoritative apostolic tradition that he passed on to the Thessalonians through his teaching and preaching.

- Paul follows up on this theme in II Thessalonians: "[F]rom the beginning God chose you to be saved through the sanctifying work of the Spirit and through belief in the truth. He called you to this through our gospel, that you might share in the glory of our Lord Jesus Christ. So then, brothers, stand firm and hold to the teachings we passed on to you, whether by word of mouth or by letter." Later, he adds the warning, "If anyone does not obey what we say in this letter, take note of that person and have nothing to do with him" – clearly a declaration that his words carry the weight of Scripture (ref. II Thess. 2:14-15; 3:14).

- Likewise, in I Corinthians 14:37-38 Paul explicitly asserts his apostolic authority: "If anyone thinks that he is a prophet, or spiritual, he should acknowledge that the things I am writing to you are a command of the Lord. If anyone does not recognize this, he is not recognized."

- In Galatians 1:6-12 Paul excoriates those who preach a "different gospel": "I am astonished that you are so quickly deserting the one who called you by the grace of Christ and are turning to a different gospel – which is really no gospel at all. Evidently some people are throwing you into confusion and are trying to pervert the gospel of Christ. But even if we or an angel from heaven should preach a gospel other than the one we preached to you, let him be eternally condemned!...

  "I want you to know, brothers, that the gospel I preached is not something that man made up. I did not receive it from any man, nor was I taught it: rather, I received it by revelation from Jesus Christ."

- Particularly noteworthy are the words of the apostle Peter in II Peter 3:15-16 in reference to Paul's writings as "Scripture": "Bear in mind that our Lord's patience means salvation, just as our dear brother Paul also wrote you with the wisdom that God gave him He writes the same way in all his letters, speaking in them of these matters. His letters contain some things that are hard to understand, which ignorant and unstable people distort, as they do the other Scriptures, to their own destruction."[27]

- In Revelation 1:1-3 John claims that he is recording the prophecy of Jesus Christ as delivered to him by an angel (1:1). Consequently, there is a divine blessing incorporated into this book: "Blessed is the one who reads the words of this prophecy, and blessed are those who hear it and take to heart what is written in it, because the time is near" (Rev. 1:3). Furthermore, the authority of the book is accentuated by the inclusion of an "inscriptional curse" at the end, warning the reader neither to add anything to the text nor take anything away from it lest they suffer divine judgment (Rev. 22:18-19).

As the Anglican bishop N.T. Wright comments, it used to be alleged that the New Testament authors "didn't think they were writing Scripture," but that position is unwarranted. The fact that their writings were often "occasional" – i.e., written in a particular time and place to a specific audience to address certain concerns – misses the point because it is in such scenarios of urgent need (for instance, when writing Galatians or II Corinthians) that "Paul is most conscious that he is writing as one authorized, by the apostolic call he had received from Jesus Christ, and in the power of the Spirit, to bring life and order to the church by his words."[28]

The Church Fathers of the 2nd and 3rd centuries certainly regarded the gospels as divinely-inspired accounts of Jesus' life and the epistles as divinely-inspired exhortations. This was the whole basis for the later canonization of these books. The authority of these apostolic writings was accepted by the Church Fathers as equal to that of the ancient Hebrew prophets. Authority precedes canonicity, and had the words of Christ and his apostles not been accorded supreme authority, there would have been no motivation on the part of early church leaders to canonize these written records of their words.

---

[27] The authorship and dating of II Peter is controversial. Some biblical scholars accept it as authentically Petrine, while others assign it to the 2nd century. Although none of the reasons put forth by skeptics are particularly convincing, it should be noted that no Christian scholars mention the book until the time of Origen (c. 230), who was unsure of its apostolic authenticity and thereby assigned it to the "disputed" category of books.

[28] N.T. Wright, *The Last Word: Beyond the Bible Wars to a New Understanding of the Authority of Scripture* (HarperSanFrancisco, 2005), p. 51.

2. To complete the story of God's redemption throughout history.

The early Christians were convinced that Jesus was the eschatological fulfillment of the ancient prophecies regarding God's redemption of his people. Therefore, it followed that a written record of his life would provide a proper conclusion to the Old Testament. In *The Canon of Scripture*, F. F. Bruce comments on the connection between these two covenants:

> Over six hundred years after the ratification of the covenant of Moses' day at the foot of Mount Sinai, the prophet Jeremiah announced that, in days to come, the God of Israel would establish a new covenant with his people to replace that which he had made with the Exodus generation when he "took them by the hand to bring them out of the land of Egypt" (Jer. 31:31-34). That ancient covenant made the divine will plain to them, but did not impart the power to carry it out; for lack of that power they broke the covenant. Under the new covenant, however, not only the desire but the power to do the will of God would be imparted to his people: his law would be put within them and written on their hearts. "In speaking of a new covenant," says the writer to the Hebrews, "he treats the first as obsolete." (Heb. 8:13). And he leaves his readers in no doubt that the new covenant has already been established, ratified not by the blood of sacrificed animals but by the blood of Christ, a sacrifice which effects not merely external purification from ritual defilement but the inward cleansing of the conscience from guilt....
>
> Each of these covenants – the ancient covenant of Sinai and the new covenant inaugurated by Jesus – launched a great spiritual movement. Each of these movements gave rise to a special body of literature, and these books of literature came to be known in the Christian church as 'the books of the ancient literature' and 'the books of the new covenant'. The former collection came into being over a period of a thousand years or more; the latter collection has a more inaugural character. Its various parts were written within a century from the establishment of the new covenant; they may be regarded as the foundation documents of Christianity. It was not until the end of the second century AD that the two collections began to be described, briefly, as the Old Covenant (or Testament) and the New Covenant (or Testament). [Bruce, *The Canon of Scripture*, pp. 20-21.]

It is instructive to note that the first book of the New Testament, Matthew, begins with a genealogy with a strong Davidic theme (Matt 1:1*ff*) – as does the (likely) last book of the Hebrew canon, Chronicles (I Chron. 1:1-9:1). A reasonable deduction is that Matthew is seeking to connect Jesus, the Messiah of Israel, with the history of Israel, the restoration of the Davidic dynasty, and God's developing plan of salvation for his people. Therefore, Jesus continues the ongoing biblical narrative. Early Christians believed Jesus' life inaugurated a new covenant relationship between God and mankind (Jer. 31:31*ff*and II Cor. 3:6), and covenants are by nature written contracts.

3. To preserve orthodoxy in the face of heresy.

Conservative Christians often tend to overlook the diversity in early Christianity, while theological liberals usually exaggerate these differences. But history is clear that rivalries, factionalism and partisanship plagued the Jesus movement from the outset. For instance, the apostle Paul had to contend with legalistic Judaizers and other "false brothers" who threatened not only his ministry but his very life (ref. II Cor. 11:26). Likewise, the apostle John writes of heretics and schismatics in the churches, referring to such people as "false prophets" and even "antichrists" (ref. I John 2:18*ff*; 4:1; II John 7; and III John 9-10.) Early heresies such as Docetism, Nicolaitanism, Gnosticism, Marcionism, and others required that the mainstream church set forth a well-articulated rule of faith based on a generally accepted corpus of inspired Scriptures and in keeping with the apostolic tradition.

Around 150 A.D. **Marcion** (c. 90-160), a prominent member of the church in Rome, was excommunicated for teaching heresy. In response, he set up a rival sect, and in the process he compiled what was probably the first attempt in Christian history to establish a set canon of Scriptures – a "purified" collection of sacred books composed of two parts: (1) *The Gospel*, an edited version of the Gospel of Luke; and (2) the *Apostolikon,* an edited collection of 10 of Paul's epistles, excluding I and II Timothy and Titus. In addition, he wrote *Antithesis*, a doctrinal handbook in which he argued that Christianity should sever all connections to Judaism, which he dismissed as a false religion. Marcion rejected the legitimacy of the ancient Hebrew writings, and in his book he claimed that the god of the Old Testament was not the Divine Father of Jesus. In fact, he argued, YHWH was actually an evil "Demiurge" who had created the physical world.

Around the same time as Marcion, another pseudo-Christian heretic, **Valentinus** (c. 100-160) sparked further controversy in Rome. According to Tertullian, Valentinus was extraordinarily gifted and charismatic to the point that at one time he was even considered a potential successor to the bishop of Rome. But Valentinus had a Gnostic orientation and eventually separated from the apostolic church to found his own theological school. Two Gnostic works, the *Gospel of Truth* and the *Epistle to Rheginus*, are associated with Valentinus and his followers.

Like Marcion, Valentius recognized certain apostolic writings as inspired and authoritative, but he rejected others. His list of acceptable books included the gospels of Matthew, John and Luke (probably including Acts), the Pauline epistles (other than the Pastorals), I John, Hebrews, and Revelation. However, he believed such books should be interpreted in a highly allegorical sense according to his own enlightened understanding.

In response to sectarians and schismatics such as Marcion and Valentinus, mainstream church leaders recognized the necessity of identifying those writings that set forth an orthodox "rule of faith" based on the true apostolic tradition. As mentioned previously, various "apocryphal gospels" were written and circulated in the first 300 years of Christian history using the names of notable apostles such as Peter, Paul, John, and James. Although not all of these books were necessarily heretical, some incorporated legendary and mythical elements into the Christ story. In addition, numerous Gnostic and quasi-Gnostic "gospels" masqueraded as Christian writings with titles such as the *Gospel of Thomas*, the *Gospel of Mary [Magdalene]*, the *Gospel of Philip*, the aforementioned *Gospel of Truth*, and *The Apocryphon of John*. One can imagine that all of this could have been quite confusing to the average neophyte Christian or the naive spiritual seeker, and it was a contributing factor in the efforts of church leaders to reach some kind of general consensus regarding those writings that were authentic and authoritative (or at least theologically orthodox) and those that clearly were not. As Lee Martin McDonald observes, "This widespread concern for the truth – that is, the correct understanding of the story of Jesus – was significant in the church's decision about what literature to read in its worship. What did not conform to this tradition was eventually considered heresy and rejected."[29]

4. To preserve orthodoxy in the face of persecution.

Periodically, Christians were subjected to intense persecution and their Scriptures collected and confiscated. During such times it was essential that church officials distinguish between those books which might be, as a last resort, surrendered to the authorities, and those that had to be preserved at all cost. In 303 the pagan emperor Diocletian (r. 284-305) launched the last and worst empire-wide persecution of the church. Among other measures, he demanded that the Christian Scriptures be destroyed. This was a major factor in the efforts of church leaders to forge a consensus on the content of the biblical canon so as to identify and preserve the sacred texts.

---

[29] McDonald, *The Biblical Canon*, p. 292.

The Criteria for Inclusion

For nearly 300 years various Christian scholars and clerics regarded certain books as authoritative Scripture that were eventually excluded from the canon of the New Testament for various reasons. It is important to note, however, that like the Old Testament Apocrypha, none of these disputed texts, however popular they might have been in certain churches, were ever regarded as core Christian writings. Over time, in considering which Christian books should be accepted as canonical, three criteria prevailed: apostolicity, orthodoxy, and catholicity (or general acceptance).

1. Apostolicity.

The primary criterion for canonicity was apostolic authorship: Was the book written by an apostle or a close associate of an apostle? From the early years forward, the church's spiritual legitimacy was rooted in the apostolic tradition, which assured that its oral and written message was a true representation of the life and teachings of Christ. After all, Jesus himself was the true and perfect "canon" – the ultimate standard for orthodoxy and orthopraxy. Early Christians believed that Jesus was the climax of all history, and naturally they looked for guidance and authority to those whom he had chosen, equipped, and commissioned for leadership in the church. They rightly believed that the writings that most accurately related the life, the teachings, and the meaning of Jesus were those authored by the apostles and their associates.

By necessity, the criterion of apostolicity required that a book be written in the 1st century. For example, the Muratorian Fragment (c. 180) excluded *The Shepherd* of Hermas from its list of approved books for reading in formal worship services in the church of Rome specifically because of its late date. As the document explained:

> But Hermas wrote *The Shepherd* very recently, in our times [i.e., within recent decades] in the city of Rome, while bishop Pius, his brother, was occupying the [episcopal] chair of the church of the city of Rome. And therefore it ought indeed to be read [privately]; but it cannot be read

publicly to the people in church either among the [ancient Hebrew] prophets... or among the apostles, for it is after [their] time.

Although the Christian scholar Tertullian (c. 160-225) was the first to explicitly emphasize this factor, there seems to have been an intuitive acceptance in the post-apostolic church that the writings of the apostles and their associates carried special authority. Gradually over the first several centuries a consensus developed among the foremost Christian scholars and clerics of the time that all post-apostolic writings were purely supplemental to those of the apostolic generation. Regardless of how insightful and inspiring these subsequent writings might be, they offered up no new revelations. At best, they simply interpreted, illuminated, reflected upon, and perhaps amplified our understanding of the foundational documents of the Christian faith, the apostolic writings of the New Testament, which alone set forth the literary "rule of faith" by which all other writings and teachings were judged. Post-apostolic writings might be extraordinarily inspiring and edifying, but they were merely supplemental. For example, in his *Epistle to the Romans* (c. 112), Ignatius of Antioch writes, "I do not command you like Peter and Paul. They were apostles" (Rom. 4:3). We find this deferential view in relation to the teachings and writings of the apostles in all orthodox Christian writings from the early 2nd century on.

Throughout the first 350 years of Christian history various post-apostolic books were sometimes regarded as canonical in certain churches and by particular scholars and clerics. For example, the *Didache* (*The Teachings of the Twelve Apostles*), *The Shepherd* of Hermas, the *Epistle of Barnabas*, and even fanciful writings such as the *Apocalypse of Peter* were commonly included in various lists for recommended reading along with the New Testament texts. But over time these works gradually slipped into secondary status as the general awareness of the unique authority of the apostolic texts became more of a determining criterion.

2. Orthodoxy.

A second factor regarding canonicity was whether a particular book conformed to the "rule of faith" – the generally-accepted core doctrines of the Christian faith as articulated by Jesus and propagated by the apostles.

The New Testament is not a treatise on systematic theology. It includes much doctrine, but primarily it is biography, history, prophecy, and a lot of personal correspondence addressing specific issues and problems in particular churches or groups of churches. Yet there are consistent theological themes that are recurrent in these writings. As the Roman Christian philosopher Justin argued in his *Dialogue with Trypho* (c. 163), "I am entirely convinced that no Scripture contradicts another."[30] From the outset of the Jesus movement heresy and fanaticism constantly plagued the church, so it should not be surprising to find warnings against aberrant beliefs and practices throughout the New Testament.

For example, in I Corinthians 12:3 Paul sets forth a basic criterion on which to judge the veracity of any teaching as he writes, "[N]o one can say, 'Jesus is Lord,' except by the Holy Spirit." Years later the apostle John, probably in reference to the Docetist heresy, was more specific. In I John 4:2 he writes, "This is how you can recognize the Spirit of God: Every spirit that acknowledges that Jesus Christ has come in the flesh is from God." Those who deny this fundamental doctrine, John says, are "antichrists" (I John 2:18). Such statements by Paul and John and other New Testament writers anticipated the later emphasis on doctrinal orthodoxy as it related to the issue of canonicity.

For the early Church Fathers, a primary consideration regarding canonicity was this: Is the book theologically sound and generally correlative with the rest of the apostolic literature? Yet the mainstream church recognized that theological orthodoxy was broad enough to encompass the different perspectives and emphases expressed, for example, in Paul's Epistle to the Romans and the Epistle of James.

According to the Church Fathers, one of the seminal errors of the Gnostics was their contention that the Holy Spirit continued to reveal new knowledge and prophecies to *pneumatics* like themselves who were spiritually "illuminated." Mainstream church leaders considered this a great deception, as true Christians were those who believed and lived in accord with the teachings of Jesus and his apostles as recorded in the apostolic texts.

To reiterate a key point emphasized by F. F. Bruce at the beginning of this chapter, canonization was more than simply an attempt to assemble "an anthology of inspired or inspiring literature." Rather, "the chief concern [was] to get as close as possible to the source of the Christian faith." As Bruce writes, "In the canon of Scripture we have the foundation documents of Christianity, the charter of the church, the title-deeds of faith." This is what renders the biblical texts unique. "In the words of Scripture the voice of the Spirit of God continues to be heard," and it is these words that provide "a living power" that has inspired, animated and motivated followers of Christ throughout the centuries.[31] As Lee Martin McDonald comments, it is the authoritative nature

---

[30] Justin, *Dialogue with Trypho* 65.2.

[31] Bruce, *The Canon of Scripture*, pp. 282-83.

of these biblical texts that distinguished them from all other writings:

An examination of the origins and development of the Bible for both Judaism and Christianity is essentially about the process of canonization that led to the stabilizing of fixed collections of writings that undergird the core beliefs and religious practices of Jewish and Christian communities of faith. The corollary to canon formation is the belief that the writings that make up those collections have their origin in God, that is, that they are inspired by God and are consequently sacred and authoritative for worship and contain instruction in core beliefs, mission activity, and religious conduct. [McDonald, *The Biblical Canon*, p. 18.]

3. Catholicity.

The third criterion for canonicity concerns the issue of acceptance. Was a particular book received over time by most orthodox/catholic churches as authentic and authoritative, and did the book prove itself to be inspirational, edifying and instructional? This is the principle of "catholicity" (or "universality") – i.e., general acceptance among the churches.

Two examples indicate how this principle played out historically. In the early 5th century the renowned Bible scholar Jerome doubted the scriptural status of the Epistle of Jude for two reasons: not only did Jude cite the apocryphal book of *I Enoch*, but he also appeared to regard it as prophetic Scripture (see Jude 14-15). However, Jerome concluded, "Nevertheless, by age and use it [Jude] has gained authority and is reckoned among the Holy Scriptures." Similarly, Augustine was skeptical initially regarding the canonical status of Hebrews because the authorship of the book was in question, but he eventually accepted it on the basis that it was received as authentic Scripture by many Latin-speaking churches in the West and virtually all the Greek-speaking churches in the East. As he noted, "I am moved rather by the prestige of the Eastern churches to include this epistle among the canonical writings."

Acceptance of the New Testament Texts

Skeptical scholars such as Bart Ehrman, influenced as they are by theological liberalism and postmodernist theories, argue that the canonization process was primarily the result of a political power struggle between competing Christian sects. This is not at all surprisingly since liberal scholars tend to challenge the very concept of Christian orthodoxy itself. For them, theological "orthodoxy" was merely an arbitrary construct forged by competing factions vying for control over the burgeoning Christian movement of the first few centuries. Just as conservative Christians often ignore or minimize the theological and ecclesiastical diversity in the early church, liberal scholars tend to exaggerate the differences. In his bestseller, *Misquoting Jesus* (2007), Ehrman misrepresents the issue when he argues that the first two centuries of the Christian era, which were "particularly rich in theological diversity," produced an intense struggle for dominance in which the triumphant faction declared itself the "orthodox" party and suppressed any further dissent.

> In fact, the theological diversity was so extensive that groups calling themselves Christians adhered to beliefs and practices that most Christians today would insist were not Christian at all....
>
> The New Testament... emerged out of these conflicts over God... as one group of believers acquired more converts than all the others, and decided which books should be included in the canon of scripture. During the 2nd and 3rd centuries, however, there was no agreed-upon canon – and no agreed-upon theology. Instead there was a wide range of diversity....
>
> Only one group eventually "won out" in these debates. It was this group that decided what the Christian creeds would be.... This was also the group that decided which books would be included in the canon of scripture....
>
> The group that established itself as "orthodox"... then determined what future Christian generations would believe and read as scripture. What should we call the "orthodox" views before they became the majority opinion of all Christians? Possibly it is best to call them proto-orthodox. [Bart D. Ehrman, *Misquoting Jesus* (HarperOne, 2007), p. 153*ff*]

Ehrman's interpretation of the historical debate over canonization far exceeds the historical evidence. In fact, it is the kind of anti-Christian conspiratorial propaganda that one might expect to find in Dan Brown's *The Da Vinci Code*. On the contrary, the historical sources are clear that the selection of the 27 books of the New Testament was not the result of intra-Christian power struggles, nor was it the product of some decree set down by an ecclesiastical synod. In reality, these books were included in the canon because their authority had already been recognized and established among orthodox Christians, as F. F. Bruce clarifies:

> It was not until the 27 books had been generally accepted by Christians throughout the known world that they were first made the subject of a decree by an ecclesiastical council – the Synod of Hippo in 393.... And when at last a church council gave a ruling on the matter, all that it did was to ratify the general consensus of Christians, who (we may well believe) had been guided in this respect by a wisdom higher than their own.
>
> Canonicity implies supreme authority in matters of faith.... [T]hey included these writings in the canon because they already recognized their authority; the writings did not acquire authority by being included in the canon. [F. F. Bruce, *The Spreading Flame* (William B. Eerdmans Publishing Company, 1958), pp. 235*ff*.]

Other scholars, including even some prominent liberals, concur. Despite the fact that many have been led to believe that an elite group of Christian bishops got together and decided which books to include and exclude, in reality there was a general consensus among leading Christian scholars and church leaders regarding what constituted reliable tradition and literature, and what clearly was not. Historian Ivor Davidson explains the realities of the situation in his book, *The Birth of the Church*:

> At one level, it might be said that Christians created their Canon, for the decisions as to which books were *in* and which were *out* were obviously made by Christians leaders over a period of time and in response to particular internal and external challenges. At another level, however, these believers would have claimed that they were simply recognizing an authority that had already come to be appreciated by a large number of Christians.... Rather than imposing legitimacy on a particular set of texts, they were, as they saw it, acknowledging and conserving the inspired authority that was already inherent in these works according to their origin, content, and proven usefulness over time. [Ivor J. Davidson, *The Birth of the Church*. The Baker History of the Church, Vol. 1 (BakerBooks, 2004), p. 178.]

In *The Biblical Canon*, Lee Martin McDonald, while taking a more liberal position on some issues related to canonization, nonetheless arrives at a similar conclusion. As he frames the issue:

> The final biblical canon for both religious communities [i.e., Judaism and Christianity] was determined not by a council so much as by widespread use of sacred literature in the communities of faith. Councils typically confirm widespread practice, and that was the case when decisions about canon were made by councils in the 4th and 5th centuries and later: they simply endorsed choices made earlier by majorities or by consensus and convenience rather than by conscious council decisions....
>
> Some people think that church councils deliberated and determined what books should be included in the biblical canon, but a more accurate view is that the church councils of the 4th and 5th centuries acknowledged those books that had already obtained prominence from widespread usage among the various Christian churches in their areas. Church council decisions reflect what the communities *recognized*, and they subsequently authorized this recognition for the church.... In other words, church councils did not create biblical canons, but rather reflected the state of affairs in such matters in their geographical location. [McDonald, *The Biblical Canon*, pp. 160, 209.]

Bruce Metzger, the dean of New Testament scholars in the last half of the 20th century, points out that liberal scholars have misrepresented the dynamics in the canonization process and have turned the facts on their head. As he puts it succinctly, "The canon is a list of authoritative books more than it is an authoritative list of books."

> What the [church] synods and councils did in the 5th century and following was to ratify what already had been accepted....
>
> [T]he canon was not the result of a series of contests involving church politics. The canon is rather the separation that came about because of the intuitive insight of Christian believers....
>
> When the pronouncement was made about the canon, it merely ratified what the general sensitivity of the church had already determined. The canon is a list of authoritative books more than it is an authoritative list of books....
>
> For somebody... to say that the canon emerged only after councils and synods made these pronouncements would be like saying, "Let's get several academies of musicians to make a pronouncement that the music of Bach and Beethoven is wonderful".... [But] we knew that before the pronouncement was made. We know it because of sensitivity to what is good music and what is not. The same with the canon. [Quoted in Lee Strobel, *The Case for Christ* (Zondervan, 1988), p. 69]

Many early Christian writers implied in their references to various New Testament books that they regarded these writings as divinely-inspired Scripture in the same sense as the ancient Hebrew prophets. A few examples include:

- In II Peter 3:16, which most conservative scholars believe was written circa 65 A.D., Peter regards Paul's epistles on par with "the other Scriptures" – i.e., the Old Testament. Notably, this comment infers that a collection of at least some of Paul's letters had already begun to circulate throughout the churches.

- In the epistle of *I Clement* (c. 95) the author, Clement of Rome, exhorts the Corinthian church, "Take up the epistle of that blessed apostle, Paul [i.e., I Corinthians]," and he adds, "To be sure, he sent you a letter in the Spirit concerning himself and Cephas [Peter] and Apollos" (*I Clem. 47:1-3*). Clement also alludes to other Pauline epistles including Romans, Galatians, Philippians and Ephesians, as well as Hebrews, and he implies that these writings carry the same weight of authority as the numerous passages that he cites from the Old Testament.

- In his seven letters written circa 112, Ignatius, the bishop of Antioch, quotes from six of Paul's epistles – Ephesians, Philippians, Colossians, I and II Thessalonians, and Philemon – inferring that these writings have scriptural authority.

- The Roman presbyter Hermas, in his book, *The Shepherd* (early 2nd century?), quotes from two gospels (Matthew and Mark), Acts, six of

Paul's epistles (I and II Corinthians, Philippians, I Thessalonians, I and II Timothy), the general epistles of Hebrews, James, I Peter, and I John, and Revelation.

- The early Christian chronicler Papias, in his *Exposition of the Oracles of the Lord* (c. 120s), refers to the gospels of Mark and Matthew and quotes from I Peter, I John, Revelation, and several Pauline epistles.

- The anonymous author of *II Clement* implies that there are two written sources of authority for the church: the "Scripture" [i.e, the Septuagint] and "the books and the Apostles" (*II Clem. 14:2*). In addition, the author specifically refers to Matt. 9:13 (or Mark 2:17) as "Scripture" (*II Clem. 2:4-6*).

- In the *Epistle of Barnabas* (c. 130), the author introduces Matt 22:14 ("Many are called but few are chosen") with the words, "It is written..." – the same language used when citing various Old Testament passages (*Barn. 4:14*).

- Polycarp (c. 150), the renowned bishop of Smyrna, quotes from all of the four gospels, Acts, most of Paul's epistles (other than II Timothy, Titus and Philemon), and the general epistles of I Peter and I and II John. In his *Epistle to the Philippians* he cites both Psalm 4:4 and Ephesians 4:26 as "Scripture."

- Justin Martyr (c. 150) refers to the gospels as "the memoirs of the apostles" that were "drawn up by [Christ's] apostles and those who followed them." In his writings Justin quotes from all four of the gospel accounts.

- Theophilus of Antioch (c. 177) argued that the gospel writers and apostles were spokesmen for God in the same sense as the ancient Hebrew prophets, and he regarded the Christian writings of the New Testament to be equal in authority to those of the Old Testament.

Early New Testament Canonical Lists

Based on Peter's comments about Paul's letters in II Peter 3:16 and other early references, many scholars believe that the Pauline corpus of epistles was circulating as a collection by at least the end of the 1st century. In the mid-2nd century the Christian philosopher **Justin Martyr** wrote that the "memoirs of the apostles" [i.e., the gospels] were read on Sundays in the church in Rome. Furthermore, according to **Tertullian** and **Valentinian**, by about the year 140 collections of apostolic writings were being preserved both in Rome and Ephesus that were, for the most part, similar to our New Testament. However, the history of canonization was neither a simple nor a smooth process, and over the next 250 years church leaders often disagreed regarding the exact parameters of the Christian Scriptures.

One of the earliest collections of Christian writings was the **Muratorian Fragment** (a.k.a. the Muratorian Canon, c. 170), a list of books approved for public reading in the church of Rome in the late 2nd century that included comments on the authorship and origins of several of the texts.[32] Unfortunately, the manuscript is mutilated at the beginning – hence no reference to the first two gospels of Matthew and Mark. Nonetheless, the document mentions all New Testament books except Hebrews, James, and I and II Peter. (In all likelihood the exclusion of I Peter was by mistake as its authenticity was never in doubt.) The apostolic authorship of Hebrews was often questioned in the early centuries because it was written anonymously, and the Epistle of James might have received limited circulation in the early church due to the fact that its target audience was Jewish Christians. As for II Peter, as mentioned earlier, there is no mention of the epistle prior to the time of Origen.

The Muratorian Fragment contains several anomalies. The 2nd century apocryphal gospel, the *Apocalypse of Peter*, is included in the list, as is the intertestamental Jewish writing, the *Wisdom of Solomon*. In addition, *The Shepherd* of Hermas is recommended for private edification but not for reading in the church.

Irenaeus (c. 180), the scholarly bishop of Lyons in France, never compiled a set list of sacred books. But like his contemporary, Melito, he distinguished between the "Old Testament" and the "New Testament" in his monograph, *Against Heresies*. Irenaeus also referred to the "canon" in his writings, but in the context of an apostolic "rule of faith" (i.e., doctrinal orthodoxy), not as a body

---

[32] The Muratorian Fragment was first published in 1740 by the antiquarian scholar Cardinal L.A. Muratori, and the text was a 7th century copy made at a monastery in Bobbio in Lombardy and later lodged in the Ambrosian Library in Milan.

of literature. A century-and-a-half later the church historian Eusebius referenced Irenaeus' comments on Scripture and noted that he cited all New Testament books other than James, II Peter, III John, and Jude. (Of course, the fact that he doesn't mention these texts is not necessarily a convincing argument that he was either unaware of them or that he rejected their apostolic legitimacy.) Irenaeus characterized the four gospels as the "Pillars of the Church," and in contradistinction to all the spurious "gospels' circulating at the time, he insisted upon "these four and no more." Understandably, he held *I Clement* in high esteem, but he seems also to have accepted the apocryphal *Wisdom of Solomon* and even *The Shepherd* of Hermas as "Scripture."

Irenaeus' admiration for *The Shepherd* is particularly odd because the book implies an adoptionist view of Jesus, and Irenaeus was one of the most fastidious proponents of TC (Theological Correctness) in the 2nd century. In his classic work, *Against Heresies* (*Adversus Haereses*, c. 180), he provides a summary of the basic tenets of the orthodox Christian faith that became a standard for later creedal formulations. These core principles also influenced the decisions of later scholars and church leaders regarding the canonical status of various Christian writings:

> The Church, though dispersed throughout the whole world... has received from the apostles and their disciples this faith: It believes in one God, the Father Almighty, Maker of heaven and earth... and in one Christ Jesus, the Son of God, who became incarnate for our salvation; and in the Holy Spirit, who proclaimed through the prophets the dispensations of God, the advents, the birth from a virgin, the passion, the resurrection from the dead, and the ascension into heaven in the flesh of the beloved Christ Jesus, our Lord. He also proclaimed through the prophets his future manifestation from heaven in the glory of the Father "to gather all things in one," and to raise up anew all flesh of the whole human race. [This will take place] in order that to Christ Jesus, our Lord, God, Saviour, and King, according to the will of the invisible Father, [so that] 'every knee should bow... and every tongue confess' him. And he will execute just judgment towards all, sending into everlasting fire "spiritual wickednesses," and the angels who transgressed and became apostates, together with the ungodly, the unrighteous, the wicked, and the profane among men. But he will, in the exercise of his grace, confer immortality on the righteous and holy, and those who have kept his commandments, and have persevered in his love, some from the beginning of their Christian course, and others from the time of their repentance. He will surround them with everlasting glory. [Irenaeus, *Against Heresies* I:10.1]

In light of the above, it is important to keep in mind that Irenaeus' objective was not to set forth the parameters of Scripture but to define the essential core doctrines of the faith. In that regard he emphasized the Old and New Testament writings as divinely inspired and authoritative in the same sense as the apostolic tradition that was transmitted through the "apostolic succession" of orthodox bishops in the churches. Taken together, these factors defined the "canon" – the "rule of faith" for all "catholic" Christians. But none of this was imposed upon individual Christians and church leaders by outside authorities such as church councils. Instead, the consensus regarding theological orthodoxy was based on spiritual discernment derived from two sources: the apostolic tradition, and the corpus of divinely inspired writings that were circulated, preserved and venerated in the churches. As a result, amid all the diversity that otherwise existed in the early church, there was a general consensus regarding the core beliefs of the Christian faith.

The historical evidence confirms that by at least the middle of the 2nd century most Christian scholars and church leaders accepted most of the books of the New Testament. As Hans von Campenhausen notes, "the critical period between Marcion and Irenaeus" (circa 140-180) was "the period in which the 'New Testament' as such emerged."[33] There were still differences of opinion over a few books such as Hebrews, James, II Peter, II and III John, Jude and Revelation, but the essential core of the New Testament was well established.

Nonetheless, some Christian scholars had a more expansive view of Scripture than others. In his book, *Stromata* (*Miscellanies*), **Clement of Alexandria** (c. 200) provided a brief synopsis of the writings he regarded as Scripture. Clement's list included the four gospels, Acts, thirteen Pauline epistles, I Peter, I and II John, and Revelation. Regarding Hebrews, he believed that Paul originally composed the epistle in the Hebrew language, after which Luke translated and published it in Greek. According to Clement, Paul refrained from affixing his name to the letter because many Jews were prejudiced against him, so he "very wisely" chose not to sign it so as "not to repel them."[34]

In addition to these books Clement also included other "disputed writings" such as Jude, the *Epistle of Barnabas*, and the *Apocalypse of Peter*. He quoted freely from several other sources including *I Clement*, the *Didache*, *The Shepherd* of Hermas, the *Preaching of Peter,* the *Acts of Paul*, and even the *Sibylline Oracles*, although he apparently never considered these books to be scriptural. Furthermore, he referred to quasi-gnostic works such as the *Gospel of the Egyptians*, the *Gospel of the Hebrews*, and the *Traditions of Matthias* without

---

[33] Hans von Campenhausen, *The Formation of the Christian Bible.* (E.T., 1972), p. 37.

[34] See McDonald, *The Biblical Canon*, p. 302.

categorizing them as heretical. As for the remaining three books of the New Testament – James, II Peter, and III John – he never mentioned them.

In the early 3rd century **Hippolytus** of Rome (c. 170-235) was the greatest Western scholar of his day. Although he never compiled a list of specific books that he regarded as canonical, he defined "all Scripture" as including "the prophets, the Lord, and the apostles." In his writings he quoted from the Epistle to the Hebrews but did not consider it Scripture, apparently putting it on the same level as *The Shepherd* of Hermas, the *Didache*, and the *Epistle of Barnabas*.

Like his predecessors Melito and Irenaeus, **Tertullian** (fl. 196-212) also used the term "the New Testament" to designate the second part of the Christian Bible. Although he never compiled a formal list of books, in his writings he made it clear that he considered the four gospels, Acts, Paul's thirteen epistles, I Peter, I John, Jude and Revelation to be inspired Scripture. Tertullian attributed the authorship of Hebrews to Barnabas, and he defended the authenticity of Jude despite its reference to the book of *I Enoch*. (In fact, he apparently seemed to think that *Enoch* was actually an antediluvian book that survived the Great Flood.) He made no mention of James, II Peter, II and III John, and he expressed a rather low view of *The Shepherd* of Hermas, which many scholars and churchmen held in high esteem at the time.

Cyprian of Carthage (c. 200-258), one of the leading bishops of his day, cited in his writings the four gospels, Acts, eleven of Paul's epistles, I Peter, I John, and the Apocalypse of John. He never mentions II Timothy, Philemon, James, II Peter, II and III John, or Jude. He probably was familiar with Hebrews but did not regard it as Scripture due to the fact that its author was unknown. However, in his published homily, "Against Dice-Players," he called *The Shepherd* of Hermas "divine Scripture."

Sometime around the year 220 the great scholar **Origen** compiled a set list of Old Testament books that he regarded as Scripture, but curiously he never did the same for the New Testament. However, he did recognize a New Testament canon in principle, and a century later Eusebius collected Origen's comments on various Christian writings. Origen seems to have been the first Christian scholar to regard all 27 books of the New Testament as Scripture, although he conceded that five of them were "disputed." Among the "undisputed" books were the four gospels and Acts, fourteen of Paul's epistles (including Hebrews), I Peter, I John, and the Apocalypse of John. In *Homilies on Joshua*, he noted:

> So too our Lord Jesus Christ... sent his apostles as priests carrying
> well-wrought trumpets. First **Matthew** sounded the priestly trumpet in his
> Gospel, **Mark** also, and **Luke**, and **John**, each gave forth a strain on their

priestly trumpets. **Peter** moreover sounds with the two trumpets of his Epistles; **James** also and **Jude**. Still the number is incomplete, and **John** gives forth the trumpet sound through his Epistles [and Apocalypse]; and **Luke** while describing the deeds of the apostles. Latest of all, moreover, that one [**Paul**] comes who said, "I think that God has set us forth as the apostles last of all" [I Cor 4:9], and thundering on the fourteen trumpets of his Epistles he threw down, even to their very foundations, the wall of Jericho, that is to say, all the instruments of idolatry and the dogmas of the philosophers. [Origen, *Homilies on Joshua* 7.1]

Among the books that Origen characterized as "disputed" were II Peter, II and III John, "the reputed epistle of James," and Jude. Regarding II Peter, he commented, "Peter... has left one acknowledged epistle, perhaps a second also, but it is doubtful."[35] As noted earlier, Origen is the earliest Christian writer to mention II Peter, and as F. F. Bruce observes, the book "does not appear to have been known much before his day."[36] [Note: The earliest manuscript to contain the text of II Peter is the Bodmer manuscript P72 (see Chapter 5), which was probably copied in Origen's lifetime.]

In his remark that "some doubted" the authenticity of Hebrews, James, II Peter, II and III John, and Jude, Origen implies that the majority of scholars, including himself, accepted these books as genuine. But he also apparently considered the *Didache* and *The Shepherd* of Hermas to be Scripture, and he referred to the *Epistle of Barnabas* as "a catholic epistle." In addition, he held a high opinion of the *Gospel According to the Hebrews*, although he never labeled it "Scripture." But unlike his predecessor Clement of Alexandria, he was more skeptical of books such as the *Preaching of Peter* and the *Acts of Paul*, and he dismissed the *Gospel According to the Egyptians*, the *Gospel of the Twelve*, and the *Gospel According to Basilides* as demonstrably "false" (i.e., heretical).

In the history of biblical canonicity the **Clermont List** is the connecting link in the century between Origen and Eusebius. In 303 the emperor Diocletian (284-305) ordered all Christian writings to be surrendered to authorities for confiscation, which made it imperative that Christians know which books were sacred Scripture and therefore worth dying for. In this context, the *Codex Claromontanus* was a list of sacred books that was compiled around Alexandria, Egypt circa 300. The New Testament portion included 23 books and omitted only Philippians, Hebrews, and I and II Thessalonians. Since Philippians and Thessalonians had never been in doubt, these were probably left off by mistake.

---

[35] Quoted in Eusebius, *Ecclesiatical History* 6.225.8.

[36] Bruce, *The Canon of Scripture*, p. 193.

The Clermont List also included the *Epistle of Barnabas*, *The Shepherd* of Hermas, the *Acts of Paul*, and the *Apocalypse of Peter*, but these books are separated from the rest as if to indicate their secondary status.

Circa 325 the church historian **Eusebius** drew up a list of canonical books, and like Origen he divided the texts into three categories:

(1) *Homologoumena* – books that were universally accepted;

(2) *Antilegomena* – disputed books; and

(3) *Nothos* – spurious books.

The *Homologoumena* included the four gospels, Acts, fourteen epistles of Paul (including Hebrews), I John, I Peter, and Revelation (the Apocalypse of John). Regarding Hebrews, Eusebius noted that it was "disputed by the Church of Rome on the ground that it was not written by Paul." Personally, he was skeptical of Revelation for two reasons: uncertainty regarding its authorship (was it the apostle John or another man, "John the Elder?"), and its millenarian theme.

Eusebius considered the *Antilegomena* to include James, II Peter, II and III John, and Jude. However, despite their controversial status, Eusebius conceded that many churches accepted these writings as apostolic and authoritative.

Among the spurious (*Nothos*) books that were generally rejected as canonical, Eusebius listed the *Acts of Paul*, "the so-called *Shepherd* [of Hermas]," the *Apocalypse of Peter*, the *Epistle of Barnabas*, "the so-called *Teachings of the Apostles* [the *Didache*]," and the *Gospel According to the Hebrews*.

As for the various heretical and Gnostic writings that masqueraded under apostolic titles such as the *Gospel of Thomas*, the *Gospel of Philip*, the *Gospel of Mary [Magdalene]*, the *Gospel of Truth*, and others, Eusebius commented, "None of these has been deemed worthy of citation in the writings of any of the succession of churchmen." He dismissed them summarily as illegitimate, unorthodox, and "the figments of heretics," and concluded, "they are not to be reckoned even among 'spurious' books but must be shunned as altogether wrong and impious."[37]

At this point it seems reasonable to summarize the writings of the New Testament which have been quoted. In the first place should be put the holy tetrad of the Gospels. To them follows the writing of the Acts of the Apostles. After this should be reckoned the Epistles of Paul. Following them the Epistle of John called the first, and in the same way should be recognized the Epistle of Peter. In addition to these should be put, if it seems desirable, the Revelation of John.... These belong to the

---

[37] Quoted in Bruce, *The Canon of Scripture*, p. 200.

Recognized Books [*Homologoumenois*].[38]

Of the Disputed Books *[Antilegomenon]* which are nevertheless known to most are the Epistle called of James, that of Jude, the second Epistle of Peter, and the so-called second and third Epistles of John, which may be the work of [John] the evangelist or some other of the same name.

Among the books which are not genuine *[Nothois]* must be reckoned the *Acts of Paul*, the work entitled the *Shepherd*, the *Apocalypse of Peter*, and in addition to them the letter called of *Barnabas* and the so-called *Teachings of the Apostles [Didache]*.* And in addition, as I said, the Revelation of John, if this view prevail. For, as I said, some reject it, but others count it among the Recognized Books. Some have also counted the *Gospel According to the Hebrews* in which those of the Hebrews who have accepted Christ take a special pleasure. These would all belong to the disputed books, but we have nevertheless been obliged to make a list of them, distinguishing between those writings which, according to the tradition of the Church, are true, genuine, and recognized [Scriptures], and those which differ from them in that they are not canonical but disputed, yet nevertheless are known to most of the writers of the Church, in order that we might know them and the writings which are put forward by heretics under the name of the apostles, containing gospels such as those of Peter, and Thomas, and Matthias, and some others besides, or Acts such as those of Andrew and John and the other apostles. To none of these has any who belonged to the succession of the orthodox ever thought it right to refer in his writings. Morever, the type of phraseology differs from apostolic style, and the opinion and tendency of their contents is widely dissonant from true orthodoxy, and clearly shows that they are the forgeries of heretics. They ought, therefore, to be reckoned not even among spurious books but shunned as altogether wicked and impious. [Eusebius, *Ecclesiastical History* III.25.1-7.]

It is clear that by the time of Eusebius at least twenty of the New Testament writings were universally accepted, and the status of the remaining seven books – Hebrews, James, II Peter, II and III John, Jude, and Revelation – was increasingly favorable. Nonetheless, the debate over some of these books continued throughout most of the 4th century. After Eusebius numerous other canonical lists circulated among the churches, but a comparison of the contents of the two great 4th century codices, **Codex Sinaiticus** and **Codex Vaticanus** (both dated c. 350), reveals that there was still no definitive consensus. Codex Sinaiticus (see Chapter 6) is the oldest extant manuscript to contain most of the entire Bible, and it includes nearly all of the New Testament. The text of the

---

[38] On two occasions Euesbius referred to *I Clement* as "recognized" [*Homologoumena*], although he never called the book "testamented" – his preferred term for Scripture.

Old Testament follows the Septuagint translation and includes the Apocrypha. The New Testament portion contains all 27 books, but it also includes the *Epistle of Barnabas* and *The Shepherd* of Hermas. Codex Vaticanus originally contained the entire New Testament, although the latter part of Hebrews is missing along with I and II Timothy, Titus, Philemon and Revelation. Most scholars speculate that some of the non-canonical Christian writings were also included in the manuscript as a kind of appendix, as in the case of Sinaiticus and the later Codex Alexandrinus (c. 425).

In 363 thirty or so clerics attended the **Synod of Laodicea** in Asia Minor, at which time they issued a number of "canons" or decrees. Most of these declarations addressed issues related to liturgical practices and codes of conduct for the clergy and laity. Canon 59 stated that only canonical books should be read in worship services, and a final decree, Canon 60 (which some scholars believe was a later addition), contained a list of canonical books that included all Old and New Testament books except the Apocalypse of John.

The Cheltenham List (a.k.a. the Mommsen List), discovered in 1885, was probably drawn up in North Africa around the year 365. It included the same New Testament books that Origen and Eusebius had labeled "undisputed" while it excluded the "disputed" books of Hebrews, James, II and III John, II Peter, and Jude.

In retrospect, the parameters of the New Testament canon were essentially set in 367 when **Athanasius**, the influential bishop of Alexandria, issued his annual Festal letter to the churches of Egypt in which he named the books that he regarded as canonical. His list included all 27 New Testament books, which he called "the springs of salvation." In addition, he commented that the *Didache* and *The Shepherd* of Hermas, while not being part of the canon, "were appointed from the time of the [church] fathers to be read," and were efficacious for catechetical purposes. Athanasius was particularly impressed by *The Shepherd*, which he called "a most profitable book."

Again, we must not hesitate to name the books of the New Testament. They are as follows:

Four gospels – according to Matthew, according to Mark, according to Luke, according to John.

Then after these the Acts of the Apostles and the seven so-called catholic epistles of the apostles, as follows: one of James, two of Peter, three of John, and... one of Jude.

Next to these are fourteen epistles of the apostle Paul, written in order as follows: First, to the Romans; then two to the Corinthians; and after these to the Galatians and next to the Ephesians; then to the Philippians and the Colossians, and the two to the Thessalonians and that to the

Hebrews. Next are two to Timothy, one to Titus, and last the one to
Philemon.

Moreover, John's Apocalypse.

These are the "springs of salvation," so that one who is thirsty may be
satisfied with the oracles which are in them. In these alone is the teaching
of true religion proclaimed as good news. Let no one add to these or take
anything from them....

But for the sake of greater accuracy I must needs, as I write, add this:
there are other books outside these, which are not indeed included in the
canon, but have been appointed from the time of the [church] fathers to be
read to those who are recent converts to our company and wish to be
instructed in the word of true religion. These are... the so-called *Teaching
of the Apostles* [the *Didache*] and *The Shepherd* [of Hermas]. But while
the former are included in the canon and the latter are read [in church], no
mention is to be made of the apocryphal works [i.e., so-called "Gnostic
gospels"]. They are the invention of heretics, who write according to their
own will, and gratuitously assign and add to them dates so that, offering
them as ancient writings, they may have an excuse for leading the simple
astray. [Quoted in Bruce, *The Canon of Scripture*, pp. 208-9.]

In the years following Athanasius' pronouncement, several more influential
church leaders weighed in on the issue of the canon. In one of his catechetical
lectures, **Cyril of Jerusalem** (c. 313-86) urged his congregants to "Learn
diligently from the church what are the books of the Old Testament, and what
are those of the New. But read none of the apocryphal [i.e., Gnostic/ heretical]
writings."[39] However, the debate over the status of Revelation was still not
resolved. According to Cyril, the book should be consigned to the "secondary
rank." Likewise, **Gregory of Nazianzus'** (c. 329-90) put forth a list of "genuine
books of inspired Scripture" that included 26 of the 27 New Testament texts –
the sole exception being Revelation. Around this same time **Amphilochius of
Iconium** (c. 340-400) compiled a canonical list that included all 27 books of the
New Testament, although with some reservations. He commented that "some
say the epistle to the Hebrews is spurious; but this is not correct as its grace is
genuine." He then added, "Of the catholic epistles some say there are seven,
others that three only are to be received: one of James, one of Peter and one of
John." Regarding the status of Revelation, he remarked that some included the
book, "but the majority say it is spurious."*

Meanwhile, two other influential clerics, **Epiphanius** (c. 315-403) and **John
Chrysostom** (c. 347-407), accepted the divine inspiration of Revelation without
reservation, as did **Rufinus of Aquileia** (345-410) in his Exposition on the

---

[39] Quoted in Bruce, *The Canon of Scripture, p 210.*

[Apostles] Creed. Like Athanasius, Rufinus also recommended two additional "ecclesiastical" books: *The Shepherd* of Hermas and the *Didache.*

By the end of the 4th century there was a general consensus in the Western (Latin-speaking) Church regarding the 27 books of the New Testament, and a century later the same was true in the Eastern (Greek-speaking) Church. The most notable exception was the ambivalence in the Eastern Church regarding the authorship and authenticity of the Book of Revelation. However, it should be noted that at least some Christians – mostly those associated with fringe groups – continued to value other works such as Tatian's harmony of the Four Gospels, *The Diatessaron,* and even apocryphal gospels such as the *Protoevangelium of James.*

The Official Lists

Damasus I, the bishop of Rome from 366-84, is considered by Roman Catholic historians and theologians to be the "father of the Catholic canon." According to tradition, Damasus convened a **Council of Rome** in 382 that officially sanctioned the Athanasian list. (Oddly, the council regarded II and III John as legitimate, but it questioned whether these books had been written by the apostle John.) With the official backing of the Roman church, the **Damasian List** effectively ended the debate over the New Testament canon.

In 383 Damasus I commissioned the renowned scholar **Jerome** (c. 347-420) to standardize the various Old Latin translations of the Bible into an official Latin Vulgate edition based on the available Greek texts. Jerome included the same 27 books that Athanasius had listed and the Council of Rome had approved, and with the publication of the Latin Vulgate the boundaries of the New Testament canon were officially fixed in the Western church. In a letter in 394 to Paulinus, bishop of Nola, Jerome set forth his views on the proper parameters of the New Testament. Regarding Revelation, Jerome was effusive in his praise of the book: "The Apocalypse of John has as many mysteries as it has words. I have said too little in comparison with what the book deserves; all praise of it is inadequate, for in every one of its words manifold meanings lie hidden."[40] Addressing the age-old controversy over the Johannine epistles, he attributed I John to the apostle John but thought II and III John were written by another John, "John the Elder."

Unlike many earlier Christian scholars, Jerome considered the *Epistle of Barnabas* to be the authentic work of Paul's apostolic colleague, but since the book had generally been regarded in recent generations as apocryphal, Jerome

---

[40] Quoted in Bruce, *The Canon of Scripture*, p. 213.

conceded to the majority opinion. Likewise, while noting that *The Shepherd* of Hermas is "a useful book, and many of the ancient writers quote from it as authoritative," he acknowledged that most of the churches relegated it to non-canonical status.

Augustine (c. 354-430), the most eminent scholar in the first four centuries of the church, considered the debate over the canon to be a settled issue. In his 4-volume work, (397-426), he replicated the Athanasian and Damasian lists.

That of the New Testament... is contained within the following: Four books of the gospel – according to Matthew, according to Mark, according to Luke, according to John. Fourteen epistles of the apostle Paul – one to the Romans, two to the Corinthians, one to the Galatians, to the Ephesians, two to the Thessalonians, one to the Colossians, two to Timothy, one to Titus, to Philemon, to the Hebrews. Two [epistles] of Peter, three of John, one of Jude, and one of James. One book of the Acts of the Apostles, and one of the Revelation of John. [Bruce, *The Canon of Scripture*, p. 230.]

Regarding the ongoing debate over the authorship of Hebrews, Augustine insisted that it was Pauline in origin, although in his latter years he modified his position and called the book "anonymous." Commenting on the criteria for canonicity, Augustine noted that the issue should be decided on the basis of the consensus opinion of "all the catholic churches."

Three church councils, all of which were dominated by Augustine, officially sanctioned the consensus view of the New Testament canon. The **Synod of Hippo** (393) formally ratified a set list of canonical books, and under the leadership of Augustine the Synod approved the same books that Origen, Eusebius, Athanasius, Damasus I, Jerome and Augustine had previously endorsed. Four years later the **Third Council of Carthage** (397) incorporated into Canon 47 the Synod of Hippo's decree on canonicity. In its statement the Council noted: "And further it was resolved that nothing should be read in church under the name of the divine Scriptures except the canonical writings" – whereupon it listed the books of the Old and New Testaments along with the deuterocanonical writings. Likewise, a **Fourth Council of Carthage** in 419 issued a similar pronouncement.

In the interim **Pope Innocent I** (r. 401-17) declared in 405 that only the 27 books of the New Testament were to be considered canonical. As for "the rest of the books" [i.e., the so-called Gnostic Gospels], they "are to be not only rejected but also condemned." However, in reality the status of some books remained in question throughout the 5ᵗʰ century. In fact, there never was a time when the entire church accepted as Scripture the 27 books of the New Testament exclusively. When the **Codex Alexandrinus** (c. 425) was published about twenty years after Innocent I, it still included along with the standard Bible *I-II Clement* and the *Psalms of Solomon*. **Codex Claramontanus**, a bi-lingual Greek-Latin Bible dated circa 500, includes *The Shepherd* of Hermas, the *Acts of Paul*, and the *Apocalypse of Peter*. Five hundred years later, **Codex Hierosolymitanus** (c. 1050) still contained the *Didache*, *I-II Clement*, the *Epistle of Barnabas*, and even the epistles of Ignatius.

Throughout the medieval era there was little if any debate over the composition of either the Old or New Testaments. However, official pronouncements on the parameters of the canon were not made until it became a contentious issue during the Reformation era. In response, all major branches of Christianity eventually drafted official statements on the scope of the biblical canon. Among the more notable declarations were...

- The Roman Catholic Canon of Trent, drafted in 1546;
- The Gallic Confession of Faith of 1559, drafted by John Calvin for French Protestants;
- The Church of England's Thirty-Nine Articles of 1563; and
- The Synod of Jerusalem of 1672 for the Greek Orthodox Church.

Even today there are variations in the canons of the Syriac Orthodox Church, the Armenian Orthodox Church, the Georgian Orthodox and Apostolic Church, the Coptic Church, and the Ethiopian Orthodox Church. For example:

- The Syriac Church, in its Doctrine of Addai (c. 400), approved seventeen Christian books including Tatian's *Diatessaron*, the Acts of the Apostles, and fifteen Pauline epistles including Hebrews and *III Corinthians* (a pseudepigraphical book written circa 160-70 based on Paul's comments in I Cor. 5:9 and 7:1). However, the Church later anathematized Tatian as a heretic, and his *Diatessaron* was replaced by the Four Gospels.
- By the 5ᵗʰ century the Syrian Bible, called the Peshitta, included the disputed books of Philemon, James, I Peter and I John (while omitting *III Corinthians*), but it still excluded II Peter, II and III John, Jude and Revelation.
- The Armenian Bible omitted Revelation from its canon until the 13ᵗʰ century, and until recent times it included *III Corinthians*. As late as 1290 some clerics in the Armenian Church continued to lobby for the

inclusion of the *Epistle of Barnabas*, the *Advice of the Mother of God to the Apostles*, and the *Books of Criapos* – in addition to the *Testaments of the Twelve Patriarchs* in its Old Testament.

- The Copic Bible continues to include the epistles of *I* and *II Clement*.
- The Revelation of John has never been included in the official lectionary of the Greek Orthodox Church.

The Protestant Canon

In the years immediately preceding the Reformation, the biblical scholar **Erasmus** of Rotterdam (1466-1536) reopened the historical controversy over the authorship of several New Testament books. Based on his study of the original Greek texts, Erasmus concluded that Paul was not the author of Hebrews, nor was Revelation the work of the apostle John. Erasmus' contemporary, the theologian **Cardinal Thomas Cajetan** (1469-1534), likewise doubted the Pauline authorship of Hebrews as well as the traditional authorship of James, II and III John, and Jude. However, neither Erasmus nor Cajetan challenged the canonical legitimacy of any of these books.

When **Martin Luther** (1483–1546) published a German translation of the New Testament in 1522, he considered omitting the books of Hebrews, James, Jude and Revelation from the New Testament canon. Instead, he essentially separated the apostolic writings into two sections – an inner canon and an outer canon – and he placed these four books after III John.

Luther noted in his preface to Hebrews that the book was written by "an excellent man of learning, who had been a disciple of the apostles... and who was very well versed in Scripture." (He later speculated that the author was probably Apollos.) He objected to the Epistle of James for theological reasons – i.e., its emphasis on good works – claiming that it contradicted Paul's central message of justification by grace through faith alone. (Later in life Luther came to accept the book.) He regarded Jude as a superfluous document and an abstract of II Peter, and like many of the early Church Fathers he was troubled by its reference to *I Enoch*. Regarding Revelation, he considered it too opaque, quipping that "a revelation should be revealing," and adding that the book "lacks everything that I hold as apostolic and prophetic."

The great English Bible scholar **William Tyndale** (1494-1536) followed a similar pattern in his 1525 translation of the New Testament, separating Hebrews, James, Jude and Revelation from the rest of the apostolic writings. This arrangement was perpetuated in subsequent English-language Bibles such as the **Coverdale Bible** (1535) and the **Matthew's Bible** (1537). Beginning with the publication of the **Great Bible** of 1539, the traditional order was restored wherein Hebrews and James were placed between Philemon and I Peter, with Jude and Revelation following III John.

John Calvin (1509-64) also doubted the Pauline authorship of Hebrews, reasoning that it was probably written either by Luke or Clement of Rome. He doubted that Peter had written II Peter, opting for the theory that it was probably the work of one of Peter's disciples. But unlike Luther, he had no problem reconciling the theology of James with the rest of the New Testament, although he speculated that the book might have been written by James the son of Alphaeus rather than James "the Just," the half-brother of Jesus. Calvin never commented on the authorship of II and III John or Revelation.

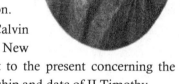

Few Protestant scholars after Luther and Calvin challenged the apostolic authorship of any New Testament book, although questions persist to the present concerning the Petrine authorship of II Peter and the authorship and date of II Timothy.

The Summa

As mentioned at the outset of this chapter, the process of canonization was a long, complicated and sometimes contentious process. However, the popular myth that the compilation of the biblical canon was the result of power struggles between various factions within the church to define and control the parameters of orthodoxy is historically unsupportable. The books that eventually were accorded canonical status were chosen on the basis of accepted criteria – apostolicity, orthodoxy, and catholicity – and over a period of several generations they demonstrated conclusively their divine authority. In retrospect, it is apparent that church leaders were guided by the Holy Spirit to the point that they ultimately reached a sensible consensus – or more accurately, a providential consensus.

6

Composition of the Bible and the Earliest Extant Manuscripts

The Biblical Texts

In the ancient world relatively few people were literate, and writing materials were expensive and often in short supply. Compared to modern times, very few books (actually, scrolls) were written, and those that were produced were typically revered as works of profound wisdom. The tacit assumption was that if something was "written," it was true. Particularly when a manuscript purported to be an oracle from God, it carried an aura and a mystique that virtually assured that it would be treasured and preserved – at least by those who accepted its message.

The sixty-six books that comprise the Bible were written over a period of about 1500 years by some forty authors including kings, peasants, philosophers, poets, scribes, priests, prophets, apostles, and associates of the apostles. As II Peter 1:21 declares, the individual authors "spoke from God as they were inspired by the Holy Spirit," and the texts were composed in three languages. Virtually all of the Old Testament was written in Hebrew with the exception of part of Daniel and two passages in Ezra that were in Aramaic, the official language of the old Assyrian Empire and the common language of Western Asia from about the 8th century B.C. to the time of Christ. The New Testament was written in Greek, the acknowledged international language in the 1st century A.D., but it also includes a few Aramaic words and expressions.

Currently, there are about 7,000 extant copies of Greek manuscripts of the Bible, mostly New Testament texts but also including some from the Old Testament. Of these, less than ten ever contained the entire Bible, and all are incomplete with missing pages and sometimes even entire books. Only four of these original Bibles predate the 10th century.

Based on extensive manuscript evidence augmented by the discovery of the Dead Sea Scrolls in 1947, scholars can verify that the text of the Old Testament was preserved without significant alteration for more than 2000 years – or from before the time of Christ down to the present. Likewise, as discussed in Chapter 7, literally thousands of extant New Testament manuscripts provide overwhelming evidence that the New Testament has also been preserved and transmitted accurately through the centuries.

The Production Process

Generally-speaking, the term **"manuscript"** (singular MS, or plural MSS) refers to a hand-written document. In most cases a manuscript would predate the advent of the printing press – i.e., the mid-to-late 1400s. "Extant" manuscripts are those that have been preserved (at least in part) over the centuries to the present, while those that have been lost are "extinct."

The earliest Biblical manuscripts were written on **papyrus** (paper), an aquatic reed that grew in the marshy lands of the Egyptian delta with a stem that resembles a stalk of corn. Papyrus is capable of

Cyperus papyrus

surviving for millennia in hot, dry climates such as Egypt and Dead Sea area, as exemplified by the fact that there are extant papyrus fragments (none of which are biblical manuscripts) that date back as early as 2400 B.C. The production process for preparing papyrus was a careful and time-consuming ordeal:

- First, papyrus reeds were stripped of their outer rind and cut into pieces about 18" long;
- Next, the inner pith was cut into narrow slices, each of which was placed vertically side by side on a table with their edges slightly overlapping;
- A second layer of slices was laid horizontally over the first layer, and the two layers were pressed and beaten until the plant's natural juice fused them into a single sheet;
- Once the sheet was dried, the surface was polished with a rounded object such as a stone until it became perfectly smooth; and
- Finally, the edges were cut in order to make the sheet straight and rectangular.

Typically, papyrus sheets were about 15" high and 9" wide (or a little larger than a legal-size sheet of paper), and the horizontal lines of the top layer of papyrus provided guidelines for scribes to write on. To make a roll or scroll, sheets were overlapped and glued together. In ancient times the foremost center for producing scrolls was the Syrian port city of Byblos. Therefore, manuscripts were commonly referred to generically as *byblos*, or books. Later, Christians referred to the ultimate *byblos* as "the Bible."

Scholars believe that the first Jewish scribal academies were established in Israel in the late 6th century B.C. following the Babylonian Exile. At first single books, and then major sections of the ancient Scriptures were written on scrolls that sometimes measured 30 feet or longer. Until much later, perhaps the 5th century A.D., Jewish scribes continued to use a separate scroll for the Law (the Torah or Pentateuch) so as to distinguish it from the rest of the Scriptures. Some scholars believe that separate scrolls were also devoted to the other two sections of the Hebrew Bible, the Prophets (Nevi'im) and the Writings (Ketuvim).

Expensive manuscripts were written on **parchment** or **vellum**. Parchment is the leather skins of cattle, sheep, goats, or sometimes antelopes, while vellum is a finer quality of parchment produced from the skins of young calves. Parchment was first developed in the 2nd century B.C., and since it was thicker and more durable than papyrus, it could be written on both sides. Beginning in the 4th century A.D., parchment replaced papyrus as the material of choice for high-quality books. For example, two of the oldest and most complete extant biblical manuscripts, Codex Vaticanus and Codex Sinaiticus, were written on vellum. As with papyrus, the production process for preparing parchment manuscripts was an exacting art form:

• Only fine, unflawed skins were chosen;

• Skins were soaked in vats in a solution of slaked lime for several days, after which the wet, slippery skins were scooped out of the vat and draped over a concave frame of wood, hair side up;

• The parchmenter scraped away the hair with a long, curved knife, after which the skin was turned over on the frame and the parchmenter pared away the residue of flesh on the inside of the skin;

- The smooth skin was rinsed in fresh water to wash away the lime;
- The skin was stretched taut on a wooden frame and dried;
- The parchmenter repeatedly scraped the skin until the surface was thin and smooth;
- Finally, the parchment was cut into sheets – usually about 15" high and 9" wide.

The most common **ink** for papyrus was a carbon-based mixture of charcoal and water. However, since carbon inks do not stick well to parchment, a better kind of ink was developed from oak galls and ferrous sulfate. Very expensive **deluxe editions** of manuscripts were sometimes made of vellum dyed a deep purple and written with gold and silver inks.

Scrolls were made by gluing together sheets of papyrus or stitching sheets of parchment and winding these long strips around two dowels. In the case of parchment manuscripts, the pages were stitched together using the tendon fibers of animals. Scrolls could be any length, but they became virtually unmanageable when longer than about 30 feet. (The two longest books in the New Testament, the Gospel of Luke and Acts of the Apostles, would have each filled a papyrus scroll about 30 feet long.) The writing on scrolls was usually arranged in a series of columns approximately 2½ to 3½ inches wide, and in most cases only the lighter side of the writing surface was utilized. Since the text was not divided into chapters and verses, scrolls were cumbersome when it came to finding specific passages.

In Jewish synagogues, scrolls were often covered by a decorated cloth cover and kept in the ark, an indentation in the building's outer wall that faced toward Jerusalem. Archaeological evidence indicates that in early Christian churches, scrolls (and later codices) were kept in a chest.

By the late 1ˢᵗ century A.D. Christian writers and scribes were replacing the scroll with the **codex** as the preferred form for biblical manuscripts. However, scrolls were still used for most non-biblical manuscripts until well into the 3ʳᵈ century, although by the 4ᵗʰ century about 75% of manuscripts were codices. Originally, the codex was developed by the Romans and used for nonliterary texts such as business documents and personal notes. With the codex, sheets of papyrus were folded in half, inserted one inside another, and stitched together to form a **quire**. In the case of more elaborate codices, two or more quires would be glued together at the edge and bound in a leather cover. The codex represented a considerable advancement in the writing, storage and preservation of manuscripts in that it was more compact, more convenient, and more economical as scribes could write on both sides of each page.

A re-creation of an early Gospel of John codex.

Some scholars believe the apostle Paul wrote most of his epistles in papyrus or parchment codices. For instance, in II Timothy 4:13 Paul requests "the books" (Greek: *ta biblia*) and "the parchments" (Greek: *tas membranas* – literally, "animal skins"), a reference to parchment codices. When Paul's letters were collected and passed around among the various churches in the late 1st century, it is likely that the use of the codex made it possible to circulate these texts in a single volume. As Harry Gamble notes in *Books and Readers in the Early Church*, codices functioned as "the handbooks of the Christian community."[1]

Codex Vaticanus, dated to circa 350, divided the Bible into **chapters**, as did the later Codex Alexandrinus (c. 425). This made the process of accessing particular passages considerably more efficient, and around 900 a new edition of the Latin Vulgate incorporated both **chapter and** (unnumbered) **verse divisions** in both the Old and New Testaments. Modern chapter divisions were organized in 1227 by Stephen Langton, a professor at the University of Paris and later Archbishop of Canterbury, but it wasn't until 1551 that chapters were sub-divided into numbered verses when Stephanus (Robert Estienne) produced a new edition of the Greek New Testament. In 1924 Helen Barrett Montgomery edited and published the Centenary Translation of the Bible, which divided the text into paragraphs and included the verse numbers in the margins. Montgomery was a gifted Greek scholar and the first female president of the Northern Baptist Convention (later the American Baptist Churches USA), and her translation may also have been the first to assign titles to chapters and sections of the Bible, which subsequently became a standard practice.

---

[1] Harry F. Gamble, *Books and Readers in the Early Church: A History of Early Christian Texts* (Yale University Press, 1995), p. 50.

Part 1:
Old Testament Manuscripts

The Hebrew National Archives

Compiled over a period of perhaps a thousand years, the **Tanakh** (or Old Testament in the Christian Bible) was essentially the national archives of the Hebrew/Jewish people. Most scholars believe the text of the Old Testament was not static and that these Scriptures were subject to redactions and additions over time. For example, the account of Moses' death and burial in Deuteronomy 34 was an epilogue added some time after the composition of the book itself. The discovery of the Dead Sea Scrolls verified what scholars always suspected: there were several editions of the Hebrew Scriptures in use at the time of Jesus. However, the differences between the various texts were minor, and comprised mostly of differences in spelling and syntax and insignificant copying errors.

Targum. As Aramaic replaced Hebrew as the common language among Jews following the Babylonian Captivity, it eventually became necessary to translate the Tanakh into Aramaic. The targumim were originally oral commentaries on the Tanakh in the Aramaic language, but by the mid-1st century A.D. some rabbis were incorporating these commentaries into paraphrased translations of the Scriptures themselves. The text was never settled, and there is no reliable information regarding who the authors and compilers of the targumim were. Interestingly, all Old Testament books were included in these commentaries except Ezra, Nehemiah, and Daniel.

The Septuagint (c. 250 B.C.). The first translation of the Hebrew Scriptures into another language was the Greek Septuagint (LXX), dated around the middle of the 3rd century B.C. The manuscript evidence indicates that for the most part the Septuagint was not a literal translation. In particular, anthropomorphic references to God were down-played – probably to emphasize the distinctive concept of God in Jewish theology from the mainstream pagan polytheism of other cultures.

In addition to the traditional Hebrew canon, the Septuagint included various intertestamental (or "apocryphal") books, including:

- Greek translations of 3 Hebrew originals – *Tobit*, *Wisdom of Sirach (Ecclesiasticus)*, and *I Maccabees*;

- Several Greek originals, including the *Wisdom of Solomon* and *II*, *III*, and *IV Maccabees*;
- Some supplemental material, including...
  - **Additions to Esther** (the Hebrew version has 167 verses, while the LXX version has 107 additional verses);
  - **Additions to Daniel**, including "Susanna," "Bel and the Dragon," and "The Song of the Three Hebrew Children;" and
- Some abridgements:
  - In the LXX, the Book of Job is about 16% shorter than in the Hebrew text; and
  - The Book of Jeremiah is about 12% shorter.

In addition, the sequential order of books in the LXX differed from the traditional Hebrew Bible, and in this respect it became the model for the Christian Bible.

Christians adopted the Septuagint as their preferred translation of the Hebrew Scriptures, and it essentially functioned as the "Bible" of the early church. When the ancient Jewish Scriptures are quoted in the New Testament, they are usually taken from the LXX version. Christians used the Septuagint to propagate and defend their faith, and some early Church Fathers even declared that the LXX had been divinely inspired and was more accurate than the preserved copies of the Hebrew Bible itself. Therefore, the veracity of the LXX became a central point of contention in the theological disputes between Christians and orthodox Jews. In the mid-2nd century the Christian scholar Justin Martyr charged that Jewish rabbis had altered the texts in subsequent translations of the Septuagint to obscure prophetic references to Christ, and eventually Jews abandoned it completely. As a result, after the 2nd century manuscript copies of the Septuagint were made and preserved by Christian scribes alone.

The Talmud (c. 100-500 A.D.). For several centuries after the Zealot Revolt (66-73 A.D.) and the destruction of the Temple in Jerusalem, Jewish scholars and rabbis wrote extensive commentaries on topics ranging from the Torah to history, philosophy, ethics, and social customs. In the process, Talmudist scribes exercised extreme care in copying the ancient Scriptures. So meticulous were they that the new manuscripts were actually valued more than the older ones because the older copies tended to become defaced and damaged over time and were therefore deemed "unclean."

The Masoretic Text (c. 500-700). Prior to the discovery of the Dead Sea Scrolls in 1947, the Masoretic text was the oldest extant Hebrew version of the Tanakh. (The Hebrew term *masorah* means "transmission.") The Masoretic text was compiled between the 6th and 8th centuries, and it became the standard Hebrew text that is still in use today – including in most modern translations of the Christian Bible. The Masoretic text included 22 books divided into three sections:

(1) The Torah (or Pentateuch): Genesis, Exodus, Leviticus, Numbers, and Deuteronomy.

(2) The Nevi'im (the Prophets): Joshua, Judges, Samuel, Kings, Isaiah, Jeremiah (including Lamentations), Ezekiel, and "The Twelve" (Minor Prophets) – Hosea, Joel, Amos, Obadiah, Jonah, Micah, Nahum, Habakkuk, Zephaniah, Haggai, Zechariah, and Malachi.

(3) The Ketuvim (the "Writings"): Psalms, Proverbs, Job, Song of Songs, Ruth, Esther, Ecclesiastes, Daniel, Ezra/Nehemiah, and Chronicles.

Masorete scribes (literally: the "conveyors of tradition") were meticulous perfectionists who revered the written word. They numbered the verses, words and letters of every book, and as Sir Frederick Kenyon has noted, "These trivialities... had the effect of securing minute attention to the precise transmission of the text.... The Masoretes were indeed anxious that not one jot nor tittle, not one small letter nor one tiny part of a letter of the Law should pass away or be lost."

Masoretes were also diligent textual critics. In the margins of manuscripts they added detailed notes on textual (orthographic) variants and even statistical information on the frequency of certain words. This compendium of marginal notes is referred to as the **Masorah Parva** ("small Masorah"). In addition, they included more extensive notes, the **Masorah Magna** ("large Masorah"), at the top and the foot of each page. This is significant because a comparison of the Masoretic Text to extant copies of the Septuagint shows that there were no substantive alterations of the text through 1300 years of transmission.

Extant Manuscripts

Aleppo Codex (c. 930). One of the oldest Masoretic texts is the Aleppo Codex, which according to tradition was edited by the renowned medieval Jewish scholar Aaron ben Moses ben Asher. The Aleppo Codex is regarded as the most authoritative document in the *masorah* – the tradition of transcribing and preserving the ancient Hebrew Scriptures. But unfortunately, this manuscript is only about 60% complete as large portions have been lost since

1947, including most of the Torah. Hebrew scholars consider the Aleppo Codex to be the most accurate representation of the Masoretic scribal tradition, and it contains very few errors among its 2.7 million orthographic details.

The Aleppo Codex has an interesting history. In the mid-11th century, about a hundred years after it was produced, the Karaite Jewish community in Jerusalem purchased the codex from Israel ben Simha of Basra. A few decades later, in 1099, the synagogue in Jerusalem was plundered during the First Crusade and the codex, along with other manuscripts and hundreds of Jewish survivors, was held ransom. About a year later it was purchased along with 230

Codex Aleppo

other Bible codices, eight Torah scrolls, and a hundred other books by Jews in Cairo, Egypt, where it was preserved in the Rabbanite synagogue and consulted by Jewish scholars. According to our sources, it served as the model for paragraphing and other details of formatting for subsequent transmissions of the Hebrew Scriptures. Reportedly, the great scholar Maimonides used the Aleppo Codex as his model when he wrote his rules for copying Torah scrolls – "The Laws of the Torah Scroll" – in his *Mishneh Torah*.

In 1375 a Jewish scholar took the codex to Aleppo, Syria, where it got its present name. The book remained closely guarded in an iron safe in the synagogue in Syria for nearly 600 years, and was rarely seen by outsiders. In the 1920s the Hebrew scholar Paul Kahle, who was revising the text of the Biblia Hebraica, requested a photographic copy of the codex, but his overtures were rebuffed. Then in 1947 Syrian rioters, enraged by the United Nations' decision to establish a Jewish state in Palestine, burned down the synagogue that housed the Codex Aleppo. The Jews of Aleppo claimed the book was damaged in the

fire, with less than 300 pages of the original 487 pages having survived –
including only the last few pages of the Torah. Curiously, though, forensic
analysis of the manuscript shows no evidence that the fire actually damaged it,
which has led some scholars to suspect that Jews in Aleppo probably tore out
pages to keep as souvenirs. Over the years two "missing" leaves have turned up,
so perhaps more will eventually surface. Fortunately, the codex resurfaced in
1958 when it was smuggled into Israel by a Syrian Jew and presented to the
Israeli president, Yitzhak Ben-Zvi, and it was at this time that it was discovered
that nearly 40% of the book was missing. The Aleppo Codex is currently
housed in the Shrine of the Book at the Israel Museum.

Codex Leningradensis (c. 1008). The oldest complete copy of the
Hebrew Bible is the Codex Leningradensis. A high-quality parchment
manuscript, the book was bound in leather. According to the colophon, the
codex was copied in Cairo from manuscripts written by Aaron ben Moses ben
Asher. Other than Codex Aleppo, which was supposedly edited by ben Asher
himself, Codex Leningradensis is considered the manuscript most faithful to
ben Asher's tradition. Remarkably, the book has been preserved in excellent
condition through the centuries, and it features intricate medieval Jewish art
work. Sixteen of the pages contain decorative geometric patterns – including
one particularly famous graphic on the signature page showing a Star of David
with the names of the scribes on the edges and a blessing written in the middle.

A former owner of the manuscript, Abraham Firkovich, left no information
regarding how, when or where he acquired the book, but we know that in 1838
it was taken to Odessa in Russia, and in 1863 it was transported to the Imperial

Codex Leningradensis signature page

Library in St. Petersburg. Originally called the Codex Petersburgensis, after the Bolshevik Revolution it was renamed the "Leningrad Codex" – an unfortunate irony in that one of the oldest and most treasured of all biblical manuscripts is named for one of the world's most ruthless and notorious atheists. The manuscript is currently preserved in the National Library of Russia in St. Petersburg.

Like the Aleppo Codex, Leningradensis follows the Tiberian textual tradition in the order of its books – except that it includes two additional divisions:

(1) The Torah (or Penteteuch): Genesis, Exodus, Leviticus, Numbers, and Deuteronomy.

(2) The Nevi'im: Joshua, Judges, Samuel, Kings, Isaiah, Jeremiah, Ezekiel, and the "Twelve Prophets" – Hosea, Joel, Amos, Obadiah, Jonah, Micah, Nahum, Habakkuk, Zephaniah, Haggai, Zechariah, and Malachi.

(3) The Ketuvim: Chronicles, Psalms, Job, and Proverbs.

(4) The "Five Megilot" ("Five Scrolls"): Ruth, Song of Songs, Ecclesiastes, Lamentations, and Esther; and

(5) Other "Writings": Daniel and Ezra/Nehemiah.

The Dead Sea Scrolls. Prior to the discovery of Dead Sea Scrolls (DSS) in 1947, scholars understandably questioned the accuracy of the Masoretic text. But with the discovery of the cache of texts near Qumran, skepticism was no longer warranted. Written between 100 B.C. and 50 A.D. – a thousand years before Codex Leningradensis – the Dead Sea Scrolls verify that the ancient texts have been copied and preserved nearly perfectly for at least the past 2,100 years.

The first cluster of Dead Sea Scrolls was discovered in 1947, and eventually some 40,000 fragments were uncovered from more than 500 books. Most of the fragments are portions of non-biblical books, including the "Zadokite documents" and a *Manual of Discipline* for the Qumran community, assumed to have been Essenes. There are about a hundred fragments from Old Testament books, with only the Book of Esther missing. There are multiple fragmentary copies of Genesis, Deuteronomy, and Isaiah, along with various commentaries on the Tanakh.

Perhaps the most significant find was a complete text of the Book of Isaiah, which provided additional confirmation to the accuracy of the Masoretic version. As the Old Testament scholar Gleason Archer later wrote, the Isaiah copies of the Qumran community "proved to be word-for-word identical with our standard Hebrew Bible in more than 95% of the text," and "the 5% variation consisted chiefly of obvious slips of the pen and variations in spelling."

The Isaiah Scroll

The Biblia Hebraica Stuttgartensia (BHS, 1977). The BHS, completed in 1977, is the standard edition of the Hebrew Bible in use today. Based primarily on the Codex Leningradensis, each page contains footnotes on textual variants that are found in the oldest and best Hebrew manuscripts available. Many modern translations of the Christian Bible are also based on the Masoretic text of the Hebrew Bible as found in the Biblia Hebraica.

Part 2:
New Testament Manuscripts

A Wealth of Manuscripts

By comparison to any other ancient texts, the sheer number of New Testament manuscripts is overwhelmingly large.[2] Furthermore, the time interval between the composition of these books and our earliest extant copies is relatively brief by ancient history standards. In fact, several papyrus manuscripts and numerous citations in the writings of the early Church Fathers date to within a century or so of the composition of the original texts.

As of 2016 there were more than 5,850 Greek manuscripts (see the chart on page 254) – about a thousand of which predate the Latin Vulgate translation of the Bible (i.e., circa 390 A.D.). The vast majority of the manuscripts are fragments, and only about sixty contain the entire New Testament, of which the Codex Sinaiticus is the oldest (c. 350 A.D.) and the sole majuscule manuscript. The Book of Revelation is the least attested part of the New Testament, having been preserved in about 300 Greek manuscripts.

In addition to these Greek manuscripts, there are an estimated 12,000 Latin Vulgate translations that date from 390-1500 and fifty Old Latin manuscripts, many of which pre-date the Vulgate. Furthermore, there are more than 8,000 New Testament manuscripts in other languages (see the following section on Extant Vernacular Versions). Adding to this vast collection of documents are thousands of quotations and comments from the Church Fathers of the first four centuries. This is significant because the biblical citations from these sources shed light on the oldest forms of the texts that were in common usage in the second, third and fourth centuries A.D. This is also particularly important to note because even if no manuscripts from the first four centuries had survived, scholars could still reconstruct most of the New Testament from quotations and comments by Christian scholars alone during that period. As the New Testament scholar Bruce Metzger of Princeton Seminary has written:

---

[2] For a comprehensive list of significant New Testament manuscripts, see the website for the Center for the Study of New Testament Manuscripts (CSNTM) at www.csntm.org. Also, see Bruce M. Metzger and Bart D. Ehrman, *The Text of the New Testament: Its Transmission, Corruption, and Restoration.* Fourth Edition (Oxford University Press, 2004).

So extensive are these citations that if all other sources of our knowledge of the text of the New Testament were destroyed, they would be sufficient alone for the reconstruction of practically the entire New Testament. [Metzger and Ehrman, *The Text of the New Testament*, p. 126]

Another valuable but overlooked textual source is **Tatian's** *Diatessaron* (c. 160 A.D.), the first harmony of the four gospels that blended the various accounts into a single narrative. In the process of creating his work, Tatian preserved virtually the entire contents of the four gospels. [Note: Unfortunately, due to the fact that Tatian later associated with a heretical sect, most of his work was destroyed by zealous Christians. Therefore, no complete copy of the *Diatessaron* has survived. A small fragment, dated prior to 250 A.D., was discovered in 1933 in Dura-Europos that indicates that he was working from four separate manuscripts of the gospels. There are also portions of the *Diatessaron* quoted by the Church Fathers.]

New biblical manuscripts are still being discovered. For example, on a 2010 trip to Greece and Romania, Daniel Wallace of the Center for the Study of New Testament Manuscripts (CSNTM) discovered ten new manuscripts, including a 7th century majuscule codex and an 800-page, 20-pound 11th century lectionary. In February 2012 Wallace also announced that a fragment of the Gospel According to Mark had recently been discovered which, if verified as authentic, would be not only the oldest New Testament manuscript ever preserved but the only one that dates to the 1st century. (Presently, our earliest copy of Mark's gospel dates to around 200 A.D.)

Scrolls and Codices. As mentioned earlier, Christian writers were among the first to adopt the codex. Codices were compact, relatively economical, and ideal for circulating collections of books such as the four gospels and the corpus of Paul's epistles. In their book, *Birth of the Codex*, C. H. Roberts and T. C. Skeat contend that it was not until the 4th century that all the books of the Old and New Testaments were combined into a single codex. Prior to that, the most that could be circulated together in a single codex were the four gospels, comprising a little more than 200 pages (or about 100 leaves).[3]

---

[3] C. H. Roberts and T. C. Skeat, *Birth of the Codex* (Oxford University Press, 1987), pp. 62-66.

Extant Vernacular Versions

Greek Manuscripts.

Greek manuscripts can be divided into 4 groups:

(1) **Papyri** are the oldest Greek manuscripts, dating from the 2nd to the 7th centuries. As of 2016 there were 131 papyri manuscripts that had been preserved and catalogued that contain portions of most of the books of the New Testament, a dozen of which date as early as the 2nd century.

(2) **Majuscule** (or **uncial**) manuscripts are written on parchment (or vellum) in all capital letters. This kind of manuscript dates from the 4th to the 9th centuries, and as of 2016 there were 323 of these manuscripts.

(3) **Minuscule** manuscripts were also written on parchment, and the text resembles the Greek equivalent of cursive writing. As of 2016 there were more than 2,900 of these manuscripts. [Note: Why the transition from majuscule to minuscule script? Minuscule letters are smaller, take up less space and could be written more rapidly.]

(4) **Lectionaries**, usually written in minuscule form, are not New Testament manuscripts per se, but they include New Testament passages used in church liturgies or as devotionals or commentaries. As of 2016 nearly 2,500 such lectionaries had been preserved and catalogued.

Of the approximately 5,850 Greek manuscripts catalogued as of 2016:

- Fifty-nine are complete New Testaments – the average length of which is 475 pages;
- Eighteen are 2nd century manuscripts, including 6 discovered within the last decade; and
- More than sixty manuscripts predate 300 A.D.

Fragments from the Dead Sea Scrolls? In 1972 Jose O'Callaghan (1922-2001), a Jesuit Bible scholar and professor of papyrology at the Pontifical Biblical Institute in Rome, analyzed a small fragment from the Dead Sea Scrolls (DSS) and concluded that the text corresponded to Mark 6:52. The fragment, designated 7Q5, contained only 20 Greek letters on 5 lines of text, and came from cave 7 at Qumran, which had been sealed around the year 68 AD during the Zealot Revolt. Over the next few years O'Callaghan thought that 7 other DSS fragments corresponded to various New Testament passages, including 7Q4/I Timothy 3:16-4:3 and 4Q8/James 1:23.

O'Callaghan's sensational claims were controversial, to say the least. If these fragments were actually portions of early Christian writings, they would be the earliest New Testament manuscripts ever discovered. As the *New York Times* reported, "If O'Callaghan's theory is accepted, it would prove that at least one of the Gospels, that of St. Mark, was written only a few years after the death of Jesus." In 1982 the German bibliologist Carsten Peter Thiede (1952-2004) came out in support of O'Callaghan's hypothesis, summarizing his arguments in a 1992 book, *The Earliest Gospel Manuscript? The Qumran Fragment 75Q and Its Significance for New Testament Studies*. However, 7Q5 is so small and of such poor quality that positive identification even of the individual letters is difficult, and most Bible scholars remain skeptical of the claim.

Old Latin Manuscripts (c. 175-400).

The origins of the early Old Latin versions of the New Testament are unknown, but it is likely that the Bible was first translated into Latin in the latter half of the 2nd century A.D. Most of these translations pre-date Jerome's Latin Vulgate of 390 A.D., and they seem to have been the translations used by Latin-speaking Church Fathers such as Irenaeus, Tertullian, and Justin Martyr. There was a proliferation of these versions, and since there are substantial differences between quotations of the same passages, it appears that there was no standard text. In the late 4th century Jerome complained that there were "almost as many forms of the text as there are manuscripts."

Historical records indicate that Old Latin versions of the Scriptures were in circulation in North Africa by circa 200 A.D., and internal evidence reveals that the translations of the Old Testament were based on the Septuagint rather than the Hebrew text. Therefore, the Old Latin versions included the Apocrypha, a tradition that was carried over into the Latin Vulgate. In the New Testament, the gospels were presented in the "Western order" – Matthew, John, Luke and Mark – thereby giving preference to the accounts written by Jesus' disciples.

The Latin Vulgate (c. 390).

The Latin Vulgate was the official Latin (and Roman Catholic) version of the Bible for some 1600 years. In 383 **Damasus I** (r. 366-84), the bishop of Rome, commissioned **Jerome**, one of the most gifted biblical scholars of his generation, to produce an official Latin version of the Bible. For the next thirty years Jerome labored to produce his Latin translation. As a master of Latin and Greek, he based his work on the best Greek and Old Latin manuscripts available. In the process he noted that his greatest challenge came in translating ancient Hebrew into Latin. Therefore, he consulted regularly with a learned Palestinian rabbi, bar-Anina, who visited him at night for fear of his fellow-Jews. Scholars observe that Jerome's translation of some books was better than others: for example, he spent only a single day on apocryphal books such as *Tobit* and *Baruch*.

Jerome strove to produce a translation that was what modern scholars call a "functional (or dynamic) equivalent" of the original languages. He understood that one cannot simply transfer a sentence word-for-word from one language to another as each language has its own unique characteristics, and the challenge of the translator is to rewrite the sentence in accordance with its original intended meaning. In his journal, Jerome noted the rather loose translation of many passages in the Septuagint and the freedom with which New Testament writers often quoted Old Testament passages.

In the process, Jerome set the limits of the Old Testament canon. Out of respect for the Hebrew tradition he delineated the "canonical" books from the "apocryphal" ones – and in fact he would not have bothered to translate the Apocrypha at all had it not been that his benefactor, Bishop Damasas, insisted upon it. [Note: A thousand years later many Protestant reformers preserved this distinction and often omitted the Apocrypha from their vernacular translations.]

Jerome's final product, the Latin Vulgate, was a formidable accomplishment. It served as the standard Roman Catholic version of the Scriptures until well into the 20th century, and it was the first Bible to be produced by Johann Gutenberg on his printing press in 1456. To date, an estimated 12,000 Vulgate manuscripts have been preserved.

Syriac (c. 200).

Sometime around 200 A.D. parts of the New Testament began to circulate in Old Syriac, the common language of Syria and a branch of Aramaic that was akin to Hebrew. Only two manuscripts of this version have survived – the **Sinaitic Syriac** (4th century) and the **Curetonian** (5th century) manuscripts.

Over time, the standard form of the Syriac Bible was called the **Peshitta** ("simple" or "common"). The Peshitta remains the authoritative biblical text of Eastern Syriac churches, including the Syrian Orthodox Church, the Chaldean Church, and the St. Thomas Catholic Church in India. The Peshitta contains only twenty-two New Testament books, excluding the "disputed" books of II Peter, II and III John, Jude and Revelation. A few centuries later the Western Syriac churches incorporated these five books into their **Philoxenian** version of the New Testament in the 6th and 7th centuries. Cumulatively, more than 350 copies of Syriac manuscripts are extant.

Coptic (c. 275).

Until the 3rd century A.D. the Egyptian language was still being written in hieroglyphics and hieratic script, and it was Egyptian Christians who developed the Coptic written language. The first Coptic translations of the Bible were made sometime around the year 300. The Old Testament was probably translated from the Septuagint, and the New Testament portions seem to be based on the Old Latin text. Almost a thousand Coptic manuscripts survive in various dialects, including several fragments of the four gospels that date to the late 3rd century. In the early 20th century archaeologists discovered a large collection of Coptic biblical manuscripts dating from the early 9th century, but many extant copies of Coptic manuscripts were written as recent as the 19th century.

Gothic (c. 300-600).

The Goths were a loose confederation of Germanic tribes that settled in Roman territory between the Rhine and Danube rivers in the late 4th century. Over the next hundred years they were periodically at war with the Romans, and they played a key role in the fall of the Western Empire throughout the 5th century. Nonetheless, under the influence of **Ulfilas** (c. 311-81), the "Apostle to the Goths," large numbers of Goths converted to Arian Christianity in the 4th century. As part of his missionary efforts, Ulfilas developed a Gothic alphabet (composed primarily of Greek and Latin characters) and translated the Bible into the Gothic language. Over time, as the various Gothic tribes were absorbed into other nations, the Gothic language itself became extinct.

Of the six Gothic manuscripts that survive, **Codex Argenteus** (the **Silver Codex**, c. 525) is the most substantive and impressive, and it is one of the premier deluxe copies of the Bible from the entire early medieval era. The Codex contains portions of the four gospels and was written with silver ink on purple parchment. The gospels are presented in the "Western order" – Matthew, John, Luke, and Mark – and the first three lines of each book are written in golden letters. Of the manuscript's original 336 leaves, 188 have survived. With the exception of the Codex Argenteus, all the other Gothic Bible manuscripts are palimpsests. After the Gothic language became extinct, scribes erased or scraped off the writing from these manuscripts and reused the parchment for some other text, leaving only remnants of the former writing still visible.

Codex Argenteus

Armenian (c. 414).

Armenia was the first kingdom to accept Christianity as its official religion. The person most responsible for bringing Christianity to Armenia was **Gregory the Illuminator** (c. 257-331), a member of the royal family who converted to Christianity while living in Caesarea in Cappadocia in the 290s. Toward the end of the 3rd century Gregory returned to Armenia to spread the Gospel, and among his converts was Tiridates I, king of Armenia, who ordered all his subjects to adopt Christianity and be baptized.

The Armenian alphabet and the subsequent translation of the Bible were developed in the early 400s century under the leadership of two men: **Sahak** (c. 350-439), the *catholicos* (primate) of the Armenian Church and a descendant of Gregory the Illuminator; and **Mesrop** (Mesroh or Mashtotz, c. 361-439), a former military officer who became a monk and dedicated his life to scholarship and missionary activity. After creating the Armenian alphabet, Mesrop gathered a team of scholars who he dispatched to Constantinople, Rome, and other Christian centers to procure biblical and other important manuscripts, and an Armenian translation of the Bible was completed around the year 414.

More than 2,000 Armenian manuscripts have been catalogued – more than any ancient version other than the Latin Vulgate and the various Slavonic texts. The earliest manuscript is a copy of the four gospels that dates to 887.

A distinctive of the Armenian Bible is the inclusion of certain books that have otherwise been regarded as apocryphal. The Armenian Old Testament includes the *History of Joseph and Asenath* and the *Testaments of the Twelve Patriarchs*, while the New Testament incorporates the *Epistle of the Corinthians to Paul* and *III Corinthians* – none of which have been accepted as authentic by most Christian scholars or other denominations. Armenian manuscripts also preserve other non-canonical writings such as *The Book of Adam, The History of Moses, The Deaths of the Prophets, Concerning King Solomon, A Short History of the Prophet Elias, Concerning the Prophet Jeremiah, The Vision of Enoch the Just*, and *III Esdras*. [Note: Interestingly, Armenian is the only ancient language that has not changed substantially over the past 2,000 years.]

Georgian (c. 450).

Georgia is located north of Armenia between the Black and Caspian Seas. According to tradition, Christianity was brought to the land in the mid-4th century by Nino, a slave woman who was taken captive by Bakur, the pagan king of Georgia. (Despite some legendary details concerning miracles performed by Nino, historians believe that Christianity first came to Georgia sometime around 350 A.D.)

According to tradition, the same Mesrop who had created an Armenian alphabet and supervised the translation of the Bible into Armenian did the same for the Georgians. Historical specifics aside, most scholars believe the New Testament was translated into Georgian by the mid-5th century, and of the forty-three extant Georgian manuscripts the earliest dates from the late 9th century.

Ethiopic (6th century).

As in most other regions outside the Roman Empire, the origins of Christianity in Ethiopia are obscure. In Acts 8, Philip the Evangelist converted an Ethiopian who was chamberlain to the Candace (or queen) of the Ethiopians, and according to tradition, once he returned home he introduced Christianity to Ethiopia. However, other traditions credit various apostles for evangelizing the Ethiopians.

These traditions aside, the first firm literary evidence for the presence of Christianity in Ethiopia comes from the late 300s. According to Rufinus' *Ecclesiastical History*, during the time of Constantine (r. 312-37) **Frumentius** and **Aedesius** traveled to Axum, the capital of Ethiopia, and converted the royal family. Frumentius then visited Alexandria, where he recruited missionary co-workers and was consecrated the bishop of Ethiopia by Bishop Athanasius. Unlike the stories associated with Armenia, there is no indication that the king of Ethiopia ordered the conversion of all his subjects.

In the latter half of the 400s Monophysite Christians, having been condemned by the Council of Chalcedon in 451 and persecuted by Byzantine officials, found refuge in Ethiopia. In the early 6th century a Christian traveler, Cosmas Indicopleustes, visited Ethiopia and reported that it was thoroughly Christianized. Later in the 500s various evangelists, monks, nuns and hermits migrated into Ethiopia from Egypt and Syria including the so-called **"Nine Saints"** – nine monks who founded monasteries and actively evangelized the populace. According to tradition, the Nine Saints also developed an Ethiopian alphabet and translated the Bible into the native language.

About 600 Ethiopic manuscripts containing portions of the New Testament have survived over the centuries and been catalogued by modern scholars. However, many believe that within Ethiopia perhaps as many as 5,000 manuscripts are yet to be discovered, including several hundred that pre-date the 17th century. The earliest catalogued manuscript dates to the 10th century, and two others date to the 11th century.

Arabic (c. 700s).

Historians have no idea when the first Christian missionaries visited Arabia. Almost certainly, there were Christian churches in the region by the early 200s when the renowned scholar Origen was invited to Arabia to participate in doctrinal discussions over various pseudo-Christian heresies. Some time after that, Christian missionaries, perhaps from Ethiopia, attempted to evangelize among the nomadic bedouin tribes.

Likewise, historians are uncertain when the Scriptures were first translated into Arabic or who was responsible. The assumption is that the earliest translations probably date from sometime in the 8th century.

Slavonic (c. 860s).

According to tradition, two brothers, **Methodius** (c. 815-85) and **Constantine** (later **Cyril**, c. 826-69), traveled to Moravia in the early 860s to evangelize among the various Slavic groups such as the Bulgarians, Serbians, Croats, and Eastern Slavs. Known as "the Apostles to the Slavs," the brothers were Orthodox Christians from Thessalonica, a city that included many Slavic residents at the time.

Constantine gained a university education in Constantinople and became the librarian of the Church of Hagia Sophia. Sometime around 860 a Moravian prince, Rostislav, requested that the Byzantine Emperor Michael III ("The Drunkard") send missionaries to convert and instruct his people. The emperor dispatched Constantine and Methodius, who commenced their ministry in Moravia around 863. The brothers trained Moravians for the clergy, and Constantine devised an alphabet for the Slavonic language and translated the New Testament and various liturgical books into Slavonic.

Almost from the outset the brothers became embroiled in religious turf wars. Catholic authorities in Austria, arguing that only Latin, Greek, and Hebrew were proper liturgical languages, objected to the translation of the liturgy into Slavonic, and eventually the dispute was resolved when Pope Hadrian II ruled in the brothers' favor.

After five years the brothers traveled to Rome, whereupon Constantine fell ill, took monastic vows, and changed his name to Cyril before dying a few weeks later. Methodius returned to Moravia as archbishop, but once more the Catholic hierarchy in Bavaria interfered in his ministry. In fact, he was imprisoned for 2-1/2 years before Pope John VIII intervened and ordered his release. After Methodius died in 885, German Catholic officials banned the use of the Slavonic liturgy in Moravia and suppressed the Orthodox mission. They expelled some of Methodius' followers and sold others into slavery.

The oldest extant Slavic Bible manuscripts date from the late-10th or early-11th centuries. Current estimates of the total number of Slavonic manuscripts vary widely, but scholars agree there are more than 4,000.

Major Greek Manuscripts

Manuscripts (abbreviated MS for singular, MSS for more than one) are classified according to the **CRG** (Caspar Rene Gregory) system, named for the American-born German theologian and papyrologist who in 1908 standardized the taxonomy for biblical manuscripts in *Die Griechischen Handschriften des Neuen Testaments* (*The Greek Manuscripts of the New Testament*).

- **P** indicates a papyrus manuscript;
- Most major parchment codices are assigned a capital letter ('**A**', '**B**', '**C**,' etc.); and
- Zero (**0**) indicates a vellum manuscript.

Extant Ancient Manuscripts

Author	Date	Earliest Fragment or Copy	Time Span	No. of MSS
Homer	c. 900 BC	c. 400 BC	500 years	1,757
Herodotus	c. 440 BC	c. 950 AD	1400 years	109
Thucydides	c. 400 BC	c. 250 BC	150 years	8
Plato	c. 380 BC	c. 900 AD	1280 years	210
Julius Caeser	c. 50 BC	c. 850 AD	900 years	250
Livy	c. 10 AD	c. 420 AD	400 years	160
Tacitus	c. 110 AD	c. 850 AD	750 years	33
New Testament *	c. 50-95 AD	c. 125 AD	30 years	25,000+

Extant Greek New Testament Manuscripts

Type	Approx. dates	No. of MSS (1965)	No. of MSS (2016)
Papyri	c. 2nd - 7th century	78	131
Majuscule	c. 4th - 9th century	247	323
Minuscule	c. 8th -15th century	2,623	2,936
Lectionaries	2nd century and later	1,968	2,465
Total		4,916	5,855

* This figure includes an estimated 12,000 Latin MSS, more than 8,000 MSS in other languages (Syriac, Coptic, Gothic, Armenian, Georgian, Ethiopic, Arabic, Slavonic, etc.), and approximately 5,850 Greek MSS.

Sources: Clay Jones, "The Bibliographical Test Updated." *Christian Research Journal*, Vol. 35, No. 3 (2012), and William Warren, Center for New Testament Textual Studies.

John Rylands Manuscript (P52, c. 125)

The John Rylands manuscript (P52), a portion of John 18, is the oldest verified fragment of the New Testament that has been discovered. The scrap is tiny, measuring only 2½" x 3½", and it contains portions of 5 verses, including Jesus' testimony before Pilate: "...[F]or this I came into the world, to testify to the truth. Everyone on the side of truth listens to me" (John 18:37). The manuscript seems to confirm the traditional belief that John's gospel was composed near the end of the 1ˢᵗ century, and quite appropriately, the text itself serves as a testimony to the truth of the Gospel of Jesus Christ!

P52 was discovered in Egypt and purchased in 1920 by Bernard Grenfell, who donated it to the John Rylands Library in Manchester, England. For several years it lay unnoticed in a file cabinet until C. H. Roberts of Saint John's College, Oxford, noticed it in 1934 while sorting through papyri fragments in the library. Based on the style of its script, Roberts dated it to the first half of the 2ⁿᵈ century, and most scholars today accept a date of between 120-130.

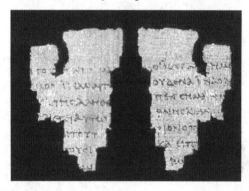

Chester Beatty Papyri (c. 200-250)

Most of the Chester Beatty Papyri are housed in the Chester Beatty Library in Dublin, Ireland. Discovered in 1930, the CBP are estimated to be about 100-150 years older than the Codex Sinaiticus, which verify that the New Testament text of the early 3ʳᵈ century was essentially identical to that of later translations. The CBP include 3 codices that contain major portions of the New Testament:

- **Papyrus I (P45**, c. 220) is 30 leaves out of an original 220-page papyrus book, consisting of parts of the Four Gospels and Acts including our earliest manuscript of Mark's Gospel.[4]

---

[4] For an in-depth analysis of P45, see Michael Horton, ed., *The Earliest Gospels: The Origins and Transmissions of the Earliest Christian Gospels – The Contribution of the Chester Beatty Gospel Codex P45* (T&T Clark International, 2004).

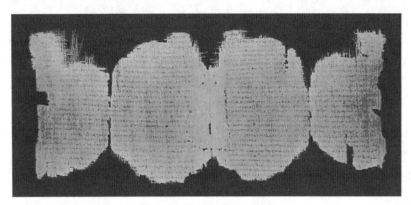

Chester Beatty Papyrus I

- **Papyrus II (P46,** c. 200) has 86 pages of what was originally a 104-page papyrus book, and contains the oldest extant copy of 8 Pauline epistles and part of the Epistle to the Hebrews. Dated slightly earlier than Papyrus I, it probably originated around the year 200. The manuscript is a single quire, and the epistles are arranged in order of decreasing length (as in the New Testament).

Chester Beatty Papyrus II

- **Papyrus III (P47,** c. 250) is a portion of the Book of Revelation, consisting of 10 leaves of what was originally a 32-page quire. This is the oldest extant manuscript of John's Apocalypse other than some small earlier fragments.

Bodmer Manuscripts (c. 175-300)

The Bodmer collection of papyri, purchased by the Swiss bibliophile Martin Bodmer, are located in the Bodmer Library of World Literature in Geneva, Switzerland.

- **Papyrus P66** (c. AD 200) contains nearly all of the first 14 chapters of the Gospel of John – about 108 pages. Several passages in P66 include unique readings not found in other manuscripts. [See Bruce Metzger and Bart D. Ehrman, *The Text of the New Testament*, p. 57.]

- **Papyrus P75** (c. 175-225) is a single-quire codex of Luke and John. The codex includes 102 pages of an original text of 144 pages. This is the earliest-known copy of Luke and one of the earliest of John.

- **Papyrus P72** (3rd century) contains the epistles of Peter and Jude.

Bodmer MS
P66

Oxyrhynchus Papyri (c. 150-500)

The Oxyrhynchus Papyri are thousands of Greek and Latin documents that were discovered in 1896 in a garbage dump near Oxyrhynchus in Egypt (modern-day el-Bahnasa). Many of these documents were first discovered by the archaeologists Bernard Pyne Grenfell and Arthus Surridge Hunt, and the manuscripts date from the 2nd to the 6th centuries. The collection is currently housed in several libraries and museums around the world, with the Ashmolean Museum at Oxford University having the largest single collection.

The Oxyrhynchus Papyri include some of the earliest extant fragments of some New Testament manuscripts. For example, on only their second day of excavation, Grenfell and Hunt discovered P1, a portion of Matthew 1 that dates to circa 250.

Among the many Old Testament papyri fragments are an Old Latin version of Genesis (Vol. VIII, No. 10723). There are also Septuagint versions of Genesis (IV, 656; VII, 1007; VIII, 1073; IX, 1166; IX, 1167); fragments of Exodus (VIII, 1074; VIII 1075; LXV, 4442); Leviticus 16 (X, 1225); Joshua 4-5 (IX, 1168); Esther 6-7 (LXV, 4443); Job 42:11-12 (L, 3522); Psalm 1 (XV, 1779); Psalms 7-8 (X, 1226); Psalm 68 (VI, 845); Psalm 75 (LX, 4011); Psalms 82-84 (XI, 1352; XXIV, 2386); Psalm 90 (XVI, 1928; XVII, 2065); Ecclesiastes 6-7 (XVII, 2066); and Amos 2 (VI, 846).

In addition, portions of the Old Testament Apocrypha include *Baruch, II Esdras, Tobit, Wisdom of Sirach* (*Ecclesiasticus*), *I Enoch*, and the *Wisdom of Solomon*.

Included among the Oxyrhynchus Papyri are 124 registered New Testament fragments, including...

- Matthew 1 (P1) – circa 250;
- Matthew 6 (0170) – circa 500;
- Matthew 10-11 (P19) – c. 400;
- Matthew 10-11 (071) – c. 500;
- Matthew 12 (P21) – c. 400;
- Matthew 21(?) (P104) – c. 150;
- Mark 10-11 (069) – c. 500;
- Luke 22 (P69) – c. 250;
- John 1 (P5) – c. 250;
- John 2 (0162) – c. 300;
- John 15-16 (P22) – c. 250;
- Acts 26 (P29) – c. 250;
- Romans 1 (P10) – c. 350;
- I Corinthians 7-8 (P15) – c. 250:
- I Thess. 4-5 and II Thess. 1 (P30) – c. 250;
- Galatians 1 (P51) – c. 400;
- Philippians 3-4 (P16) – c. 300;
- Hebrews 2-5, 10-12 (P13) – c. 250;
- Hebrews 9 (P17) – c. 350;
- James I (P23) – c. 250;
- James 2-3 (P20) – c. 250;
- I Peter 5 (0206) – c. 350;
- I John 4 (P9) – c. 250;

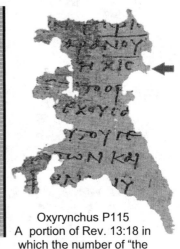

Oxyrynchus P115
A portion of Rev. 13:18 in which the number of "the Beast" is 616 rather than the more common 666.

- Jude (P78) – c. 300;
- Revelation 13:18 (P115) – c. 300;
- Revelation 1 (p18) – c. 300;
- Revelation 3-4 (0169) – c. 350;
- Revelation 5-6 (p24) – c. 350; and
- Revelation 16 (0163) – c. 450.

Among the approximately 20 non-canonical Christian works are...

- *The Shepherd* of Hermas (P404) – 3rd or 4th century;
- *The Didache*;
- *Gospel According to the Hebrews* (P655) – 3rd century;
- *Protoevangelium of James*;
- *Acts of Paul and Thecla*; and
- "The Letter of Abgar to Jesus."

Supplemental to these Christian writings are various manuscripts containing prayers, hymns and letters.

Several Gnostic writings are also part of the Oxyrhynchus collection:

Oxy 654 – a fragment of the earliest-known *Gospel of Thomas* (c. 225)

- *Gospel of Mary [Magdalene]*;
- *Gospel of Peter*;
- *Acts of Peter*;
- *Acts of John*;
- *Acts of Paul*;
- *Sophia of Jesus Christ*; and
- *The Gospel of Thomas*. The three Thomas manuscripts are particularly significant because they are the only extant Greek translations of the book in existence – the only other version being a nearly complete Coptic manuscript from the Nag Hammadi collection.

The Oxyrhynchus collection also includes many significant extra-biblical works of antiquity, including the oldest and most complete diagrams from Euclid's *Elements*; poems by the celebrated poet, Pindar; fragments of the works of Sappho and Alcaeus; fragments of the works of the Athenian playwright Menander (342-291 BC); and 7 of the 107 lost books of the Roman historian Livy.

Codex Sinaiticus ('א', c. 350)[5]

Codex Sinaiticus, a high-quality parchment manuscript that contains most of the Old Testament and all of the New Testament, is the most significant biblical manuscript ever discovered. In fact, it is the only complete edition of the Greek New Testament in majuscule script. Some scholars believe that it might have been one of the 50 deluxe edition pulpit Bibles commissioned by the Roman Emperor Constantine (r. 312-37) in 331 for placement in prominent churches throughout the empire.

The text of Codex Sinaiticus is a true work of art, laid out beautifully in four columns per page. The Old Testament portion of the book is the Septuagint translation (including the Apocrypha), and the manuscript includes two extra-biblical Christian texts: the *Epistle of Barnabas* and *The Shepherd* of Hermas.

Discovered in 1844 by Constantin von Tischendorf, a professor at the University of Leipzig, Codex Sinaiticus essentially laid the foundation for the most accurate text of the New Testament ever known. (See the following sidebar, "Constantin von Tischendorf and the Codex Sinaiticus.") Most of the manuscript is housed in the British Library in London.

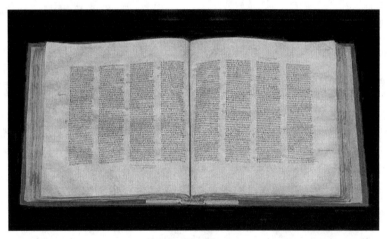

Codex Sinaiticus

---

[5] Since the time of Bishop Brian Walter of Chester, England and the publication of his popular *Polyglot Bible* (*Biblia Sacra Polyglotta*, 1655-57), capital letters of the alphabet had been used to designate majuscule manuscripts (e.g., 'A' for Codex Alexandrinus, 'B' for Codex Vaticanus, etc.). However, when Tischendorff discovered Codex Sinaiticus, he regarded the manuscript as so significant that he assigned it the letter *Aleph* (א), the first letter of the Hebrew alphabet.

Constantin von Tischendorf and The Codex Sinaiticus

One of the most impressive and extensive collections of ancient Biblical manuscripts is in the library of the University of Glasgow in Scotland. The Glasgow collection was purchased from Trinity College in Glasgow, which originally bought the collection of Constantin von Tischendorf (1815-74), a professor at the University of Leipzig in Germany, in 1877 for £460. Although a prized collection, the papers were locked away in a library cupboard, uncatalogued and all but forgotten, for a hundred years. Then in 1974, when Trinity College had fallen into a state of disrepair and was nearly collapsing, the papers were rediscovered and presented to the University of Glasgow.

The papers told a fascinating story that began in 1839 when the young Tischendorf started his search for ancient manuscripts in order to reconstruct as accurately as possible the original text of the New Testament. Many of the great libraries of Europe had lain undisturbed for centuries, and Tischendorf had a hunch that if he could gain access to some of them he would be able to rediscover ancient biblical manuscripts that had been ignored or forgotten for generations.

Tischendorf was a dedicated and passionate scholar who saw his work as a ministry. While still in his twenties he had written his fiancé, "I am confronted with a sacred task, the struggle to regain the original form of the New Testament." To that end, he made numerous trips around Europe and into the Middle East, transcribing and publishing the manuscripts he located.

At the National Library of Paris, he came across the **Codex Ephraemi**, one of the oldest extant New Testament manuscripts. The vellum codex had originally contained the entire Bible, but much has been lost. However, all of the New Testament was still intact other than II Thessalonians and II John. The codex was originally a 5th century Greek manuscript of the New Testament, but it had been erased in the 12th century so its pages could be reused to record sermons by the Syriac church father Ephraim. Although the pages had been erased, some of the underwriting was still visible, although most of it was illegible. By the time Tischendorf encountered the document, chemical reagents had been developed that could help expose the underwriting. Tischendorf painstakingly applied the reagents and produced the first transcription of the text.

Buoyed by this discovery, Tischendorf decided to scour the monasteries of North Africa and the Middle East in search of more. He traveled first to Venice, Modena, Milan, Verona, Turin and Rome, searching their libraries. In the process he discovered many significant manuscripts. In Florence he came across a copy of the Bible translated into Latin by the 4th-century Italian scholar Jerome while living in a cave in Bethlehem.

In 1844 Tischendorff arrived on camelback at the **Monastery of St. Catherine** at the base of **Mt. Sinai**, where he came across fragments of some of the most valuable ancient manuscripts ever discovered. As he related the story:

It was at the foot of Mt. Sinai, in the Convent of St. Catherine, that I discovered the pearl of all my researches. In visiting the library of the monastery.... I perceived in the middle of the great hall a large and wide basket full of old parchments; and the librarian who was a man of information told me that two stacks of papers like these, mouldered by time, had already been burned....

To Tischendorff's amazement, these old papers were fragments of the Septuagint written in majuscule script – and among the oldest fragments he had ever seen. When he attempted to persuade the monks to give him all the papers in the trash basket, they became suspicious and only allowed him to take about forty pages, including portions of I Chronicles, Jeremiah, Nehemiah and Esther. Fortunately, he did succeed in persuading them not to burn any more of the manuscript.

For the next several years he corresponded occasionally with the monks at St. Catherine's, but was unable to obtain the documents. Nine years later he returned to the monastery to hand-copy the documents, but although the monks received him with great hospitality he could find no trace of the manuscripts he sought. Finally, he appealed to Tsar Alexander II of Russia for assistance, under whose authority the monastery at Mt. Sinai functioned. Due to the fact that he was a Protestant, many Orthodox Church officials in St. Petersburg opposed the project, but in 1859 he finally secured the support of the Tsar and returned to the monastery. After several days of fruitless searching, he finally found what he had come for. In a conversation with the convent's steward, Tischendorf brought up the issue of the Septuagint, which prompted the monk to remark, "I too have read a Septuagint" – whereupon he retrieved from a closet in the room a manuscript wrapped in red cloth. As Tischendorf later recounted...

I unrolled the cover and discovered, to my great surprise, not only those very fragments which, fifteen years earlier, I had taken out of the basket, but also other parts of the Old Testament, the complete New Testament, and in addition, the *Epistle of Barnabas* and part of *The Shepherd* of

Hermas. [Note: Until this time *The Shepherd* of Hermas was known only by its title, as it was often mentioned in the writings of the Church Fathers.] Full of joy, which this time I had the self-command to conceal from the steward and the rest of the [monastic] community, I casually asked for permission to take the manuscript into my sleeping chamber to look over it more closely at my leisure. There by myself I could give way to the great joy which I felt. I knew that I held in my hand the most precious biblical treasure in existence....

The next morning Tischendorf attempted to buy the manuscript, but his offer was rebuffed. Likewise, over the next few months he continued to negotiate but to no avail. Finally, after assuring the monks that his patron, Tsar Alexander II, would reciprocate with generous gifts to the monastery, he was allowed to take the manuscript back to Leipzig. There, he edited and prepared a lavish four-volume edition of the Codex Sinaiticus that he presented to the Tsar in 1862 on the one thousandth anniversary of the founding of the Russian empire. [Note: For their part, the monks of St. Catherine's Monastery contended that Tischendorf was never actually given the manuscript, but absconded with it.]

Tischendorf received worldwide acclaim, and he was convinced that God had used him to preserve this ancient treasure. As he described it:

While so much had been lost in the course of centuries, by time or by the carelessness of ignorant monks, an invisible eye watched over this treasure and when it was on the point of vanishing in the fire, the Lord decreed its deliverance.

In 1933 the Soviet government, desperate for capital and disinterested in biblical artifacts, sold the Tischendorf collection to the British Museum for £100,000.

Codex Sinaiticus laid the foundation for the most accurate text of the New Testament ever known. The manuscript was written in Greek circa 350 A.D. and contains all the New Testament as well as most of the Old. Since then, even more significant papyrus manuscripts have been discovered, some of which predate the Codex Sinaiticus by as much as 150 years, although most are fragmentary. But the Codex Sinaiticus is still the most complete ancient Bible manuscript in existence.

Post-script: In 1975 many more manuscripts were discovered at the Monastery of St. Catherine. Biblical scholars gained access to a sealed room in the compound and found more than 1,000 manuscripts in various languages, of which 836 were Greek New Testament manuscripts – including 12 more missing leaves from the Codex Sinaiticus.

Codex Vaticanus ('B', c. 350)

Codex Vaticanus is a high-quality parchment text and, along with Codex Sinaiticus, one of the two most important biblical manuscripts in the world. Originally, Vaticanus was a complete Bible, but portions have been lost over the centuries, including most of Genesis, thirty of the Psalms, the latter part of Hebrews, and all of I and II Timothy, Titus, Philemon, and Revelation. As with Sinaiticus, some scholars believe that Vaticanus could be one of the premier vellum Bibles that Constantine commissioned Eusebius to produce in the early 330s.

Like Codex Sinaiticus, Vaticanus includes all the books of the intertestamental Apocrypha except the books of the Maccabees. This is odd because *I and II Maccabees* were regarded as among the most revered of the Apocryphal texts.

Originally written in small and thin majuscule script, the beauty of the text was spoiled by a later corrector who traced over every letter to darken the script.

The manuscript has been housed in the Vatican Library in Rome since at least 1475.

[Note: Vaticanus is dated about the same time as Sinaiticus and is similar, but there are thousands of variants between the two manuscripts.]

A page from Codex Vaticanus

Codex Alexandrinus ('A' / c. 425)

Codex Alexandrinus, dated about 75 years after Sinaiticus and Vaticanus, was originally a complete Bible, but several sections have been lost. The manuscript contains virtually the entire Old Testament and most of the New Testament except for Matt. 1-25:6; John 6:50-8:52; and II Cor. 4:13-12:6.

In addition to the canonical Bible, Alexandrinus includes three other texts: *I Clement*, *II Clement*, and the *Psalms of Solomon*.

In 1627 the patriarch of Constantinople presented the manuscript to King Charles I of England, and the manuscript is currently housed in the British Library.

Codex Alexandrinus

Codex Ephraemi ('C' / c. 450)

Housed at the National Library in Paris, Codex Ephraemi is a vellum codex that originally contained the entire Bible, although much has been lost. The manuscript includes portions of all New Testament books other than II Thessalonians and II John.

Codex Ephraemi is a palimpsest. Originally, it was a 5th century Greek manuscript of the New Testament, but the words were scraped off in the 12th century so it could be reused to record the texts of some sermons by the Syriac church father, Ephraem. Although the original words had been "erased" and were illegible, some of the underwriting was still visible. By the time Constantin von Tischendorf (1815-74) came across the document in 1843, chemical reagents had been developed that could help expose the underwriting. Tischendorf applied the reagents and was able to produce the first transcription of the text.

A portion of Codex Ephraemi

Codex Bezae ('D' / c. 450)

Codex Bezae is a unique manuscript that features parallel Greek and Latin texts on opposite pages. The manuscript contains most of the Four Gospels and Acts, along with a small fragment of III John. The Gospels are arranged in the "Western Order" – Matthew, John, Luke, and Mark – that gives preference to the narratives written by apostles.

Many text scholars believe the manuscript originated in France in the mid-to-late 5th century, and Bezae is known for its bizarre and eccentric variant readings. The text includes numerous additions and/or deletions of words, sentences, and even entire *pericopes* (a set of verses or a single passage that form a coherent unit or thought). For example, the text of the Acts of the Apostles is nearly 10% longer than the generally accepted text. The manuscript's unusual features have baffled scholars for centuries, and as Bruce Metzger admits, "There is still no unanimity of opinion regarding the many problems that the manuscript raises."

Codex Bezae is named for Theodore Beza, the French Reformation scholar and successor to Calvin who presented the manuscript to the Cambridge University Library in 1581.

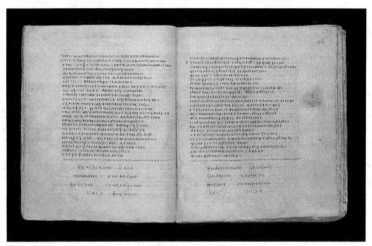

Codex Bezae

Codex Washingtonianus ('W' / c. 475?)

Codex Washingtonianus is an intriguing manuscript. It was discovered in Hierapolis, Egypt in 1906, and sold by an Arab antiquities dealer to Charles L. Freer of Detroit, Michigan. Since 1906 it has been housed in the Freer Gallery of Art of the Smithsonian Institution in Washington, D.C.

The manuscript contains all Four Gospels but none of the epistles. Like Codex Bezae, the Gospels are arranged in the "Western Order" of Matthew, John, Luke, and Mark, and like Codex Sinaiticus and Codex Vaticanus, 'W' does not include the controversial *Pericope Adulterae* of John 7:53-8:12. But unlike those two codices, 'W' includes a longer ending to Mark 16 – the so-called "Freer Logion" of 89 words inserted between Mark 16:14-15.

[14]Afterward He appeared to the eleven as they were eating and reproved them for their lack of faith and stubbornness because they had not believed those who saw Him after He had risen. *[14a] And they made excuses, saying,"This age of lawlessness and unbelief is under Satan, who by means of unclean spirits does not allow men to grasp the truth and power of God. Therefore, reveal now your righteousness." Thus they spoke to Christ. [14b] And Christ replied to them,"The term of years of Satan's power is completed, but other terrible things draw near. [14c] And for those who have sinned I was handed over to death, in order that they might return to the truth and sin no more; in order that they might inherit the spiritual and incorruptible glory of righteousness which is in heaven."*

[15]Then He said to them, "Go into all the world and preach the gospel to every creature...."

[Note: In 2006 two biblical scholars, Lee Woodard and James Rutz, announced that Codex 'W' actually contains the original 1st century autographs. According to them, "The Greek text of 'W' is... the original hub from which all other ancient versions of the gospels are drawn." They also claimed that "roughly 80 pages of the 372-page codex contain tiny explanatory notes in Aramaic Hebrew, written for the benefit of Christian Jews in Egypt and elsewhere who were less familiar with Greek," and that "by A.D. 150-165, that language was so nearly displaced by other languages that no substantial community of believers remained who would have benefitted from the many notes."

Woodard and Rutz also asserted that Irenaeus, Clement of Alexandria, and Origen all cited verses peculiar to Codex 'W' exclusively. But their most sensational claim is that each of the gospels in Codex 'W' was signed by the original author and dated using the old Roman dating system! Woodard and Rutz are lobbying to have the manuscript carbon-14 dated to determine its age, but suffice it to say that no notable Bible scholars have yet accepted their hypothesis.]

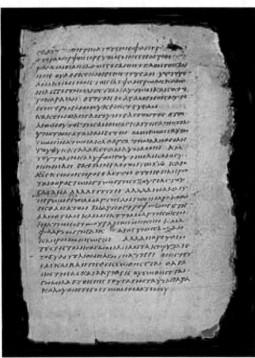

7

Biblical Textual Criticism

Has the Bible Been Accurately Preserved and Transmitted Through the Centuries?

Introduction

Biblical Textual Criticism

When you read the Bible or hear it referred to in church as "the Word of God," how do you know what you're reading or hearing is what the authors of the Bible originally wrote? Are there good reasons to believe that the Bible has been accurately preserved and transmitted through the centuries, or has the biblical text been seriously corrupted over time? This is the field of study known as biblical textual criticism, and it is one of the most controversial and important areas in the whole field of Bibliology.

For most Christians the term biblical textual criticism is an unfamiliar concept, and in fact it can be quite misleading. "Criticism" usually connotes something negative – as in "to find fault with," but as it is used by biblical scholars it simply refers to biblical textual evaluation or analysis. Stated succinctly: **Biblical textual criticism is the art and science of comparing the variant readings in biblical manuscripts so as to restore, as closely as possible, the original wording in the original text.**

Biblical textual criticism is a tedious and complex process, but it is absolutely essential for two reasons:

(1) None of the original biblical documents is extant.

(2) The existing copies that we have all contain variant readings. In other

words, in the process of being hand-copied from generation-to-generation, the texts were altered. Therefore, it is necessary to compare the variant readings in order to determine as accurately as possible what the texts originally said.

Furthermore, there are three reasons why biblical textual criticism is such a crucial issue for Christians:

(1) The Christian faith makes exclusive claims which, if valid, renders it the only belief system in the world that is true. If these claims are untrue, the Christian faith is a fraud.

(2) These truth claims – including virtually everything we believe about God, the human condition, the character and mission of Christ, and the path to salvation – depend upon the veracity of the Bible.

(3) If the biblical texts have been corrupted in the transmission process through the centuries, then the Christian faith is on very shaky ground and we can have little confidence in terms of what the Bible teaches about the nature of God, the condition of man, the meaning and purpose of life, objective morality, how we can be spiritually related to God, or our eternal destiny. In other words, if the Bible is not a reliable source for what to believe and how to live our lives, everything is relative and subjective, and we are truly adrift on the vast ocean of life.

The Controversy

Biblical textual criticism has been a contentious controversy for over 200 years and a major line of demarcation between theological conservatives and liberals. This is not a minor issue, as theological conservatism and liberalism represent diametrically opposite interpretations of the Bible that have both theological and moral ramifications.

In brief, theological conservatives generally hold to the following beliefs about the Bible:

- The Bible is unique among all religious texts in that its authors were divinely-inspired by the Holy Spirit;
- The Bible is historically reliable;
- The Bible is doctrinally authoritative;
- The Bible includes moral absolutes that are universally applicable; and
- God has preserved the integrity of the biblical texts throughout history.

In contrast, theological liberals, while representing a wide range of views, generally hold to the following precepts:

- The Bible is one of the great religious texts in history, but nonetheless a book of purely human origins;
- The Bible contains some accurate history, but also much legend and mythology;
- The Bible is not necessarily doctrinally authoritative when it comes to our understanding of God and humanity;
- The Bible contains some profound moral wisdom, but also some antiquated social and moral values that are no longer appropriate; and
- The Bible has been so corrupted in the transmission process through the centuries as to be unreliable.

All biblical textual scholars, both conservative or liberal, agree that there are substantial variations in the ancient manuscripts that have been passed down to us. Most of these variations in the texts resulted from copying accidents as a result of poor eyesight, poor hearing, or poor concentration due to fatigue on the part of copyists. However, some variants were intentional and resulted from attempts to clarify vague passages, correct syntax, grammar, and spelling, harmonize parallel passages, or correct historical or geographical references that were thought to be erroneous. Other changes were theologically motivated as when copyists modified a passage to emphasize a particular doctrine or to counter a particular heresy – an issue discussed in more detail in Part 2.

This has led liberal scholars to make some exaggerated and unsupportable claims regarding what they consider to be the corruption of Scripture. For example, Robert Funk, the former chair of the radical Jesus Seminar, wrote in the Introduction of the group's seminal work, *The Five Gospels*, "Even careful copyists make mistakes, as every proofreader knows. So we will never be able to claim certain knowledge of exactly what the original text of any biblical writing was."[1]

The controversies over textual criticism have even spawned conspiracy theories regarding the writing and preservation of the Bible, such as this bit of absurd revisionism from the popular 1980s book, *Holy Blood, Holy Grail* (one of the major influences on Dan Brown's infamous *Da Vinci Code*):

> In A.D. 303... the pagan emperor Diocletian had undertaken to destroy all Christian writings that could be found. As a result Christian documents – especially in Rome – all but vanished. When Constantine commissioned new versions of these documents, it enabled the custodians of orthodoxy to revise, edit, and rewrite their material as they saw fit, in accordance with

---

[1] Robert W. Funk, *The Five Gospels: What Did Jesus Really Say? The Search for the Authentic Words of Jesus* (HarperOne, 1996), p. 6.

their tenets. It was at this point that most of the crucial alterations in the New Testament were probably made and Jesus assumed the unique status he has enjoyed ever since. [Michael Baigent, Richard Leigh, and Henry Lincoln, *Holy Blood, Holy Grail* (Dell, 1983), pp. 368-69.]

This kind of crackpottery aside, the issue of textual variants is a legitimate issue that deserves serious treatment. We shall do this at length later in this chapter. But at this point, I should simply note that the ultimate issue – and the point to be emphasized – is that the controversy has nothing to do with whether there are variant readings in various biblical manuscripts. That fact is undeniable. **But what matters is this: How significant are these changes, and do they alter our understanding of Christ or affect any fundamental Christian doctrine?** My contention is that they are not significant, nor do they necessitate a reevaluation of any traditional core belief that true Christians have held throughout history.

Part 1:
The Case for Biblical Deconstructionism...
and Reconstructionism

Bart Ehrman and Misquoting Jesus

One of the latest and most influential contemporary scholars to weigh-in on the subject of biblical textual criticism is Bart D. Ehrman, chair of the Religious Studies Department at the University of North Carolina. Ehrman typifies what conservative New Testament scholar Craig Blomberg of Denver Seminary describes as "the most radical wing of New Testament scholarship," a position that has received a disproportionate amount of publicity in recent years. A prolific and best-selling author, Ehrman argues for a radical revisionist (or deconstructionist) view of the Bible in books such as *The Orthodox Corruption of Scripture* (1993), *Lost Christianities* (2003), and most notably, *Misquoting Jesus: The Story Behind Who Changed the Bible and Why* (2005).

Part of Ehrman's appeal is his personal testimony in which he claims that he was once a Bible-believing Christian who drifted away from the faith once he began studying the origins and transmission of the Bible in depth. Now, as a passionate apostle of skepticism, he contends that the Bible has been so corrupted over time in the transmission process as to be unreliable. Being a New Testament scholar, Ehrman rarely addresses issues related to the Old Testament, but it is reasonable to assume that his skepticism regarding the historical and textual reliability of the New Testament would apply even more to the ancient Hebrew Scriptures. According to Ehrman, we can have little confidence that what we read today correlates to what was actually written 2,000 years ago by the gospel writers and apostles. This is a controversial position but one that appeals to a large segment of the public that eagerly embraces any scholarly (or pseudo-scholarly) claims that tend to discredit the Bible and the Christian faith. His audacious critiques of the Bible are also guaranteed to propel him into the limelight as a popular media celebrity, just as they assure that his books will top the bestseller charts.

When *Misquoting Jesus* debuted, the *Dallas Morning News* hailed Ehrman as "a new breed of biblical scholar." In fact, nothing could be further from the truth. Bible skeptics have been around since the 2nd century, but especially in the last 250 years there is absolutely nothing novel or original about biblical deconstructionism. Nonetheless, scholars such as Ehrman generate considerable excitement among secularists and skeptics. As *Publishers Weekly* gushed in its review of the book, "Readers might never read the gospels or Paul's letters the same way again."[2] Certainly, the cover blurb of *Misquoting Jesus* emphasized the provocative nature of the book:

> When world-class Bible scholar Bart Ehrman first began to study the texts of the Bible in their original languages he was startled to discover the multitude of mistakes and intentional alterations that had been made by earlier translators.
>
> In *Misquoting Jesus*, Ehrman tells the story behind the mistakes and changes that ancient scribes made to the New Testament and shows the great impact they had upon the Bible we use today. He frames his account with personal reflections on how his study of the Greek manuscripts made him abandon his once ultraconservative views of the Bible.
>
> Since the advent of the printing press and the accurate reproduction of texts, most people have assumed that when they read the New Testament they are reading an exact copy of Jesus's words or Saint Paul's writings. And yet, for almost 1500 years these manuscripts were hand copied by scribes who were deeply influenced by the cultural, theological, and political disputes of their day.
>
> Both mistakes and intentional changes abound in the surviving manuscripts, making the original words difficult to reconstruct.
>
> For the first time [!] Ehrman reveals where and why these changes were made and how scholars go about reconstructing the original words of the New Testament as closely as possible.
>
> Ehrman makes the provocative case that many of our cherished biblical stories and widely held beliefs concerning the divinity of Jesus, the Trinity, and the divine origins of the Bible itself stem from both intentional and accidental alterations by scribes – alterations that dramatically affected all subsequent versions of the Bible.

In the text, Ehrman questions whether we can trust that the Bible has been properly translated over time:

> How do we know what was originally in the Bible?.... How do millions of people know what is in the New Testament? They "know" because scholars with unknown names, identities, backgrounds, qualifications, predilections, theologies, and personal opinions have told them what is in the New Testament. But what if the translators have translated the text wrong? [Bart D. Ehrman, *Misquoting Jesus* (HarperOne, 2005), p. 208*ff.*]

[2] http://www.amazon.com/Misquoting-Jesus-Story-Behind-Changed/dp/0060859512/ref=sr_1_1?s=books&ie=UTF8&qid=1398871312&sr=1-1&keywords=bart+d.+ehrman%2C+misquoting+jesus

Problematic Manuscripts

Skeptics such as Ehrman argue that the fact that we have no original biblical manuscripts presents an insurmountable problem for belief in the Bible. As he frames the issue:

> How does it help us to say that the Bible is the inerrant word of God if in fact we don't have the words that God inerrantly inspired, only the words copied by the scribes – sometimes correctly but sometimes (many times!) incorrectly? What good does it say that the autographs [i.e., the originals] were inspired? We don't have the originals! We have only error-ridden copies, and the vast majority of these are centuries removed from the originals." [Ibid., p. 7.]

These and other allegations by liberal scholars present serious challenges to the textual integrity, the reliability, and the authority of the Bible. Until the dawn of the printing press in the last half of the 15th century, all copies of the Bible had been hand-copied by either amateur or professional scribes. All the early New Testament manuscripts were written in Greek, and most early Greek script was written in *scriptio continua* in which all the words ran together with no spaces between, no capital letters, no punctuation marks, etc. An example in modern English would look something like this:

INEARLYGREEKSCRIPTMOSTWORDSRUNTOGETHERAND
SOMEAREABBREVIATEDWITHNOSPACESBETWEENTHEMNO
CAPITALLETTERSANDNOPUNCTUATIONMARKSETC

Because the early scribes who copied the Christian Scriptures were amateurs, they made numerous errors in the process. As Ehrman explains:

> Because the early Christian texts were not being copied by professional scribes... we can expect that in the earliest copies... mistakes were commonly made in transcription. Indeed, we have solid evidence that this was the case. [Ibid., p. 51.]

Copying errors, both accidental and deliberate, had been a problem dating back to the dawn of written communication. Note, for instance, Moses' warnings in Deuteronomy 4:2 and 12:32 – directed no doubt to those who would pass on God's commands either orally or in written form: "You shall not add to the word which I command you, nor take from it.... See that you do all that I command you; do not add to it or take away from it." But probably the best-known admonition to copyists is what we find in Revelation 22:18-19 in which the author, John the Elder, issues a stern warning to those who would copy his manuscript:

I warn everyone who hears the words of the prophecy of this book: If anyone adds anything to them, God will add to him the plagues described in this book. And if anyone takes words away from the book of this prophecy, God will take away from him his share in the tree of life and the holy city, which are described in this book.

Similarly, the 2nd century Christian scholar Irenaeus cautioned those who reproduced his works to exercise the utmost care:

I adjure you who shall copy this book, by our Lord Jesus Christ and by his glorious advent when he comes to judge the living and the dead, that you compare what you transcribe, and correct it carefully against this manuscript from which you copy; and also that you transcribe this adjuration and insert it in the copy. [Cited in Bruce M. Metzger and Bart D. Ehrman, *The Text of the New Testament: Its Translation, Corruption and Restoration.* Fourth Edition (Oxford University Press, 2005), p. 33]

In his anti-Christian polemic, *The True Word* (c. 177), the pagan skeptic Celsus maligned Christians for altering their Scriptures to serve an apologetical purposes. According to Celsus:

Some believers, as though drunk, go so far as to oppose themselves and alter the original text of the gospel... several times over, and they change its character to enable them to deny difficulties in face of criticism. [Cited in Origen, *Against Celsus* 2.27]

In the following century the Christian scholar Origen wrote the following complaint regarding the numerous errors in the manuscripts to which he had access. [Note: Some scholars think that Origen may have been directing his comments not toward Christian copyists but Gnostics and other heretics who arbitrarily altered the texts as they copied them.]

The differences among the manuscripts have become great, either through the negligence of some copyists or through the perverse audacity of others; they either neglect to check over what they have transcribed, or, in the process of checking, they make additions or deletions as they please. [Commentary on Matthew 15:14, as quoted in Bruce M. Metzger, "Explicit References in the Works of Origen to Variant Readings in New Testament Manuscripts," in Robert Pierce and Robert W. Thomson, eds., *Biblical and Patristic Studies in Memory of Robert Pierce Casey* (Herder, 1963), p. 78.]

Later, in the Preface to Origen's book, *On First Principles*, the Christian scholar Rufinus issued this dire warning:

Truly in the presence of God the Father and the of the Son and of the Holy Spirit, I solemnly warn everyone who may either transcribe or read these books, by his belief in the kingdom to come, by the mystery of the resurrection from the dead, and by that everlasting fire prepared for the devil and his angels, that, as he would not possess for an eternal inheritance that place where there is weeping and gnashing of teeth and where their fire is not quenched and their spirit does not die, he add nothing to what is written and take nothing away from it, and make no insertion or alteration, but that he compare his transcription with the copies from which he made it. [Cited in Ehrman, *Misquoting Jesus*, p. 54]

Textual Accretions

To support his allegation that biblical manuscripts have been altered through the centuries, Ehrman offers up two examples of additions to scriptural texts.

(1) The *Pericope Adulterae* (John 7:53-8:11) – the passage in which Jesus encounters the woman who was caught in adultery; and

(2) Mark 16:9-20 – the "Long Ending" to Mark's Gospel.

Virtually all New Testament scholars, conservative or liberal, agree that these passages are accretions that were added at some point to the texts, and that neither are in our oldest and best manuscripts. However, there are considerable differences of opinion as to whether these passages were outright fabrications or venerable oral traditions that were later incorporated into the texts. Predictably, Ehrman is confident that they are fabrications, whereupon he then charges that these are merely two examples of "thousands of places in which the manuscripts of the NT came to be changed by scribes." He also speculates that the original version of the Gospel of John ended with chapter 20, and that chapter 21 "appears to be a later add-on" and an "afterthought." Likewise, based on stylistic analysis, he contends that the prologue (verses 1:1-18) originally came from a different source. Nonetheless, he concedes that "all our Greek manuscripts contain the passages in question."

Tampering With Theology

All biblical text critics understand that the manuscripts were altered to some extent in the process of transmission. But to reiterate a key point, what really matters is whether any fundamental Christian doctrine or our understanding of Jesus has been affected in the process. Unsurprisingly, Ehrman argues that Christian theology has indeed been altered, and he contends, "It would be wrong... to say – as people sometimes do – that the changes in our text have no real bearing on what the texts mean." Furthermore, he asserts, these variant readings affect various "theological conclusions" that one might draw from the texts, and that in some instances "the very meaning of the text is at stake. As evidence, he puts forth several examples.

(1) The "Johannine Comma" (1 John 5:7-8). In the King James Version this passage reads:

> For there are three that bear record in heaven, the Father, the Word, and the Holy Spirit; and these three are one; and there are three that bear witness on earth, the Spirit, the water, and the blood, and these three are one.

This verse appears to be a strong endorsement of the doctrine of the Trinity, but there is a problem: This is not how it reads in our earliest and best manuscripts. Clearly, the reference to "the Father, the Word, and the Holy Spirit" was a later addition to the text. According to the earliest manuscripts, the text should simply read:

> For there are three that testify: the Spirit, the water, and the blood; and the three are in agreement.

As in the two examples cited previously, New Testament scholars are virtually unanimous in this opinion. In all likelihood, a well-meaning scribe at some point in the 5th century took it upon himself to alter the text in order to emphasize the doctrine of the Trinity. But in doing so, and regardless of his motive, he committed an egregious violation of scholarly ethics.

(2) Mark's Angry Jesus (Mark 1:41). As Jesus was traveling throughout Galilee, preaching in synagogues and exorcizing demons, a leper approached him and pleaded, "If you are willing, you can make me clean." Then in Mark 1:41 we read that Jesus, "filled with compassion, reached out his hand and touched the man," and pronounced him "clean" – whereupon he was cured. With that, Jesus sent him on his way, but warned him not to tell anyone what happened. But instead, he "went out and began to talk freely, spreading the news." As a result, Jesus could no longer enter a town openly but "stayed outside in lonely places, yet "the people still came to him from everywhere."

Nearly all of our early manuscripts say that Jesus felt "compassion" for the leper and healed him, but one of the oldest manuscripts, Codez Bezae, states that Jesus became "angry." [Note: The Greek words for "compassion" (*splangnistheis*) and "angry" (*orgistheis*) are somewhat similar.] Ehrman thinks this is probably what Mark originally wrote because, after all, "Which is more likely, that a scribe copying this text would change it to say that Jesus became wrathful instead of compassionate, or to say that Jesus became compassionate instead of wrathful?" He concludes, "When seen from this perspective, the latter is obviously more likely."[3]

---

[3] Ehrman, *Misquoting Jesus*, p. 134, 135.

Putting Ehrman's speculative reasoning aside, why would it matter if Jesus felt "compassion" or "anger?" Well, it matters a lot to Ehrman because he sees an opportunity here to challenge the sinless nature of Christ. He notes, correctly, that Matthew and Luke borrowed heavily from Mark in writing their gospels, but in their versions of this story they omit Jesus' emotion when he heals the man. Furthermore, Ehrman points out that elsewhere in Mark, Jesus is described as angry, but Matthew and Luke always modify (i.e., sanitize) these accounts. His conclusion: Jesus had a temper that Matthew and Luke are reluctant to admit. Therefore, according to Ehrman, this alters our perception of Jesus as perfectly in control of his emotions.

(3) Luke's Imperturbable Jesus (Luke 22:39-46). According to Ehrman, Luke always portrays Jesus as cool and calm and never angry. However, there is one passage in this gospel in which Jesus appears to lose his composure – "and that, interesting enough, is in a passage whose authenticity is hotly debated among textual scholars."[4]

Ehrman is referring to Jesus' prayer on the Mount of Olives prior to his arrest, in which we are told that "being in anguish, he prayed... earnestly, and his sweat was like drops of blood falling to the ground." Strangely, some of the earliest manuscripts do not include this verse, although others do.

Ehrman seriously doubts that Jesus ever sweat drops of blood, and he observes that three of the key words in this passage – "agony," "sweat," and "drops" – occur nowhere else in Luke's gospel, nor are they used in the Acts of the Apostles. According to Ehrman...

> Nowhere else in Luke's Gospel is Jesus portrayed in this way. Quite the contrary, Luke has gone to great lengths to counter precisely the view of Jesus that these verses embrace. Rather than entering his passion with fear and trembling, in anguish over his coming fate, the Jesus of Luke goes to his death calm and in control, confident of his Father's will....
> [Ibid., p. 142]

Moreover, according to Ehrman, this verse is suspect because it interrupts the literary flow of the passage:

> The passage appears to be deliberately structured as what scholars have called a chiasmus. When a passage is chiastically structured, the first statement of the passage corresponds to the last one; the second statement corresponds to the second to last; the third to the third to last, and so on. In other words, this is an intentional design; its purpose is to focus attention on the center of the passage as its key. [Ibid., p. 140]

---

[4] Ibid., p. 139.

As Ehrman observes, the center of the passage is Jesus' prayer itself. "But what happens, though, when the disputed verses (vv. 43-44) are injected into the passage?" The answer is that Luke's masterful narrative is disrupted: "On the literary level, the chiasmus that focuses the passage on Jesus' prayer is absolutely destroyed. Now the center of the passage, and hence its focus, shifts to Jesus' agony."[5] In Ehrman's mind, this appears to be an unpardonable violation of literary aesthetics that Luke would never have committed.

According to Ehrman, these examples are only a few of many such corruptions in the texts. He writes, "The more I studied the manuscript tradition of the New Testament, the more I realized just how radically the text had been altered over the years at the hands of scribes, who were not only conserving scripture but also changing it."[6] In fact, he declares, there are literally "thousands of places in which the manuscripts of the New Testament came to be changed by scribes."[7]

One of the most cited passages from *Misquoting Jesus* is one in which Ehrman writes that there are about 130,000 words in the New Testament, yet there are perhaps 300,000-400,000 variants in our manuscripts. He observes, "We do not know for sure because, despite impressive developments in computer technology, no one yet has been able to count them all." But regardless of the exact number, "There are more variations among our manuscripts than there are words in the New Testament[!]"[8] The implication is that virtually every word in the New Testament is questionable to the point that we cannot possibly know what was originally written.

While conceding that most of these alterations are not important, Ehrman charges that the corruption of the text is nevertheless serious enough to affect some basic Christian doctrines.

> To be sure, of all the hundreds of thousands of textual changes found among our manuscripts, most of them are completely insignificant.... It would be wrong, however, to say – as people sometimes do – that the changes in our text have no real bearing on what the texts mean or on the theological conclusions that one draws from them.... In some instances, the very meaning of the text is at stake, depending on how one resolves a textual problem. [Ibid., pp. 207-08]

---

[5] Ibid., p. 141.

[6] Ibid., p. 207.

[7] Ibid., p. 68.

[8] Ibid., pp. 10, 90.

The Collapse of Faith

Misquoting Jesus is anything but a dry, scholarly tome on a ponderous academic subject. Ehrman is a gifted and provocative writer, and part of the book's appeal is the fact that he personalizes the relevance of the material by working in an anti-testimony of sorts – i.e., how his study of biblical textual criticism led to the collapse of his faith.

According to Ehrman, he was raised in a nominally-Christian Episcopalian family, but as a teenager he experienced a spiritual conversion through the ministry of Young Life. Full of zeal, he attended the ultra-conservative Moody Bible Institute where he was taught the doctrines of biblical inerrancy and verbal, plenary inspiration, after which he transferred to Wheaton College, one of America's premier evangelical colleges. It was while he was at Wheaton that he became interested in biblical textual criticism, a field of study that he pursued as a graduate student at Princeton Seminary.

In one of his seminar courses at Princeton, Ehrman wrote a paper in which he attempted to reconcile an apparent discrepancy in two biblical texts regarding the name of the high priest at the time of David. In Mark 2:23-27, Jesus referred to Abiathar as the high priest at the time when David took consecrated bread from the tabernacle to feed himself and his followers, but in I Samuel 21:1-6 the author identifies Abiathar's father, Ahimelech, as the high priest at the time. (II Sam. 8:17 also mentions Ahimelech as the priest during David's reign.) At the end of Ehrman's paper, his professor, Dr. Cullen Story, wrote a terse comment: "Maybe Mark just made a mistake." Ehrman implies that the comment came as a bolt out of the blue, and that for the first time he had to face the startling possibility that the Bible might not be inerrant after all.

He writes, "Once I made that admission, the floodgates opened."

A few years later, while teaching a course at Rutgers University entitled "The Problem of Suffering in the Biblical Tradition," Ehrman states that he finally renounced Christianity, confessing that his faith had become "a dead end." The crucial factor was his skepticism regarding the divine inspiration of Scripture. He recounts his thinking at the time:

> As I realized... in graduate school, even if God had inspired the original words [of the Bible], we don't have the original words. So the doctrine of inspiration was in a sense irrelevant to the Bible as we have it, since the words God reputedly inspired had been changed and, in some cases, lost.... The only reason... for God to inspire the Bible would be so that his people would have his actual words; but if he really wanted people to have his actual words, surely he would have miraculously preserved those words, just as he had miraculously inspired them in the first place. Given

the circumstance that he didn't preserve the words, the conclusion seemed inescapable to me that he hadn't gone to the trouble of inspiring them. [Ibid., p. 211.]

According to Ehrman, "I was basing my entire life on the literal meaning of the Bible, but then I started realizing the Bible isn't divinely inspired – it's a very human book."[9] Relieved of the burden of adhering to traditional Christian doctrines, he has since pronounced himself "a happy agnostic." In a profile in the *Carolina Alumni Review*, he is quoted as saying...

For me, life is good. If everybody had my life, there'd be no problem of suffering [in the world]. I make a lot of money. I have a fantastic job. I've got a great wife, my kids are fantastic, life's great! I'm happy, but I don't know if God exists or not. And if God does exist, I don't think the God that I used to believe in exists. [Quoted in Kathleen Kearns, "The Happy Agnostic." *Carolina Alumni Review* (May/June 2006), p. 30]

High Stakes

In *Misquoting Jesus*, Bart Ehrman offers a radical deconstructionist critique of the divine inspiration, historical reliability, and doctrinal authority of the Bible. For much of 2006 the book was near the top of the *New York Times* Best Seller list, and it probably ranks as one of the more influential religious books of the past 25 years. But if Ehrman's allegations are true, the Bible has been so

thoroughly corrupted as to render it totally unreliable, and by extension the Christian faith is essentially a fraud.

For Christians, the stakes could not be higher. Since virtually everything we believe about the nature and character of God, the human condition, the meaning and purpose of life, right and wrong, and our eternal destiny is derived from Scripture, it is imperative that we take the criticisms of Ehrman and other skeptics seriously. Either the authority and integrity of the Bible is defensible, or it is not. In particular,

---

[9] Ibid., p. 11.

has the Bible been accurately preserved and transmitted through the centuries? I believe there are good reasons to answer affirmatively. But first, the deconstructionist arguments put forth by skeptics such as Ehrman need to be addressed and themselves deconstructed.

Critiquing *Misquoting Jesus*

Before responding to *Misquoting Jesus*, some prefatory comments are in order. First, the title of the book is a total misnomer. The book has virtually nothing to do with "misquoting Jesus." Other than Jesus' comments in the story of the woman caught in adultery, all the other "errors" he cites have nothing to do with what Jesus did or did not say. In addition, the subtitle, *The Story Behind Who Changed the Bible and Why*, is misleading. Ehrman never attempts to address that issue directly because, frankly, we have absolutely no idea who was responsible for the various (and as I'll argue, insignificant) textual variants that we find in the manuscripts. Second, Ehrman contradicts himself throughout the book at key points, often tempering (if not totally invalidating) some of his key arguments. The book suffers either from very poor editing, or else Ehrman's views on the subject are perplexingly erratic.

Third, the book is unduly (not to mention pretentiously) sensationalistic. As Dillon Burroughs has noted in his critique of the book, *Misquotes in Misquoting Jesus: Why You Can Still Believe*, "*Misquoting Jesus* has a tendency to create controversies where they do not exist."[10] Daniel Wallace, a respected New Testament scholar at Dallas Theological Seminary and the executive director of the Center for the Study of New Testament Manuscripts, charges that Erhman's arguments are simplistic and exaggerated, and that the book is little more than "New Testament textual criticism 101."[11] In other words – and contrary to the sensationalistic claims by the book's publisher – there is nothing particularly new or revelatory in terms of the basic facts that Ehrman puts forth. Much of this information is common knowledge in the field of biblical textual criticism. His interpretations of the facts, however, are often disingenuous, misleading, and subject to criticism.

---

[10] Dillon Burroughs, *Misquotes in Misquoting Jesus: Why You Can Still Believe* (Nimble Books, 2006), p. 8.

[11] Quoted in Kathleen Kearns, "The Happy Agnostic." *Carolina Alumni Review* (May/June 2006), p. 29.

The Ultimate Issue

No textual scholar, conservative or liberal, doubts that there were errors in the copying and transmission process of the New Testament. After all, it was hand-copied by humans, and "to err is human." Furthermore, no serious scholar doubts that later copyists added and subtracted from the texts for various reasons – some legitimate, some not. As Timothy Paul Jones comments in *Misquoting Truth: A Guide to the Fallacies of Bart Ehrman's Misquoting Jesus,* "The ancient manuscripts were not copied perfectly. Yet they were copied with enough accuracy for us to comprehend what the original authors intended."[12]

As stated previously, the ultimate issue is whether any fundamental Christian doctrines or our understanding of Jesus have been affected in the process. Ehrman argues that fundamental doctrines have in fact been affected, as has our understanding of the character and nature of Christ. His supporting evidence, however, is speculative and unconvincing.

The Issue of Original Manuscripts

Regarding the issue of no original manuscripts, even Ehrman admits that this is not a significant problem. In fact, he concedes that we can, with reasonable accuracy, be assured that our earliest manuscripts are "very closely related to what the author originally wrote."[13]

Interestingly, one of Ehrman's professors at Princeton, the renowned New Testament scholar, Bruce Metzger, contradicts virtually all of Ehrman's skeptical contentions. When interviewed by Lee Strobel for his book, *The Case for Christ,* Metger commented on the fact that there are no original biblical manuscripts, and why this poses no great crisis when it comes to determining what they original authors originally wrote:

Bruce Metzger

> When I first found out that there are no surviving originals of the New Testament, I was really skeptical. I thought, If all we have are copies of copies of copies, how can I have any confidence that the New Testament we have today bears any resemblance whatsoever to what was originally written?

---

[12] Timothy Paul Jones, *Misquoting Truth: A Guide to the Fallacies of Bart Ehrman's Misquoting Jesus* (IVP Books, 2007), pp. 31*ff.*

[13] Ehrman, *Misquoting Jesus,* p. 62.

This isn't an issue that's unique to the Bible; it's a question we can ask of other [ancient] documents.... But what the New Testament has in its favor... is the unprecedented multiplicity of copies that have survived....

The more often you have copies that agree with each other, especially if they emerge from different geographical areas, the more you can cross-check them to figure out what the original document was like....

We have copies commencing within a couple of generations from the writings of the originals. In addition to Greek manuscripts, we also have translations of the gospels into other languages at a relatively early time – into Latin, Syriac, and Coptic [among others]. [Quoted in Lee Strobel, *The Case for Christ* (Zondervan, 1999), pp. 58-59.]

Many other New Testament experts have emphasized the same points. F. F. Bruce is quoted in Strobel's *The Case for Christ* as saying, "There is no body of ancient literature... which enjoys such a wealth of good textual attestation as the New Testament."[14] Similarly, Sir Frederick Kenyon, the former director of the British Museum, is cited in Bruce's book, *The New Testament Documents: Are They Reliable?*, attesting to the historical veracity of the Four Gospels in particular:

The interval between the dates of the original composition [of the gospels] and the earliest extant evidence [is] so small as to be negligible, and the last foundation for any doubt that the Scriptures have come down to us substantially as they were written has now been removed. [F. F. Bruce, *The New Testament Documents: Are They Reliable?* (William B. Eerdmans Publishing Company, 1972), p. 20.]

The Case for Careful Copying

Most all scholars agree that early Christian scribes would have treated the New Testament texts with utmost respect. After all, these were sacred Scriptures – not just the common ordinary writings of men. And of course copying errors, both accidental and deliberate, had been a problem since the dawn of written documents. For example, as cited previously, note Moses' warnings in Deuteronomy 4:2 and 12:32 – "You shall not add to the word which I command you, nor take from it" – directed no doubt to those who would pass on these commands either orally or in writing. Also, early Christian copyists, cognizant of John's warning in Revelation 22:18-19, would not have changed the texts in a casual and cavalier way.

Later in history, during and after the Constantinian era, Christian copyists might well have exercised similar care as Jewish Masorete scribes used in

---

[14] Quoted in Strobel, *The Case for Christ*, p. 63.

transcribing the sacred texts of the Tanakh (the Old Testament).[15] Even Ehrman, after arguing previously in his book that there are "thousands of places in which the manuscripts of the NT came to be changed by scribes," admits that the changes are largely insignificant.

> [T]he copying of early Christian texts was by and large a 'conservative' process. The scribes... were intent on 'conserving' the textual tradition they were passing on. Their ultimate concern was not to modify the tradition, but to preserve it.... Most scribes, no doubt, tried to do a faithful job in making sure that the text they reproduced was the same text they inherited. [Ehrman, *Misquoting Jesus, p. 177*]

Ehrman is quite correct that early manuscripts contained many errors and that "there are more variations among our manuscripts than there are words in the New Testament." However, although technically correct, this statement is misleading. As Bruce Metzger commented in *The Case for Christ*, the contention that ancient manuscripts contained 200,000 variants or more sounds devastatingly serious, but in fact one must consider the large number of texts involved and the way variants are counted. For example, if a single word is misspelled in 2,000 manuscripts, it is counted as 2,000 variants. This puts the issue in an entirely different context as more than 99% of textual variants are related to syntax and grammatical errors or insignificant miscues such as misspellings. Even Ehrman concedes that "the more manuscripts one discovers, the more the variant readings; but also the more the likelihood that somewhere among those variant readings one will be able to uncover the original text."[16] So for example, the first edition of Ehrman's own book, *Misquoting Jesus*, contained at least 16 documented errors. Reportedly, the book sold about 100,000 copies, which means that if we use the same method to determine the number of errors in *Misquoting Jesus* that Ehrman applies to biblical manuscripts, we can declare authoritatively that his book contains 1.6 million errors! – even though not a single one of these affects the message of the book.[17]

More significantly, on the correlation between scribal errors and doctrinal alterations, Metzger points out that Greek, unlike English, is an inflected language. In English, word order in a sentence can make all the difference – for example, it matters whether we say, "The dog bit the man" or "The man bit the dog." But as Metzger explains:

---

[15] See the sidebar: "The Jewish Transmission of the Tanakh – and Its Implications," in Part 2 : "The Transmission Process."

[16] Ehrman, *Misquoting Jesus*, p. 177.

[17] See Norman L. Geisler and Patty Tunnicliffe, *Reasons for Belief* (Bethany House Publishers, 2013), p. 101.

But in Greek [word order] doesn't [matter]. One word functions as the subject of the sentence regardless of where it stands in the sequence; consequently, the meaning of the sentence isn't distorted if the words are out of... order. Some variations among manuscripts exist, but generally they're inconsequential variations. [Quoted in Strobel, *The Case for Christ*, p. 83.]

When asked by Strobel, "How many [biblical] doctrines... are in jeopardy because of variants?" Metzger replied, "I don't know of any doctrine that is in jeopardy." Timothy Paul Jones concurs:

From my perspective, a significant alteration would be one that requires Christians either to rethink a vital belief about Jesus Christ – a belief we might find in the Apostles' Creed, for example – or to doubt the historical accuracy of the New Testament documents. Yet, when I look at the changes in the Greek manuscripts of the New Testament, I find no 'highly significant' alterations. [Jones, *Misquoting Truth*, p. 54.]

According to Daniel Wallace, more than 99% of textual variants are insignificant, and none of the others affect any basic Christian doctrine.[18] It would appear, as Dillon Burroughs charges in *Misquotes in Misquoting Jesus*, that Ehrman has tried to manufacture a controversy where none exists.

The Witness of the Church Fathers

Another major problem with Ehrman's thesis is that he devalues the significance of the Ante-Nicene Church Fathers (a.k.a. the "Patristic Fathers"), those Christian scholars and clerics of the 2nd and 3rd centuries who preserved the biblical texts and commented extensively on them. In the writings of the Church Fathers there are more than a million citations of the New Testament, and as Metzger has pointed out, much of the New Testament could actually be reconstructed just from their commentaries alone. As he explains in *The Case for Christ*, "Even if we lost all the Greek manuscripts and the early translations, we could still reproduce the contents of the New Testament from the multiplicity of quotations in commentaries, sermons, [and] letters of the early Church Fathers."[19] For example, Irenaeus (c. 135-202) quotes more than a thousand passages from the New Testament and treats these writings as sacred Scripture. This is particularly noteworthy because some of the Church Fathers probably had access to early-generation copies of many of the original manuscripts. In

---

[18] Daniel B. Wallace, "The Gospel According to Bart." *Journal of the Evangelical Theological Society* 49 (June 2006), p. 330.

[19] Quoted in Strobel, *The Case for Christ*, p. 69. See also Metzger and Ehrman, *The Text of the New Testament*, p. 126.

addition to these works, we also have portions of Tatian's *Diatessaron*, written circa 160 and the first attempt to harmonize the four gospels.

In *Prescription Against Heretics* (c. 203), Tertullian (c. 160-225) scolded his theological opponents for their doubts about what the texts originally said. Writing more than a century after the apostle Paul, he notes that the "authentic writings" [Latin: *authenticae*] of some of Paul's letters are still being held in Rome, Corinth, Ephesus, Philippi, and Thessalonica, and he urges his readers to visit these churches and view these epistles for themselves. [Note: It is unclear whether Tertullian is arguing that the original manuscripts are still preserved or if these are copies of the originals. The fact that no scholars after Tertullian make this claim indicates that the original autographs had probably all disappeared by the early 3rd century.]

Early Christian scholars took textual criticism seriously. Irenaeus wrote in the late-2nd century that he had examined copies of the Book of Revelation, making notes on which manuscripts were written earlier in order to determine the correct wording of the text. Two centuries later Augustine (354-430) comments in a letter to the biblical scholar Jerome that if he encountered an apparent error in the biblical texts, "I decide that either the text is corrupt, or the translator did not follow what was really said, or that I failed to understand it." There is no reason to think that these scholars took their work any less seriously than honest scholars do today. Convinced that they were working with the divinely-inspired written Word of God, they exercised all due diligence to assure that the texts were preserved and transmitted as accurately as possible.

Deconstructing Ehrman

In *Misquoting Jesus* Ehrman focuses on five New Testament passages that he considers to be prime examples of his thesis that the texts have been altered and key Christian doctrines have been affected. However, he greatly exaggerates the issues at stake, and none of these passages is as problematic as he contends.

[Note: Ehrman's argument that the Authorized (King James) Version of the Bible is riddled with errors is old news. Text critics have known this for more than 300 years, which is why scholars have produced newer and better translations in the 20th century. One serious deficiency of the KJV is that it was based on the *Textus Receptus*, as discussed in Part 3 of this chapter.]

1. The *Pericope Adulterae* (John 7:53-8:11). As mentioned earlier, Ehrman's "revelations" regarding John 8, Mark 16, and 1 John 5:7-8 are nothing new. Virtually all New Testament scholars and any good new translation of the Bible make it clear that these passages are textual accretions that are not found in the oldest and best manuscripts. However, scholars differ as to whether these passages were outright fabrications or based on venerable oral traditions that were later incorporated into the texts.

In the case of the *Pericope Adulterae*, some modern translations place the passage in brackets (RSV, NSRV, GNB, ESV, NET), while others set it off from the rest of the text with an explanatory comment (NIV), print it in a smaller font (TNIV, NET), or incorporate it into a footnote. Many scholars have pointed out that the story interrupts the flow of the verses that come before and after, and that stylistically it is different from that of the rest of John's gospel. Although the story of Jesus and the woman caught in adultery was cited by Greek writers in the 2nd century *Gospel of the Hebrews*, the earliest extant Greek biblical text in which it appears is dated to the 5th century.

[Note: In 2007 Daniel Wallace examined four New Testament manuscripts from the National Archive in Albania that dated from the 9th and 10th centuries. The archive had been off-limits to Western scholars for decades, so the collection was a source of great interest to contemporary biblical scholars. Wallace found that the *Pericope Adulterae* was absent from three of the texts and that it had been tacked on to the end of the fourth text.]

Some liberal scholars believe this narrative was purely a fictitious fable, but there is no reason necessarily to dismiss it as an authentic oral tradition that was eventually inserted into the text. According to Bruce Metzger, there are elements of the story that sound authentic:

> The story of the woman taken in adultery... has many earmarks of historical veracity; no ascetically minded monk would have invented a narrative that closes with what seems to be only a mild rebuke on Jesus' part: "Neither do I condemn you; go, and do not sin again...."
>
> The Church preserved many traditions of the deeds and sayings of Christ that had not been included in the Gospels. It would be natural for these to slip into the text of the Gospels, either from the margins of other manuscripts or from the living memory of the Church. [Metzger and Ehrman, *The Text of the New Testament*, pp. 319; 213]

All the stories about Jesus began as oral transmissions, so it is certainly possible that this particular story eventually got written down much later. Even Ehrman concedes, "Most scholars think that it was probably a well-known story circulating in the oral tradition about Jesus, which at some point was added in the margin of a manuscript." So as he is prone to do, Ehrman cites the story as if it seriously compromises the credibility of Scripture, only to admit that it is probably inconsequential.[20]

---

[20] Ehrman, *Misquoting Jesus*, p. 65.

2. Mark 16 – the "Long Ending." In the case of the mysterious "Long Ending" to Mark 16, there are three possible reasons why the passage ends so abruptly after verse 8: "Trembling and bewildered, the women went out and fled from the tomb. They said nothing to anyone, because they were afraid."

(1) The author intentionally left the rest of the story open-ended. The problem here is rather apparent: Would Mark write a "Good News" account of Jesus that ended with the women fleeing the tomb in fear? Nonetheless, many scholars believe this was indeed the case.

(2) The gospel was never finished – a theory that is highly unlikely.

(3) The last leaf of the original manuscript was lost. This argument is based on the fact that subsequent copyists attached three different endings to the gospel. Even Ehrman speculates that "possibly, the last page of Mark's gospel, one in which Jesus actually did meet the disciples in Galilee, was somehow lost," and that all our copies of Mark's gospel go back to this one truncated manuscript.[21]

3. The "Johannine Comma" (I John 5:7-8). Regarding the controversy surrounding 1 John 5:7-8, the case for the doctrine of the Trinity is not jeopardized by the addition of the words, "the Father, the Word, and the Holy Spirit" to the text. In fact, the doctrine of the Trinity is clearly implied in several New Testament passages.

- At the time of Jesus' baptism he hears his Father speak from heaven, and the Holy Spirit descends upon him in the form of a dove. (Matt. 3:13-17; Mark 1:9-11; Luke 3:21-22; John 1:31-34.)
- In John 14-16, Jesus repeatedly equates himself with God the Father and speaks of the coming of the Holy Spirit.
- In Matthew 28:18-20, Jesus instructs his disciples to baptize "in the name of the Father and of the Son and of the Holy Spirit" – thereby equating the three persons of the Trinity.
- In Romans 1:1-4, Paul refers to Christ, "who through the Spirit of holiness was declared with power to be the Son of God by his resurrection from the dead: Jesus Christ, our Lord."
- In Ephesians 1:3-14, Paul implies that Jesus Christ, God the Father, and the Holy Spirit, although distinct persons, are one in nature.

Certainly, the Church Fathers of the 2nd and 3rd centuries regarded Jesus as divine, so the doctrine was never in doubt among orthodox Christians operating within the apostolic tradition.

---

[21] Ibid., p. 68.

4. Mark's Angry Jesus (Mark 1:41). As mentioned previously, one ancient manuscript, Codex Bezae, describes Jesus as "angry" prior to healing the leper. Of all ancient manuscripts, Codex Bezae (c. 450) is known for its unique and eccentric peculiarities, and it certainly should not be considered the standard when it deviates from the norm. The codex features many variant readings not found in most other early texts, including numerous additions and deletions including even entire pericopes. For example, the text of the Acts of the Apostles is nearly 10% longer in Codex Bezae than in any other manuscript. According to Bruce Metzger, the manuscript is an enigma, and there is no consensus among scholars regarding the document's peculiarities.

Ehrman's contention that this variant reading presents a problem is patently absurd. Even if he were correct that Jesus became "angry" prior to healing the man, what would it mean? It would seemingly be out of character for Jesus to be angry at the poor victim of the disease, so perhaps he was angry because of the ravaging effects the leprosy had on the man's body. In any event, this says nothing of Jesus' character, and other passages in Mark clearly demonstrate that Jesus was exceedingly compassionate toward the unfortunate (Mark 6:34; 8:2; 9:22-23). So in effect, Ehrman's argument is a non-issue.

5. Luke's Imperturbable Jesus (Luke 22:39-46). Likewise, Ehrman's arguments regarding Jesus sweating blood in this passage are extremely weak. Regarding Jesus' agony in the garden, this was obviously a unique experience in his life. He was, after all, a human being who was on the verge of being beaten and tortured to death. Why should we find it usual that he displayed intense emotions unlike anything else recorded during his life?

Ehrman is sadly mistaken if he thinks that Luke was more concerned with employing a clever literary technique, a chiasmus, than with relating the simple facts of the event. Luke was a physician and a biographer who was scrupulously (and extraordinarily) fastidious in terms of presenting an accurate account of Jesus' life in his gospel, just as he shows himself to be a first-rate ancient historian in the Acts of the Apostles. Although he might very well have had a sense for aesthetic literary construction, he is neither a poet nor a panegyric eulogist. His narratives are typically straightforward, well-crafted, and unembellished by artificial literary devices.

But that point aside, whether Jesus actually sweat drops of blood or not – and whether this clause was in the original text or not – does nothing to detract from Jesus' character. Ehrman's strained effort to discredit the historicity of Luke's account of Jesus' agony in the garden is speculative and unconvincing. It probably says far more about the character of Bart Ehrman than about Jesus.

Case Closed

There is, of course, a fundamental logical inconsistency in Ehrman's whole argument: If he is correct that we can have no idea what the texts originally said, then how would he know that these passages (and others) have been altered?

Despite its provocative and sensationalistic claims, Ehrman's book (not to mention his whole approach to biblical textual criticism) is underwhelming, to say the least. He utterly fails to prove his case, he never directly addresses "who changed the Bible and why," and he certainly never demonstrates that changes in the texts alter basic Christian doctrines or our understanding of Jesus.

Ultimately, Ehrman's failure is not so much scholarly or intellectual as it is a moral problem. As Ben Witherington has commented, "I am... glad Bart is honest about his [religious] pilgrimage. If only he could be equally honest and admit that in his scholarship he is trying now to deconstruct orthodox Christianity... rather than do 'values-neutral' text criticism."[22]

Bart Ehrman abandoned his Christian faith for agnosticism, but in many respects he is still a fundamentalist at heart. In the theological equivalent of the domino effect, his brittle fundamentalist faith shattered once he discovered a minor (and insignificant) historical "error" in the biblical text. His whole house of cards collapsed, and eventually he was left with no faith at all.

Dale Martin, a longtime friend of Ehrman who teaches religious studies at Yale, is quoted in Timothy Jones' *Misquoting Truth* as saying, "Bart was, like a lot of people who were converted to fundamental evangelicalism, converted to the certainty of it all, of having all the answers. When he found out they were lying to him, he just didn't want anything to do with it."[23] So now, rather than being a fundamentalist Christian, Ehrman is a fundamentalist skeptic. His all-or-nothing epistemology is astonishingly unsophisticated for such an erudite and highly-educated scholar. Like extremists of every persuasion, his tendency is to throw the metaphorical baby out with the bath water.

[Note: Regarding the incident that initially shook his faith – the alleged discrepancy between Mark 2:23-27 and I Samuel 21:1-6 concerning the name of the high priest in the time of David, one possible solution is that Jesus' reference to Abiathar might simply indicate the position that Abiathar

---

[22] Ben Witherington, "Misanalyzing Textual Criticism: Bart Ehrman's 'Misquoting Jesus'." http://benwitherington.blogspot.com/2006/03/misanalyzing-text-criticism-bart.html.

[23] Jones, *Misquoting Truth*, p. 145.

eventually attained. According to I Samuel 22:20, Abiathar was present in the tabernacle during the scenario described in I Samuel 21, although he didn't actually become high priest until later. This would simply be analogous to someone saying, "I knew President George W. Bush when we were in college" – chronologically and technically incorrect since it would be many years later before Bush was elected president, but not exactly an egregious historical error that would necessarily invalidate the narrator's credibility. In any event, for most Christians their faith is probably sufficient to encounter a dilemma such as Mark 2:26 and I Samuel 21:1 and still emerge intact.]

In an October 2011 debate between Ehrman and Daniel Wallace of the Center for the Study of New Testament Manuscripts, Wallace asked Ehrman what kind of evidence he would need in order to believe that we have an accurate text of the New Testament. Ehrman replied that he would need to see 10 manuscripts of the Gospel of Mark, all written within a week of the original and having no more than 0.001% deviation (one letter in every 100,000). Since there are only 57,000 letters in the entire Gospel of Mark, this presumably means that Ehrman would not accept the text as authentic if there were half-a-letter deviation. Assuming that he was in fact serious and was not merely speaking in jest, this is either extraordinarily high standards or an extraordinarily low understanding of the threshold for truth.[24]

In *Misquoting Truth* Timothy Jones implies that Ehrman lost his faith not because he delved so deeply into the background of Christianity but because he gained his understanding of Christian faith in a fundamentalist context that allowed little if any space for questions, variations, or rough edges. But life is messy and complicated – which is why we are called to live by faith. Life is full of ironies, paradoxes and ambiguities. These things make life all the more challenging, but also more interesting. In their efforts to eliminate the perplexing ironies, paradoxes and ambiguities of life, fundamentalists also inadvertently resist reality. This seems to be the case for all varieties of fundamentalists – whether religious or rigid political ideologues.

A Lesson To Be Learned

Ironically (and certainly unintentionally), Bart Ehrman has done the church a favor by bringing to the forefront – and in the process, helping to popularize – such a vitally important field of study as biblical textual criticism. This is long overdue, and one lesson to be learned from this controversy is that the gap between the church and the academy must be

---

[24] Ibid., p. iv.

closed. To paraphrase the venerable Yale church historian Jaroslav Pelikan, **"The church [should always be] more than a school; but the church [should never be] less than a school."**[25] **Christians need to be educated on the tough apologetical issues of our day. Instead of trying to shield believers from these controversies – and in the process reducing Christian education to the lowest common denominator – church leaders should be preparing Christians to actively engage these issues intelligently and effectively.**

The dumbing-down of Christian education is condescending, disgraceful and self-defeating. Not only do we end up forfeiting the great intellectual battles of our day, but we bore mature Christians and reduce the Gospel to relative insignificance. This is a key point that Timothy Jones makes in *Misquoting Truth*. In 2005 Jones was asked, "Why do you think Dan Brown, author of *The Da Vinci Code*, is such a threat to the Christian faith?" In response, Jones remarked, "He isn't.... The real danger isn't Dan Brown. The real danger is our own ignorance of how Christianity... came into existence." Jones continued: The real danger is "a faith that refuses to deal with the tough questions about the church's history and about Scripture. What *The Da Vinci Code* has provided is an opportunity to help millions of people who are asking these questions."[26]

Jones applies the same principle to the challenges posed by Bart Ehrman and other radical biblical deconstructionists. Far from being devastating attacks on the credibility of the Bible and the Christian faith, these critiques only expose the factual inaccuracies and the shallow thinking of these skeptics, and provide an excellent opportunity for informed Christians to present an effective apologetic in defense of the historic Christian faith. As Jones writes:

> Ehrman poses no ultimate threat to Christian faith. What he poses is an opportunity for believers to become more aware of the beautiful struggles by which God brought us to where we are today. Ehrman has created an opportunity for us to ask difficult questions – questions like, What do I mean when I say that the Bible is God's Word? and What are we actually claiming when we declare that the Scriptures are without error? [Jones, *Misquoting Truth*, p. 143.]

Finally, much Good News emerges from this controversy. If this is the best evidence the skeptics can produce for deconstructing the Bible, Christians can rest assured that we have a very solid basis for believing that the Bible we currently read is trustworthy, and that it has been accurately preserved and transmitted through the centuries.

---

[25] Jaroslav Pelikan, *The Emergence of the Catholic Tradition (100-600)* (University of Chicago Press, 1971), p. 1.

[26] Jones, Misquoting Truth, pp. 142-43.

Part 2:
The Transmission Process

The Original Autographs

Were the apostles literate? One of the first questions that skeptics raise regarding the authenticity of the New Testament relates to whether the apostles were even literate. After all, weren't Jesus' initial followers, the Twelve Disciples, uneducated Galilean peasants and fishermen?

Internal evidence in the New Testament itself indicates that some of the authors personally wrote the books attributed to them, while others probably dictated their thoughts to a scribal secretary. In all likelihood at least some of the disciples and apostles were literate. For example, if Matthew was a tax collector and Luke a physician, they almost certainly could read and write. Furthermore, no reputable scholar doubts that the apostle Paul was well-educated and capable of writing the epistles attributed to him.

In the case of the other two gospel writers, Mark and John, they may or may not have been literate, but they certainly could have dictated their accounts to a scribal secretary (an *amanuensis*), as Paul did in some of his epistles. (For example, Paul's scribe in the Epistle to the Romans identifies himself as Tertius in Romans 16:22.) Likewise, the apostle Peter could have used an *amanuensis* in writing his epistles. As for James "the Just" and Jude, reputed to have been the half-brothers of Jesus, there is no reason to think they were illiterate. After all, the gospels record the stories of Jesus reading from the scroll of Isaiah in his hometown synagogue in Nazareth (Luke 4:14-21) and writing a message on the ground while dialoguing with the woman who was caught in adultery (John 7:53-8:11). So it stands to reason that if Jesus was literate, his half-brothers James and Jude, who grew up in the same family, could also probably read and write. If not, there were plenty of other followers of Christ who could have recorded their thoughts.

According to Alan Millard's *Reading and Writing in the Time of Jesus* (2000), literacy was fairly common among Jewish males in the 1st century. At least in pious Jewish families, there was a strong tradition of education that dated back many centuries. Both Josephus and Philo relate that Jewish sons were taught to read the Torah at an early age so they could later serve as elders in the local synagogue and take their turn reading from the holy Scriptures.

Skeptics cite Acts 4:13, in which Peter and John were characterized by members of the Sanhedrin as being "uneducated," as evidence that they were illiterate. But the word used does not imply that they were illiterate so much as they were "untrained" in the Jewish law – in other words, they were not professional rabbis or scholars. Furthermore, modern scholars believe that most people living in Israel in the time of Christ were probably multi-lingual, at least to some extent. The common language was Aramaic, but many would also have been conversant in Greek, the cosmopolitan language of business and commerce in their day. In addition, those who had regular dealings with the Romans would have known at least some Latin, and it is also likely that pious Jewish families such as the one in which Jesus was raised spoke ancient Hebrew.

In the case of apostles such as Paul, Peter, and John, one can assume that their amanuenses took great care to record as accurately as possible what was dictated to them. The apostles were highly revered, and their official correspondences were considered divinely-inspired revelations. Considering the importance of these manuscripts, it is likely that the writings of their scribes would be proofread for accuracy by the apostle himself or another literate associate.

As discussed in Chapter 5, by the turn of the 2nd century most major churches probably had a collection of books that they considered sacred. This would have included the Septuagint (the Greek version of the Jewish Scriptures), along with some of the Four Gospels, the epistles of Paul, and perhaps a few other apostolic writings. These special books were often kept in an *armarion* (book chest), just as similar collections were commonly kept in Jewish synagogues.

What became of the original autographs? Most of the original *autographa* probably didn't last long. Numerous copies would have been made from each original, and the autograph itself might have been circulated far and wide. If the original autographs had been preserved, many of the 2nd century disputes over variant readings in the texts would easily have been resolved by appeals to the originals.

As cited previously, Tertullian indicated in *Prescription Against Heretics* (c. 203) that some of Paul's "authentic writings" [Latin: *authenticae*] were still held in Rome, Corinth, Ephesus, Philippi, and Thessalonica, and he urged his theological opponents to check these out if they doubted what Paul had originally written. However, it is unclear whether Tertullian is referring to the original autographs themselves or to carefully preserved copies, but it is unlikely that he would have urged skeptics to examine mere copies of the writings in question. The fact that no scholars after Tertullian make this claim indicates that all of the originals had probably disappeared by the early 3rd century.

Over time the original manuscripts and virtually all of the second- and third-generation copies were eventually lost or discarded due to several factors:

- The normal wear and tear on the fragile papyrus manuscripts as they were passed around from person-to-person or church-to-church.

- The preference for new copies over the old. Unlike modern scholars, most ancient scribes preferred a new manuscript over an old, tattered one. Older manuscripts were often discarded after new copies were produced.

- During times of persecution copies of Christian Scriptures were confiscated and burned. The last and worst period came under the emperor Diocletian in the early 4th century. We do not know how many early biblical manuscripts were destroyed at this time, but undoubtedly it was hundreds if not thousands.

Biblical Transmission and the Issue of Quality Control

To err is human. Once the original autographs were in circulation, quality control became problematical. As mentioned previously, most early Greek writing was in *scriptio continua* – i.e., all the words run together with no spaces between them, no capital letters, no punctuation marks, etc. In the process of copying and recopying manuscripts, changes in the text were inevitable. Most of these variants were accidental, while some were intentional. Once a change was made in a manuscript, it was probably passed on in all subsequent copies based on that particular text. Therefore, the variants often became permanent. The next scribe to copy the manuscript probably reproduced the mistakes of his predecessor, along with adding new ones of his own. And somewhere in the process the original autograph got worn out or lost.

As this process was repeated in generation after generation of copies, mistakes tended to multiply. In some cases a scribe might have more than one manuscript to compare, in which case he might correct a variant copy. But the evidence indicates that errors and changes in the texts were more common in the first three centuries than later, and the problem of copying errors, both accidental and intentional, was often addressed by ancient authors and scribes. (See the previous section, "Problematical Manuscripts.")

Nonetheless, the historical sources are clear that early Christian scholars took textual criticism seriously. Irenaeus, bishop of Lyons, wrote in the late-2nd century that he had examined copies of the Book of Revelation, making notes on which manuscripts were written earlier in order to determine the correct wording of the text. Two centuries later Augustine (354-430) comments in a letter to his fellow-scholar Jerome that if he encountered an apparent error in the biblical texts, "I decide that either the text is corrupt, or the translator did not follow what was really said, or that I failed to understand it."

Since most texts were copied locally, it was common for the same errors to show up repeatedly in various "families" or (*stemma*) of texts. Scribes in some areas were more conscientious and competent than in others. For example, as discussed in Part 3 of this chapter, Alexandrian manuscripts were generally of high quality. Fortunately, beginning in the 4th century, the process of copying Scripture became more standardized and professionalized, such that in the year 331 the emperor Constantine commissioned Eusebius, the bishop of Caesarea, to produce 50 high-quality Bibles for placement in prominent churches throughout the empire.

The copying profession. Beginning in the 4th century the copying of Scriptures (along with other books) became a common activity of monks in monastery scriptoriums. Bruce Metzger describes the production process in a typical scriptorium:

> Sitting in the workroom of a scriptorium, several trained scribes, each equipped with parchment, pens, and ink, would write a copy of the book being reproduced as the reader, or lector, slowly read aloud the text.... In this way, as many copies could be produced simultaneously as scribes were working in the scriptorium. [Metzger and Ehrman, *The Text of the New Testament*, p. 25]

Monks were required to keep their work stations clean and neat, and those who did a sloppy job could be reprimanded or even punished. But as Metzger concedes, mistakes were still common even for professional scribes. (After all, eyeglasses were not invented until the 14th century, and hearing aids even centuries after that!)

> Errors of transmission would almost inevitably occur. Sometimes the scribe would be momentarily inattentive or, because of a cough or other noise, would not clearly hear the lector. Furthermore, when the lector read aloud a word that could be spelled in different ways... the scribe would have to determine which word belonged in that particular context. [Ibid., p. 25.]

Nonetheless, there was a degree of quality control built into the system, as texts were commonly proofread by a corrector. In the case of serious errors, the scribe would have to recopy the whole page. In other instances the corrector would make notes in the margins of the manuscript. The process was arduous, tedious and fatiguing, and following the completion of a manuscript some scribes would add a colophon such as, "The end of the book. Thanks be to God!"

Yet despite the exhausting nature of the process, most scribes seem to have taken their work seriously and considered it a true ministry and a "praiseworthy industry." Scribes such as the 5th century scholar Cassiodorus regarded their work not only as a scholarly discipline but a form of spiritual warfare:

> By reading the divine Scriptures [the scribe] wholesomely instructs his own mind, and by copying the precepts of the Lord he spreads them far and wide. What happy application, what praiseworthy industry... to fight the Devil's insidious wiles with pen and ink! For every word of the Lord written by the scribe is a wound inflicted on Satan.... [Ibid., p. 30]

Similarly, a colophon at the end of one early Coptic manuscript notes...

> There is no scribe who will not pass away, but what his hands have written will remain forever. Write nothing with your hand but that which you will be pleased to see at the resurrection.... May the Lord God Jesus Christ cause this holy copy to avail for the saving of the soul of the wretched man who wrote it. [Ibid., p. 31]

Bruce Metzger observes that the degree of calligraphic precision and artistry involved in the production of many ancient manuscripts is indicative that scribes considered their work to be a true act of spiritual service to God. As he notes, "In view of the difficulties involved in transcribing ancient books, it is... remarkable how high was the degree of achievement of most scribes." Metzger points out, for example, that in most manuscripts the size of the letters and the ductus [width] of the script "remain surprisingly uniform" throughout even a lengthy document. This is all evidence that the scribes not only took their work seriously, but that they regarded it as a true labor of love.[27]

---

[27] Ibid., p. 30.

Regarding the issue of textual variants, as discussed earlier, more than 99% are totally insignificant. Furthermore, none of the others affect in any way our understanding of the message and meaning of Jesus Christ or any other basic Christian doctrine. Commenting on the copying profession and the issue of quality control, Ed Komoszewski, James Sawyer and Daniel Wallace emphasize in *Reinventing Jesus: How Contemporary Skeptics Miss the Real Jesus and Mislead Popular Culture*, "There are two attitudes to avoid when it comes to the text of the New Testament: absolute certainty and total despair."[28] (See the following essay, "The Jewish Transmission of the Old Testament – and Its Implications.")

The Jewish Translation of the Tanakh – And Its Implications

Historically, Jewish scribes took Moses' admonition in Deut. 4:2 with utmost seriousness: "You shall not add to the word which I command you, nor take from it." They applied this standard not only to the Pentateuch but to the entire Tanakh (Old Testament) – all the ancient writings that they revered as divinely-inspired.

Scribes such as the **Talmudists** (AD 100-500) took extreme care in copying ancient manuscripts and synagogue scrolls. In fact, they were so exacting in their work that when they finished transcribing a manuscript, they gave the new copy equal authority to the older text and even valued it more because the older documents tended to become defaced and damaged over time. As Sir Frederick Kenyon has noted, "A damaged or imperfect copy was at once condemned as unfit for use.... Far from regarding an older copy of the Scriptures as more valuable, the Jewish habit has been to prefer the newer, as being the most perfect and free from damage."

Prior to the discovery of the Dead Sea Scrolls in 1947, the **Masoretic Texts** of the Tanakh were the oldest extant Hebrew versions of the Old Testament. These texts were compiled between the 6th and 8th centuries and became the standard Hebrew text that is still used today.

---

[28] Ed Komoszewski, James Sawyer and Daniel Wallace *Reinventing Jesus: How Contemporary Skeptics Miss the Real Jesus and Mislead Popular Culture* (Kregel Publications, 2003), p. 66.

Masorete scribes were meticulous perfectionists who revered the written word, as Wheeler Robinson comments in *The Bible in Its Ancient and English Versions*: "They treated the text with the greatest imaginable reverence, and devised a complicated system of safeguards against scribal slips. They counted, for example, the number of times each letter of the alphabet occurs in each book; they pointed out the middle letter of the Pentateuch and the middle letter of the whole Hebrew Bible."

Kenyon adds: "[The Masorete scribes] numbered the verses, words, and letters of every book. These trivialities... had the effect of securing minute attention to the precise transmission of the text.... The Masoretes were indeed anxious that not one jot nor tittle, not one small letter of the Law should pass away or be lost."

Masoretes were also diligent textual critics. In the margins of manuscripts they added detailed notes on textual (orthographic) variants and even statistical information on the frequency of certain words – a compendium of marginal notes known as the *Masorah Parva* ("Small Masorah"). In addition, they included more extensive notes, the *Masorah Magna* ("Large Masorah"), at the top and the foot of each page.

The significance of the Masoretic system of textual transmission cannot be overemphasized. A comparison of the Masoretic Text to the extant copies of the Dead Sea Scrolls proves that there were no significant alterations of the text over a period of more than a thousand years of transmission. And while no biblical scholar would argue that the monks and scribes who copied the New Testament texts were as meticulous and exacting as the Masoretes, they would still have regarded the transmission of the gospels and the other apostolic writings as a sacred trust.

Textual Variants: Accidental Changes

Although some scriptural variants were intentional (see the following section), the vast majority were accidental due to several factors.

Poor eyesight. In an age before eyeglasses, scribes who were afflicted with astigmatism found it difficult to distinguish between Greek letters that resemble one another, particularly if the previous copyist had written sloppily. For example, in majuscule script the sigma (Σ) and the epsilon (ϵ) were easily confused, as were the theta (Θ) and the omicron (O).

When two lines being copied happened to end with the same word or words, the scribe might accidentally copy the first line and omit the second. For example, in John 17:15 Codex Vaticanus reads: "I do not pray that you take them from the *[world, but that you keep them from the]* evil one."

An old monastic joke holds that a young monk, new to the monastery, noticed that the scribes were copying the Scriptures from copies, not originals. He expressed his concern to the abbot that any mistakes in the copies would be passed on, and over time the Scriptures would become corrupted. The abbot replied that this is the way it had always been done, but he conceded that the young man's point was valid and promised to check into it. He then descended into the vaults to check the originals, and when he didn't return after a long time, the young monk went looking for him. He found the abbot sitting in stunned silence, his eyes glazed over and wet with tears. "What's the matter, Father?" asked the monk – to which the abbot choked out, "In the original, the word was 'celebrate'!" [Note: In the scribal profession, "haplography" is the term used for words with accidental omitted letters.]

Poor hearing. When scribes in a scriptorium produced copies from dictation, confusion sometimes arose over words that are pronounced the same but have a different spelling and meaning – as in English words such as "their" and "there," "great" and "grate," or "eminent," "immanent," and "imminent." For example, in Rev. 15:6 the text should read: "Out of the temple came the seven angels with the seven plagues. They were dressed in clean, shining linen...." Several early manuscripts read instead: "They were dressed in clean, shining stone...."

Lack of concentration. Between glancing at the manuscript being copied and writing down the text, scribes sometimes forgot the exact wording of a clause or a sequence of letters. Occasionally, words or notes written in the margin of an older copy might even be incorporated into the text of a new manuscript.

For example, this was probably what happened in the case of the story of Jesus healing the man at the pool of Bethesda recorded in John 5:3-4. Apparently, a later scribe incorporated into the text a marginal reference to an angel coming down and periodically stirring the water, with the result that whoever got into the water first would be healed.

Changes in spelling, grammar and syntax. These constitute the vast majority of textual variants, and they include variations in spelling, variations on names, and transpositions (changes in the word order). Of course, these changes are insignificant and have no bearing on the meaning of a passage.

Textual Variants: Intentional Changes

An expanded text. Between the years 100-1500, about 2,500 words were added to the New Testament – or about 2% of the 138,000 total words in the text. Most of the additions were inserted to clarify certain passages, to enrich the text, or to harmonize parallel passages.

Clarifying the text. In Matthew 9:13 Jesus says: "For I came not to call the righteous, but sinners." Some scribes added the words, "unto repentance" – as in keeping with Luke 5:32. Likewise, in Matthew 26:3, as Jesus is denouncing the chief priests, some copyists couldn't resist adding, "and the scribes."

Jerome complained about copyists who "write down not what they find but what they think is the [true] meaning, and while they attempt to correct the errors of others, they make new errors." But in other cases, scribes were loathe to tamper with the received text even if it contained mistakes. For example, in the margin of Codex Vaticanus at Hebrews 1:3, a proofreader reprimanded a scribe for changing the text even though he had actually corrected an error in the older copy. The supervisor wrote in the margin, "Fool and knave, leave the old reading. Don't change it!"

Harmonizing parallel passages of Scripture. Since many scribes knew portions of the Bible by heart, they often tried to harmonize discordant parallels or quotations in certain passages. For example, in some later manuscripts the shorter form of the Lord's Prayer in Luke 11:2-4 was expanded to correlate with the longer form in Matthew 6:9-13.

In Matthew 9:11, Pharisees ask Jesus' disciples, "Why does your rabbi eat with tax collectors and sinners? Some Greek manuscripts add "and drink" to conform with the parallel passage in Luke 5:30. Similarly, the comment in John 19:20 that the *Titulus Crucis* (the inscription that hung above Jesus' head on the cross) "was written in Hebrew, in Latin, and in Greek" was also inserted into the text of many manuscripts at Luke 23:38.

Rectifying historical or geographical problems. Earlier manuscripts of Mark 1:2 read: "As it is written in Isaiah the prophet...." Actually, the reference is a composite taken from Malachi 3:1 and Isaiah 40:3. Later scribes, realizing the problem, edited the passage to read, "As it is written in the prophets...."

The reference in Matthew 27:9 to the chief priests using the 30 silver coins to buy the potter's field is cited as a fulfillment of Jeremiah's prophecy. Actually, it was Zechariah 11:12-13 that specifically relates to the incident. Therefore, some later scribes changed the reference from "Jeremiah" to "Zechariah," while others simply omitted the name altogether.

Expanding or enriching the text. As discussed previously, the *Pericope Adulterae* (John 7:53-8:12) is not included in the earliest and best manuscripts, and even when it does appear in some later texts its location changes. Perhaps, as Bruce Metzger concluded, this was simply an authentic oral tradition that was later inserted into the text. Even the ultra-critical Bart Ehrman has written that "most scholars think that it was probably a well-known story circulating in the oral tradition about Jesus, which at some point was added in the margin of a manuscript." (See the previous section, "Deconstructing Ehrman.") According to the church historian Eusebius (c. 320s), the story was included in the 2nd century *Gospel of the Hebrews,* portions of which have been preserved in the writings of the Church Fathers.

In most early manuscripts Jesus' words from the cross, "Father, forgive them, for they do not know that they are doing" (Luke 23:34), are not in the text. The addition may have been based on an early oral tradition.

The most extended expansion of a New Testament text is the epilogue to Mark's gospel in which the earliest manuscripts end abruptly with Mark 16:8 – "Trembling and bewildered, the women went out and fled from the tomb. They said nothing to anyone because they were afraid." As discussed earlier, there are three possible reasons for the abrupt ending:

(1) The author intentionally left the rest of the story open-ended;

(2) The book was never finished; or

(3) The last leaf of the manuscript was lost. As Ehrman concedes, "possibly, the last page of Mark's gospel, one in which Jesus actually did meet the disciples in Galilee, was somehow lost, and that all our copies of the gospel go back to this one truncated manuscript without the last page."[29]

---

[29] Ehrman, *Misquoting Jesus*, p. 68.

Regarding the "long ending" to Mark, ancient and medieval manuscripts feature three variations:

(1) The standard version that includes verses 9-20 in most Bibles. This includes Jesus' appearance to Mary Magdalene and her testimony to Jesus' other followers. "Later," we are told, Jesus appeared to the Eleven [disciples] as they were eating, and gave them a modified version of the Great Commission. In his charge, Jesus declared many "signs" that would accompany those who believed – including healing the sick, driving out demons, speaking "in new tongues," handling deadly snakes, and immunity to drinking poison. Following these exhortations, Jesus ascended into heaven.

(2) A few texts from the 7th, 8th and 9th centuries add a succinct postscript:

> All that they were told, they reported briefly to Peter and those around him. After these things, Jesus sent out by means of them, from east to west, the sacred and immortal message of salvation unto the ages.

(3) At least one manuscript, Codex Washingtonius (c. 475), includes a longer version of the epilogue called the Freer Logion that is an expansion of verse 14:

> [14] Afterward He appeared to the eleven as they were eating and reproved them for their lack of faith and stubbornness because they had not believed those who saw Him after He had risen. [14a]And they made excuses, saying, "This age of lawlessness and unbelief is under Satan, who by means of unclean spirits does not allow men to grasp the truth and power of God. Therefore, reveal now your righteousness." Thus they spoke to Christ. [14b] And Christ replied to them, "The term of years of Satan's power is completed, but other terrible things draw near." [14c] And for those who have sinned I was handed over to death, in order that they might return to the truth and sin no more; in order that they might inherit the spiritual and incorruptible glory of righteousness which is in heaven.'
>
> [15] Then He said to them, "Go into all the world and preach the gospel to every person...."

[Note: A few scholars contend that the original Gospel of Mark included both a prologue and an epilogue that were lost. See N. Clayton Croy, *The Mutilation of Mark's Gospel* (Abingdon Press, 2003).]

Theologically-motivated changes. Ancient and medieval manuscripts include many accretions that were intended to clarify or emphasize a particular doctrine or refute a particular heresy. For example, the 2nd century heretic, Marcion, in his heavily-edited Gospel According to Luke, eliminated all references to Jesus' Jewish heritage. In addition, Tatian's *Diatessaron* included several alterations that emphasized asceticism.

In the prologue to Luke's Gospel (Luke 1:3), the author notes that "it seemed good to me to write an orderly account" of the life of Christ. But some later copyists thought this didn't sound spiritual enough, so they added, "it seemed good to me and to the Holy Spirit to write an orderly account."

In I Timothy 3:16 – "Who appeared in a body, was vindicated by the Spirit,..." a copyist changed "who" to "God" – either intentionally to clarify the text or accidentally because the two words are similar. In Greek, "who" is spelled ΟΣ, and the abbreviation for "God" is ΘΣ.

Matthew 1:16 reads, "Jacob was the father of Joseph, the husband of Mary..." A later copyist, wanting to emphasize Jesus' immaculate conception, altered the verse to read, "Jacob was the father of Joseph, to whom was betrothed the virgin Mary...."

In John 7:8, Jesus tells his disciples, "I am not going to this festival [in Jerusalem], for my time has not yet fully come," but two verses later John notes, "But after his brothers had gone up to the feast, then he also went up, not publicly but in private." Some scribes, apparently embarrassed by the implications that Jesus was being duplicitous, changed the reading to say, "I am not *yet* going up...." [Note: Interestingly, the NIV, which usually excludes later additions to the texts, also inserts "yet" into the text of John 7:8, although a text note explains that "Some early manuscripts do not have 'yet'."]

In Matthew 24:36, Jesus says regarding his return: "But about that day and hour no one knows, neither the angels in heaven, nor the Son, but only the Father." Some scribes, unable to reconcile Jesus' ignorance with his divinity, omitted the phrase, "nor the Son." Curiously, all of the manuscripts include "nor the Son" in the parallel passage in Mark 13:32.

In Mark 9:28-29, when the disciples ask Jesus why they could not exorcize a demon, he replies, "This kind can come out only by prayer." Some later manuscripts add, "This kind can come out only by prayer and fasting."

In the version of the "Lord's Prayer" in Matthew 6:9-13, our earliest texts end with: "And lead us not into temptation, but deliver us from the evil one" – to which some later manuscripts added a phrase borrowed from David's prayer in I Chron. 29:11: "...for yours is the kingdom and the power and the glory forever. Amen."

In the story of Philip and the Ethiopian eunuch recorded in Acts 8, we read: [36]"As they traveled along the road, they came to some water and the eunuch said, 'Look, here is water. Why shouldn't I be baptized?' [38]And he gave orders to stop the chariot. Then both Philip and the eunuch went down into the water and Philip baptized him." A scribe, perhaps fearing that readers would think that the eunuch received baptism without believing in Jesus, later added the sentences that became Acts 8:37 – "Philip said, 'If you believe with all your heart, you may [be baptized].' The eunuch answered, 'I believe that Jesus Christ is the Son of God.'"

As discussed earlier, regarding the "Johannine Comma" of I John 5:7-8, the text should simply read: "For there are three that testify: the Spirit, the water, and the blood; and the three are in agreement." In the later Byzantine *stemma* of texts, the verses were altered to emphasize the doctrine of the Trinity: "For there are three that bear record in heaven, the Father, the Word, and the Holy Spirit; and these three are one; and there are three that bear witness on earth, the Spirit, the water, and the blood, and these three are one." When the Dutch scholar Erasmus produced his Greek New Testament in the early 1500s, he originally omitted the "Johannine Comma" but later bowed to pressure and reinserted it.

In addition to these examples, a few later changes seem to have been motivated by a bias against women. In Acts 18:26, the names "Priscilla and Aquila" were switched in some later manuscripts so the husband's name would be listed first. In Romans 16:7 some later manuscripts changed "Junia," whom Paul refers to as "outstanding among the apostles," to the male "Junias." In Acts 17:4 a scribe changed "prominent women" to "wives of prominent men."

Maintaining Perspective

Regarding the issue of variant readings in the manuscripts, three important points should be reemphasized:

(1) Very few variants are significant. In fact, most are not even noticeable when the text is translated into other languages. Less than 1% change the meaning of the text, and few of those are consequential. For example, in Romans 5:1, does Paul write, "We have peace" (indicative mood) or "Let us have peace" (subjunctive mood)? – a difference of a single letter. Is this truly significant?

In I Thessalonians 2:7, does Paul describe himself and his colleagues as "gentle" or "little children"? – a difference of a single letter (*epioi* or *nepioi*). Does this matter?

In I John 1:4, does John write, "...we are writing these things so that our joy may be complete" or "...we are writing these things so that your joy may be complete"? How important is this difference?

(2) It is almost always possible to compare manuscripts and determine where the changes were made. For instance, suppose you write an essay and ask five friends to produce a handwritten copy of it.

- Next, your friends ask five more people to do the same – down to the fifth generation.
- The first generation of copyists will inevitably make some errors, which will be reproduced by each of the succeeding four generations.
- Furthermore, each succeeding generation will make additional errors of their own.
- By the fifth generation, there would be about 4,000 copies of your essay – all with numerous errors.
- Now consider: The first generation of copyists made errors, but it would be unlikely that they all made the same mistakes.
- If you compared the copies, you would find that one group contained the same mistakes, while the other four did not – which would make it relatively easy to reconstruct the original from the copies.
- Furthermore, most of the errors would be obvious – misspellings, punctuation marks, etc.
- Therefore, even if you lost the original, it would be possible to reproduce the original essay provided you had access to a sufficient number of copies.

(3) There is no evidence that later copyists introduced any new or novel doctrines into the texts, or that any of the changes alter our understanding of Jesus. It is important to keep in mind that the transmission process was primarily motivated by a desire to reproduce the sacred texts faithfully and accurately, as Bruce Metzger notes:

> Lest the foregoing examples of alterations should give the impression that scribes were altogether willful and capricious in transmitting ancient copies of the New Testament, it ought to be noted that other evidence points to the careful and painstaking work on the part of many faithful copyists. [Metzger and Ehrman, *The Text of the New Testament*, p. 271.]

Infamous Bibles

The invention of the printing press and the transition from hand-copied manuscripts to printed Bibles did not totally eliminate the problem of accidental errors in biblical texts. Here are a few examples of some of the more infamous Bibles of the past 500 years.

The "Bug Bible." The 1535 Coverdale Bible translation of Psalm 91:5 reads, "Thou shall not nede to be afrayed for eny bugges by night." (In Middle English, "bugge" meant a ghost or a "spectre that haunts." The King James Bible replaced "bugges" with "terror.")

The "Placemakers Bible." The second edition of the Geneva Bible (1562) translation of Matthew 5:9 reads, "Blessed are the placemakers [peacemakers]; for they shall be called the children of God."

The "Debased Bible." The 1815 Douai-Rheims Bible translates Philippians 2:7 as Christ "debased [emptied] himself."

The sinful **"Printers Bible."** The 1612 edition of the KJV translates Psalm 119:161 as, "Printers [Princes] have persecuted me without cause."

The "Unrighteous Bible." In the 1653 edition of the KJV published by Cambridge Press, I Corinthians 6:9 reads, "Know ye not that the unrighteous shall [not] inherit the kingdom of God?"

The infamous **"Wicked Bible"** (or **"Sinner's Bible"**). A 1631 edition of the KJV translates Exodus 20:14 as, "Thou shalt commit adultery." The printers, Barker & Lucas, were fined £300 and all copies were recalled. Only 11 copies are known to exist today.

The "Sin On Bible." The 1716 KJV translation of John 8:11 reads, "Go and sin on more" rather than "Go and sin no more."

The "Fool's Bible." The 1763 KJV translates Psalm 14:1 as, "The fool hath said in his heart there is a God." The printers were fined £3,000 and all copies were ordered recalled and destroyed.

The "Wife-Hater Bible." The 1810 KJV translation of Luke 14:26 reads, "If any man come to me, and hate not his father, and mother, and wife, and children, and brethren, and sisters, yea, and his own wife also, he cannot be my disciple."

The "Wife-Beater Bible." In the Matthew's Bible of 1537, a footnote to I Peter 3:7 reads, "And if she be not obedient and healpeful unto him, endevoureth to beat the fear of God into her head, that thereby she may be compelled to learn her duty and do it." (It should be noted that footnotes are neither divinely-inspired nor infallible!)

The "Prostitutes Bible." Mistakes still occasionally happen in Bible publishing. In the New English Bible (NET Bible, 2001), Prov. 2:16 reads, "To deliver you from the adulteress, from the sexually loose woman who speaks flattering words." In the first printing of the NET Bible, a footnote at the end of the verse referenced a 1-800 number. As it so happened, the translator was writing the notes for this verse on his computer when he received a phone call and, without a pen at hand, typed the call-back number into the notes – after which he forgot to delete it!

Part 3:
A Brief History of Biblical Textual Criticism

First Phase

The advent of the printing press in the latter half of the 1400s opened up fortuitous opportunities not only for the mass production of Bibles, but for the standardization and the exact replication of the biblical text.

The Complutensian Polyglot (1522). The first "modern" version of the Greek New Testament in Western Europe was the Complutensian Polyglot, completed in 1517 but not published until 1522. This "polyglot" version was a multi-lingual edition in which the Old Testament was presented in Hebrew, the Latin Vulgate, and the Greek Septuagint translations, side by side in parallel columns. The book was translated by an editorial team of Spanish scholars headed by **Stunica** (Diego Lopez de Zuniga), and it was printed in the university town of Alcala, or "Complutum" in Latin – hence, the Complutensian Polyglot. Unfortunately, the Greek manuscripts on which the editors based their translation have never been identified.

Desiderius Erasmus (1515). Before the Complutensian Polyglot edition could be published the Dutch scholar, Erasmus of Rotterdam, published his own version of the Greek New Testament in 1515. Lacking access to many early Greek manuscripts, Erasmus relied upon about half a dozen copies – mostly from the late Medieval period. Nonetheless, his New Testament became a publishing sensation and he became a celebrity and a best-selling author.

There were some significant deficiencies in Erasmus' research. None of his manuscripts predated the 10th century, and he based his edition of the gospels primarily upon a single 12th century manuscript. His versions of Acts and the epistles were based mostly upon another 12th century text, and his sole source text for Revelation lacked the final leaf – whereupon he improvised and simply translated the final six verses of the book directly from the Latin Vulgate version. His book was augmented by a revised edition of the Latin Vulgate.

The Textus Receptus. Despite its shortcomings, Erasmus' Greek New Testament became the standard for subsequent Greek editions – the so-called

Textus Receptus tradition. For the next 200 years Greek editions were based not on the oldest or best manuscripts but on the "received text" as filtered primarily through Erasmus.

The *Textus Receptus* served as the standard version for the earliest vernacular translations, including Luther's German-language New Testament and English-language translations such as Tyndale's New Testament and the Authorized (King James) Version.

Not until the 19th century did scholars begin applying the scientific principles of textual criticism and basing translations on the oldest and best manuscript evidence rather than simply deferring to the *Textus Receptus* tradition. In 1550 a new Greek New Testament produced by **Stephanus** (Robert Estienne) included margin notes citing some of the textual variations in the manuscripts consulted, but no substantial changes to the *Textus Receptus* were incorporated into his edition. [Note: Stephanus' fourth edition, published in 1551, divided the text into numbered verses for the first time.]

Theodore Beza (1519-1605), an eminent Protestant scholar and close associate of John Calvin, published nine editions of the Greek New Testament between 1565-1604, but his text varied little from Stephanus' 1551 edition.

In 1624 **Bonaventure and Abraham Elzevir** published a Greek New Testament in their printing shop in Leiden that was based primarily on Beza's edition. In the preface to the second edition (1633), they declared that the reader was holding "the text now received by all, in which we give nothing changed or corrupted." This became the basis for the designation, *Textus Receptus* – considered at the time to be the commonly received, standard text of the Greek New Testament. But as Bruce Metzer comments, "Yet, its textual basis is essentially a handful of late and haphazardly collected minuscule manuscripts, and in a dozen passages its rendering is supported by no known Greek witness."[30]

The Authorized (King James) Version of 1611. Like its predecessors and its successors for more than the next 200 years, the popular King James Version of the Bible was also based on the *Textus Receptus*. It should be noted that modern translations have access to a hundred times more manuscripts than the number used in producing the KJV – including more than 400 that predate the earliest texts used by Erasmus. Strangely (or more correctly, ignorantly), contemporary advocates of the KJV argue that the earliest manuscripts were all corrupt and that the later manuscripts were superior – an absurd premise that no reputable scholar today would endorse.

---

[30] Metzger and Ehrman, *The Text of the New Testament*, p. 152.

Second Phase

Beginning in the mid-1600s, the second phase in the history of New Testament textual criticism was marked by serious scholarly efforts to catalogue variant readings from as many Greek manuscripts and commentaries of the Church Fathers as possible. For the next couple of centuries scholars scoured libraries and museums in Europe and the Middle East, accessing and often purchasing ancient texts. However, most editors of the New Testament during this period were content to reprint variations on the *Textus Receptus*.

In the 1650s **Brian Walton** (1600-61) edited a English-language Polyglot Bible based on Stephanus' 1550 edition, with slight alterations. Walton included footnotes with variant readings from the Codex Alexandrinus (which the patriarch of Constantinople had recently presented to King Charles I) and several other texts.

In 1675 **John Fell** (1625-86), the bishop of Oxford, published a Greek Testament in which he claimed to have consulted more than a hundred manuscripts. However, his basic text was still virtually indistinguishable from the *Textus Receptus*.

Third Phase

John Mill (1645-1707). John Mill, a renowned Oxford scholar, published an edition of the Greek New Testament in 1707 that revolutionized the field of biblical textual criticism. Over a 30-year period Mill collected and accessed over a hundred Greek manuscripts, comparing their texts to the Scripture commentaries by the early Church Fathers. Whenever possible, he also accessed early versions of the New Testament in Coptic and Syriac. When Mill finally published his findings, he cited some 30,000 variations in the texts.  Inexplicably, he did not construct a new text based on his research but simply reprinted Stephanus' 1550 text without variation.

Daniel Whitby (1638-1726). Mill was a theological conservative, but his research nonetheless alarmed many clerics and Bible scholars who feared that his findings might undermine fundamental doctrines of the faith. This prompted the Anglican Arminian theologian, Daniel Whitby, to publish a rebuttal in 1710 in which he argued correctly that although minor scribal errors had obviously crept into the texts over time, they did not alter or corrupt anything significant including any key doctrines of the faith.

Richard Simon (1638-1712). Whitby had an additional concern: He feared Roman Catholic scholars would use Mill's conclusions as propaganda against Protestants, arguing that Scripture alone was an insufficient basis for authority for the Christian faith. In fact, this had already happened. In *A Critical History of the Text of the New Testament* (1689), the French Catholic priest and scholar Richard Simon argued that the reason Jerome was inspired to produce the Latin Vulgate was precisely because the ancient texts had already become corrupted and unreliable. Therefore, he asserted, the Vulgate is more accurate and authoritative than the manuscripts that preceded it. According to Simon, it is not Scripture itself that ultimately matters (since it has been corrupted), but the interpretation of Scripture as found in the apostolic tradition as transmitted through the Roman Catholic Church. Therefore, he declared, "the great changes that have taken place in the manuscripts of the Bible... since the first originals were lost, completely destroy the principle of the Protestants."

[Note: Simon's argument provided a clever apologetic for Catholics, but it is fundamentally flawed. In effect, he was arguing that our oldest surviving manuscripts cannot be trusted, but that the revision of those manuscripts can be trusted as reliable. But this is circular reasoning. Obviously, Jerome revised his text on the basis of earlier manuscripts which, apparently, he trusted to a sufficient extent.]

Anthony Collins (1676-1729). The concern that John Mill had opened up a pandora's box was soon confirmed when, just three years after Whitby's rebuttal, the English philosopher Anthony Collins referenced Mill's research to push a deistic agenda. In his pamphlet, *Discourse on Free Thinking* (1713), Collins argued that the Bible had been supernaturally inspired but was nonetheless unreliable, and that reason rather than revelation should be our ultimate guide to belief and practice.

Edward Wells (1667-1727). In 1719 Edward Wells, an Anglican vicar and theologian, published the first Greek Testament that abandoned the *Textus Receptus* altogether in favor of the new scholarship based on the more ancient manuscripts. Although his edition was largely ignored at the time, Wells was influential in setting the process of textual criticism on a new course.

Richard Bentley (1662-1742). In the intense scholarly debates that followed, Richard Bentley, the Master of Trinity College of Cambridge University, set forth a reasonable and orthodox position on the issue. Bentley observed that textual variants were unavoidable given the fact that there were so many Greek New Testament manuscripts transcribed over the centuries. However, he asserted, considering the large number of manuscripts available, a systematic analysis of their variant readings rendered it likely that in most cases the original texts could be determined within a high degree of probability.

In fact, this was Bentley's goal: to restore as closely as possible the original text of the New Testament. Assuming that Jerome had used the best Greek manuscripts available in his day, Bentley reasoned that by comparing the oldest extant manuscripts of the Vulgate with the oldest manuscripts of the Greek New Testament, one could determine the content of the best texts of the 4th century and therefore skip over the 1200 years of textual transmission in which the text was repeatedly changed. It was an ambitious undertaking, and unfortunately Bentley died before completing the project.

Johann Albrecht Bengel (1687-1752). Like Daniel Whitby and many other conservative scholars, Johann Albrecht Bengel, a Lutheran pastor and professor, was seriously disturbed by the implications of Mill's research and the 30,000 or more variants he had found in the ancient and medieval manuscripts. As a strict biblical literalist, Bengel's theology and hermeneutics depended upon the exact wording in the original manuscripts. Therefore, he devoted his career to studying the history of the transmission of the biblical texts in an effort to reconstruct the original New Testament.

As an intense textual critic, Bengel developed two important methodological principles that text critics still use today.

- **Principle #1: There are "families" of manuscripts that stand in a kind of genealogical relationship to each other.** In theory, a scholar can set up a kind of family tree (or *stemma*) and trace the lineage of various documents back to their source. [Note: About 150 years later, Westcott and Hort would state the basic presupposition regarding the identification of a *stemma* of manuscripts as "Identity of reading implies identity of origin."]
- **Principle #2: The more difficult reading is preferable to the easier one.** This presupposition is based on the rational assumption that when

scribes changed the texts, they were more likely to try to improve, simplify, or harmonize them than otherwise.

In 1734 Bengel published a new edition of the Greek New Testament based primarily upon the *Textus Receptus* but also citing variant readings in the text that he considered superior. In the process he also standardized punctuation and divided the NT text into paragraphs. While acknowledging the variants in the manuscripts, Bengel concluded that (1)they were fewer in number than might have been expected given the large number of extant manuscripts, and (2)these variants affected no fundamental articles of faith.

[Note: Bengel had some eccentric interpretations, particularly in relation to Bible prophecy. He was convinced that the pope was the Antichrist, that Freemasons represented the False Prophet of Revelation, and that the Second Coming of Christ would occur in 1836.]

Johann Wettstein (1693-1754). Johann Wettstein, a contemporary of Bengel, was convinced as a young scholar that the core salvific message of the Bible was unaffected by the variant readings in the early manuscripts. In 1715, however, while examining the Codex Alexandrinus in England, he noticed a variant reading for I Timothy 3:16. In most manuscripts, the text referred to Christ as "God made manifest in the flesh, and justified in the Spirit." However, Alexandrinus referred to Christ as he "who was made manifest in the flesh, and justified by the Spirit." Wettstein was troubled that the passage did not refer specifically to Christ as divine.

Over the next 15 years as he continued his studies, Wettstein noticed other instances in which various manuscripts had been altered to clarify the divine nature of Jesus Christ – most notably the "Johannine Comma" in I John 5:7-8. Wettstein drifted toward a liberal/critical view of Scripture until he was fired from his faculty position at the University of Basel for holding "rationalistic" views on the inspiration of the Bible and the doctrine of the Trinity in particular.

In 1752 he published a new edition of the Greek New Testament based on the *Textus Receptus* but also including copious editorial notes derived from variant readings in numerous manuscripts. Over the course of his career he came to the odd conclusion that all the early Greek manuscripts had been contaminated by the Latin versions and that, therefore, the later Greek manuscripts were more representative of the authentic original text.

Johann Jakob Griesbach (1745-1812). Subsequent 18th century scholars such as **William Bowyer** and **Edward Harwood** regularly deserted the *Textus Receptus* tradition for alternate readings found in earlier manuscripts.

Likewise, Johann Jakob Griesbach largely abandoned the *Textus Receptus* in favor of the results of his own research. Griesbach was a New Testament professor at the University of Jena (Holland) who studied not only the ancient Greek texts and the Church Fathers but also other versions of the New Testament that had been largely overlooked such as the Syriac, Armenian, and Gothic.

Griesbach was also gifted systematizer who further developed Bengel's theory of manuscript groupings into family trees (*stemma*), and based on his research he concluded that extant manuscripts could be divided into three *stemma*: the **Alexandrian**, the **Western**, and the **Byzantine**.

Karl Lachmann (1793-1851). In 1831 a German philologist, Karl Lachmann, produced the first Greek New Testament based exclusively on the earliest-known manuscript evidence rather than the *Textus Receptus*. Lachmann concluded that recovering the original text of the New Testament was an exercise in futility since our earliest extant texts were 4th or 5th century manuscripts. Therefore, the best that could be done was to produce the Greek New Testament in the time of Jerome, circa 380. Using no minuscule manuscripts, he based his text on several of the earliest majuscules, the Old Latin and Jerome's Vulgate, and the scriptural citations in the writings of the Church Fathers.

Lachmann's edition launched a new era in biblical textual criticism and marked the first systematic effort to utilize "scientific methods" in New Testament scholarship rather than subjective educated opinions

Constantine von Tischendorf (1815-74). Some of the most remarkable discoveries in the 19th century were made by Constantine von Tischendorf, a passionate and dedicated scholar who considered his life's calling to be "a sacred task": the recovery of "the original form of the New Testament." (See page 190*ff.*) To this end, Tischendorf scoured the libraries and monasteries of Europe and the Middle East seeking lost and neglected manuscripts. He succeeded brilliantly in his quest, recovering more manuscripts and publishing more critical editions of the Greek Bible than any other scholar in history. Over the course of his career, he  published 22 editions of early Christian texts and published 8 separate editions of the Greek New Testament. Among his discoveries, two manuscripts in particular are noteworthy:

- In 1840 he accessed the Codex Ephraemi (c. 450) in the Biliotheque Nationale in Paris and deciphered it.

- Beginning in 1844 he was able to retrieve the Codex Sinaiticus (c. 350) from St. Catherine's Monastery at the foot of Mt. Sinai. This Greek manuscript, containing the entire New Testament and most of the Old, and is still the most complete ancient Bible manuscript ever discovered, and its text became the basis for the most accurate translations of the New Testament.

In 1881 **Brooke Foss Westcott** (1825-1901) and **Fenton John Anthony Hort** (1828-1892), published one of the most significant works in biblical textual criticism, The New Testament in the Original Greek. Both men were professors of divinity at Cambridge University.

The result of 28 years of collaborative effort, their two-volume text presented analytical methods that set the standard in the field of textual criticism, and the Greek text that they produced is very similar to the one that scholars still use today.

One of their major contributions to the field came in their cataloguing of genealogical groupings of manuscripts. Nearly 150 years earlier, Bengel had recognized that manuscripts could be sorted out by *stemma*, Westcott and Hort deduced that manuscripts that have the same wording must derive from a common source – either the original manuscript or a particular copy of it (a principle that is sometimes stated as "Identity of reading implies identity of origin.") In their research, Westcott and Hort concluded there were 4 major families of texts:

(1) The Neutral text. These manuscripts represent very closely the original texts and were relatively free from later corruption or revision in the course of their transmission. Wescott and Hort considered Codex Sinaiticus (c. 350) and Codex Vaticanus (c. 350), the two oldest manuscripts available to them, to be part of this tradition. [Note: Most contemporary scholars no longer use the term "Neutral" text.]

(2) The Alexandrian text. Produced in Alexandria, Egypt, these copies are high-quality, standardized, and probably the products of professional copyists. Quotations in the Alexandrian Church Fathers – Clement,

Origen, Dionysius, and Cyril – indicate that this was the text they used. The Alexandrian manuscripts includes occasional alterations in the texts to make them grammatically and stylistically more acceptable. Examples include two of the Bodmer papyri, P66 and P75, and Codex Ephraemi.

(3) The Western text. These are early manuscripts from the 2nd century and are thought to be based on the original texts. There are copious copying errors in these texts, indicating that they were produced before manuscript copying became more professionalized and standardized. In many passages, the Western text is closer to a paraphrase than a literal translation. Westcott and Hort noted the extent to which "words, clauses, and even whole sentences" were altered or inserted into the text in order to clarify various passages.

The Western text is best represented by P38 (late 2nd century), P48 (3rd century), Codex Bezae (c. 450) and the Old Latin manuscripts. Also, early scholars such as Marcion, Tatian, Justin, Irenaeus, Hippolytus, Tertullian, and Cyprian accessed the Western form of text. [Note: The term, "Western text," is somewhat of a misnomer. Scholars believe these manuscripts were written and circulated primarily in Italy and Gaul, but also in North Africa.]

(4) The Byzantine (or Syrian) text. This text originated in and around Constantinople, from where it was disseminated throughout the Eastern Roman Empire. In time, it became the dominant form of the Greek New Testament in the Byzantine Empire. The Byzantine text is found in rudimentary form as early as the late 4th century in the commentaries of Basil the Great and John Chrysostom, and is best represented by Codex Alexandrinus, the later majuscule manuscripts, and most of the minuscule manuscripts that proliferated during the Middle Ages.

These manuscripts are numerous, but they are considered the farthest removed in wording from the original texts. Westcott and Hort noted the "lucidity and completeness" of the Byzantine text, along with its conflation and harmonization of parallel readings. Erasmus' Greek New Testament and the *Textus Receptus* were based on these Byzantine manuscripts. [Note: Most contemporary scholars agree with Westcott and Hort that the Byzantine text post-dates the other *stemma* of texts. According to Bruce Metzger, none of the patristic writers prior to Basil the Great and John Chrysostom (i.e., late 300s) had any acquaintance with the Byzantine text. (See Metzger and Ehrman, *The Text of the New Testament*, p. 222.)]

The Current State of Textual Criticism

The proliferation of manuscripts. Whereas early textual critics such as Mill and Bentley had access to about 100 Greek manuscripts, today more than 5,700 manuscripts have been catalogued. As discussed in Chapter 6, these manuscripts include everything from tiny fragments to a few complete New Testaments.

- There are 18 manuscripts from the 2nd century – 6 of which were recently discovered and not yet catalogued.
- More than 60 manuscripts pre-date the year 300.
- Only about 60 manuscripts contain the entire New Testament, of which Codex Sinaiticus is the oldest and the only complete majuscule text.
- A recently-discovered 1st century manuscript of Mark's gospel is scheduled to be published by E. J. Brill in 2015. (Previously, the earliest copy of Mark's Gospel dated to circa 200).

In addition to the Greek texts, there are hundreds of early manuscripts in other languages such as Latin, Syriac, Coptic, Gothic, Armenian, etc., as well as the voluminous scriptural references in the writings of the Church Fathers.

A new taxonomy. The taxonomy that Westcott and Hort developed has been revised based on discoveries of many more early papyri manuscripts in the 20th century. In 1924 **B. H. Streeter**, in *The Four Gospels: A Study of Origins*, concluded that Westcott and Hort's "Neutral" and "Alexandrian" groups were in fact one and the same. Since then, most scholars accept a triadic division of manuscripts:

(1) Alexandrian – including Codex Vaticanus; Codex Sinaiticus; two Bodmer papyri (P66 and P75); and Codex Ephraemi.

(2) Western – including P38, P48, and Codex Bezae.

(3) Byzantine (or Syriac) – including Codex Alexandrinus.

It should be noted that most contemporary scholars regard the classification of texts by *stemma* to be considerably more complex than was generally accepted in previous generations. By the second decade of the 4th century, once the emperor Constantine had legalized the Christian religion, manuscripts could be freely exchanged throughout the empire. The result was an extensive cross-pollination of biblical texts, and the geographical variations of the past generally vanished. Furthermore, some early texts appear to have had a mixed ancestry as a result of copyists integrating two or more manuscripts.

Some fundamentalist scholars have challenged the mainstream assumption that the Alexandrian manuscripts are the qualitative standard for textual criticism. They argue that the original text is best preserved in the medieval Byzantine manuscripts which constitute the vast majority of extant manuscripts. According to this view, God providentially preserved the essential purity of the type of text that eventually became the *Textus Receptus* – and hence their argument that the Authorized (King James) Version of the Bible should be regarded as the standard and superior English-language translation.

Computer-based textual analysis. In the past 20 years the computer has revolutionized the field of biblical textual studies in four key areas:

(1) The availability of digitized copies of manuscripts on the worldwide web;

(2) The collation of manuscripts;

(3) The analysis of manuscript data; and

(4) High-resolution images of thousands of pages of early manuscripts.

With the publication of manuscripts on the internet, scholars now have access to the whole range of extant manuscripts. The text of every biblical manuscript is stored in a database, making it possible to analyze and calculate every variation in every one of these documents. Computers are capable of doing complicated statistical analyses at blinding speed – an astonishing development when one considers that until the mid-1990s scholars still tabulated scriptural agreements and variations by hand – a laborious, tedious and time-intensive endeavor.

Part 4:
The Methodology of Biblical Textual Criticism

Biblical Textual Criticism: The Science and the Art

The process of biblical textual criticism is as much an art as a science. In lieu of verifiable, original manuscripts – of which we have none – the process of restoring the original wording of the texts is an exercise in probabilities and the educated assumptions of textual critics. As the English classical scholar A. E. Housman explained:

> Textual criticism is not a branch of mathematics, nor indeed an exact science at all. It deals with a matter not rigid and constant... but fluid and variable; namely the frailties and aberrations of the human mind and of its insubordinate servants, the human fingers. It is therefore not susceptible to hard-and-fast rules. [Quoted in Metzger and Ehrman, *The Text of the New Testament*, p. 315.]

Nonetheless, it is a valuable and essential undertaking, and over the years scholars have developed sensible guidelines to make the process more systematic and scientific based on external and internal evidence. Even many skeptical scholars such as Bart Ehrman acknowledge the positive potential of textual criticism:

> For my part... I continue to think that even if we cannot be 100 percent certain about what we can attain to, we can at least be certain that all the surviving manuscripts were copied from other manuscripts... and that it is at least possible to get back to the oldest and earliest stage of the manuscript tradition for each of the books of the New Testament.... And so we must rest content knowing that getting back to the earliest attainable version is the best we can do.... This oldest form of the text is no doubt closely (very closely) related to what the author originally wrote. [Ehrman, *Misquoting Jesus*, p. 62.]

External Evidence

When assessing the relative value of a manuscript and adjudicating between variant readings, text critics consider four external criteria: (1) the age of the manuscript; (2) the number of comparable manuscripts; (3) the geographical distribution of comparable manuscripts; and (4) the genealogy of the manuscript.

1. Age of the manuscript. Generally-speaking – and based on the sensible principle that the more the texts are copied and recopied, the more changes accrue – the oldest manuscripts are the most reliable. Of course, the rule doesn't always apply for two reasons:

- A text from the 6th century may be based on a 5th century manuscript, while a text from the 8th century may be based on a 4th century document – in which the latter (8th century) manuscript may be superior.

- The earliest period of textual transmission was, unfortunately, also the least controlled. For the most part amateur scribes copied the earliest manuscripts, making many mistakes and alterations (both intentional and inadvertent) in the process.

It is important to note that text critics, regardless of their theological orientation, generally agree on the established principles for determining the relative age of manuscripts:

- As discussed in Chapter 6, the oldest Greek manuscripts are **papyrus**, dating from the 2nd to the 7th centuries. To date, there are 116 papyri manuscripts containing portions of most of the books of the NT.

- *Majuscule* manuscripts, made of parchment and vellum (animal skins), contain all capital letters and date from the 4th to the 9th centuries.

- *Minuscule* manuscripts, also written on parchment, date from the 9th to the 15th centuries.

2. Number of comparable manuscripts. The sheer number of manuscripts bears little correlation to the quality of the texts. The mere fact that a majority of manuscripts read a particular way does not necessarily mean they are superior. For example, there are many more medieval-era (Byzantine) manuscripts than earlier texts, but they are generally considered to be the least reliable. As the following chart illustrates, if manuscript "A" is superior to "B" (i.e., it contains fewer errors and/or variant readings), then the 8 offspring of "B" are inferior to the 2 offspring of "A" even though there are more of them.

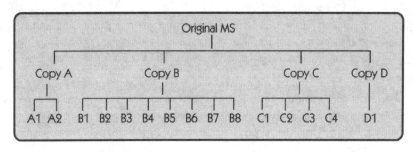

If the majority of the earliest manuscripts support a particular reading, scholars usually consider that reading to be superior to alternative readings.

3. Geographical distribution of comparable manuscripts. The geographical range of manuscripts often determines the preferability of a particular reading. For example, if a particular variant reading is found in a number of manuscripts but all these manuscripts originated in one location, text critics might conclude that it was a local variant in which the same mistake was recopied multiple times – in which case scholars would prefer the variant reading from texts that came from a wider geographical range of manuscripts.

4. Genealogy of the manuscript. For a particular reading to be considered "original," it should be found in the best manuscripts and the best groups of manuscripts. As Johann Albrecht Bengel theorized, certain *stemma* can be shown, for a variety of reasons, to be superior to others. Later, Westcott and Hort identified the "Neutral" or "Alexandrian" text as the oldest and best text, and the one to be preferred when comparing variant readings.

Internal Evidence

Along with the foregoing external factors, text critics also consider two relevant criteria related to the internal quality of a manuscript.

1. What is the most likely reading of the passage considering the specific characteristics of the author? When comparing variant readings, which alternative makes the most sense considering the author's particular writing style, vocabulary and theology? Furthermore, the general theme of the book along with the immediate context of a passage can shed light on which variant reading is more likely.

2. What is the most likely reading that a scribe would have created in order to clarify or alter the passage? In keeping with Bengel's principle that the more difficult reading is more likely to be closer to the original – and all other factors being equal – the more obscure reading is usually assumed to be the more authentic. This principle is based on the sensible assumption that scribes would be more likely to try to correct mistakes or clarify the meaning of a vague passage than to complicate it. This criterion is sometimes stated as, "The reading that best explains the existence of the others is more likely to be original."

This principle usually infers that the shorter reading is to be preferred over the more expanded or more explanatory alternative. For example, the shorter form of the Lord's Prayer in Luke 11:2-4 is generally preferred to the longer version of Matthew 6:9-13. But of course, regarding this particular example,

Jesus might very well have prayed a similar prayer on several occasions – sometimes in an abbreviated form and other times in a more extended version.

An associated corollary to this principle is that in passages with a parallel in another gospel, that reading is preferred which stands in verbal dissidence with the other – the assumption being that scribes regularly altered passages to bring them into harmony with other similar passages. This principle also applies to the citation of Old Testament passages. In addition, it was common for scribes to replace an obscure or unfamiliar word with a more familiar synonym, or to add words or connecting clauses to make the text more readable and understandable.

A Parting Question

Considering all the scholarly and technical issues related to the art and science of biblical textual criticism, what has been the role of the Holy Spirit in this whole history of biblical transmission?

There is no question that the history of biblical transmission, like all human endeavors, has been a messy, complicated, and error-ridden process. Nothing that human beings do is ever perfect or problem-free. But consider: What exactly *is* the Bible, and exactly what do we mean by divine inspiration (or revelation)? As discussed in previous chapters, in II Timothy 3:16 the apostle Paul used the term *theopneustos* ("God-breathed") to describe the phenomenon of divine inspiration, which raises the question: What matters most – the literal words of God in the original language or the essential truths that are being conveyed? Many Bible scholars would argue that what ultimately matters is retaining the seminal essence and intention of God's revealed message.

Unlike the Muslim doctrine of inspiration as it relates to the Quran, Christian scholars reject the idea of a mechanical (or dictation) process of inspiration. The Bible is a book of divine origin and human authorship. The Holy Spirit superintended the process but did not by-pass the mind of the apostles, the prophets or the chroniclers who wrote the texts. Therefore, the written Word of God is the thoughts of God expressed in the words of man. Although inspired by the Holy Spirit, the Bible is expressed in the vocabulary and thought forms of men who were products of their time and culture.

Interestingly, the history of biblical translations itself reinforces this truth. The Septuagint was not a word-for-word (verbal/plenary) translation of the Hebrew Scriptures, and New Testament citations of the ancient Hebrew texts are often expressed in functional (or dynamic) equivalents or even paraphrases. This is not to deny that certain key words and names and concepts are innately sacred. But what ultimately seems to matter most is that the message and intent of God be communicated as clearly and explicitly as possible from the original to the receptor language.

So to what extent has the Holy Spirit been involved in the preservation and transmission of the Bible through the centuries? I would say that the Holy Spirit has been integrally involved in this process in the same way that he initially inspired the biblical texts themselves and to the same extent that he has worked in Christian history in general. Undeniably, the Holy Spirit has been a guiding force, but his influence is often so subtle as to be virtually undetectable. In other words, he has been involved historically in the same sense and to the same degree that he is involved in our lives today. To the extent that we submit our will to him, he works symbiotically and synergistically within us and through us to transform our heart, our mind, and our actions. While not overriding or violating our will, God nonetheless providentially accomplishes his will and purpose in our individual lives and, by extension, in history in general.

The bottom line is that the art and science of biblical textual criticism provides ample evidence that the biblical text has been accurately preserved through the centuries. Just as no historical fact or archaeological discovery has ever refuted or contradicted the Bible, no copying errors or textual variants in the manuscripts have ever altered any core Christian doctrine or our understanding of the character and redemptive work of Jesus Christ. That is what matters, and in that regard we can rest assured that when we read the Bible, we can be confident that what we are reading is what the Holy Spirit originally inspired the authors to write.

◼

Recommended Reading

As mentioned in the Introduction, this work is merely an introduction to the vast field of Bibliology. For every topic and issue addressed in this work, there is an extensive bibliography that can be referenced. However, for the sake of efficacy and manageability, the following is a list of sources cited in this book for those who desire to explore in more depth any or all of these areas of study.

Some of the sources listed below directly address issues related to Bibliology, while others are supplemental to this study. Most of these sources are highly recommended, others are recommended with some reservations, and a few (marked with an asterisk*) are unduly skeptical. Nonetheless, all are helpful in terms of acquiring an understanding of the scope and depth of the field of Bibliology.

Baigent, Michael, Leigh, Richard, and Lincoln, Henry, *Holy Blood, Holy Grail* (Dell, 1983).*

Barna Group Survey, "What Do Americans Really Think About the Bible" (2013). https://www.barna.org/barna-update/culture/605-what- do-americans-really-think-about-the-bible#.U0WjIvldX.

Barna Group Survey, "The State of the Bible: Six Trends for 2014." https://www.barna.org/barna-update/culture/664-the-state-of-the-bible-6-trends-for- 2014#.U0WigPldXTo.

Bloom, Alan, The Closing of the American Mind (Simon & Schuster, 1987).

Breshears, Jefrey D., *Natural Law: The Moral Foundation for Social and Political Civility* (Areopagus Publishing, 2011)

Bruce, F. F., *The Canon of Scripture* (InterVarsity Press, 1988).

F. F. Bruce, *The New Testament Documents: Are They Reliable?* (William B. Eerdmans Publishing Company, 1972).

Bruce, F. F., *The Spreading Flame* (Wm. B. Eerdmans Publishing Company, (1958).

Budziszewski, J., *What We Can't Not Know* (Spence Publishing Company, 2003).

Bultmann, Rudolph, *Jesus and the Word* (Scribner's, 1934).*

Burroughs, Dillon, *Misquotes in Misquoting Jesus: Why You Can Still Believe* (Nimble Books, 2006).

Calvin, John, *The First Book of Moses Called Genesis*.

Campenhausen, Hans von, *Formation of the Christian Bible* (Fortress, 1972).

Carson, D. A., *Collected Writings on Scripture* (Crossway, 2010).

Copan, Paul, *That's Just Your Interpretation* (Baker Books, 2001).

Copan, Paul, *When God Goes to Starbucks: A Guide to Everyday Apologetics* (Baker Books, 2008).

Copan, Paul, ed., *Will the Real Jesus Please Stand Up?* (Baker Books, 1998).

Cowan, Steven B., *Five Views on Apologetics* (Zondervan Publishing House, 2000).

Croy, N. Clayton, *The Mutilation of Mark's Gospel* (Abingdon Press, 2003).

Ehrman, Bart D., *Forged: Writing in the Name of God – Why the Bible's Authors Are Not Who We Think They Are* (HarperCollins, 2011).*

Ehrman, Bart D., *Lost Christianities* (Oxford University Press, 2003).*

Ehrman, Bart D., *Misquoting Jesus: The Story of Who Changed the Bible and Why* (HarperOne, 2005).*

Fee, Gordon and Stuart, Douglas, *How To Read the Bible Book by Book* (Zondervan, 2002).

Fee, Gordon D. and Stuart, Douglas, *How To Read the Bible for All Its Worth* (Zondervan, 2003).

Finegan, Jack, *Handbook of Biblical Chronology*. Revised Edition (Hendrickson Publishers, 1964, 1998).

Foster, Richard J., *Celebration of Discipline: The Path to Spiritual Growth*. Twentieth Anniversary Edition (HarperSanFrancisco, 1978, 1998).

France, R. T., *Jesus and the Old Testament* (InterVarsity Press, 1977).

Funk, Robert W., *The Five Gospels: What Did Jesus Really Say? The Search for the Authentic Words of Jesus* (HarperOne, 1996)

Galileo Galilei, "Letter to the Grand Duchess Christian of Tuscany." Quoted in Mark Noll, *The Scandal of the Evangelical Mind* (William B. Eerdmans Publishing Company, 1994).

Gamble, Harry F., *Books and Readers in the Early Church: A History of Early Christian Texts* (Yale University Press, 1995).

Geisler, Norman L., and Nix, William E., *A General Introduction to the Bible* (Moody Publishers, 1968, 1986).

Geisler, L. Norman, and Tunnicliffe, Patty, *Reasons for Belief* (Bethany House Publishers, 2013).

Glueck, Nelson, *Rivers in the Desert* (Farrar, Strous and Cudahy, 1959).

Grant, Frederick C., *An Introduction to New Testament Thought* (Abingdon, 1950).

Halley, Henry H., *Halley's Bible Handbook*. Deluxe Edition (Zondervan, 2000, 2007).

Harris, R. Laird, *Inspiration and Canonicity of the Bible* (Zondervan Publishing House, 1957, 1969).

Hirsch, E. D., *Cultural Literacy: What Every American Needs To Know* (Vintage Books, 1988).

Brand, Chad, Draper, Charles, and England, Archie, eds., *Holman Illustrated Bible Dictionary* (Holman Bible Publishers, 2003).

Holmes, Arthur F., *Contours of a World View* (Eerdmans, 1983).

Horton, Michael, ed., *The Earliest Gospels: The Origins and Transmissions of the Earliest Christian Gospels – The Contribution of the Chester Beatty Gospel Codex P45* (T&T Clark International, 2004).

Johnson, Luke Timothy, *Faith's Freedom* (Augsburg Fortress Publishers, 1990).

Johnson, Luke Timothy, *The Real Jesus* (HarperOne, 1997).

Johnson, Luke Timothy, *The Writings of the New Testament* (Fortress Press, 1986).

Jones, Timothy Paul, *Misquoting Truth: A Guide to the Fallacies of Bart Ehrman's Misquoting Jesus* (IVP Books, 2007).

Kearns, Kathleen, "The Happy Agnostic." *Carolina Alumni Review* (May/June 2006).*

Keller, Werner, *The Bible As History* (Hodder & Stoughton, 1965).

Komoszewski, Ed, Sawyer, James, and Wallace, Daniel, *Reinventing Jesus: How Contemporary Skeptics Miss the Real Jesus and Mislead Popular Culture* (Kregel Publications, 2003).

Kreeft, Peter, *A Summa of the Summa* (Ignatius Press, 1990).

Lewis, C. S., "Christian Apologetics," in Walter Hooper, ed., *God in the Dock: Essays on Theology and Ethics* (William B. Eerdmans Publishing Company, 1970).

Lewis, C. S., *Mere Christianity* (HarperSanFrancisco, 1952, 1980).

Licona, Michael R., *The Resurrection of Jesus: A New Historiographical Approach* (IVP Academic, 2010).

Lindsell, Harold, *The Battle for the Bible* (Zondervan, 1976).

Loosely, Ernest, *When the Church Was Young* (Christian Books Publishing House, 1989).

Maier, Paul L., ed., *Eusebius: The Church History* (Kregel Publications, 1999).

Maier, Paul L., ed., *Josephus: The Essential Works* (Kregel Publications, 1988).

Mangalwadi, Vishal, *The Book That Made Your World: How the Bible Created the Soul of Western Civilization* (Thomas Nelson, 2011)

Markos, Louis, *Apologetics for the 21st Century* (Crossway, 2010).

McDonald, Lee Martin, *The Biblical Canon: Its Origin, Transmission, and Authority* (Hendrickson Publishers, 2007).

McDonald, Lee Martin, and Sanders, James A., eds., *The Canon Debate* (Hendrickson Publishers, 2002).

McDowell, Josh, *New Evidence That Demands a Verdict* (Thomas Nelson Publishers, 1999).

Merrick, J., Garrett, Stephen M., and Gundry, Stanley N., eds., *Five Views on Biblical Inerrancy* (Zondervan, 2013).

Merton, Thomas, *Opening the Bible* (The Liturgical Press, 1970).

Metzger, Bruce M., *The Bible in Translation* (Baker Academic, 2001).

Metzger, Bruce M., *The Canon of the New Testament: Its Origin, Development, and Significance* (Oxford University Press, 1987).

Metzger, Bruce M., and Ehrman, Bart D., *The Text of the New Testament: Its Transmission, Corruption, and Restoration.* Fourth Edition (Oxford University Press, 2004).

Metzger, Bruce M., and Murphy, Roland E. Murphy, eds., *The New Oxford Annotated Apocrypha* (Oxford University Press, 1991)

Mickelsen, A. Berkeley, *Interpreting the Bible* (Wm. B. Eerdmans Publishing Company, 1963).

Millard, Alan, *Reading and Writing in the Time of Jesus* (NYU Press, 2000).

Naugle, David, *Worldview: The History of a Concept* (Eerdmans, 2002).

Newman, Robert C., "The Council of Jamnia and the Old Testament Canon" (1983). http://www.ibri.org/RRs/RR013/13jamnia.html.

Pascal, Blaise, *Pascal's Pensees* (E. P. Dutton & Company, 1958).

Pelikan, Jaroslav, *The Emergence of the Catholic Tradition* (100-600) (University of Chicago Press, 1971).

Pinnock, Clark, *Set Forth Your Case: An Examination of Christianity's Credentials* (Moody Press, 1971).

Prothero, Stephen, *Religious Literacy: What Every American Needs To Know – and Doesn't* (HarperOne, 2007).

Rhodes, Ron, *Answering the Objections of Atheists, Agnostics & Skeptics* (Harvest House Publishers, 2006).

Roberts, C. H., and Skeat, T. C., *Birth of the Codex* (Oxford University Press, 1987).

Robinson, Wheeler, *The Bible in Its Ancient and English Versions* (Praeger, 1970).

Rogers, Jack, *Biblical Authority* (Word Books, 1977).

Rogers, Jack B., and McKim, Donald K., *The Authority and Interpretation of the Bible: An Historical Approach* (Harper & Row Publishers, 1979).

Rogerson, John, *Atlas of the Bible* (Facts on File, 1985, 1994).

Ross, Hugh, *Why the Universe Is the Way It Is* (BakerBooks, 2007).

Sire, James W., *The Universe Next Door: A Basic Worldview Catalogue*. Fourth Edition (IVP Academic, 1976, 2004).

Smith, Houston, *The World's Religions* (HarperSanFrancisco, 1958, 1991).*

Strobel, Lee, *The Case for Christ* (Zondervan, 1998).

Tolstoy, Leo, *A Confession and Other Religious Writings* (Penguin Classics, 1987).

Tozer, A. W., *The Pursuit of God* (WingSpread Publishers, 1948).

Wallace, Daniel B., "The Gospel According to Bart." *Journal of the Evangelical Theological Society* 49 (June 2006).

Witherington, Ben, "Misanalyzing Textual Criticism: Bart Ehrman's 'Misquoting Jesus'." http://benwitherington.blogspot.com/2006/03/misanalyzing-text-criticism-bart.html.

Wright, N. T., *The Last Word: Beyond the Bible Wars to a New Understanding of the Authority of Scripture* (HarperSanFrancisco, 2005).

Wright, N. T., *The Resurrection of the Son of God* (Fortress Press, 2003).

Index

A note on biblical passages: For practical reasons, I have omitted listing in this Index most of the Bible passages and verses cited in this study. There are simply too many of them. Therefore, references to certain books and passages are included only if they are particularly relevant to key issues and controversies related to bibliology – for example, books such as Esther, Ecclesiastes, II Peter, Revelation, etc.